IN SEARCH OF CERTAINTY

THE SCIENCE OF OUR INFORMATION INFRASTRUCTURE

Mark Burgess

In Search of Certainty, Second Edition

by Mark Burgess

Printed in the United States of America.

Published by O'Reilly Media, Inc., 1005 Gravenstein Highway North, Sebastopol, CA 95472.

O'Reilly books may be purchased for educational, business, or sales promotional use. Online editions are also available for most titles (*http://safaribooksonline.com*). For more information, contact our corporate/institutional sales department: 800-998-9938 or *corporate@oreilly.com*.

Editors: Mike Loukides and Brian Anderson

Proofreader: Jasmine Kwityn

Cover Designer: Edie Freedman

September 2013:   First Edition
April 2015:   Second Edition

Revision History for the First Edition

September 2013:   First edition published in ebook format by χtAxis Press, Oslo, Norway
January 2014 and March 2014:   Reprinted with corrections

Revision History for the Second Edition

April 2015:   First Release

978-1-491-92307-8

[LSI]

Dedicated to my friends,
who helped me to understand a little over the years.

"Let the future tell the truth, and evaluate each one according to his work and accomplishments. The present is theirs; the future, for which I have really worked, is mine."

–Nikola Tesla

"For a successful technology. reality must take precedence over public relations, for Nature cannot be fooled.

–Richard Feynman

"I don't want knowledge, I want certainty"

– David Bowie, Law (*Earthling*)

Dynamics
Concerning forces and changes in the world.

Semantics
Concerning meaning, interpretation and intent.

Foreword

Over the years I've noticed that many people working on performance, capacity planning, and configuration of large scale systems think differently, and are particularly effective because they have a background in physics. Personally I have a degree in Applied Physics and enjoy the way Mark introduces scientific concepts, and applies them to computer systems, in this book. Unlike many books in the general area of systems administration, which are tied to specific tools or platforms, and which date over time, the fundamental scientific concepts described here aren't going to change. As time passes, more people are finding the path that leads in search of certainty to the ideas around promise theory, and—over time—I believe this book will be seen as an important landmark in the development of our craft.

Mark is both a practitioner and an academic, and he has brought rigor, clarity and a deep understanding of the physics of complex systems to the world of systems administration. Where the state of the art used to be "type in the commands in the installation manual or run book by hand", he built CFEngine to repeatably automate configuration steps, and inspired several generations of tools that create infrastructure with code. Moving on from "hack it until it appears to work and don't touch it until it breaks again", he implemented the idea that a large collection of systems should actively maintain a desired configuration. Now, with this updated second edition of *In Search of Certainty*, he sets out a physics-based foundation for reasoning about the complex state of large-scale distributed systems. By inverting the concept of externalized service level agreement *obligations* into decentralized local *promises*, "Promise Theory" provides a scalable and robust approach to systems management. There is no such thing as certainty in a distributed system, but there are good and bad approximations to certainty, and this book is a valuable guide to those of us who want to build large scale distributed systems that promise to behave themselves most of the time.

In 2009 and 2010 I was lucky to be part of a very experienced team of managers and engineers at Netflix who went back to first principles to come up with an architecture that would be very agile, automated, self service, highly available, and cloud based. We internalized the principles that Amazon Web Services (AWS) was promoting, and synthesized ideas from our backgrounds at Google, eBay, Yahoo and Sun, along with anti-patterns from our experience at Netflix that we wanted to avoid. One of the recurring problems in our data-center deployment was that individual machine failures could break the service. In addition intermittent problems were traced to configuration drift, where supposedly identical installations weren't. Our solution for this was to move up a level, and ban individual "snowflake" or "pet" machines. Instead, any change we made was baked into a machine image and replicated into a "herd" of identical instances. To ensure that these instances remained ephemeral, with immutable code, and didn't maintain local state between requests, we also created a "chaos monkey" process that would delete them from time to time, and use the AWS auto-scaler to replace them automatically. In effect, in our own search for certainty, we were able to make strong assertions, or promises, that a group of machines were always executing identical code, and immunize the group so that it would self-repair.

In 2015 many of the radical ideas and patterns we argued about five years ago have become well established and now have names. Using a DevOps organization to deliver auto-scaled microservices, based on immutable containers, is becoming a common pattern. As we model and reason about the behavior of large-scale collections of microservices, this book on certainty, and how promise theory came about, is an important addition to our bookshelf.

– Adrian Cockcroft, Los Gatos 2015.

Author preface to second edition

In preparing the second edition of the book, I have made as few changes as possible to the text. My goal is not to update or correct it, as much as to repair some deficiencies in the first attempt at explaining an intricate topic. I prefer that the book remain a cultural document, a child of its time, however naive that might prove to be in the long run.

Some obvious points failed to come through the text at first attempt, especially with regard to material structure of infrastructure in chapter 12. For the sake of keeping the promise of the introduction, I was embarrassed enough to want to improve on that. The republication by O'Reilly seemed like the perfect opportunity to do that. Minor improvements have been made throughout, and substantial changes made to sharpen chapter 12. I have also added a summary of points from each chapter at the end of the book, as a comprehension aid to all readers, and perhaps as a study aid for college students.

This book is an ambitious project, and there is a lot to swallow in its pages. However, like the books that were just a little beyond my reach (and hence inspired me to learn) as a teenager, I hope that this will be a book readers can revisit multiple times to discover new insights, over several years. No one can absorb the entirety of such a story in one sitting.

One interesting historical point seems worth noting. Following the release of the first edition, it was pointed out to me by Jeff Sussna how the writings of William Ross Ashby on the nascent subject of cybernetics [Ash52, Ash56], in the 1950s, parallels much of the first part of this book. Having recovered copies of these forgotten works, long since out of print, I was amazed to see how closely his thinking tracked my own. Some terms naturally differ. His mention of 'over-stability', for instance, is what is referred to here as fixed point convergence. Ashby (who was contemporary with Asimov's robot stories) described an analogue kind of cybernetics. Such a viewpoint was also my first instinct, given a similar background in physics. However, it is not the right approach for today's machinery, as readers will discover in these pages. I believe that the true insights came from realizing the digital nature of information, leading to what we might call a modern cybernetics. There is a tendency to grant historical insights, ahead of their time, almost mystical truth, especially amongst laymen—whether it be Ashby or Hobbes, as examples. However, it would be wrong to think that nothing new has been learnt in the intervening years. Far from it. While words are easily compared and assigned significance by a modern reader, precise scientific understandings are harder won, and always slower to emerge. One could say that the digital version of Ashby's work was covered in monograph *Analytical Network and System Administration* [Bur04a]. The later addition of functional semantics through Promise Theory [BB14] then went beyond the scope of what Ashby could address in his analogue form, though he seems to have appreciated that the problem existed. His work was remarkable for its time, and its insights, but it is surpassed by modern knowledge.

Finally, I would like to give humble thanks to all the readers, and reviewers, who expressed glad tidings about the first edition. Their remarks exceeded my wildest expectations, and that makes the efforts expended in writing all the more rewarding.

– Mark Burgess, Oslo 2015.

Contents

8   **The Equilibrium of Knowing**
       Or how not to disagree with yourself   **176**

9   **Clockwork Uncertainty**
       The arms race between reason and complexity   **199**

       Part III: Promises

       The chemistry of autonomous cooperation   **237**

10   **The Concept Of Promises**
       Or why behaviour comes from within   **239**

11   **The Human Condition**
       How humans make friends to solve problems   **263**

12   **Molecular and Material Infrastructure**
       Elastic, plastic and brittle design   **314**

13   **Orchestration And Creative Instability**
       Or why the conductor does not promise to blow every trumpet **341**

14   **Epilogue**   **385**

       References   426

       Index   440

Introduction: The Hallowed Halls

"Our great computers
Fill the hallowed halls"

– Neil Peart, Rush, 2112

Quite soon, the world's information infrastructure is going to reach a level of scale and complexity that will force scientists and engineers to think about it in an entirely new way. The familiar notions of command and control, which have held temporary dominion over our systems, are now being thwarted by the realities of a faster, denser world of communication, a world where choice, variety, and indeterminism rule. The myth of the machine, that does exactly what we tell it, has come to an end.

Many of the basic components of information infrastructure, including computers, storage devices, networks, and so forth, are by now relatively familiar; however, each generation of these devices adds new ways to adapt to changing needs, and what happens inside them during operation has influences that originate from all over the planet. This makes their behaviour far from well understood even by the engineers who build and use them. How does that affect predictability, their usefulness?

It is now fair to draw a parallel between the structures we build to deliver information, and the atomic structure of materials that we engineer for manufacturing, like metals and plastics[1]. Although these things seem far removed from one another, occupying very different scales, they have a basic similarity: physical materials are made of atoms and molecules networked through chemical bonding into structures that give them particular properties. Similarly, information infrastructures are made up of their own components wired into networks, giving them particular properties. Understanding what those properties are, and why they come about, requires a new way of thinking. In this book, I

1

will attempt to explain why this analogy is a fair one, why it is not the full story, but what we can learn from the limited similarity.

At the engineering level, we put aside the details of *why* a structure behaves as it does, and rather make use of what properties the materials promise. We become more concerned with how to use them, as 'off-the-shelf' commodities, and describe their promises in terms of new terms like strength, elasticity, plasticity, and so on, qualities far removed from raw atoms and chemical bonds. The useful properties of materials and infrastructure lie as much in the connections between parts, as in the parts that get connected, but we prefer to think of them as continuous reliable stuff, not assemblages of tiny pieces.

The parallels between information infrastructure and the physics of matter go deeper than these superficial likenesses, and I have studied some of these parallels in my research over the past twenty years. This book will describe a few of them. Understanding this new physics of information technology is going to be vital if we are to progress beyond the current state of the art. This is not the physics of silicon wafers, or of electronics, nor is it about ideas of software engineering; rather, it's about a whole new level of description, analogous to the large scale thermodynamics that enabled the steam age, or the economic models of our financial age. Only then, will we be able to build predictably and robustly, while adapting to the accelerating challenges of the modern world.

What does this mean to you and me? Perhaps more than we might think. Every search we perform on the Internet, every music download piped to our earplugs from an embedded mobile hotspot, or more speculatively every smartphone-interfacing self-driving hybrid car purchased with a smart-chip enabled credit card, sends us careering ever onwards in the uncontrolled descent of miniaturization and high density information trawling that we cheer on as The Information Revolution.

We no longer experience information-based technology as thrilling or unusual; the developed world has accepted this trajectory, expects it, and even demands it. In the developing world, it is transforming money, communications and trade in areas where more traditional alternatives failed for a lack of physical infrastructure. The ability to harness information, to process it, and at ever greater speeds, allows the whole world to fend off threats, and exploit opportunities.

As information technology invades more and more parts of our environment, we are going to experience it in unexpected ways. We won't always see the computer in a box, or the remote control panel, but it will be information technology nevertheless. New smart materials and biologically inspired buildings already hint at what the future might look like. Yet, if we are to trust it in all of its varied forms, we have to understand it better.

For years, we've viewed information technology as a kind of icing on our cake, something wonderful that we added to the mundane fixtures of our lives, with its entertainment systems and personal communications channels; but, then these things were no longer the icing, they were the cake itself. Information systems began to invade every aspect of our environments, from the cars we drive to the locks on the front door, from the way we read books to the way we cook food. We depend on it for our very survival.

Artificial environments support more of our vital functions for each day that passes. Few in the developed world can even remember how to survive without the elaborate infrastructure of electricity, supply networks, sanitation plants, microwave ovens, cars and other utilities. So many of us rely on these for their day to day lives. Some have hearts run by pacemakers, others are reliant on technology for heating or cooling. Our very sense of value and trade is computed by technology, which some parts of our planet would consider magic. We 'outsource' increasing amounts of our survival to a 'smart' environmental infrastructure, and hence we become more and more dependent on it for each day that passes.

What makes us think we can rely on all this technology? What keeps it together today, and how might it work tomorrow? Will we even know how to build the next generation of it, or will be become lulled into a stupor of dependence brought about by its conveniences? To shape the future of technology, we need to understand how it works, else what we don't understand will end up shaping us.

As surely as we have followed the trajectory, we have come to rely on it, and thus we must know what it takes to make the next steps, and why. Some of those details are open to choice, others are constrained by the physical nature of the world we live in, so we'll need to understand much more than just a world of computers to know the technology of tomorrow.

Behold the Great Transformation, not just of technology but of society itself, adapting to its new symbiosis! It is happening now, at a datacentre near you! (Or in a test tube, or under an etching laser.) Vast halls of computing power, and laboratories of microscopic bio-chemical machinery, have supplanted the mechanisation and civil engineering of the industrial age, as the darlings of change. What will be the next thing? Nanotechnology? Human enhancement? Where will our sense of adventure set out next?

In 1997, I visited San Diego, California, for the 11th Annual Conference in Large Installation System Administration, as something of an outsider. It was a conference not for the designers of information systems, but for those who keep such systems running, on behalf of society at large. As a physicist by training, relatively new to technological research, I was excited to present some work I'd been doing on new ways to ensure the reliability of large computer systems. I presented a rather technical paper on a new kind of smart process-locking mechanism to make computers more predictable and maintainable.

To a physicist, reliability looks like a kind of stability. It is about enabling an equilibrium to come about. To me, the work I presented was just a small detail in a larger and more exciting discussion to make computer systems self-governing, as if they were as ordinary a part of our infrastructure as as the self-regulating ventilation systems. The trouble was, no one was having this discussion. I didn't get the response I was hoping for. A background in science had not prepared me for an audience with different expectations. In the world of computers, people still believed that you simply tell computers what to do, and, because they are just machines, they must obey.

I left the conference feeling somewhat misunderstood. My paper had been related to a piece of software called CFEngine that I had started developing in 1993 to configure and maintain computers without human intervention. It had become unexpectedly popular, spreading to millions of computers in datacentres and small environments, and it is still widely used today.

On the plane going home, my misery was compounded by becoming ill, and began to think about the human immune system and how smart it seemed to be in repairing a state of health. There was an answer! I became inspired to explain my work in terms of the analogy of health, and I spent much of the year thinking about how to write a paper 'Computer Immunology' which I submitted to the next conference, spelling out a manifesto for building self-healing computers[2].

The following year, 1998, the conference was in Boston, Massachusetts. This time, I was delighted to win the prize for best paper at the conference, and was immediately thrust into a world keen to know about the concepts of self-regulating, self healing computers—though it would take another ten years for the ideas to become widely recognized. The experience underlined the importance of bridging the awareness gap between cultures in different fields, even in science and technology. It underlined, perhaps, a need for books like this one.

After the conference, I was taken on a trip of honour by a former colleague Demosthenes Skipitaris from Oslo University College, to a high security, state-of-the-art datacentre facility run by a Norwegian search engine called FAST, just outside of Boston. After surrendering my passport on the way for security validation, and being frisked by over-dressed guards, we were led into a vast hall of computer racks the size of several football pitches.

Computers on top of computers, accompanied by the deafening noise of thousands of fans whirring, disks spinning and air blowing, all mounted in racks and stacked up to the ceiling. Row upon row of black boxes, separated by narrow walk-spaces, just wide enough for a person, for as far as the eye could see. We were listening to the roar of all the web searches of people from across the world being processed before our eyes, but there were no humans in sight. In the whole building I saw a single keyboard and a single screen for emergency use[3].

"All this is run by your software CFEngine," my host told me. CFEngine is essentially a collection of software robots embedded into each machine's operating system. I told him about my computer health analogy, and he commented that with the software running, the most common failure in the machines was that the vibration from all the computer disks would cause the removable disks to work their way out of the chassis, causing a machine to stop now and then. That was the only time a human needed to touch the machines—just push the disk back in and restart.

Then, as we passed one of the racks, he pointed to a small cable emerging from a socket. "That," he said, "is our single point of failure. If I pull that plug, we're offline." We stopped there for a moments to pay our respects to the gods of fragility.

It was a telling reminder that, even with the most advanced systems at our fingertips, the smallest detail can so easily be overlooked and result in a fatal flaw.

How would we even know about a tiny error, a minute design flaw, an instability waiting to grow into a catastrophic failure? Standing amongst the anonymous array of whirring machines in that hallowed hall, it was evident that finding a needle in a haystack might be easy by comparison. In a world of software, there is nothing to even get hold of and feel a prick of a needle.

In 2012, I visited a datacentre ten times the size of the one in Boston, and was shown a room where 40 humans still sat and watched screens, in what looked like an enactment of NASA's mission control. They were hoping to see some advance warning of signs of trouble in their global operations, still using the methods of a decade before in a pretence of holding together a system that was already far beyond their ability to comprehend—as if a few shepherds were watching over all of the wildlife in Earth's oceans with their crooks. Those 40 humans watched with naked eye graphs of performance, somewhat like medical monitors for tens of thousands of computers spread around the globe.

I recall thinking how primitive it all was. If a single machine amongst those tens of thousands were to develop an instability, it could bring everything to a halt, in the worst case, like pulling out an essential plug. Watching those screens was like trying to locate a single malignant cell in a patient's body just by measuring a pulse. The mismatch of information was staggering. I began to wonder what role CFEngine's immune principles already played in preventing that from happening. I hope that this book can help to shed some light on what makes a system well-behaved or not.

For two decades, the world's most advanced datacentres have been run largely by automated robotic software that maintains their operational state with very little human intervention. Factories for manufacturing are manned by robot machines, and familiar services like banking, travel, and even vending machines have been automated and made more widely available than ever before. The continuity of these services has allowed us to trust them and rely on them.

How is this even possible? How is it that we can make machines that work without the need to coax and cajole them, without the need to tell them every detail of what to do? How can we trust these machines? And can we keep it up? So far, we've been lucky, but the long term answers have yet to be revealed. They can only emerge by knowing the science behind them.

If information systems are going to be mission critical in the society of today and tomorrow, then the mission controls of this increasingly 'smart' infrastructure need principles more akin to our autonomous immune systems than to nurses with heart monitors. We have to understand how continuous operation, how dependability itself, can emerge from the action of lots of individual cellular parts, and follow a path of continuous adaptation and improvement. To even grasp a knowledge of such speed, scale and complexity is beyond any human without technological assistance.

We build software systems every day, and extend the depth of this dependency on technology. We suffer sometimes from the hubris of believing that control is a matter of applying sufficient force, or a sufficiently detailed set of instructions. Or we simply hope for the best. How shall we understand the monster we are creating, when it is growing so rapidly that it can no longer be tethered by simple means, and it can no longer be outsmarted by any human?

Such a Frankensteinian vision is not as melodramatic as it sounds. The cracks in our invulnerability are already showing as tragedies emerge out of insufficiently understood systems. We have thrown ourselves into deep water with only a crude understanding of the survival equipment. Clearly, the adventure *could* go badly, in a worst case scenario. Luckily, this need not happen if we build using the best principles of science, and base technology on proper knowledge about how the world really works, adapting to its limitations.

This book is about that science, and how we may use it to build reliable infrastructure. It is about the tension between stability, witting and unwitting, and pride in a sense of control and certainty. In a sense, it is the story of how I conceived CFEngine, or if you prefer, of how to implement Computer Immunology.
The book is in three parts:

- Part I Stability: describes the fundamentals of predictability, and why we have to give up the idea of control in its classical meaning.

- Part II Certainty: describes the science of what we can know, when we don't control everything, and how we make the best of life with only imperfect information.

- Part III Promises: explains how the concepts of stability and certainty may be combined to approach information infrastructure as a new kind of virtual material, restoring a continuity to human-computer systems so that society can rely on them.

I have chosen to focus especially on the impact of computers and information on our modern infrastructure, yet the principles we need for managing technology did not emerge from computer science alone. They derive from an understanding of what is all around us, in the natural world. The answers have emerged from all those sciences that learned to deal with fundamental uncertainty about the world: physics, chemistry, economics and biology. Emergent effects, so often mysticized, are really not so mysterious once one takes the time to understand. They are inevitable consequences of information-rich systems. We must understand how to harness them for safe and creative purpose.

When civil infrastructure meant gas lamps and steam locomotives, and computers were still a ghost in the punch-card looms of the industrial revolution, the denizens of history wrestled with fundamental questions about the nature of the physical world that we still find hard to comprehend today. Without those questions and the discoveries they led to, none of what we take for granted today would have been possible.

So, to unearth the roots of this story about technological infrastructure, I want to delve into the roots of science itself, into the principles that allow us to understand system operation and design, to reveal the advances in thinking that led to modern, information rich methods of fending off *uncertainty*. Above all, this is a fascinating story of human endeavour, from a personal perspective. Just beyond reach of most of us, there is a treasure trove of understanding that has propelled humanity to the very limits of imagination. That is surely a story worth telling.

How to read this book

This book introduces concepts that will be new to a majority of readers. To do so, it builds from fundamental ideas that might initially seem to stray from the topic of information, and builds towards the more contemporary aspects of information infrastructure today. Some readers might be impatient to get to the final answers without all the basics, but science does not work that way. I have committed myself to explaining, as plausibly as I can, how this edifice of thought emerged, with cultural and historical context, in the hope that it will make sense to the committed reader. The panorama and intricacies of scientific thought are truly rewarding for those who are willing to climb the mountain.

I have provided a level of technical depth for readers who are conversant with science and technology. However, no one should feel defeated by these details. In all cases, it should be straightforward to skip across details that seem too difficult, and rejoin the train of thought later. I encourage readers to exercise personal judgement and skip over sections that seem difficult, and I cross my fingers that the book might still be enjoyed without every nuance rendered with complete fidelity.

– Mark Burgess, Oslo, 2013

Part I
Stability

Or how we base technology on science

1

King Canute and the Butterfly

How we create the illusion of being in control.

"If the doors of perception were cleansed every thing would appear to man as it is, infinite. For man has closed himself up, till he sees all things thro' narrow chinks of his cavern."
- William Blake, *The Marriage of Heaven and Hell*

Imagine a scene in a movie. A quiet night on the ocean, on the deck of a magnificent ship, sailing dreamily into destiny. Moonlight reflects in a calm pond that stretches off into the distance, waves lap serenely against the bow of the ship, and – had there been crickets on the ocean, we would have heard that reassuring purring of the night to calm the senses.

The captain, replete with perfectly adjusted uniform, comes up to the night helmsman and asks: "How goes it, sailor?" To which the sailor replies: "No problem. All's quiet, sir. Making a small course correction. Everything's ship-shape and under control."

At this moment, the soundtrack stirs, swelling into darker tones, because we know that those famous last words are surely a sign of trouble in any Hollywood script.

At that very moment, the camera seems to dive into the helmsman's body, swimming frantically along his arteries with his bloodstream to a cavernous opening, where we view a deadly parasite within him that will kill him within the hour. Then the camera pulls back of him and pans out, rising above the ship, up into the air to an altitude at which the clear, still pond of the ocean seems to freckle and soon becomes obscured by clouds. The calm sea, it turns out, is just the trough of a massive wave that, miles away, reaches up to ten times the height of the ship, and is racing across the planet with imminent destruction written all over it. As we rise up, and zoom out of the detail, we see the edge of a massive storm, swirling with fierce intensity and wreaking havoc on what is now a hair's

11

breadth away on the screen. And then, pulling even farther out, just beyond the edge of the planet, is a swarm of meteorites, firing down onto the human realm, one of which is the size of Long Island (it's always Long Island), and will soon wipe out all life on Earth. Picking up speed now, the camera zooms back and we see the solar system spinning around a fiery sun, and see stars and galaxies and we return to a calm serenity, where detail is mere shades of colour on a simple black canvas. Then the entire universe is swallowed into a black hole.

Shipshape and under control?

Well, don't worry. This scene is not a prediction of anyone's future, and hopefully you recognized the smirk of irony injected for humorous effect. What the imaginary scene is supposed to convey is that our perceptions of being 'in control' always have a lot to do with the scale at which we focus our attention— and, by implication, the information that is omitted. We sometimes think we are in control because we either don't have or choose not to see the full picture.

Is this right or wrong?

That is one of the questions that I want to offer some perspectives on in this book. How much of the world can we really control and harness for our purpose? To make infrastructure, we need to make certain assurances. From the parody presented above, one has the sense that we can control some parts of the world, but that there are also forces beyond our control, 'above' and 'below' on the scale of things.

This makes eminent sense. The world, after all, is not a continuous and uniform space, it is made of bits and pieces, of enclosed regions and open expanses – and within this tangle of environments, there are many things going on about which we often have very limited knowledge. In technical language, we say that we have *incomplete information* about the world. This theme of missing information will be one of the central ideas in this book.

Some of the missing information is concealed by distance, some by obstacles standing in our way. Some is not available because it has not arrived yet, or it has since passed, and some of the information is just occurring on such a different scale that we are unable to comprehend it using the sensory apparatus that we are equipped with. Using a microscope we can see a little of what happens on a small scale, and using satellites and other remote tools we can capture imagery on a scale larger than ourselves, but when we are looking down the microscope we cannot see the clouds, and when we are looking through the satellite, we cannot perceive bacteria.

Truly, our capacity for taking in information is limited by scale in a number of ways, but we should not think for a moment that this is merely a human failing. There is more going on here.

Sometimes a lack of information doesn't matter to predicting what comes next, but sometimes it does. Phenomena have differing sensitivities to information, and that information is passed on as an *influence* between things. So this sensitivity to information is not merely a weakness that applies to humans, like saying that we need better glasses: the ability to interact with the world varies hugely with different phenomena – and those interactions themselves are often sensitive to a preferred scale. We know this from physics itself, and it is fundamental, as we shall see in the chapters ahead.

Let's consider for a moment why scale should play a role in how things interact. This will be important when we decide how to successfully build tools and systems for the world. Returning for a moment to our ship on the sea, we observe that the hull has a certain length and a certain width and a certain height, and the waves that strike it have a certain size. This is characterized by a wavelength (the distance between one wave and the next), and an amplitude (the mean height of the wave). Intuition alone should now tell us that waves that are high compared to height of the ship will have a bigger impact on it when they hit the ship than waves that are only small compared to its size. Moreover, waves that are much shorter in length compared to the length and width of the ship will strike the ship more often than a long wave: bang bang bang instead of gradually rising and falling. Indeed, if a single wave were many kilometres in wavelength, the ship would scarcely notice that anything was happening as the wave passed it, even if the wave gradually lifted the ship a distance of three times its height. Relative scales in time and in space matter.

The ship is a moving, physical object, but could we not avoid the effects of scale by just watching a scene without touching anything? In fact, we can't because we cannot observe any without interacting with it somehow. This was one of the key insights made by quantum theory founder Werner Heisenberg, at the beginning of the 20th century. He pointed out that, in order to transfer information from one object to another, we have to interact with it, and that we change it in the process. For instance, to measure the pressure of a tyre, you have to let some of the air out of the tyre into a pressure gauge, reducing the pressure slightly. There are no one-way interactions, only mutual interactions. In fact, the situation is quite similar to that of the waves on the ship, because all matter and energy in the universe has a wavelike nature.

Knowing your scales is a very practical problem for information infrastructure. To first create, and then maintain information rich services, we have to know how to extract accurate information and act on it cheaply, without making basic science errors. For example, to respond quickly to phone coverage demand in a flash crowd, you cannot merely measure the demand just twice daily and expect to capture what is going on. On the other hand, rechecking the catalogue of movies on an entertainment system every second would be a pointless excess.

One has to use the right kind of probe to see the right level of detail. When scientists take picture of atoms and microstructures, they use small wavelength waves like X-rays and electron waves, where the wavelength is comparable to the size of the atoms themselves. The situation is much like trying to feel the shape of tiny detail with your fingers. Think of a woollen sweater. Sweaters have many different patterns of stitching, but if you close your eyes and try to describe the shape of the stitching just by feeling it with your fat fingers, you would not be able to because each finger is wider than several threads. You can see the patterns with your eyes because light has a wavelength much smaller than the width of either your fingers or the wool.

Now suppose you could blow up the sweater to a much greater size (or equivalently shrink your fingers), so that the threads of wool were like ropes; then you would be able to feel the edges of each thread and sense when one thread goes under or over another. You would be able to describe a lot more information about it. Your interaction with the system of the sweater would be able to *resolve* detail and provide *sufficient information*[4] .

To develop a deep understanding of systems, we shall need to understand information in some depth, especially how it works at different scales. We'll need to discuss control, expectation and stability, and how these things are affected by the incompleteness of the information we have about the world. We need to think bigger than computers, to the world itself as a computer, and we need to ask how complete and how certain is the information we rely on.

Information we perceive is limited by our ability to probe things as we interact with them—we are trapped between the characteristic scales of the observer and the observed. Infrastructure is limited in the same way. This is more than merely a biological limitation to be overcome, or a problem of a poorly designed instrument. In truth, we work around such limitations in ingenious ways all the time, but it is not just that. This limitation in our ability to perceive is also a benefit. We also use that limitation purposely as a tool to understand things, to form the illusion of mastery and control over a limited scale of things, because by being able to isolate only a part of the world, we reduce a hopeless problem to a manageable one.

We tune into a single frequency on the radio, we focus on a particular distance, zoom in or zoom out, looking at one scale at a time. We place things in categories, or boxes, files into folders, we divide up markets into stalls, and malls into shops, cities into buildings, and countries into counties, all to make our comprehension of the world more manageable by limiting the amount of information we have to interact with at any time. Our experience of the world can be made comprehensible or incomprehensible, by design.

Analogies will be helpful to us in understanding the many technical issues about information. Thinking back to the ship, our fateful helmsman, who reported that everything was under control, was sitting inside a ship, within a calm region of ocean with sensory devices that were unable to see the bigger picture. Without being distracted by the inner workings of his body, he was able to observe the ship and the ocean around him and steer the ship appropriately within this region. By being the size that he was, he could fit inside the safety of the ship, avoiding the cold of the night, and by fitting into the calm trough of the ocean's mega-wave, the ship was able to be safely isolated from damage caused by the massive energies involved in lifting such an amount of water.

The mental model of the ship on the ocean seemed pretty stable to observers at that scale of things, with no great surprises. This allowed the ship to function in a controlled manner and for humans to perceive a sense of control in the *local* region around the ship, without being incapacitated by *global* knowledge of large scale reality. How would this experience translate into what we might expect for society's information infrastructure?

Scale is thus both a limiter and a tool. By shutting out the bigger (or smaller) picture, we create a limited arena in which our actions seem to make a difference[5]. We say that our actions *determine* the outcome, or that the outcomes are *deterministic*. On a cosmic scale, this is pure hubris—matters might be wildly out of control in the grand scheme of things, indeed we have no way of even knowing what we don't know; but that illusion of local order, free of significant threat, has a powerful effect on us. If fortune is the arrival of no unexpected surprises, then fortune is very much our ally, as humans, in surviving and manipulating the world around us.

The effect of limited information is that we perceive and build the world as a collection of containers, patches or environments, separated from one another by limited information flow. These structures define characteristic *scales*. In human society, we make countries, territories, shops, houses, families, tribes, towns, workplaces, parks, and recreation centres. They behave like *units* of organization, if not physically separated then at least de-marked from one another; and, within each, there are clusters of interaction, the molecules of human chemistry. Going beyond what humans have built, we have environments such as micro-climates, ponds, the atmosphere, the lithosphere, the magnetosphere, the atomic scale, the nuclear scale, the collision scale or mean free path, and so on. All of these features of the world that we identify can be seen as emerging from a simple principle: a finite range of influence, or limited transmission of information, relative to a certain phenomenon.

There are really two complementary issues at play here: perception and influence. We need to understand the effect that scale has upon these. The more details we can see, the less we have a sense of control. This is why layers of management in an organization tend to separate from the hands-on workers. It is not a class distinction, but a skill separation. In the semantic realm, this is called the *separation of concerns*, and it is not only a necessary consequence of loss of resolution due to scale, but also a strategy for staying sane[6]. Control seems then to be a combination of two things:

Control → Predictability + Interaction

To profit from interactions with the world, in particular the infrastructure we build, it has to be predictable enough to use to our advantage. If the keyboard I am typing on were continuously changing or falling apart, it would not be usable to me. I have to actually be able to interact with it—to touch it.

Rather than control, we may talk about certainty. How sure we can we be of the outcomes of our actions? Later in the book, I will argue that we can say something like this:

Certainty → Knowledge + Information

where knowledge is a relationship to the history of what we've already observed in the past (i.e. an expectation of behaviour), and information is evidence of the present: that things are proceeding as expected.

Predictability and interaction: these foundations of control lie at the very heart of physics, and are the essence of information, but can we guarantee them in sufficient measure to build a world on top? Even supposing that one were able to arrange an island of calm, in which to assert sufficient force to change and manipulate the world, are we still guaranteed absolute control? Will infrastructure succeed in its purpose?

The age of the Enlightenment was the time of figures like Galileo Galilei (1564-1642) and Isaac Newton (1642-1727), philosophers who believed strongly in the idea of reason. During these times, there emerged a predominantly machine-like view of the world. This was in contrast with the views of Eastern philosophers. The world itself, Newton believed, existed essentially as a deterministic infrastructure for God's own will. Man could merely aspire to understand and control using these perfect laws.

The concept of determinism captures the idea that cause and effect are tightly linked to bring certainty, i.e. that one action inevitably causes another action in a predictable fashion, to assure an outcome as if intended[7]. Before the upheavals of the 19th and 20th century discoveries, this seemed a reasonable enough view. After all, if you push something, it moves. If you hold it, it stops. Mechanical interaction itself was equated with control and perfectly deterministic outcome. Newton used his enormous skill and intellect to formalise these ideas.

The laws of geometry were amongst the major turning points of modern thinking that cheered on this belief in determinism. Seeing how simple geometric principles could be used to explain broad swathes of phenomena, many philosophers, including Newton, were inspired to mimic these properties to more general use. Thomas Hobbes (1588-1679) was one such man, and a figure whom we shall stumble across throughout this story of infrastructure. A secretary to Francis Bacon (1561-1626), one of the founders of scientific thinking, he attempted to codify principles to understand human cooperation, inspired by the power of such statements of truth as 'two straight lines cannot enclose a space'. He dreamt not just of shaping technology, but society itself, by controlling it with law and reason.

Information, on the other hand, as an idea and as a commodity, played an inconspicuous role during this time of Enlightenment. It crept into science more slowly and circuitously than determinism, through bookkeeping ledgers of experimental observation, but also implicitly through the new theory for moving objects. Its presence, although incognito, was significant nonetheless in linking descriptive state with the behaviour of things. Information was the key to control, if only it could be mastered.

Laws, inspired by geometry then, began to enter science. Galileo's law of inertia, which later became co-opted as Newton's first law of motion, implicitly linked information and certainty with the physics of control, in a surprising way. It states that, unless acted upon by external forces, bodies continue in a state of rest or uniform motion in a straight line. This is basically a statement that bodies possess motional *stability* unless perturbed by external influences. Prior to this, it had seemed from everyday experience that one had to continually push something to make it move. The concepts of friction and dissipation were still unappreciated. Thus Newton's insights took science from a general sense of motion being used up, like burned wood, to the idea that motion was a property that might be conserved and moved around, like money.

Newton's first law claimed that, as long as no interactions were made with other bodies, there could be no payment, and thus motion would remain constant. Thus emerged a simple accounting principle for motion, which is what we now call *energy*. The concept of energy, as book-keeping information, was first used formally by German philosopher Gottfried Wilhelm Leibniz (1646-1716), Newton's contemporary and rival in scientific thought, though Thomas Young is recorded as the first person to use the modern terminology in lectures to the Royal Society in 1802.

Newton's second law of motion was a quantification of how these energy payments could be made between moving bodies. It provided the formula that described how transmission of a form of information altered a stable state of motion. The third law said that the transmission of influence between bodies had to result in a mutual change in both parties: what was given to one must be lost by the other. In other words, for every force given there is an equal and opposite back-reaction on the giver.

The notion of physical law emerging was that the world worked basically like a clockwork machine, with regular lawful and predictable behaviour, book-keeping its transactions as if audited by God himself. It all worked through the constant and fixed infrastructure of a *physical law*. If one could only uncover all the details of that law, Man would have total knowledge of the future. Information could become a tool, a technology. This was Newton's vision of God, and there is surely a clue in here to the search for certainty.

These thoughts were essential to our modern view of science. They painted a picture of a world happening, like a play, against a cosmic backdrop, with machine-like predictability. They still affect the way we view the separation of 'system' and 'environment', such as the activities of consumers or users from society's background infrastructure. Universality of phenomena independent of environments allowed one to reason, infer and plan ahead.

When Galileo dropped balls of different mass from the Tower of Pisa in the 16th century, predicting that they would hit the ground at the same time, he codified this as a law of nature that all masses fall at the same rate[8]. The original experiment was said to have been a hammer and a feather[9], which had not worked due to the air resistance of the feather. The experiment was repeatable and led to the promise that the same thing would happen again if the experiment were repeated. His experiment was repeated on the Moon by Apollo 15 astronaut David Scott, actually using a hammer and a feather. He proved that if one could eliminate the interfering factors, or separate the concerns, the rule remained true. (Note how the concept of promises seems to be relevant in forming expectations. This theme will return in part III of the book.)

We might choose to take this continuity of physical behaviour as an axiom, but the example illustrates something else important: that what seems to be a law often needs to be clarified for the context in which it is made. On Earth, dropping a hammer and a feather would not have the same result because of the air resistance of the feather. In outer space, the lack of uniform gravitation would prevent the objects from falling at all. Had we simply made the promise (or more boldly, the 'law') that says hammers will fall at a constant acceleration, it would have been wrong. The way we isolate effects on a local scale and use them to infer general rules is a testament to the homogeneity of physical behaviour.

But how far does this go? Still there is the issue of scale. Is the world truly clockwork in its machinations, and at all scales, and in all contexts? During Newton's time, many philosophers believed that it was[10].

The desire to control is a compelling one that has seduced many minds over the years. A significant amount of effort is used to try to predict the stock market prices, for instance, where millions of dollars in advantage can result from being ahead of competitors in the buying and selling of stocks. We desire an outcome, and we desire the ability to determine the outcome, so that we can control things. Yet this presupposes that the world is regular and predictable with the continuity of cause and effect. It presupposes that we can isolate multiple attempts to influence the behaviour of something so that the actual thing *we* do is the deciding factor for outcome —with no interference from outside. Noise and interference (radio noise, the weather, flocks of birds at airports, etc.), are constant forces to be reckoned with in building technologies for our use.

Shutting things into isolation, by separating concerns is the classic strategy to win apparent control from nature. This is reflected in the way laws of physics are formulated. For example: "A body continues in a state of rest or uniform motion in the absence of net external forces". This is a very convenient idealization. In fact, there is no known place in the universe where a body could experience exactly no external force. The law is a fiction, or – as we prefer to say – a *suitably idealized approximation* to reality. Similarly, examples of Newtonian mechanics talk about perfectly smooth spheres, with massless wires and frictionless planes. Such things do not exist, but, had they existed, they would have made the laws so much simpler, separating out only the relevant or dominant concerns for a particular scale. Physics is thus a creative work of abstraction, far from the theory of everything that is sometimes claimed.

For about a century, then, determinism was assumed to exist and to be the first requirement to be able to exert precise control over the world. This has come to dominate our cultural attitudes towards control. Today, determinism is known to be fundamentally false, and yet the illusion of determinism is still clung onto with fervour in our human world of bulk materials, artificial environments, computers and information systems.

The impact of Newton and Leibniz on our modern day science, and everyday cultural understanding of the world, can hardly be overestimated. The clockwork universe they built is surely one of the most impressive displays of theoretical analysis in history. If we need further proof that science is culture, we only have to look at the way their ideas pervade every aspect of the way that we think about the world. Words like energy, momentum, force and reaction creep into everyday speech. But they are approximations.

The problem was this: the difficult problems in physics from Newton's era were to do with the movements of celestial bodies, i.e. the physics of the very large. Seemingly deterministic methods could be developed to approximate these large scale questions, and today's modern computers make possible astounding feats of prediction, like the Martian landings and the Voyager space probe's journey through the solar system, with a very high degree of accuracy. What could be wrong with that?

The answer lay in the microscopic realm, and it would not be many years following Newton, before determinism began to show its cracks, and new methods of statistics had to be developed to deal with the uncertainties of observing even this large scale celestial world of tides and orbits. For a time science could ignore indeterminism. Two areas of physics defied this dominion of approximation, however, and shattered physicists' views about the predictability of the natural world. The first was quantum theory, and the second was the weather.

The 20th century saw the greatest shift away from determinism and its clockwork view of the universe, towards explicitly non-deterministic ideas. It began with the development of statistical mechanics to understand the errors in celestial orbits, and the thermodynamics of gases and liquids that lay behind the ingenious innovations of the industrial revolution[11]. Following that, came the discovery that the physics of the very small could only be derived from a totally new kind of physical theory, one that did not refer to actual moving objects at all, but was instead about different states of information.

That matter is made up of atoms is probably known by everyone with even the most rudimentary education today. Many also know that the different atomic elements are composed of varying numbers of protons, neutrons and electrons, and that even more particles were discovered after these, to form part of a sizable menagerie of things in the microscopic world of matter. Although commonplace, this knowledge only emerged relatively recently in the 20th century, a mere hundred years ago, and yet its impact on our culture has been immense[12]. What is less well known is that these microscopic parts of nature are goverened by the dynamics of states rather than smooth motion.

A *state* is a very peculiar idea, if you are used to thinking about particles and bodies in motion, but it is one that has, more recently, become central in information technology. A state describes something like a signal on a traffic light, i.e. its different colour combinations. We say that a traffic light can exist in a number of allowed states.

For example, in many countries, there are three allowed states: red, amber and green. In the UK and some European and Commonwealth countries, however, it can exist in one of four states: red, amber, red-amber, and green. The state of the system undergoes transitions: from green to amber to red, for instance.

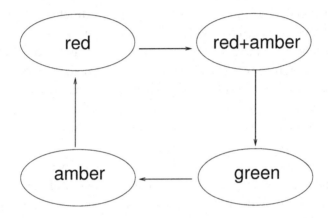

Fig. 1.1. The traffic light cycle is made up of four distinct states. It gives us a notion of orbital stability in a discrete system of states, in the next chapter.

What quantum science tells us is that subatomic particles like electrons are things that exist in certain states. Their observable attributes are influenced (but not determined) by states that are hidden somewhere from view. Even attributes like the positions of the particles are unknown *a priori*, and seem to be influenced by these states. At the quantum level, particles seem to live *everywhere* and nowhere. Only when we observe them, do we see a snapshot outcome. Moreover, instead of having just three or four states, particles might have a very large number, and the changes in them only determine the *probability* that we might be able to observe the state in the particle.

It is as if we cannot see the colour of nature's states directly, we can only infer them indirectly by watching when the traffic starts and stops. These are very strange ideas, nothing like the clockwork universe of Newton.

The history of these discoveries was of the greatest significance, gnawing at the very roots of our world view. It marked a shift from describing outcomes in terms of forces and inevitable laws, to using sampled information and chance. The classical notion of a localized point-like particle was obliterated leaving a view based just on information about observable states. The concept of a particle was still 'something observable', but we know little more than that. Amazingly, the genius of quantum mechanics has been that we also don't need to understand the details to make predictions[13]. We can get along without knowing what might be happening 'deep down'. Although a bit unnerving, knowing that we have to let go of determinism has not brought the world to a standstill.

There are lessons to be learnt from this, about how to handle the kind of uncertainties we find today in modern information infrastructure, as its complexity pushes it beyond the reach of simple methods of control.

The way 'control' emerges in a quantum mechanical sense is in the manipulation of guard-rails or constraining walls, forces called *potentials*: containers that limit the probable range of electrons to an approximately predictable region. This is not control, but loading the dice by throwing other dice at them. Similarly, when building technologies to deal with uncertainty, we must use similar ideas of constraint.

We don't experience the strangeness of the quantum world in our lives because, at the coarse scale of the human eye, of many millions of atoms, the bizarre quantum behaviour evens out—just as the waves lapping onto our ship were dwarfed by the larger features of the ocean when zooming out. We can expect the same thing to happen in information systems too. As our technology has become miniaturized to increasingly atomic dimensions, the same scaling effect is happening effectively in our information infrastructure today, thanks to increased speed and traffic density.

Determinism is thus displaced, in the modern world, from being imagined as the clockwork mechanism of Newtonian 'physical law', to merely the representing the intent to measure: the interaction with the observer[14]. This is a symptom of a much deeper shift that has shaken science from a description in terms of ballistic forces to one of message passing, i.e. an information based perspective. We'll return further to this issue and describe what this for infrastructure means in chapter 3.

Our modern theory of matter in the universe is a model that expressly disallows precise knowledge of its internal machinery. Quantum Mechanics, and its many founders[15] throughout the first half of the 20th century, showed that our earlier understanding of the smallest pieces of the world was deeply flawed, and only *seemed* to be true at the scale of the macroscopic world. Once we zoom in to look more closely, things look very different. Nevertheless, we can live with this lack of knowledge and make progress. The same is true modelling information infrastructure, if we only understand the scales in the right way. This presents a very different challenge to building technology: instead of dealing with absolute certainty, we are forced to make the best of unavoidable *uncertainty*[16].

But there is more. As if the quantum theory of the very small weren't enough, there was a further blow to determinism in the 1960s, not from quantum theory this time, but rather from the limits of information on a macroscopic scale. These limits revealed themselves during the solving of complicated hydrodynamic and fluid mechanical models, by the new generation of digital computers, for the more mundane purpose of the weather forecast.

What makes weather forecasting difficult is physics itself. The physics of the weather is considerably harder than the physics of planetary motion. Why? The simple answer is scale. In planetary motion, planets and space probes interact weakly by gravitational attraction. The force of attraction is very weak, which has the effect that planets experience a kind of calm ocean effect, like our imaginary ship. What each celestial body experiences is very predictable, and the time-scales over which major changes occur are long in most cases of interest.

The atmosphere of a planet is a thin layer of gases and water, frothing and swirling in constant motion. Gas and liquid are called fluids, because they flow (they are not solids). They experience collisions (pressure), random motion (temperature) and even internal friction and stickiness (viscosity), fluids can be like water or like treacle, and unlike planets their properties change depending on how warm they are. The whole of thermodynamics and the industrial revolution depended on these qualities. The timescales of warming and cooling and movement of the atmosphere are similar to the times over which large bodies of fluid move. All of this makes the weather a very complex fluid dynamics problem.

Now, if we zoom in with a microscope, down to the level of molecules, the world looks a little bit like a bunch of planets in motion, but only a superficially. A gas consists of point-like bodies flying around. So why is a fluid so much harder to understand? The answer is, again, the scales at work. In a gas, there are billions of times more bodies flying around than in a solar system, and they weigh basically nothing compared to a planet. Molecules in a gas are strongly impacted when sunlight shines onto them – because they are so light, they get a significant kick from a single ray of light. A planet, on the other hand, is affected only infinitesimally by the impact of light from the sun.

So when we model fluids, we have to use methods that can handle all of these complex, strong interactions. When we model planets, we can ignore all of those effects as if they were small waves lapping against a huge ship. The asteroid belt is the one feature of our solar system that one might consider modelling as a kind of fluid. It contains many bodies in constant, random motion, within a constrained gravitational field. However, even the asteroid belt is not affected by the kind of sudden changes of external force that our atmosphere experiences. All of these things conspire to make the weather an extremely difficult phenomenon to understand. We sometimes call this chaos.

The Navier-Stokes equations for fluid motion were developed in the 1840s by scientists Claude-Louis Navier (1785-1836) and George Gabriel Stokes (1819-1903), on the basis of a mechanical model for idealized incompressible fluids. They are used extensively in industry as well as in video games to simulate the flowing of simple and complex mixtures of fluids through pipes, as well as convection cells in houses and in the atmosphere. As you might imagine, the equations describing the dynamics of fluids and all of their strongly interacting parts are unlike those for planetary motion, and contain so-called non-linear parts. This makes solving problems in fluid mechanics orders of magnitude more difficult than for planetary motion, even with the help of computers. The reason for this is rather interesting.

The problem with understanding it was that its tightly coupled parts made computational accuracy extremely important. The mixing of scales in the Navier-Stokes equations was the issue. When phenomena have strongly interacting parts, understanding their behaviour is hard, because the details at one scale can directly affect the details at another scale. The result is that answers become very sensitive to the accuracy of the calculations. If couplings in systems are only weak, then a small error in one part will not affect another part very strongly and approximations work well. But in a strongly connected system, small errors get amplified. For example, planets are only weakly coupled to one another, so an earthquake in California (which is a small scale phenomenon) does not affect the orbit of the Moon (a large scale phenomenon).

Suppose our ship was not floating on the water with a propeller, but being pushed across the water by a metal shaft from the land, like a piston engine. Then the ship and the land would have been strongly coupled, and what happened to one would be immediately transmitted back to the other. Another way of putting it is that what would have remained short-range and local to the ship, suddenly attained a long-range effect. So long- and short-scale behaviour would not separate.

The coupling in a fluid is not quite as strong as a metal shaft, between every atom, but it is somewhere in between that and a collection of weakly interacting planets. This means that the separation of scales does not happen in a neat, convenient way.

What does all this have to do with the weather forecast? Well, the simple answer is that it made calculations and modelling of the weather unreliable. In fact, the effects of all of this strong coupling came very graphically into the public consciousness when another scientist in the 1960s tried to use the Navier-Stokes equations to study convection of the atmosphere. American mathematician and meteorologist Edward Lorenz (1917-2008) developed a set of equations, called naturally the Lorenz equations to model the matter of two dimensional convection, derived with the so-called Boussinesq approximation to Navier-Stokes. On the surface of the Earth, which is two dimensional, convection is responsible for driving many of the processes that lead to the weather.

The Lorenz equations, which look deceptively simple compared to the Navier-Stokes equation, are a set of mutually modulating differential equations which, through their coupling, become *non-linear*. Certain physical processes are referred to as having non-linear behaviour, which means that the graph of their response is not a straight line, giving them an amplifying effect. The response of such a process to a small disturbance is disproportionately larger than the disturbance itself, like when you whisper into a microphone that is connected to a huge public address system and blow back the hairstyles of your audience. Disproportionately means, again, not a proportional straight-line relationship, but a superlinear curve which is therefore 'non-linear'.

Non-linearity makes amplification of effect much harder to keep track of because it amplifies different quantities by different amounts, and makes computations inaccurate in inconsistent ways. When you combine those results later, the resulting error is even harder to gauge and so the problems pile up. Everything is deterministic all the way, but neither humans nor computers can work to unlimited accuracy, and the methods of computation involve approximation that gets steadily worse. The problem is not determinism but instability.

When not much is happening in the weather, the calculational approximation is good and we can be more certain of an accurate answer, but when there is a lot of change, amplification of error gets worse and worse. That is why predicting the weather is hard. If it looks like there will be no change, that is a reliable prediction. But if it looks like change is afoot (which is what we are really interested in knowing), then our chances of getting the calculations right are much smaller.

Lorenz made popular the notion of the *butterfly effect*, which is well known these days as an illustration of chaos theory. It has appeared in popular culture in films and literature for many years[17]. The butterfly effect suggests somewhat whimsically that a delicate and tiny movement like the flapping of a butterfly wing in the Amazon rain forest could, through the non-linear amplification of the weather processes, be imagined to lead to a devastating storm or cataclysm[18] on the other side of the planet. Such is the strength of the coupling – as if an earthquake could shake the Moon. Although his point was meant as an amusing parody of non-linearity, it made a compelling image that popularized the notion of the amplification of small effects into large ones.

Strong coupling turns out to be a particular problem in computer-based infrastructure, though this point needs further explanation in the chapters to come. Chaos is easily contained, given the nature of information systems, yet systems are often pushed beyond the brink of instability. We do not escape from uncertainty so easily.

Prediction is an important aspect of control, but what about our ability to influence the world? You can't adjust the weather with a screwdriver, or tighten a screw with a fan. That tells us there are scale limitations to influence too. I would like to close this section with a story about the effect of scale on control.

The presumably apocryphal tale of King Canute, or Knut the great, who was a king of Denmark, England, Norway, and parts of Sweden at the close of the first millennium, is well known to many as a fable of futility in the face of a desire to control. Henry of Huntingdon, the 12th century chronicler, told how Canute set his throne on the beach and commanded the waves to stay back. Then, as the waves rolled relentlessly ashore, the tide unaffected by his thought processes, or the stamping of his feet, Canute declared: "Let all men know how empty and worthless is the power of kings!"

Written in this way, with a human pitting himself against a force of nature that we are all familiar with, has a certain power to capture our imaginations. It seems like an obvious lesson, and we laugh at the idea of King Canute and his audacious stunt, but we should hold our breaths. The same mistake is being made every day, somewhere in the world. Our need to control is visceral, and we go to any lengths to try it by brute force, before reason wins the day.

Many of us truly believe that brute force is the answer to such problems: that if we can just apply sufficient force, we will conquer any problem. The lessons of non-predictability count for little if you don't know them. Force can be an effective tool in certain situations, but scale plays a more important role.

Canute could not hold back the ocean because he had no influential tools on the right scale. Mere thought does not interact with anything outside of our brains, naturally, so it had little hope of holding back the water. As a man, he could certainly have held back water. He had sufficient force—after all, we are all mostly made up of water, so holding back water requires about the same amount of force as holding back other people. However, unlike other people, water is composed of much smaller pieces that can easily flow around a man. Moreover, the sheer size of the body of water would have simply run over him as a finger slides over woollen threads – the water would barely have noticed his presence. A futile mismatch of scales – he could never even have used the force he was able to exert against an army because the interaction between a solid man and liquid water is rendered so weak as to be utterly ineffective.

As humans, we forget quickly the natural disasters after they have happened and go back to believing we are in control[19]. Control is important to us. We talk about it a lot. It is ultimately connected with our notions of free will, of intent and of purpose. We associate it with our personal identity, and our very survival as a species. We have come to define ourselves as a creative species, and one that has learnt to master its environments. Much of that ingenuity gives us a sense of control.

A central theme of this chapter is that control is about information, and the scale or resolution at which we can perceive it. Surely, using today's information systems, we could build a machine to do what Canute could not? If not actually hold back the tide, then at least adapt to it so quickly as to keep dry in some smart manner? Couldn't windows clean themselves? Couldn't smart streets in developing countries clear stagnant water and deploy agents to fight off malaria and other diseases? Couldn't smart environments ward off forces on a scale that we as individuals cannot to address? These things might be very possible indeed, but would they be stable? The bounds of human ingenuity are truly great, but if such things are possible, it still begs an important question: would such smart technologies be stable to such a degree that we could rely on them to be safe?[20].

Now think one step further than this, not to a modified natural world, but to the artificial worlds of our own creation: our software and information systems. These systems are coupled to almost every aspect of human survival today. They have woven themselves into the fabric of society in the so-called developed world and we now depend on them for our survival, just like our physical environment. Are these systems stable and reliable?

In a sense, they are precisely what King Canute could not accomplish: systems that hold back a deluge of communication and data records, on which the world floats, from overwhelming us, neutralizing information processing tasks that we might have tried to accomplish by brute force in earlier generations, or could not have done at all without their help. Even if it is a problem of our own making, without computers we would truly drown in the information that our modern way of living needs to function.

What can we say about the stability of our modern IT infrastructure? Software systems do not obey the laws of physics, even though they run on machines that do. The laws of behaviour in the realm of computers are not directly related to the physical laws just discussed. Nevertheless, the principles we've been describing here, of scale and determinism, must still apply, because those principles are about information. Only the realization of the principles will be different.

Scale matters.

Will our future, information-infused world be safe and reliable? Will it be a calm moonlit ocean or a chaotic mushroom cloud? The answer to these questions is: it will be what we make it, but subject to the limitations of scale and complexity. It will depend on how stable and reliable the environment around it is. So we must ask: are the circumstances around our IT systems (i.e. the dominant forces and flows of information at play) sufficiently predictable that we can maneuver reliably within their boundaries? If so, we will feel in control, but there are always surprises in store—the freak waves, the unexpected flapping of a butterfly's wings in an unwittingly laid trap of our own making. How can we know?

Well, we go in search of certainty, and the quest begins with the key idea of the first part of this book: stability.

2

Feedback Patterns and Thresholds

How the relative sizes of things govern their behaviours

Astronomy is 1derful,
And interesting 2,
The Ear3volves around the sun,
That makes a year 4 you.
The Moon affects the sur5 heard,
By law of phy6 great,
It7 when the stars, so bright,
Do nightly scintill8.
If watchful providence be9,
With good intentions fraught,
Would not been up her watch divine,
We soon should come to 0 (nought).
– Unknown[21]

Before we can argue how stable systems ought to be, we have to be able to measure how stable they actually are[22]. That is a surprisingly difficult thing to do. To understand better, we need to cover some more of the basic science of scales, and explore how these affect stability.

There are two essential reasons for wanting to measure stability: the first is to be able to put a practical figure on the result for the sake of comparison. The other is to know how it arises so that one might diagnose failures of stability. By understanding how to measure a thing, we also hope to learn something about it in the process. From the previous chapter, it should come as no surprise that stability is closely related to scales in the system[23].

Consider some examples. A computer program crashes, or undergoes a failure, when the amount of memory it needs approaches the scale of total amount of memory available in the computer. It reaches a limit for its container. The size of the container influences the functioning of the software. Even though the container is designed by humans, and is immunized against the laws of physics by existing only in software, there is no escaping the limitations of scale.

Instability can also be benign. The division of a cell during reproduction (a process called mitosis) happens by partitioning an existing single cell, while drawing nutrients from the environment. After some time, the processes within it have duplicated the contents of the original cell and the cell reaches a point of instability at which it splits. Was the split caused by the absorption from the environment, or a result of genetic programming from within? The scales at work here involve both time and space: the rate of the process of creating internal molecular structure, by absorbing material from outside the cells takes time and uses up space. We might measure the stability of a cell by the presence of a critical level of signalling proteins called growth factors, which are believed to initiate the cell division process[24].

A radioactive atom on the other hand, like Uranium 234, decays spontaneously by alpha emission to Thorium 230. No outside influence is needed, but a certain time must elapse for quantum processes to wait for this 'random' decay event to happen. We measure the stability of a so-called 'random' decay process by its *half-life*. That is the length of time we expect to elapse for half of the material to decay[25].

Instability does not have to result in a sudden 'event', like an explosion. Such a change is called a *catastrophe* in mathematics, which is not to place any moral judgement on the change: a catastrophe is a break in the continuity of a system— a change of its structure. Other kinds of change happen more smoothly than this. We might say that the water level in a bucket is stable, if it does not change; but, if we discover a leak, it will start to sink gradually. There is no sudden catastrophe, but rather a gradual process of decay. We could even top up the bucket to keep it full, as we do with the air in our tyres.

To put it into perspective, we find the emptying of the bucket disturbing mainly because it has a finite size and we know that there will be and end to the whole process. The size of the bucket defines a lifetime for the process: a timescale. If the level could simply continue falling slowly forever, we would think this was normal and there would be no problem. We say that nitroglycerine is unstable, for instance, because the smallest nudge can cause it to explode. The revolution counter (RPM meter) on cars, has red band, above a certain level, indicating when engine revolutions per second have become higher than recommended for the engine under normal working conditions. You don't expect the car to explode at this point, but prolonged use at this level might cause wear, which in turn could precipitate a catastrophe. Given the potential for instability, we look for ways to prevent the approach of the relevant threshold by observing.

The great fire of London in 1666 precipitated the invention of the first automated threshold detector—a fire alarm, to prevent the spread of a flammable instability in wooden houses. The alarm comprised a string that 'stretched through each room of a house, and then extended to the basement where it was connected to a weight suspended over a gong'[26]. The idea was that a fire in this threshold monitored home would burn through the string and wake the household to a timely escape.

A slight improvement on this detector is the bi-metallic strip, which is two long pieces of metal with different thermal expansion properties, usually steel and copper, coiled so as to take up less space. When the temperature changes, the metals expand or contract at different rates causing the metal to bend. It is a transducer that converts temperature change into mechanical movement. Bi-metallic strips are still used in basic thermostats to regulate the switching on and off of central heating systems, based on a temperature setting. The arbitrary temperature setting on the thermostat dial defines a user-controlled scale. When the threshold is passed, it triggers an electrical switch to initiate heating, and when it cools, the circuit is broken.

In medical monitors, thresholds are used for a variety of vital signs, like heart rate and breathing rate, but because humans are not such simple machines as to be regulated by a single dial, multivariate thresholds are normal to provide early warning of patient crises.

Arbitrary thresholds are used to signify critical behaviour in many industrial monitoring systems. Such a reliance on what seems to be an arbitrary choice should prompt the obvious question: how can one know the threshold for the onset of instability? One answer would clearly be to measure it by trial and error – but that presupposes that we can reproduce the exact conditions in advance of every scenario which is unlikely. The answer is to look more deeply into how scales emerge in systems of all kinds.

Suppose someone asks how old you are, what do you say? You say, "I'm 25", of course. If you were a diligent scientist, you would immediately say: "25 what? 25 years, 25 seconds?" A smart aleck, trying to be funny, would reply: "Why 25 marriages of course".

Years, metres, seconds (and marriages) are all units of measurement. In America and parts of the Commonwealth, imperial units are used. Everywhere else today we use S.I. units from the French Systeme D'internationale, also known as the metric system (or sometimes the KMS, for kilogrammes, metres, and seconds). In physics, however, we care much less about units as the underlying *kind* of measurement.

One of the most remarkable things about measurements is that they can all be broken down into a small set of basic measures: mass, length, time. Sometimes others are used, like electric charge. These are the basic measures of the physical universe we live in. In the virtual world of software and computers, there are other measures like bits and bytes, CPU cycles, and others. If we know that two things represent the same kind of measurement, then we know that they must have the same kind of measurement scale.

We call such classes of length, time, and mass *dimensions*. This has nothing really to do with the four dimensions of space and time, or the extra dimensions written about in speculative physics books. Think rather about the dimensions of a television screen, i.e. its height and width. But now keep in mind that size is only one kind of extent in space. Oths might be age (which is time), or weight (which has to do with mass).

While all this might sound terribly prosaic, it is in fact one of the most powerful tools any scientist has in his or her bag of tricks for analysing the world, for it allows us to understand the world in scale, predict the behaviour of real objects like aircraft and buildings from scale models, test them in wind tunnels, with scaled forces. With care, the technique offers enormous insight about the world of scales—and we can use this in our quest to understand stability.

Physicist Jean Baptiste Joseph Fourier (1768-1830), interested in the dimensional analysis that Newton had made powerful use of in his work, was quick to point out that it does not make sense to add together numbers of different dimensions:

   3 metres + 4 metres = 7 metres,

but

   3 metres + 4 seconds = ???

doesn't make anything. Metres and seconds, he might have said, are completely separate ideas. Physicists would say the measurements were 'orthogonal', meaning literally at right angles to one another[27] – you can change length without changing time. The importance of these difference scales to science is that actual phenomena tie different scales together, and we can use them to discover when a system is going to destabilize.

For example, a moving body has a speed, which is a distance covered over a certain time. So speed has dimensions of distance per unit of time, or L/T or length over time. Acceleration is a change in speed over an interval of time, so it has dimensions of speed divided by time, or distance over time squared

$$L/(T \times T) = L/T^2.$$

Newton's second law tells us that external force is proportional to mass multiplied by acceleration, so the dimensions of force are ML/T^2, and since, by Fourier's argument, the dimensions of force must always be the same, we can infer the any force in any situation must have these dimensions.

We can go on relating measurable quantities to other measurable quantities, and always reduce a measurement to a combination of these basic dimensions: mass, length, time. At least, that is true in the physical world. In other scenarios, these measurements might not be helpful—even if they underlie some kind of basic truth about the real world. The example of bits as a unit of information is an important one. The word 'bit' is a short form of *binary digit*, the key term being *digit*. Unlike a length, which can take on a continuum of values, a bit can only have the value 1 or 0, hence it is binary in nature. From bits we get bytes (meaning 'by eight' or $\times 8$ bits), and words, and kilobits and megabytes, and so on. The digit is thus a dimension in its own right[28].

These ideas about units of measurement form the beginning of what is known as *dimensional analysis*[29], a form of analysis that allows us to see what probably ought to be obvious about system behaviour, but which might be obscured by complicated interrelationships or fancy names. As a physics student, I recall thinking that dimensional analysis seemed to be the least glamorous part of the whole undergraduate syllabus—it was certainly presented with a certain lacklustre. It was only when I attended lectures on fluid mechanics, and later quantum field theory that its significance began to emerge. Today, I think it is one of the most remarkable aspects of physics.

Dimensional analysis starts to get interesting when we consider systems with more than one scale of the same dimension, (e.g. if there are two characteristic lengths instead of just one that govern the behaviour of a system). That is the case in the bi-metallic strip, and we use that property creatively. Just as Fourier noted that it doesn't make sense to add numbers with different units, so it also makes no sense to compare them.

Comparing the size of an egg with the time it takes to boil another does not help you to compare two eggs. However, if we divide a number measured in some units by another number, measured in the same units, the result is a pure ratio that really does give us an honest comparison of the two. It is honest because it is a relative measure. Thus, for two identical eggs, the ratio of the height of one to the height of another allows us to say that they have eggsactly (sorry) the same height, similarly with weight, whiteness, or any other measure we can think of.

When you divide a length by a length, for instance, the result has no units at all. It is just a comparative scale. A ratio of any two like-dimensions is a pure number, called a *dimensionless number*. A simple example of this is the aspect ratio of a picture of computer or television screen, which is the ratio of x/y or width over height:

$$\frac{\text{Width}}{\text{Height}} = \frac{16}{9} = 1.777.$$

The height can be measured in any units of length, as long as they are the same units: 16 nanometres divided by 9 nanometres, or 16 fathoms divided by 9 fathoms—it doesn't matter. If the ratio is the same, then the shapes of the two screens are the said to be similar.

If you took a screen that was 16 metres by 9 metres and walked away from it from a safe distance, then held a 16 inch by 9 inch screen in front of your face, it would exactly cover the larger screen in the distance. It would overlap perfectly. The screens would be *similar*.

Newton, and several other scientists after him, took dimensional analysis much farther than this. They applied the idea not only to shapes, but to any pattern of behaviour in a system that could be characterized by measurements. Newton thus pioneered what, today, would be referred to as *dynamical similarity*, or in his language *similitude*. In dynamical similarity, dimensionless numbers represent invariants, or universal, unchanging qualities of systems, whereas dimensional numbers always lead to qualitative change,

For example, if a supermarket knows that 3 persons per minute enter the supermarket, then the store will begin to fill up with people unless at least 3 people per minute leave the store (the same argument applies to users arriving at a website). The queues will begin to build up at the cash registers unless these numbers are in balance. If we write down the dimensionless ratio of these rates, the result is a service ratio:

$$\frac{\text{Checkout rate}}{\text{Arrival rate}} = \frac{1 \text{ person per minute}}{3 \text{ persons per minute}} = 0.333.$$

Because arrival and checkout rates have the same dimensions (persons per unit time[30]), we can form a dimensionless ratio of them. This tells us that only a third of the people arriving are getting out of the shop, and soon it will be full as the queues grow. We might interpret this as the efficiency of processing the customers.

Suppose now everything speeds up, and 3 customers per second enter the shop, and only 1 per second leaves: then the efficiency is unchanged—we just scaled up the whole operation 60 times. But the shop fills up faster now, because the length of the queue is going to be 60 times bigger. Length is not a dimensionless number and so it is sensitive to the measurement scale.

Only dimensionless numbers are preserved when we scale. They are said to be *scale invariant*. Systems that have all the same dimensionless ratios are called *dynamically similar*.

In physics and engineering, analysis often begins by trying to write down all of the dimensionless ratios one can think of, as these will represent i) all the combinations of parameters that can belong together in a single relationship, and ii) identification of the fixed points or invariants of scaling. For instance, for the television we might write down at least these dimensionless ratios for length and time:

$$\frac{\text{height}}{\text{width}}, \frac{\text{height}}{\text{depth}}, \frac{\text{width}}{\text{depth}}, \frac{\text{time to switch on}}{\text{time to change channel}}$$

The mass of the television is the one-dimensional scale that has no comparison, so we would not expect the mass of television to play much of a role in its behaviour. To the casual onlooker, the significance of these ratios might not be very clear, but an engineer will soon see their relevance to the behaviour of the thing.

Dimensional analysis is common in engineering, where practical issues do not allow engineers to idealize scenarios in the same way that scientists can get away with. Thus there are often more actual scales to deal with: height, width, depth, distance from a wall, etc. All of these scales make a difference in engineering[31].

In our story of stability, the scales of dimensional analysis tell us about *thresholds* that matter in different systems, because invariant thresholds always come from dimensionless numbers. If we can define stability in terms of dimensionless quantities, then we know it will be universal. These insights might have been learnt by studying physical phenomena in the past, but they must also apply to information systems and software in the modern world.

Although the characteristics of stability are summarized by having a dimensionless number cross a threshold, the changes that probe instability must rely on the dimensionful quantities that make up those dimensionless numbers, otherwise they would be invariants (e.g., your age divided by 21 years describes the threshold for ordering drinks in a bar, in many countries). So let's ask, what kind of change would change a dimensionless ratio? What would tip a system over the edge of instability?

As always, we start with a simple model. Suppose we place a ball at the crest of a hill to that it is perfectly balanced, or balance a pencil on its end (see Figure 2.1). The smallest perturbation of the ball or pencil will destabilize it. It would cause the ball to roll to the bottom of the hill. A ball placed atop a hill is thus mechanical system that we say is *unstable* to small *perturbations* of its initial configuration. The smallest change in that configuration unleashes a much larger irreversible change in the system.

Fig. 2.1.   A ball in a potential can be stable or unstable to small perturbations of ball movement. A potential well (left) is stable to movement, but unstable to filling. A potential hill (right) is unstable to movement but stable to filling.

By contrast, if we place a ball at the bottom of a valley and push it slightly, it might roll a little, and then it will roll back to where it started, preserving the original condition of the system. We would say that this system is *stable* to small perturbations[32].

The difference between the two scenarios is the shape of background they are constrained to move on. Hills, wells and valleys are regions of space that exert forces because of the force of gravity. Other forces would do just as well, but gravity is easiest for us to relate to. We call these shaped forces *potentials* in physics, because they represent the potential to convert initial location into a release of later activity. The potential stores up energy that can later be withdrawn from the bank and spent as motion. This is part of the energy accounting referred to in chapter 1.

A valley forms a potential *well* or a constraining potential for a ball, because gravity tends to pull a ball downwards so that it can't escape from the container, and the sides hinder sideways motion to escape. A hill, on the other hand, forms a potential barrier to something on either side of it because a ball would not necessarily be able to roll up hill and over the the other side without meeting the resistance of gravity wanting to pull it down again. For a ball sitting on top, it is a highly precarious, unstable potential.

This simple thought experiment is one of many notions of stability used to characterize systems, and a helpful analogy. What the definitions of stability all share in common is the idea that the state of a system is not significantly altered when we perturb systems by a small amount. Stability is therefore associated with minima (the lowest part of the wells) of a potential, and unstable points are associated with maxima (the highest part of the peaks).

Isn't the idea of perturbing a system an artificial way of deciding its stability. Isn't it cheating? The idea is that, you don't need to arrange for an external perturbation. If the system is unstable, something in the environment will eventually arrange to perturb the system for you. Designers who don't believe in Murphy's law, that which can happen will happen, are irresponsible. Many mistakes have been made by assuming such perturbations could never happen. The John Hancock Tower in Boston, Massachusetts is a telling example. The tower is a high-rise building with glass windows all the way up. During the design of the building, architects did not take into account the effect of wind on the building. Wind-generated torsion on the building[33] quickly led to one of the most embarrassing crises. Torsion is a rotational, twisting force. When wind-speeds exceeded 45 miles per hour, the wind would catch the bevelled edges of the building resulting in torsional oscillations of the building's frame. This in turn caused the window frames to transmit sudden force to the glass, which then popped out and fell hundreds of feet down to the ground. Until the problem was solved, the police would have to close off the streets whenever the wind speed exceeded 45 miles per hour.

We can talk about stability that is natural or artificially maintained, stable and meta-stable. Or to put it another way, intrinsic and extrinsic stability. The valley example is an intrinsically stable system. By virtue of its configuration of parts, it is programmed to remain stable as long as the actual configuration is not obliterated by some overwhelming force. The ball atop the hill could be stabilized, for instance, by putting wedges under the ball on each side to prevent it from falling when small perturbations strike. Or we could make a small dent in the top so that it has a notch to sit in. This would be called *meta-stability* at a local minimum of the potential (see Figure 2.2). The configuration is still basically unstable to all but the very smallest perturbations.

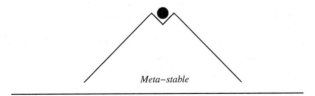

Fig. 2.2. A ball in a potential can be meta-stable, if it finds a local minimum, or dip in the potential.

Lasers are an example where meta-stability can be exploited to advantage, leading to amplification of effect. The word laser began as an acronym for Light Amplification by the Stimulated Emission of Radiation. Stimulated emission is a phenomenon in quantum theory, in which you get many electrons to balance on a kind of quantum high wire and then all jump off at the same time, to hit the ground at with combined impact, except that the high-wire is a special quantum state.

The idea of a laser is to pump atoms with photons (quanta of light) so that they end up sitting in a meta-stable state, and once they are all sitting on their high wire, to perturb them all at the same time so that all the atoms release their photons at the same time. This is called stimulated emission of light. It means that a lot of light is released in a short space of time, hence there is amplification. The idea is a bit like the less glamorous case of a toilet flush: one accumulates water in a tank, and then the flush releases all at the water at the same moment to amplify the effect of the tap feed. It only serves its purpose then the dimensionless ratio of water in the tank to the water in the basin reaches a critical threshold.

Intrinsic stability is not necessarily desirable; it might also be a nuisance. It can leave a technology unresponsive. An example of this is aircraft design. Passenger jets are designed to be as stable as possible. We basically point them in one direction and they fly in a straight line. Since they are designed to preserve human life, flight stability is a top priority. A fighter jet, on the other hand, prioritizes maneuverabilty. If a missile comes out of nowhere, it needs to be able to respond instantly. It therefore wants to operate right on the edge of stability. Fighter jets use computer-controlled flight systems that automatically compensate for minor perturbations, and the pilots do the rest. These systems correspond to someone watching the ball at the top of a hill and being ready to catch it and put it back if it should start to roll. A passenger jet can basically fly itself just as a ball can sit comfortably at the base of a valley.

The keyboard on which I am typing this text has keys that spring back and recover when I have pressed them. They spring back faster than the maximum speed of my fingers. This makes the keyboard stable and usable. Had the keys recovered much more slowly, the keyboard would have been useless to me on the timescale of my usage. If I had to wait an hour after pressing each key, I would not consider this usable under the dynamic perturbation of my fingers.

So much for the physical world, and its pitfalls. What about the unphysical worlds of our own creation: rule of law, computers and information systems all affect the functioning of complex interacting systems and they too can also be stable and unstable.

Traffic rules are a good example of this. In many countries that drive on the right hand side of the road, and before the invention of roundabouts (road circles), rules like "Wait for anyone ahead of you on your right" have been common. The idea is to allow people to enter traffic and avoid collisions, so that one of the parties knows that it has to wait for the other. Such rules are still in used many places.

A rule like this is not a physical thing, but it is easily seen to be unstable, because it tends to stop traffic rather than keep it flowing. For small side roads on non-busy trunks, this is an acceptable solution, but suppose there is a crossroads. Sooner or later four cars will arrive that this crossroads junction all together and everyone will see someone on their right, thus all of them will wait for each other. The ratio of distances from the junction have play a critical role in this instability. Assuming that the drivers actually follow the road rules, they must all stop and wait for the rest of their lives. All traffic is now dead, with no possibility to restart until someone breaks the rule.

Treated to the letter of the law, the behaviour resulting from this rule is unstable because the rule is reevaluated on a continuous basis by drivers who get stuck in a single loop of thinking. This is called negative feedback. Of course, it can easily be modified to allow the drivers to randomly wait and have a go if no one else is moving. The point is that even the careless design of rules for information systems can result in harmful behaviour. Traffic, after all, is part of the global infrastructure of our planet today.

A slightly more stable approach is the stop sign junction, as common in the United States. This uses a first-come, first-served approach: the car that arrives first gets to use the junction first. If four cars arrive at the same time, there is still a deadlock, however. The roundabout is a further improvement, designed to keep traffic moving by waiting only for traffic that is already on the roundabout itself.

What we see here is a bridge to something new: not the motion of a system running out of control, but its logic. Whenever humans are part of a system, there is the possibility of a *semantic* instability. Here, the feedback on the system is coupled by an interpretation. This will be important later in the book when we discuss economics games and the many manifestations of *reasoning*.

The semantics of a technology or system are its intended interpretation and its behavioural response to perturbations. One can imagine a sort of 'smart potential' function that adapts to different scenarios with built-in rule sets, or internal logic. Computer software behaves in this way.

The fact is that humans are not simple robotic response agents, however; we interpret and adapt and act according to a model of the world that we build on the fly, often heavily influenced by emotions. That introduces a lot of uncertainty into a feedback loop that involves humans, and there is both potential for improving and destroying stability, depending on how well placed a person is in the total system.

Here is an example of semantic instability: imagine a fearful member of tribe A, who gets caught in a trap. He sees a member of tribe B coming, who pulls out a knife to free him. The trapped tribe A member interprets this as an attack and kills the member of tribe B (the semantics of the situation are perturbed by his fear). The instability triggered by the pulling of a knife is now in motion. Tribe B declares war on tribe A and attacks, and both tribes descend into a long and protracted war over a simple misunderstanding. The escalation driven by emotional intensity creates the unstable potential for the amplification of hostilities. The threshold was perhaps fear, which could not be measured practically.

Another example of an unstable semantic or logic rule is one that was built into certain computer systems to shut down the computer if the processor began to overheat[34]. This is just like the ball atop a hill situation, waiting for a hot day to knock it off its perch—or, in fact, for hackers to perturb it.

When faced with a rule to shut something down, or deny access to a resource, in civil society[35], something will always push the wrong button, or someone will find a way to exploit it for their own benefit. That is why one usually hides such buttons out of sight. (It would be truly unfortunate if the engine stop button on a plane was located next to the intercom button.)

In several cases, hackers have been able to write computer programs to shut down systems without even having direct access to the system. This is possible if a chain of events can propagate influence indirectly, in a cascade or avalanche effect. In the case of the heat sensor, malicious software was able to perform intense calculations on the processor, generating a lot of heat which would then cause the protection system to kick in automatically—and the system would go down. Even without a malicious intent, bugs in perfectly well-intended software have also caused this to happen[36].

The most terrifying example of a feedback instability is the tragic case of Air France Flight 447, a scheduled commercial flight from Rio de Janeiro, Brazil to Paris, France. On 1 June 2009, the Airbus A330-200 airliner serving the flight crashed into the Atlantic Ocean, killing all 216 passengers and 12 aircrew[37].

Aircraft in flight are only ever meta-stable. Obviously they are poised to fall out of the sky if anything critical stops working as designed. They are extrinsically stable, held in balance by force. Even the most stable gliders that require no power can stall if they rise too steeply, or enter a dive from which they cannot recover. That was the case with the Air France Airbus flight. The aircraft crashed following an aerodynamic stall that was precipitated by a quite different failure. This precipitated failure is sometimes called an avalanche or cascade failure. It is a way of saying that, once a particular condition has occurred, the destabilization of one threshold triggers the next threshold, then the next, leading to a number of successive failures.

According to reports, ice formation in the airspeed measuring device, entering bad weather, led to an inconsistent airspeed readings. The software rules then said that the autopilot should be disengaged, as it would be unreliable. Misinterpreting the effects (a semantic instability) as a sudden loss of altitude, the pilots pulled the aircraft nose up, which further destabilized the aircraft. Despite stall warnings, this resulted in insufficient aerodynamic lift, and a complete loss of powered flight. The pilots had not received specific training in "manual airplane handling of approach to stall and stall recovery at high altitude"; this was apparently not a standard training requirement at the time of the accident. First there was the formation of ice, leading to failure of a part of the system designed to monitor airspeed. Airspeed is a controlling dimensional factor in generating lift to stay in the air, relative to angle of ascent[38]. The pilots were part of the feedback system, in charge of interpreting the semantics of the situation and responding accordingly.

From the rhyme that opens this chapter: the Moon affects the surf, I've heard, by law of physics great. Our Moon seems like the last thing to be unstable, but it too leads to a feedback system through the gravitational interaction with tides. It has been with us for four and a half billion years, yet the orbit of the Moon is also currently unstable to the tidal forces between the Earth and the Moon, on a very long timescale. Both the Earth and the Moon raise tides on each other, and this drag effect slows the Earth slightly and accelerates the Moon slightly, raising its orbit around the Earth. The Moon is thus moving away from the Earth at a measurable rate of about three centimetres per year. The system will stabilize when the Moon's orbit becomes geosynchronous.

There does not necessarily have to be physical force involved in instability. Influence requires only a transmission of information. Even messages and stories that we tell one another interact with their listeners. The concept of 'memes' was introduced by Richard Dawkins in his book *The Selfish Gene*[39]. Dawkins pointed out that certain ideas can be self-propagating. Not every idea we have is successful at being transmitted from one person to another, but certain songs, phrases of music, words, or even ideas seem to have the knack of triggering some kind of an affinity with our minds and they spread out of control. This might be called a cultural instability, though the mechanisms for memetics are not fully understood.

The foregoing examples illustrate ideas of instability using the analogy of motion around hill-valley potentials to a single perturbation. Illustrations are helpful in putting together a picture of what instability means for the short term, but for engineers to create infrastructure in our world that is stable, one needs to go beyond mere visualizations and arguments, to indisputable models that endure over time. With the discussion of scales under our belts, we can now put together a more continuous model for stability than this one-shot perturbation response.

A response to a single perturbation can be either linear or non-linear, in the sense of Chapter 1. If it is linear, the system can usually be perturbed many times and respond in a helpful, functional way. This is how we make physical tools and information-based services. A web server is a piece of computer software that receives requests and returns information in proportion to what was requested. If a web server suddenly began to return information, quite out of control based on a single request, it would be a sign of a non-linear response.

Feedback systems are part of a dialogue between something driving the input and something coming from the output. The output of the system changes and becomes part of the new input in a new iteration. This goes around and around and the system either stabilizes to a well-defined value or it blows up.

The corrective potentials are a form of what is called *feedback* in control theory. Feedback basically imagines that a dynamical system is looking at itself in a mirror and asking: are we there yet? Negative feedback tends to moderate the system, making it converge towards an equilibrium value. Positive feedback amplifies the input and feeds it back into the input again so that it grows and grows out of control. The shrieking noises from public address systems, when a microphone gets too close to the loudspeakers is an example of positive feedback.

If we are going to make infrastructure, avoiding non-linear feedback is usually an important design consideration. Non-linear systems are not predictable, as we discussed with the weather. Why do non-linear systems diverge? The answer is that they always feed back on themselves. If they feed back positively then the system is intrinsically unstable.

The idea of linear response offers a way to extract something like a signature for stability in infrastructure. To ignore non-linearity might seem over-optimistic, but to engineer a stable world, it seems clear that we must avoid non-linearity at all costs.

Consider the following symbolic representation of stability:

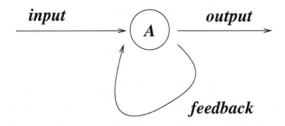

Fig. 2.3. In a feedback system, part of the response or output is fed back into the input either subtracting or adding to the input. In continuous operation this either moderates and stabilizes or amplifies.

$$(\text{Act on}) \text{ thing} \longrightarrow \text{thing}$$

I am using this to mean that when we act on a thing, we get back the same thing. We call the '(Act on)' symbol an *operator*. In mathematics, we might write something like

$$Ax \longrightarrow x.$$

It's just a way of writing the act of making a change to the object concerned (in this case: "x"). As a definition of stability, it is closing in on something sufficiently formal, but the statement is too strong. What we've defined is actually called a fixed point. A system doesn't have to be fixed in exactly the same configuration at all times, otherwise we could not allow anything to happen at all. So we revise this to an equivalence:

$$(\text{Act on}) \text{ before} \xrightarrow{equiv} \text{after}$$

We propose that the thing only has to be *dynamically equivalent* in some sense before and after the operation of being acted upon. The criterion for that equivalence must be left to the context, because it depends on the dynamics of the system concerned, as well as the level of precision we are willing to tolerate[40].

For instance, if we act on a ball by rotating it 90 degrees, the ball is not strictly in the same state, but it is in a new state that is absolutely indistinguishable from its former state. Symmetry thus plays a deep role. If we can't tell the difference before and after a change, the situation must be dynamically equivalent. It is by extending and developing this idea in a more technical and precise way that we can find other ideas of stability.

Notice that the (Act on) operator has to be dimensionless (scale free) in order to lead to a scale invariant fixed point. We can see that because an equation has to have the same dimensions on both sides of the equals sign. So if we write

$$Ax = x,$$

then, because x obviously must have the same dimensions as x on left and right, A must be dimensionless.

A similar mathematical concept with the flavour of network stability is that of *eigenstates* or *eigenvectors* and *eigenvalues*, from the German 'eigen' meaning self. These are intrinsic values that can be calculated by relatively simple mathematics, and belong to the interaction between a particular operation and the body it can acts upon. Eigenvalues crop up widely in physics, engineering and mathematical disciplines, as a method of locating stable aspects of complicated systems. Statistical methods like Principal Component Analysis, and the Principal Axes of a mechanical body use eigenvalues to determine stable configurations. Recall the strange spinning of the spaceship *Discovery* in the movie *2010*, the sequel to Arthur C. Clarke's and Stanley Kubrick's famous *2001, A Space Odyssey*. The ship seemed to be twirled like a cheerleader's baton in Jupiter's gravity. In fact this was an accurate depiction of what can happen to the spacecraft design, when a long thin shape is left in a complex perturbations like the orbit of Jupiter. It will tend to rotate about its axis of maximum moment of inertia. Eigenvector stability was also effectively used as part of Google's PageRank algorithm for ranking the importance of sites on the Web.

Fixed points and principal eigenvectors are important anchor points for technology builders. If we could always build things around fixed points to all perturbations, they would be intrinsically stable.

To examine stability in information systems, we need to develop some of these ideas. By combining the idea of operators above with the picture of the perturbations in a potential, it is straightforward to come up with a ream of examples of stability and instability. The simplest idea of stability is constancy, or invariance. A thing that has no possibility to change is, by definition, immune to external perturbations.

$$\Delta v = v_{\text{after}} - v_{\text{before}} = 0$$

If the value of something (its position, its speed, its colour, or any other verifiable property) is the same before and after an operation is applied, then we can say, without much controversy, that it is stable under that operation. In physics, one calls this *invariance* under the action of the difference operator Δ.

Invariance is an important concept, but also one that has been shattered by modern ideas of physics. What was once considered invariant, is usually only apparently invariant on a certain scale. When one looks in more detail, we find that we might only have invariance of an average. That is an idea we'll return to in Chapter 4.

The next level of stability is sometime called *covariance* (meaning varying with). If we perturb the system, it changes a little in a predictable way, but retains most of its characteristics even though some details change. This is a structural stability[41]. Galileo's inertial principle is an example of covariant stability: a free and unconstrained body will continue in a state of uniform motion in a straight line (constant velocity) unless perturbed by an external force. During the perturbed, it will shift speed or direction slightly, and thereafter continue on its uniform steady state.

The situation is different if the body is not free: for instance, if it is sitting in a confining potential, like the valley in Figure 2.1. That is the case for planets in orbit around a star, or Moons in orbit around the planets. The notion of a *steady state* can be characterized in many different ways. Indeed, in physics or mechanics constant and uniform change are basically equivalent.

A planetary orbit is a simple image that everyone can understand of something dynamically stable, yet still moving. An orbit is the balance between the inertial drag of the planet which tends to move the body in a straight line, and a sun's gravity that tends to pull it towards its centre. Planetary motion happens on such a large scale that it belongs to the scale of continuum, Newtonian motion. What about an orbit of discrete states?

The traffic lights, discussed in the previous chapter, give us this a cycle of behaviour that is stable to perturbations (see Figure 1.1). The lights always move through the same pattern of red, red and amber, amber green and back to red, regardless. If someone presses a button to cross the street, the state might change sooner than expected, but the pattern is stable. It is also a kind of orbit, but in a different arena.

Fixed cycles of behaviour, like orbits and periodic sequences, are called *limit cycles*. Rather than converging onto a single end-state, like say falling to the bottom of a well, a changing system might retain some dynamical activity and end up in a forever repeating pattern, like pendulum swinging back and forth, or a satellite going into orbit instead of crashing into the planet below. For instance, our daily circadian sleep rhythm is a cycle driven by changing levels of hormones, like melatonin, whose production is influenced by daylight. When we perturb environment by changing timezones, after a long flight, the limit cycle of our sleep is disturbed and takes some time to restabilize.

The measures of stability described above are largely about individual bodies, like planets, balls or lights, yet not everything in the world is this simple. Our bodies are complex networks of interacting cells. Materials form multitudes of different networks through chemical bonding, giving each material its characteristic properties, and humans form networks through communication.

The stability of networks thus turns out to be of enormous importance throughout science and technology. Networks are everywhere, not merely connected to our computers. Food-webs, ecosystems, economic trading patterns, chemical interactions, immune systems, and of course technologies such as water and sanitation, electricity, and all of the major infrastructure items are transport networks for something vital to our life and culture. The question of how stable networks are to perturbation is thus of key interest to human technology.

The Internet itself was envisaged as a form of network stability. Consider the simple networks depicted in Figure 2.4. Diagrams like these are called *graphs* in mathematics – they are simply nodes connected together by links, or edges. The example on the left of this figure is a 'tree' (also referred to by the more technical if less poetic name of an 'acyclic graph', meaning that it has no closed loops[42]). Tree graphs have branches and leaf nodes, but they are minimal structures that contain only a single possible path from trunk to leaf, or from any node to any other. The implication of this is that, if we block or damage on of the pathways, a part of the network becomes inaccessible.

The dashed rings in the figure show places where the destruction of a node would disconnect the graph so that it would no longer be possible to cross from one part of the graph to another. Such a point is called a *single point of failure*. That is not to say that there can only be one of them, rather that the removal of just one single point can have a catastrophic structural effect on the network.

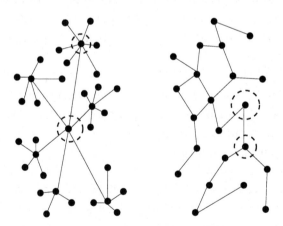

Fig. 2.4.   The reachability of one part of a network from another can be stable to the perturbation of node-removal.

A chain is a graph that is not stable to node removal. It works as a very simple model of a set of dependences. If we turn it vertically, it becomes a tower, with each successive node depending on the one beneath it[43]. Chains of dependent parts make systems fragile and unstable to catastrophic failure.

Fig. 2.5. A chain is the most fragile structure of all. The removal of any node breaks it. Thus all nodes are single points of failure.

A tree is a generalization of a chain, only with branching too. Chains and trees are the most fragile structures we can make, because they are built of many 'single points of failure'. As engineering principles go, this is not a good structure to rely on, especially if human lives are involved.

The graph or network on the right hand side of Figure 2.4 is not a tree. It contains closed loops that make it more robust. A loop means that there is more than one way around the network, i.e. there is *redundancy* or *backups* built into the multiple pathways. Networks that contain redundancy are more robust to failure, or stable to node perturbations. So, for instance, in the upper parts of the graph, the removal of a node would not disconnect the graph, we could route around an incapacitated node.

The idea that it would be possible to make networks that were robust to damaged nodes was part of the idea that spurred on the invention of the Internet as we know it today. During the 1960s, the Advanced Research Projects Agency Network (ARPANET) was the world's first operational packet switching networks, designed from conceptual studies by Paul Baran of the RAND Corporation. Baran suggested that communications could be made more stable to failures of infrastructure if messages were formed from discrete packets of information, and if the networks themselves ensured redundant pathways. The three levels of network robustness in Figure 2.6 illustrate going from a tree-like network with a critical point of failure on the left, to a *mesh* network on the right with multiple redundant pathways. The Internet was designed to be like the right hand mesh, so that, in the event of attack or other natural disaster, communications could continue uninterrupted by re-routing information. This is the system we have in use today, on an elaborate scale. We see, in action, how stability is exploited as a principle in order to make a reliant infrastructure for our society.

The foregoing examples have been continuous systems, apart from the network, which is discrete. It is also possible to generalize the initial perturbation

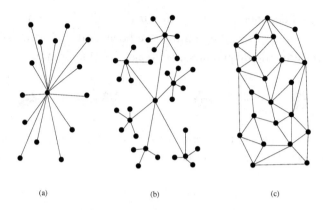

(a)   (b)   (c)

Fig. 2.6.   The reachability of one part of a network from another can be stable to the perturbation of node-removal.

argument based on Figure 2.1 so that it applies to discrete systems. Why bother? The example of the Internet is one reason, and a good illustration of the basic robustness of discrete units. Another reason is *software engineering.*

The designers of our large distributed computer systems (including the well-known Internet giants) are starting to learn about the importance of stability, not only in terms of operational stability, but also data correctness and consistency. We'll return to the details in chapter 5, but we can briefly mention the key idea of converging to a known end-state. In particular, in the world of functional programming, software engineers have begun to ask some of the hard questions about why systems become semantically unstable, especially at large scale. They refer to the problem by the name *data consistency.*

There are various formulations of the idea, but the simplest visualization is in terms of networks. Potential wells can be supplemented with a result from the theory of graphs, called internal and external stability[44]. For example, in the theory of graphs, one can identify the concept of an *externally stable* region, i.e. one in which all points outside of the graph region point into a region by a single link. Thus the smallest perturbation of position around the region would be to push something by a single hop into the region, like rolling into a potential well. It is a stable place because once in the region, there is no way out. An *internally stable* region is a place in which a perturbation of position cannot take you to any new point that is stable, i.e. it says there are no links between different stable nodes, like distinct, alternative wells. Functional programmers often appeal to the language of category theory and universal algebras, where these structures are called *semi-lattices* and *semi-groups.*

External stability tells us that we can always get to the stable region from outside it. Internal stability tells us that none of the nodes in the region are connected, so if we arrive at one of these nodes we have either reached the end of the line, or we have to leave the region again. A region that is both internally and externally stable is called the *kernel* of the graph, and it represents a trap, i.e. a place such that, if we enter, we can't leave. There might be several such traps in a network, different by some criterion, but they are all structurally stable confining potentials.

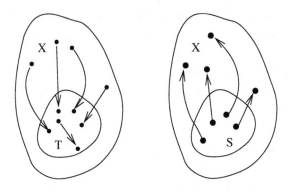

Fig. 2.7. The stability of region can be generalized from the potential well/hill view to the idea of external stability (left) and internal stability (right).

If we write the links that flow between nodes as (Flow), and the set of nodes in the region as R, then the kernel takes on the general form above:

$$(\text{Flow})R \to R$$

If you try to flow from some place in the region, you just end up back where you started, or once you're in, you're in. This is a special case of the general stability criterion: (Action) state $\to$ state, from earlier.

Each of these stable points is referred to as a *fixed point*, in mathematics. A fixed point is a place where you can end up and remain in spite of the specific perturbations that are acting. It is a self-consistent place within a system. The existence of fixed points in systems is a more or less deciding factor for the existence of a stable solution. The presence of fixed points was used to prove some of the key results in a economic game theory, for example.

When we think of networks not just as locations in a physical geography like the Internet, but as possibly abstract realms, e.g. like the map of transitions between coloured states of the traffic lights, networks become one of the most important tools in modern technology. They are used everywhere to map out the behaviour of complex interactions. They are a distinctly non-Newtonian idea, but they are a stepping stone to a deeper understanding of things that is the subject of the next chapter.

An interesting example, actually the one I came upon during my flight home from the 11th Annual Conference in Large Installation System Administration in 1997, was the human immune system. It can be regarded as having a kind of fixed-point kernel behaviour[45] that represents a state of health. Germs and viruses are perturbations to our bodies, that move us from healthy states like 'green' to poorly states like 'amber' or even deadly states like 'red'. Clearly that is a pretty simplistic view, but the principle is accurate. Viruses bring instability to our cellular processes because they re-program cells to grow and manufacture more viruses, instead of carrying out their original healthy program. They then act like cluster bombs, bursting open and releasing multiple copies of themselves to pervert neighbouring cells.

Biology has evolved stabilizing counterforces like the immune system present in vertebrates, and simpler homeostatic regulation systems in warm blooded animals[46], as a method of pseudo-intrinsic stability. It is intrinsic to our bodies, but extrinsic to the cells that are attacked, just as the CFEngine software written for computer networks was intrinsic to individual computers, but extrinsic to the files and processes it was protecting[47].

By equipping a computer with a kind of internal 'groundskeeper' or immune system, system engineers would effectively be able to architect a lasting set of *desired end-states* (like in a graph kernel) that would not immediately be attacked by the forces of decay. CFEngine accomplished this by making this groundskeeper a software robot whose specialized set of operations had to be *convergent*, meaning stable like a potential well or a graph kernel.

As long as a designer expressed all the desired system properties in terms of such fixed-point, convergent operations, the system would actually self-heal under perturbations, just by repeatedly applying the operations in a dumb manner. This is exactly what the immune system does. There is no intelligence, beyond understanding when a system is in a desired end-state. The idea was thus to create a counter-force to other, less well-behaved perturbations from outside. As long as the fixed points could be stable on the same timescale as the external perturbations, one would create an extrinsically stable state for the computer system.

These examples hint at the idea of dynamical balance, and are just cases of a more common idea: that of performing regular maintenance on structures that we build. We watch and touch up the paintwork on our houses, or dust shelves, or vacuum clean the floors. The storm drains in the streets and gutters on your house are a very simple example of a stabilizing mechanism to the perturbation of rain. All these point to a notion of dynamic stability, and are the subject of a special treatment in Chapter 4.

There is a lot to be said about stability. In one sense, it is the counterpoint of unpredictable change, and the foundation of certainty and predictability. We build on these qualities to bring reliability to the things we make. Stability takes many forms. We can approach it, as science would approach it, using abstractions and models, and we can describe it from its many exemplars. Both of these approaches will help us to understand its significance. In this chapter, I have tried to convey a little of both.

To apply these observations to technology, we need to understand the nature of the technological beast: what makes it tick, and just how clockwork is it? For that, we need to turn back a few of the pages of history, and follow its threads through the great skein of scientific understanding that led to today's technological revolution.

3
Digilogy: Cause, Effect, and Information

How transmitted information shapes the world from the bottom up.

"We are thus obliged to be modest in our demands and content ourselves
with concepts that are formal in the sense that they do not provide a visual
picture of the sort one is accustomed to require ..."
– Niels Bohr, Nobel Address

One of the running jokes, between myself and another British colleague, during the early years of founding a company around CFEngine, was my job description. "Mark is the CTO—he does *stuff* with *things*".

When two British heads come together, a wicked resonance of absurdity
known as British Humour^{TM} typically emerges, resulting in an unstoppable if
confusing force over which the remainder of the cosmopolitan workforce generally roll their eyes in pity. Doing stuff with things seemed like the most appropriate irony for the puffed up job of a Chief Technical Officer who had neither
feathers nor military honours.

Still, never missing the opportunity to ruin a good joke, the recollection of
these exchanges reminds me now of a crucial difference between stuff and things
that forms a stepping stone on the path to control over technology; and so I must
proceed now to dissect it for the good of the present story. In brief, the point is
this: there might be much stuff, but there are only so many things.

If you are still with me, 'stuff' is a *continuous* measure, like 'bread' or 'gold',
but a 'thing' is a *discrete* measure like 'a loaf' or 'a bar'. Hence: the streets are
lined with bread (or gold), and 'tis a far far better loaf I bake' (or thing I do),
and so on. All of this is highly relevant to the notion of scale, because it forces
us to confront the many different ideas we have of *atoms*.

In spite of what our senses tell us, the world is not really a continuum of stuff.
It is not the smooth and undulating world of Newton, with perfect spheres and

light strings. It is rough, granular and random, even unpredictable, when we dig down. It just appears to appear continuous to our imperfect senses, because it is a collection of very many extremely small things, too small to resolve individually. Scale, our friend. Scale, the deceiver.

We[48], of course, are made up of cells, and each cell is made up of a rich variety of molecules, each of which is made up of any number of atoms. No one quite even knows where this story ends. The key point is that, if we look closely enough, we find a world of things and not stuff. The world seems to be fundamentally *discrete*[49]. Nonetheless, we maintain the fiction of continuity, because it is convenient, both to our senses, and to the mathematical models of our world. The so-called *continuum approximation*, of discrete systems, has led to marvellous insights and advances in the science of all kinds of 'things'.

The word 'discrete' (not to be confused with 'discreet' of discretion) means separate and distinct. In other words, it can mean the opposite of continuous, which is the usual meaning in science. In order to scratch beneath the surface of technological challenge, we need to appreciate what discreteness means, and why it is fundamental to the world. Why should we care about the nature of the physical world of the very small, if we want to build smart infrastructure on the human level? The first reason is that we have to understand the true nature of discreteness, and what makes it different from the continuous world in order to understand information systems. This is the key to fully understanding technology at every scale. The second reason is that we can learn from physics how to understand the emergence of dependable continuity from a discrete foundation. The third reason is that our technology is getting so small that the quantum nature of the physical hardware is quickly becoming the one we need to think about.

Discreteness turns out to be fundamentally important for understanding almost everything about the world of information. Moreover, our modern understanding, in terms of discrete objects, has many similarities to the quantum theory (which refers to countable or quantifiable things), and also to *information theory* (which refers to the methods of communication). This chapter is about those two developments and their importance to the modern world.

The story of how we arrived at our understanding of discreteness, and its significance to the world, is one that stretches back into ancient times, to the very earliest recorded philosophers; and it ends with our modern view of information and information-based nanotechnology. It is surely as profound as the very question of why we exist at all, and it is a link between the concepts of continuum scale, put forward in the foregoing chapters, and the digital world. For context, I want to relate some of it.

Between the 19th and 20th centuries, the entire view of matter and space-time changed radically from what we might call a classical view to a quantum view. From the earliest systematic investigations about the nature of light and matter, going back to Christiaan Huygens (1629-1695) and Newton in the 17th century, it was evident that some kind of discrete, particle-like nature could be attributed to light, as well as a wavelike nature[50]. Newton supported a *corpus-cular theory* of light, originally proposed by a French scientist Pierre Gassendi, believing light to be made of discrete particles. However, phenomena like the bending of light by refraction and diffraction could only be explained in terms of waves. Thus Huygens retained his belief in a continuous wavelike nature of light, resulting in the Huygens-Fresnel principle that is key to much of modern optics.

Matter and energy: particle or wave? Discrete or continuous? That has been the question for philosophers and scientists throughout recorded history. This apparent bicameral nature of the things and stuff that make up the world remains one of the most baffling features of modern physics, right up to our present day understanding of quantum mechanics. Both views can apparently be true at the same time, and yet waves and particles are the very opposites of one another in classical thinking—the ocean versus the ship.

Resolving this mystery has been the work of a century already, one that began with the discovery of atoms. It is hard for us to imagine now, when every child with a basic education knows about the existence of atoms, how this could not be obvious. However, by following some of the history, we shall see why we continue to make the same mistakes today. Emerging from the technology of steam (in which both steam and heat seemed to behave like fluids), the idea of microscopic particles was an abstract and difficult idea to concede, and it took up to the beginning of the 20th century to approach the modern idea of atoms.

It was Democritus (460-370 BC), of ancient Greece, who coined the Greek adjective *atomos* (ἄτομος) meaning uncuttable, from which we have today's word 'atom'. Today we know that atoms are, in fact, not uncuttable at all, but may be broken down into smaller pieces, including protons, neutrons and the electrons that make up electricity.

Atoms are not only a useful concept for matter, however. The concept is also used, metaphorically, in any number of sciences and technologies for ideas or objects that cannot or should not be broken into smaller parts. An atomic transaction in banking or database engineering, for instance, is an indivisible exchange of money or data. The identification of fundamental, elemental parts, or basic building blocks, is a key part in our understanding of the way things work.

Suppose you hand somebody a coin; that is an indivisible transaction: it either succeeds or it doesn't. The person either gets the value of the coin or they don't. The coin cannot be cut in half, it is an 'all or nothing' exchange. Yet still we see on our bank print-outs that we can have fractions of a coin in value, due to interest accrued at a rate that does not respect the discreteness of monetary value. Similarly, with databases, financial transactions and other high value information, 'stuff' is handed over as 'things' in a way that ensures this 'atomicity'. The concepts of data integrity and logic are closely related to the atomicity of bits in modern computers.

The philosopher Zeno of Elea (estimated to have been born around 480 BC) fanned the flames of indivisibility in matter by suggesting the following: if the universe were in fact infinitely divisible, it would mean that the basic building blocks of stuff would have to have zero size. That meant that nothing would have size at all, and no motion would be possible. Indeed, a thing of zero size does not even exist! If one tries to construct something from nothing, one meets the embarrassing obstacle that even the sum of an infinite number of points of zero size is merely zero[51]. Zeno followed up the argument by presenting a paradox of movement in various forms, including the famous race between the tortoise and Achilles. He argued that, if distance could actually exist independently of things, then a thing trying to move in this space would have to cover an infinite number of points between the start and end of its journey, which was no more helpful than if space itself could not exist. A moving body would first have to cover half the distance, then half of the remaining distance, and half of that again, and so on. Because there would always be half left, the process of subdivision could never end, meaning the thing could never arrive at its destination.

The full discussion of Zeno's paradox is complex, and tends to subdivide as infinitely as the journey it describes, but we can make two notes about it that are somewhat practical. The first is that the notion of distance itself is not refuted by it, as we know that the sum of distances forms a geometric series that sums to the full distance. Suppose that the total distance is 1 metre, then the distance D travelled by Zeno's adventurer is:

$$D = \frac{1}{2} + \left(\frac{1}{2} \times \frac{1}{2} \right) + \left(\frac{1}{2} \times \frac{1}{2} \times \frac{1}{2} \right) + \ldots$$

The answer for this sum is known to be given by the formula $D = a/(1-r)$, with a being the first term and r being the multiplier: $a = r = \frac{1}{2}$, gives $D = 1$. In other words, the series does add up to the full journey. However, also note that the argument only works because we decomposed the journey into a number of discrete steps, without worrying about how the distance could exist in the first place.

What does not necessarily add up, however, is the cost associated with dividing up the distances and crossing them. It is somehow implicit in the formulation of the paradox that one sees the act of dividing up the distance each time as an additional step. Whether there is a real cost of dividing up the path, even if only a mental cost of thinking about it, there is nonetheless a penalty to this dissection (this is not an unreasonable idea, as most actions do not happen unimpeded in nature; there is usually some kind of penalty in time or effort). Moreover, the cutting cost does not halve with the distance. If we assumes that this penalty, in whatever units it is measured, is constant, then the infinite sum over the distances will cause the time needed to traverse the metre to be infinite, because an infinite sum of any fixed overhead is infinite—surely an important lesson for bureaucrats everywhere.

The expression 'a watched pot never boils' is related to this, as it suggests that the psychology of waiting makes us focus on smaller and smaller intervals of time, as we lose patience with increasing frustration. The mere act of thinking about waiting seems to increase the number of minutes required to boil water, in our perception, perhaps because we think faster and faster about the process, forcing a continuous revision of the dimensionless ratio of:

$$\frac{\text{Time for a unit of annoyance}}{\text{Time for water to boil}} \to \infty$$

to increase beyond some threshold of melancholy or madness.

A simple way to avoid the troubles with Zeno's paradox is to assume that space and time are in fact discrete to begin with, and that there is a minimum size, or a smallest unit that can be measured. Then all of these issues would melt away.

In fact, this might easily be true, though no one today has any detailed understanding of how it might actually work. The idea would solve many problems with our current understanding of the universe, however. This links back to the concept of scale that comes from dimensional analysis, as described in the previous chapter.

We would expect the nature space and time to be universal features of our universe. Where would a single unbalanced scale come from to define the minimum distance between two points? One possible answer is: from the laws of physics themselves. It turns out that one can combine three dimensional scales, believed to be universal constants into a value with the dimensions of length:

the speed of light in a vacuum c, the gravitational coupling strength between any two bodies G, and Planck's modified constant $\hbar$:

$$L = \sqrt{\frac{\hbar G}{c^3}} = 1.6 \times 10^{-35} \text{metres.}$$

This number is called the Planck scale. No one really knows whether it holds any significance, beyond the enthusiastic speculation of theorists (after all we don't know all the laws of physics, so there might be other scales to consider), however it is symbolic of a fundamental length-scale at work, and hence an indication of an intrinsic discreteness to the world we live in.

The unexplained constant $\hbar$ in the Planck scale is called Planck's (modified) constant, and it is the crucial value in the argument about the quantum nature of spacetime. It was introduced by Max Karl Ernst Ludwig Planck (1858-1947) to explain something quite unrelated to the discreteness of space: namely, an unexpected feature of the frequency spectrum of so-called blackbody radiation.

At the end of the 19th century, there was no inkling, in the world of physics, that the true nature of reality might really be discrete. The flagship theoretical achievements of the day were thermodynamics (of steam engines) and electrodynamics (of electricity, telegraph and radio). These were the industrial revolution's highest achievements, and both were continuum theories. Planck, however, almost under protest, turned science's view of the continuum of matter and energy upside down, and showed, with the help of Einstein, that there was a threshold scale beyond which matter and energy simply could not be treated continuously any longer. The failure of classical physics to predict this was known as the *ultraviolet catastrophe*, referring to the radiation scale at which the quantum effects revealed themselves.

Although it bears his name, the Planck *length* was not described by Planck himself, but it honours him as the father of quantum theory, because it is $\hbar$ that effectively inserts the scale at which the quantum mechanical character of nature appears. We assume therefore that it also indicates the scale at which spacetime itself would attain a quantum interpretation. The Planck length is so much smaller than anything we are able to experience that it is impossible to imagine just how small quantum effects are. The fact that we are able to observe any quantum effects is a testament to the ingenuity of humans.

As a landmark in the cultural heritage of the modern world, I think it's important to give a brief account of the discovery of discreteness in physics, and how it played into technology, because it has a profound effect on the way we think about everything today. More importantly, it is a stepping stone to our understanding of the technologies of the very small, and relates quite directly to observed computer behaviour.

Planck's early career is known from his short scientific autobiography[52]. It is relatively rare to have access to insights into the mind of a pioneer from first hand recollections, so we may consider ourselves fortunate to have so much of this history documented.

Like many other innovators, Planck was not encouraged to pursue physics, nor were his innovations received with much enthusiasm for some time. Even as early as the end of the 19th century, shortsighted individuals were naively claiming that there was nothing more to know about science[53]. One physics professor in Munich advised Planck against going into physics, saying, "in this field, almost everything is already discovered, and all that remains is to fill a few holes." Planck, however, was ripe for a challenge, and he showed no lack of courage and diligence in choosing topics to work on.

Planck studied under two other giants of physics Helmholtz and Kirchoff in Berlin, but in his own words he admitted: "I must confess that the lectures of these men netted me no perceptible gain. It was obvious that Helmholtz never prepared his lectures properly ... Kirchoff was the very opposite ... but he would sound like a memorised text, dry and monotonous"[54]. So he chose his research interests from the works of Clausius, another giant in the field of thermodynamics and entropy. His interests were the hard problems of the day: the thermodynamic properties of matter and radiation, the so-called black body radiation.

Coming out of the age of industrial steam power, kinetic theory, thermodynamics and electricity were the dominant problems of interest, although these subjects must seem terribly pedestrian today by the standards of what is trendy in physics. Yet it was time or enormous excitement not merely because of the pioneering inventors like Edison, Tesler, Faraday, but also other pioneering theoreticians like the Scottish physicist James Clarke Maxwell (1831–1879) who developed continuum mathematics of thermodynamics and electromagnetics, and Ludwig Boltzmann (1844-1906) who developed much of statistical mechanics. Boltzmann's kinetic theory of gases, for instance, basically presupposed the reality of atoms and molecules when almost all German philosophers and many scientists disbelieved their existence[55].

In 1894, Planck turned to the problem of black-body radiation, i.e. the expected energy profile for radiation of an idealized body in equilibrium with its surroundings. This was a problem where thermodynamics and electromagnetism met head on, and as with many other unification attempts in physics, it would lead to a major shift in thinking. Planck was inspired by a landmark paper by Wien who had calculated the spectrum of blackbody radiation in a limiting special case—at a particular scale. The failure of kinetic theory alone to explain the high energy behaviour of black body radiation was called the *ultraviolet catastrophe*, because at the scale of ultraviolet radiation and beyond, the results for energy flew off to infinity. Explaining this was the problem he took on.

Planck had no idea that he was about to revolutionize physics. His goal was a rather modest attempt to contribute to the new methods of statistical mechanics introduced by Boltzmann, but his fascination with the concept of entropy led him to pursue a different line of reasoning than many of his contemporaries, and he did not initially follow Boltzmann's prescription to the letter. In fact, his method was reminiscent of modern approaches to the theory of information.

He began using the standard approach in statistical mechanics, using a mathematical trick to make the calculation of thermodynamic quantities easier. One would start by assuming that the energies of light had to take multiples of a whole-number (integer) values: $E_n = \epsilon, 2\epsilon, 3\epsilon...$ and so on. This makes them countable. Later, one would take the limit $\epsilon \to 0$, to get an infinite resolution, a bit like Zeno's limit, and recover the continuity of allowed energies. But Planck found that he could only obtain an expression that agreed with experimental data for blackbody radiation if he did not take this continuity limit. Instead he had to assume that the step size ϵ was non-zero and proportional to the frequency, i.e. $\epsilon = 2\pi\hbar\nu$ at a given frequency ν of radiation, in lumps of size $\hbar$. The expression he obtained for the spectrum confirmed experimental data with great success. Planck published his work in 1900, but the work did not receive much acclaim.

Planck's hypothesis that energies were not fully continuous, but rather came in lumps proportional to a fixed scale $\hbar$, was remarkable. It was this discreteness that prevented the ultraviolet catastrophe from leading to infinities, just as in Zeno's paradox. The same approach would be used many times over the 20th century to avoid infinities in physical calculations.

In fact, it is easy to get the wrong impression about the quantization of energy from accounts of quantum mechanics. Planck's quantization did not say that energy quanta were universally discrete lumps of energy, analogous to fixed atoms. Rather, they had a size that depended upon the frequency of the waves they were part of. For every different frequency, there is a particular size of energy unit $h\nu$. Thus we have not abandoned the idea of continuous *scaling* completely—it is embedded in the formulation of the solution.

Astute readers might see a problem with this. Isn't the notion of quantization inconsistent? The frequency is a continuous classical variable that can take on any value. Can it make sense to have energy quantized, but based on a continuous quantity? Indeed, this is ultimately inconsistent, and in a full quantum theory, ν would also have to be treated as a discrete variable. To see why this worked anyway, think of it as the first level of a better approximation, which turned out to be enough for Planck's paricular case.

The following analogies might help. We already mentioned that the concept of energy is like money, so quanta are like energy coins, i.e. fixed-size units of energy-money. But there is not only one set of coins: there is a different set of coins at each frequency. We cannot divide any given coin up, so money is quantized in the fixed amounts, but at a different frequency the coins have a different size. At higher frequencies, above the ultraviolet, the quanta get very big and more noticeable; below that, they are not noticeably distinct (imagine a smooth powder). The frequency is included as a classical continuous quantity, but this can work for the same reason discussed in previous chapters, namely that there is only weak coupling between the natural frequency scale of a wave and the existence of a state of the system.

It's like saying that there is little connection between the weight of an apple and the number of people eating an apple at a given moment. The number of apples is a discrete quantity, but we can get away with treating the weight as continuous because the quanta that make up the people and the apple are so small that they are not relevant to the eating process. People on the other hand are most definitely quantized as individuals. Apples' weights are really quantized, atom by atom, but no one cares about those microscopic differences in apple weights.

The significance of Planck's discovery lay in demonstrating that experiment had probed reality in way that revealed a deeper truth about its nature. What had seemed continuous and deterministic, was in fact discrete and non-deterministic, when examined closely. Only by zooming out to a sufficiently large scale could one recover an apparent continuum. Thus, determinism is not an adequate model of discrete systems. This is a lesson we are now learning in reverse, while trying to assure predictability in information infrastructure.

Planck's result alone might not have been enough to convince anyone of the reality of quanta. It was rather technical, and the crucial insight was hard to understand. Confirmation came from Albert Einstein (1879–1955), however, in 1905 with his explanation of the *photoelectric effect* in metals.

The photoelectric effect is a phenomenon where electrons are emitted from a metal when the metal is irradiated by light. Experiments showed that electron energies in the metal depended on the frequency of incident light and not its intensity. This was another mysterious result to a classical physicist.

If the classical continuum theory of light had been true, increasing the intensity should have allowed more light to be absorbed in a continuous fashion until an electron had enough energy to escape from the metal surface. However, this was not the case. It depended only on the frequency. Einstein showed that the apparent paradox could be solved if one assumed that the light was quantized, as Planck had proposed, because then only quanta or 'coins' of sufficient size could be absorbed as a single lump. The amount of energy could not be gradually accumulated over time, as with a continuous quantity. Einstein won the Nobel prize in 1921 for his analysis of this work.

Despite the success of his discovery, Planck had much trouble accepting the physical reality of a quantum hypothesis. His own words about the struggle to reconcile these world views give us a sense of the 'quantum leap' he had to make to give up on continuity. Most likely, he worked backwards from the result, then he spent years trying to find an error in his reasoning that would allow him to refute his own hypothesis. Einstein had been less worried, because he saw that Planck had not followed Boltzmann's prescription properly, meaning that he was not able to see the truth of it. Einstein corrected the error in 1906 and showed that the result was indeed right and consistent with Boltzmann. Max Born wrote about Planck:

> "He was by nature and by the tradition of his family conservative, averse to revolutionary novelties and skeptical towards speculations. But his belief in the imperative power of logical thinking based on facts was so strong that he did not hesitate to express a claim contradicting to all tradition, because he had convinced himself that no other resort was possible."

Later Planck himself wrote:

> "My futile attempts to fit the elementary quantum of action somehow into the classical theory continued for a number of years and they cost me a great deal of effort. Many of my colleagues saw in this something bordering on a tragedy. But I feel differently about it, for the thorough enlightenment I thus received was all the more valuable."

In 1911, in epilogue of this discovery, the Belgian industrialist Ernest Solvay invited the main thinkers of the day to the first of a series of conferences on fundamental physics, which have later become enshrined in the history of quantum theory. At the first of these conferences, Planck had finally committed to the idea of quantization. Of all the physicists attending, only Planck, Einstein, and three others took the quantum hypothesis seriously.

The significance of Einstein's work did not stop there, however. It went on to be confirmed further by the developments emerging from the understanding of atomic structure. From experiments, it was known that electrons surround the nucleus of atoms somehow, but classically this was hard to understand. The only stable option for classical mechanics was to assume that electrons were in orbit about the nucleus, like the familiar planetary motion of Newton. Classical electromagnetism said that an orbiting point-like electron would have to radiate energy continuously as electromagnetic waves, and this would cause the electron to be instantly drained of energy and spiral down into the nucleus itself, causing all of matter to collapse instantly. Since this did not happen, something unknown had to be preventing it.

The answer was almost the reverse of the process imagined for the photo-electric effect. Surely enough, electrons would surround the nucleus, but not in any visual way we understand. They were not accelerating in an orbit, so they would not radiate continuously as predicted by the classical model. Instead, they would take on only very specific discrete traffic-light states with corresponding discrete energies, and these could be calculated from quantum mechanics. Radiation could only be emitted as a discrete unit of energy called a 'photon' or quantum of light, with a certain probability, making atoms stable to a very good approximation.

Planck and Einstein's work show how we owe our entire existence to the discreteness of the basic building blocks of our universe. The stability of the electron energy states, and our entire atomic infrastructure are propped up by the discreteness of energy states in matter. This shift in understanding had a profound effect on modern thinking, as the discreteness of our material world invaded scientific culture repeatedly in the years that followed.

While physicists were unravelling the connection between discrete state information and physical law during the first half of the 20th century, mathematicians were developing their own ideas, spurred on by the development of the telegraph, radio, and digital signalling. The need for creating and deciphering secret messages (cryptography) sent over radio and telegraph during the world wars, no doubt accelerated the investment of time and money that went into researching information, and ultimately led to the invention of the digital computer.

Communication was something that everyman could understand the need for. The telegraph had already taken the first steps towards globalization of trade and economy, and its development was stimulating commerce and leading to all manner of new inventions. The telegraph system was one of the technological wonders of the British Empire. It transformed communications in matters of both war and commerce[56], but no one could have imagined that so practical a concern as the signalling of intent across geographical distances would bring about such a revolution. Indeed, it led directly to the very idea that would unify our view of the most fundamental physical processes with the way we relieve ourselves of daily gossip, and then go on to propel humanity into an age of information technology. That deep and subtle unification is still being unravelled today.

The study of digital communication began, in its own right, during the 1930s and 1940s, with mathematicians such as Alonzo Church (1903-1995), Alan Turing (1912-1954)), John Von Neumann (1903-1957) and Claude Shannon (1916-2001) in the lead.

The effect of the quantum mechanics on these thinkers was likely profound. Turing and Von Neumann, two of the most well-known figures in the development of modern computation, were certainly both well versed in the modern theoretical physics of the preceding years[57], and could hardly have avoided being influenced by the deep role played by information in these theories. From statistical mechanics of Boltzmann and Einstein to the quantum mechanical formulations of Schrödinger and Dirac, discrete units of what could only be described as information (about *states* of matter) played a central role in reinterpreting our view of reality. Turing, in particular, was captivated by the meaning of reality itself and many of his arguments about computers and artificial intelligence would reflect his grasp of these ideas.

Representing information as symbolic states, and exchanging state information between participants, is the simplest of ideas, but it proves also to be the basic unifying idea to understand information systems. Claude Shannon referred to this as a communications channel, and studied it in depth. The details of his work were published under the title *The Mathematical Theory Of Communication* in 1949. Today it is also called Information Theory.

Information theory begins with the *representation*, *interpretation* and *transmission* of patterns of *data*, i.e. patterns made up of different kinds of 'things'. We attach meanings to these patterns and call the result information. Patterns of data are mainly of interest when they are transmitted from a *source* to a *receiver*, for instance:

- Morse code sent by telegraph or by lantern.

- Speech transmitted acoustically or by telephony.

- Text read from a page and transmitted to our brain.

- Data copied from hard-disk to memory.

- Data copied from memory to screen.

- DNA copied using RNA within a cell.

In each of these cases, a pattern represented in some medium, like paper, a brain, or computer memory, is transferred from one representation to another. Information is fundamentally about pattern representation.

Shannon began by defining a set of symbols, traditionally called an alphabet in the literature of coding. This might be something like the Latin alphabet A-Z: the basis of most Western writing systems. An alphabet is really just a set of reusable 'atoms' for making patterns.

Suppose we have the simple alphabet: { A,T,G,C }, recognizable as the short symbols used for nucleotides Adenine, Cytosine, Guanine, and Thymine, that make up genes. We can form any number of different messages based on these. In biology, clusters of three such nucleotides represent codons, e.g. "GUG" or "UUG", which represent different amino acids. In the context of the cellular machinery of DNA and RNA, these symbols, written in molecular form, can be copied, interpreted and treated as symbolic operators that change the states of an elaborate chemical feedback system.

If the symbols were received by a human, written on paper, we might imagine that they represented acronyms, or words in some language or other. We could equally make the same patterns out of images of fruit, as in one-armed bandit gambling machines. These sequences of symbols are just patterns that we can recognize and attach interpretation to. The symbols are often called digits, for, although the symbols represented in a channel encoding do not have to be numerical, it turns out to be sufficient to represent everything as a countable set of things. Indeed, the simplest possible representation is binary digits, consisting of only 1s and 0s.

We can convert any alphabet into any other by numbering the symbols from 1 to the maximum number. For example, in the well-known ASCII encoding of the Latin alphabet used in most computers, the association between numbers was as follows:

$$
\begin{array}{ccc}
\text{Sym} \rightarrow \text{Dec} \rightarrow \text{Bin} \\
A \rightarrow 65 \rightarrow 1000001 \\
B \rightarrow 66 \rightarrow 1000010 \\
C \rightarrow 67 \rightarrow 1000011 \\
\cdots
\end{array}
$$

Now I have sneaked in three different set of coding here: i) 'Sym', 'Dec', 'Bin' for symbolic, decimal and binary counting systems, ii) 65, 66, 67 for the ASCII values represented in decimal, and iii) the alphabet 1, 0, representing binary numbers. We are so used to handling codes today that you probably hardly noticed all of these symbolic transformations. However, technologists cannot take these things for granted when making machinery to represent and transmit information.

When actually realizing communications technology, it is much easier to represent only 1 and 0, rather than having to distinguish many distinct symbols. There is no fundamental reason for this choice, however—after all, DNA gets along just fine with four.

A reasonable question to ask is: what is the difference between information *about* something, and the thing itself? The answer is: not much. There is a direct correspondence between information about something, and the physical thing itself. In fact, we could say that the thing itself is just one possible representation of the information, but there can also be others.

For instance, we can think of a factory that makes tins of soup. We can model this using the principles of engineering and design and build the actual factory. The information is now represented both in someone's brain, and in building materials and people. Alternatively, we can represent tins of soup by symbols and numbers and model the whole process on paper, or in a computer or scraped in the mud, or indeed any other physical medium. We would call that an information system, but it is not fundamentally different from the real thing, except in what we consider to be the original. We could, after all, make a scale model where the symbols were three dimensional, but, if we are going to do that, then why not use the factory itself to track the information? In that case, how is the information different from the thing? It is just a representation.

We see that *representation* of information is a key issue. Information about something is not fundamentally different from a real thing itself, because both need a physical representation. It is only a question of how we interpret the things. Warren Weaver a contemporary of Shannon summarized three levels of information in 1949:

1. How accurately symbols can be transmitted (copying fidelity)

2. How precisely symbols convey the intended information (semantics)

3. How well understood messages are by humans.

Shannon's work pointed out that patterns of information are not always perfect, but can become distorted over time or during transmission over distance (space). His model of communication builds on the model of the so-called noisy channel (see figure 3.1). The model comes right out of the telegraph age, but it is surprisingly adaptable to almost any other situation, as it has the basic structure of all communication.

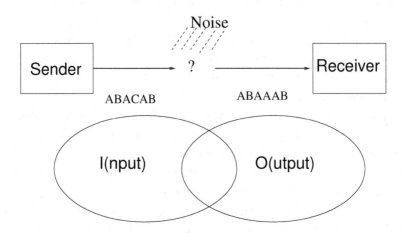

Fig. 3.1. Shannon's model of symbol transmission from sender to receiver, or source to sink. Transmission of the input message overlapped with the output message, or *mutual information* was exchanged.

The idea of the model is that some kind of generic *sender* creates a message as a stream of symbols, which are then propagated to the *receiver* at some rate. The receiver interprets the patterns and, assuming that it understands the alphabet, interprets the same message from the same alphabet. The sender might be a person, a sensor, or your fingertip when touching something. The receiver might be a microphone or a harddisk, or your brain when registering the signal.

Many signals in the physical world are really multi-leg journeys: elaborate chains of signal relays, passing messages through a variety of media. Visual signals are passed as light, then eye to brain by electro-chemical transfer. From sensor to computer is electrical, from computer to harddisk involves magnetic flux. At each stage, some kind of *transducer* is needed to convert the symbols from one representation into another. Every possible interaction between things involves the transmission of some kind of signal from one place and time to another place and time.

Even with a transducer that can transduce one medium for another, it does not guarantee communication of intent. Pouring DNA proteins into the disk tray of your laptop, for instance, would not result in a baby being born from your new 3D printer. That translation software does not yet exist at the time of writing, though it is not impossible to imagine something like it. There is thus, also a need for alphabet transformation, also known as *decryption* or *decipherment* of the stream. Ciphers or encryption methods represent a huge subject of great importance to the idea of certainty[58]. We'll revisit them in part II of the book.

A crucial principle embodied in Shannon's model is that a receiver interprets information completely independently of how the sender intends it. The sender cannot force the receiver to mirror its own intention. The receiver is not even guaranteed to receive the message. There is no determinism involved, no intrinsic, inevitable meaning. The receiver might not recognize the symbols correctly, or the symbols could have become distorted by noise in the channel, flipping bits or distorting one symbol into another. Think of message symbols as change operations, acting on the states of the receiver, changing them. Ideally, this communication would converge to the desired outcome set by the sender, but that simple deterministic idea might be spoiled by the presence of noise from the surrounding environment.

What do these messages have to do with our story of stability? The answer lies in a rephrasing of the question: what might decay look like in a discrete system? What corresponds to fading paintwork, or weeds in the flowerbed of a digital message? How could we *maintain* state over time in a discrete system? How can we make a state stable to its environment?

Shannon's answer was that noise, in a communications channel, led to symbol errors that needed correcting. The intrusion of a rogue message, during the propagation of an intended message, is what led to decay, and the subsequent need for maintenance. This, for example, is how genetic mutation takes place: copying errors in DNA cause the intended genetic message to be altered so that the interpretation of the message at the receiver leads to incorrect response, and this leads to a mutation when the genes are activated. Clearly noise is a threat to the stability of digital information.

Think of a state that is unchanging as time passes. It is just a repeated message that reiterates the same state again and again. Each time the symbol repeats is like a tick of the clock. Suppose we start with an A, then a stable unchanging state would look like this:

AAAAAAAAAAAAAAAAAAAAA ... etc.

The passage of time is marked by a new symbol in the message. A limit cycle might look like this:

ABCABCABCABCABCABCABC ... etc.

The system cycles through a fixed pattern. A noisy system with decay would look like this:

AAAAAAABBBBBBBBBBBBBBBBBCCCDDDEEEEE ...

Each time noise flips one of the symbols, it changes to a new state and remains there until more noise changes it again. Had we stabilized the state with an immunity operation, then we could correct errors in the transmission of the message. So then we might have

AAAAAAABAAAAAAAAAAAAAAAA ... etc.

The sudden occurrence of a B is now immediately corrected back to its desired state. This is sometimes possible, as long as we have a description of what the intended state actually is. This is the case for an immune system, and it is the case for the software CFEngine mentioned earlier. We often call that description a design or a *policy*. In DNA replication, most mutations lead to cells that 'crash' and die. Only if the mutation leads to a message that makes sense does the mutation survive and continue to propagate.

Now consider: what if we could not only allow a state to change, but actually control the way it changed. Then we could transform one message into another. That would be computation! The fact that puts us in charge of manipulating the world around us is this ability to identify controlled evolution of states. We call it computation or we call it medicine, or carpentry, depending on what states we are talking about. The suggestion here is a slightly incredible one: that the universe itself is a computer, whose very evolution in time has the character of a carefully programmed message.

This begins to sound like mysticism, and we should be very cautious in swallowing such a simplistic account. In fact, the universe is much more complex, much more interesting than this. Why? Because the quantum states that Planck discovered are not governed by just one message, but by a vast number of possible messages that we cannot predict. To close the loop on this story, and make this connection, we have to see how the natural world actually behaves like a highly complex computer—and how it doesn't.

You probably know the terms 'analogue' and 'digital'. Modern culture refers to information as being one or the other of these, but few of us now remember the origins of these terms.

Analogue tends to bring up vague connotations of old-fashionedness, or of being that good-old wholesome organic stuff of a pre-digital age, like vinyl records and valve amplifiers[59]. Digital, on the other hand, tends to represent cold and soulless machinery, but also high quality. But, all prejudice aside, the terms actually have very specific meanings that are quite unrelated to the images they now conjure.

Before the invention of modern computers[60], there were so-called analogue computers. These did not calculate according to the rules of arithmetic, but by analogy. The rules of modern arithmetic as we calculate today, descend from the mathematics of Chinese, Indian, and Arabic scholars. We calculate with digits (from the Latin *digitus* for finger or toe), arranged in patterns of 10 or 20 in most cultures, because that is the usual number of fingers and toes. Our methods are a variation on the Chinese abacus approach, and are also based on the method of counting.

Digital computers simulate the arithmetic approach that we humans use to count with, using symbolic manipulation. Analogue computers, on the other hand, do not use counting to compute, but work by *analogy* to certain systems of equations, using the principle of dynamical equivalence discussed in the previous chapter.

How could this work? Suppose we could construct a physical system that mimicked the behaviour of something we wanted to calculate? It might then be possible to construct a device that, by virtue of its very existence, would be a simulation of an equation, and could therefore calculate the answer to a problem. All we would have to do would be to sit back and watch the answer unfold. The laws of physics would do the work, and we could simply read off the answer at some appropriate moment. This is the idea of the analogue computer.

All measurable physical phenomena behave essentially like calculating systems, but some are more convenient to interact with than others. In electrical circuitry, there are components like resistors, capacitors, and inductors that behave like processes in a calculation. In practice, you need to be able to add and subtract, and from this anything is possible. However, electronic circuits can also perform calculus operations like integrate and differentiate. Capacitors accumulate charge and act like adders or integrators. The accumulated charge in a capacitor is proportional to the applied voltage $Q = CV$, and the charge is the integral of a current.

$$V = \frac{1}{C} \int_0^t I dt$$

Voltage and current are easily measurable, so with a multimeter, one could imagine solving integrals. Inductors, such as one finds in radios, behave like differentiators, because electric currents respond to rates of change of magnetic flux, which in turn depend on the current.

$$V = L\frac{dI}{dt}$$

By applying principles like this, and other components like transistors or operational amplifiers, clever minds were able to construct electrical circuits which would compute answers to specific problems.

Unlike digital computers, there was never a generic, multi-purpose analogue computer that ran a version of an office spreadsheet and other programs. Analogue computers had to be specially built for one specific problem at a time. At best one could hope for a 'breadboard' of components with patch-bay of connections to make the assembly easier. The user would have to build the right circuit and then set a voltage on the input contacts, and measure the outgoing voltage or current from the circuit, which would translate directly into the answer. The answer was literally computed by the analogy between the laws of electricity and mathematical operations.

Analogue computers were never a good solution because physical systems are prone to noise and non-linear effects, causing instabilities that lead to incorrect results. Their results were not discrete values, but were interpreted as continuous voltages, thus today we use the term 'analogue' to mean the opposite of 'digital'. The science has become culture.

History has produced many examples of analogue computers, using different technologies through the ages, but a particularly interesting form of analogue computation that has been explored in recent years is biological computation using DNA, because it is both an analogy engine and a digital system. This is an interesting kind of digital-analogy hybrid computer which uses DNA in bacterial colonies to perform computational operations.

Every cell has a program coded implicitly in its DNA, which receives chemical inputs from around the cell wall, and expresses proteins the same way. Cells communicate using these chemical channels in our bodies. Thus even our bodies are computational systems. The program for carrying out cellular logic is written in DNA. Unlike a digital computer, it does not have a regular clock, so time is not predictable in the same sense as it is in a digital computer. Rather, it is quantized in 'events'. i.e. the arrival of a messenger protein. Its power lies in massive parallelism. Cells are easy to copy, thanks to the mechanisms of DNA itself. Genes may be switched on and off by messenger proteins which bind to a particular site, which becomes the input. The result is a the manufacture of another protein. These proteins form a vast high-level code, written in an alphabet of amino acids. This process happens in our bodies all the time, and in that sense we can claim to be emergent effects of a physical simulation executing a program written in DNA. Progress has been made in using this process for artificial computations too.

Today, there does not seem to be a future for human-built analogue computers in the world of human technology. Digital computers offer a much more predictable approach to computation, thanks to the concept of digital error correction; they are easier to build upon to make reliable information driven systems for our human infrastructure. Analogue computers were in use up until the end of the 1980s in a variety of applications, like car and aircraft control systems, but today they are entirely replaced by more reliable digital computers.

There are two things to be taken from this. The first is that the physical world we live in is, in fact, a computer—an analogue computer. The laws of physics are literally computing our future at every moment, all over the universe. We just don't know what problem it is computing[61]. The second, and more important point, is that—no matter what approach we use to try to compute the answer to a question—every answer we come up with is an approximation in one way or another. Either the computation is performed using an indirect method, or it is carried out with finite accuracy due to the discrete nature of information in the world.

Finite resolution also means finite accuracy, and we never even get close to the fundamental limits of accuracy due to the quantum nature of matter with today's technology. However, we have chosen digital computers as the basis of modern information technology, and information technology as the extrinsic control system for almost everything else around us. Even when the applications seem to be continuous, it is hard to avoid the effects of the finiteness of the world. This is but one possible representation of information, but it is a natural one.

From the analogy between physics and computation, we have a picture of a computer as a general device which takes an input stream, and evaluates an output stream according to a set of rules. This describes pretty much any linear, physical system.

In the previous chapter, we looked at the linear rules for driving the evolution of a physical system. They had the form of

$$(\text{Act on}) \text{ thing} \longrightarrow \text{new thing}$$

It is also the transmission of a message:

$$(\text{Copy}) \text{ local state} \longrightarrow \text{remote state}$$

And, in physics, this kind of evolution crops up all the time. It was not the usual way of formulating physical problems, at least before quantum mechanics, but it is a viable representation of physics in linear cases. It represents an information viewpoint of system evolution in terms of discrete transitions, and it can usually be derived from any system of variables and constraints that represent a model of reality.

In physics, if we try to cast the evolution of the system in this form it takes the form of a 'linear response' function, also called a Green's function[62] of the previous chapter. In physics it often looks something like this[63]:

$$q(t) = \int (dt')\, G_r(t, t')\, F(t')$$

but the rather beautiful calligraphic notation is just window-dressing. This is just special notation for:

(Evolve and propagate) 'edge state F' $\rightarrow$ 'new state $q(t)$'

or

(Evolve and propagate) 'sender state' $\rightarrow$ 'receiver state'

Propagate means effectively 'follow over time'. In this form, physics recovers the operational view of states from the previous chapter, and we also see that it is just a generating loop for writing a message by repeating this propagation over and over again, marking out time. The response to the message at the source is information about the new state:

Data $G_r(t, t')$ from 'edge state F' $\rightarrow$ 'new state $q(t)$'

or, even more simply:

(Develop) Cause $\rightarrow$ Effect.

This is basically a computation:

(Compute) Input $\rightarrow$ Output.

This generalized system thus has the behaviour of a rather specific computer[64]. It evaluates only one very specific problem, i.e. how to obey this law of physics, in the form of a message of states that evolve over time. The only thing that distinguishes it from a general computer is that it is stuck on one program: integrating a simple differential equation which is physics itself. This is the basic template from which we humans are able to turn knowledge of this science into a technology to make computers of our own.

Think simply of states that can take whole number values, and imagine creating transformation operators that can perform addition and subtraction. This is possible, and indeed this is how modern computers are constructed using electronic circuits. If we let (Inc) mean increment (add one), and (Dec) mean decrement (subtract one) from a state, then here is a simple operator behaviour for elementary digital computation:

(Inc) 4 $\longrightarrow$ 5
(Dec) 4 $\longrightarrow$ 3
(Dec)(Dec) 4 $\longrightarrow$ 2
(Zero) 4 $\longrightarrow$ 0
(Zero) 0 $\longrightarrow$ 0
(Zero)(Zero) 4 $\longrightarrow$ 0

These are two of the basic operations in a modern digital computer. If we iterate a constant message of (Inc), the state will count upwards.

What jumps out from the simple formulations above is not the technical details, which are tragically simplified here, though certainly have their own beauty, but rather the underlying information structure of the relations themselves. It suggests that the world is in fact a kind if information pump, evolving states (which are measures of information) by causing transitions from one state to another. Just as the absorption of a photon in a laser would cause a change of state from one level to another, so the absorption of a message (another measure of information) from a sender would cause a change of knowledge state in the receiver. This is computation not by analogy, but by 'digilogy'[65]!

Now we might close the loop on this story of the discreteness of things and what they mean to us. Because a message is a collection of symbols, we can represent the message as a journey through a state chart, like the traffic light example in Figure 1.1, we can represent any message as a journey through a network of the different states. Such a network is called a state machine. If there is a finite number of the states, then it is called a *finite state machine*.

We can then separate the symbols into two types: operators and states.

The bold letters represent the different states of the machine: empty, stopped, playing, spooling, etc. The arrows in between show the *operations* that initiate a transition from one state to another. Thus, an empty player moves from state 'empty' to 'stopped' by inserting a tape, disk or other source medium. In the operator language, this would be written like this:

(insert) 'empty' $\rightarrow$ 'stopped'
(eject) 'stopped' $\rightarrow$ 'empty'
(play) 'stopped' $\rightarrow$ 'playing'
(stop) 'playing' $\rightarrow$ 'stopped'
(fwd) 'stopped' $\rightarrow$ 'spooling fwd'

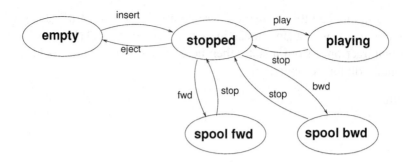

Fig. 3.2.   A finite state machine model of a video player. The bold symbols are states and the symbols on the links are operators.

(stop) 'spooling fwd' → 'stopped'
(bwd) 'stopped' → 'spooling bwd'
(stop) 'spooling bwd' → 'stopped'

Thus, when we act on the 'empty' state with an 'insert' operation, the state of the machine moved from being 'empty' to 'stopped'. Then when we press play (act on the stopped state with the 'play' operation), the state moves from 'stopped' to 'playing'.

These are called state transitions, and we can write them as a *transition matrix*, which is simply a table of all possibilities mapping all the states to all the others. If there is an arrow from one state to another, we write a 1; if there is no arrow, we write a 0. We read the state machine's graph by reading from a sender state on the left to a receiver state across the top.

(row, column)	empty	stopped	playing	spoolfwd	spoolbwd
empty	0	insert	0	0	0
stopped	eject	0	play	fwd	bwd
playing	0	stop	0	0	0
spoolfwd	0	stop	0	0	0
spoolbwd	0	stop	0	0	0

The rows and columns of the this matrix (rows go along the floor, and columns hold up the ceiling) show the transitions in and out of the states. Or, we can strip this down to bare bones and write only the transitions between in coming (row) states and outgoing (column) states:

$$T(\text{in}, \text{out}) = \begin{pmatrix} 0 & 1 & 0 & 0 & 0 \\ 0.3 & 0 & 0.5 & 0.1 & 0.1 \\ 0 & 1 & 0 & 0 & 0 \\ 0 & 1 & 0 & 0 & 0 \\ 0 & 1 & 0 & 0 & 0 \end{pmatrix}$$

where 1 means 'allowed transition' and 0 means none. This state machine is a non-deterministic state machine. There is only a certain probability of a particular transition being made.

The numbers in the table are made up, for the sake of example. One could understand them as follows. Once the tape is in the player, the probability of pressing play is slightly higher than pressing eject, but we know that we have to eject something at least once. It is not usual to feed tapes and disks into players just to eject them without playing them, but we might stop play during a movie several times before ejecting it. There is nothing programmed about these probabilities, nothing inevitable or deterministic. They represent only behavioural experience.

The signature of message passing and information propagation is evident in both the technology of communication and in many examples of physical law described above[66]. The question remains, however, how closely are these related? Are they merely inspired by one another, or is there something deeper at work? Certainly there are parallels, but there are also differences. As in the case of the ship on the ocean, a formulation of a quantum system is sensitive to the way in which we separate the big picture from the small. The alphabet of states (as we understand it) in the quantum theory is not a constant fixture for instance: it depends on a complex interplay of boundary conditions. However, before leaving this chapter, I want to return to the quantum story to reconnect the loose ends, with the benefit Shannon's perspective. This takes us back to the years following Planck and Einstein's discovery.

We left the pioneers of quantum theory at the cusp of the growing acceptance of a quantum view of the world, but little was yet understood about the structure of atoms and their interactions with light. The black-body radiation signature of Planck had been a first, semi-classical step in the analysis of the interaction between matter and radiation, where the quantum nature of energy for the first time could not be avoided.

As the idea that matter and energy were discrete sank in, a variety of models appeared to describe the behaviour of electrons confined in potential wells, or scattering through slits. Calculations of these, based on generalizations of the accounting principles for energy that Newton and Leibniz had taught us, yielded a variety of promising results to explain experimental observations, but the real difficulty lay in understanding what the theory *meant*.

The remark by Niels Bohr at the start of this chapter summarizes the frustration physicists felt with possessing an effective description of the phenomena, but having no effective understanding of why it worked. The equations of Schrödinger and Heisenberg were akin to having a slot machine that produced fortune cookies predicting experimenters' likely success in measuring results. It predicted accurately the alphabets of states that *could* be measured, but not what states *would* be measured. Newton's clockwork determinism was gone; cause and effect were no longer simply related.

During the 1930s and 1940s, developing the theoretical understanding of how quantum theory and Einstein's Special Theory of Relativity could be reconciled became a priority, as several measurable effects were related to this. Explaining the rapidly improving experiments became the chief goal of physicists. It was an effort that took many years to fully gestate, interrupted by the second world war. It began with British physicist Paul Dirac (1902-1984) and ended with the work of two Americans, and a Japanese physicist, each working independently using what seemed to be quite different approaches.

Quantum Electrodynamics (or QED for short) was pieced together by three physicists: Richard Feynman (1918-1988), Julian Schwinger (1918-1994), and Sin Itiro Tomonaga (1906-1979) between 1948 and 1949. However, their formulations of the subject seemed so radically different from one another that it took the efforts of a fourth, Freeman Dyson, to see the connection between them. All three, without Dyson, later won the Nobel prize for their efforts in 1965. The approaches used in QED to describe quantum processes are interesting because they reveal a deeper connection between physics of the small and the theory of digital communication due to Shannon.

Feynman's approach to the problem has attained the greatest popular appeal, mainly due to his greater personal flamboyance, and legendary status as a teacher. In Feynman's version of QED, he used diagrams to visualize what he believed were quantum processes, now referred to as Feynman diagrams (see Figure 3.3). Initially Feynman saw his diagrams as representing actual particle trajectories, though this became more a formality as more viewpoints emerged (Schwinger, for instance, was reported as being less than impressed), but they helped him to get past the philosophical issues with the interpretation of quantum mechanics that Bohr referred to, by not having to mystify the existence of the particles. The diagrams were not arbitrary, but came out of Feynman's own personal reformulation of quantum theory based on a principle of least action[67]. Feynman was intrigued by the experiments that showed electrons interfering, which suggested that they followed multiple paths at the same time, somewhat like a wave. This quantum interference is one of the strange and mysterious aspects of quantum theory that defies satisfactory explanation, even to this day. In his formulation, he set up a so-called 'path integral' or sum over paths that electrons might take, as if not just taking one fortune cookie but the whole machine at once.

Feynman thus did not fully give up the idea of the electron as a point object, but instead allowed it to behave in apparently unphysical ways—more like a collection of messages than a point particle. Dyson later wrote:

> Dick Feynman told me about his "sum over histories" version of quantum mechanics. "The electron does anything it likes," he said. "It just goes in any direction at any speed, forward or backward in time, however it likes, and then you add up the amplitudes and it gives you the wave-function." I said to him, "You're crazy." But he wasn't.

Whether one believes the picture he used to assemble the results, Feynman's 'sum over histories' approach turned out to give good answers. Each of his diagrams represented different kinds of processes in the sum over all possibilities—and each had the form of a message sent from a sender to a receiver.

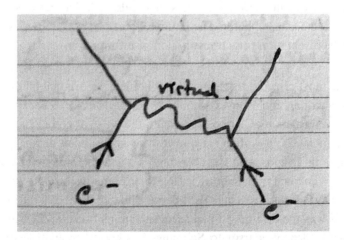

Fig. 3.3. Feynman diagram. The solid lines represent electrons, and the wavy line a photon. Electrons repel electrically by a message passed via a photon, the carrier of electromagnetic force.

Feynman was adept at intuitively writing down the processes that could go into the sums. He drew diagrams like that in figure 3.3 that seem to represent particle processes. However, in fact, each diagram did not represent a single particle process but was merely a template for a sum over all possible variations of that configuration. The lines that seemed to indicate particle trajectories to Feynman, perhaps only needed to represent the structure of causal influence, i.e. a message of information propagated from one interaction site to another, unwittingly resembling Shannon's model of communication. Being only a template message, a Feynman diagram was not like a single message, but more like a collection of similar messages, each representing a different possible version of the message machine. One couldn't know exactly what symbol is going to arrive at a particular moment, but you could add up the expected frequencies to see what was the probable outcome.

Using Tomonaga's work as a bridge, Dyson was then able to show how this picture related to an explicit and very elegant construction by Schwinger[68] that ignored the particle concept altogether. In Schwinger's formulation, the idea was to emphasize not particles, but elements of spacetime itself as the dynamical quantities. It was a quantum *field theory*, not just quantum mechanics of particles[69]. The sum over possibilities in Schwinger's work was by appeal to generating functionals, and his original formulation looked daunting and opaque to physical insight. But even though Schwinger's theory was superior in scope to Feynman's in 1948, he was aware of its deficiencies, and began to strip it down and reformulate it over the years that followed. During this time Shannon's influence became clearer. The notion of particles was quite possibly just a particular representation for a transmission of information.

One of the most prized possessions in my home is an original hardbound 1949 edition of Shannon and Weaver's book, *The Mathematical Theory of Communication*, given to me by Clarice Schwinger, the wife of Nobel Laureate Julian Schwinger in 1997, just after his unfortunate and sudden death by cancer in 1994. I became friends with the Schwingers a year before Julian's death by a lucky chance encounter[70]. While visiting their home in Bel Air, with its beautiful view overlooking Los Angeles, I perused the bookshelves during the early morning. It was the first time I had seen Shannon's book, and I was intrigued. In it, I saw a clear precursor to Schwinger's own reformulation of Quantum Theory, which he called *source theory*. Although Schwinger never acknowledged any link between the two, to my knowledge, the model of source and sink, sender and receiver, came just at the right moment and fed directly into Schwinger's formalism.

In source theory, Schwinger tried to strip away the formal details that he'd erected to prove mathematical consistency, and he reduced interactions to simple messages written in the alphabet particle processes, between a point of creation and a point of detection: a source and a sink, or a sender and a receiver. Without the actual diagrams that Feynman drew, there is an essential similarity in the formulation of a process of information transfer. In both their approaches, the word particle is empty of any real meaning. Schwinger wrote in 1970

> "Theory thus affirms, and experiment abundantly confirms, that the concept
> of a particle as an immutable object is untenable ..."[71].

What Schwinger's formulation, along with Feynman's alternative view, shows is the communication of information is the underlying mechanism for transmission of influence, even in the physics of the very small. The Newtonian idea of particles was not compatible with reality on a quantum level. It was an illusion of scale.

During the 20th century, our investigations into the fundamental nature of our world have brought about a major shift in our understanding of the nature of reality. They have influenced the way we view natural processes around us, and also led to technological innovations inspired by those processes.

The discreteness of matter and energy is a gift of understanding, that links the physical world to the virtual world of information in unexpected ways. Rather than closing a door on a dream of infinite resolution, it opens our minds to new ways of understanding the stability on which our world is built. Those insights have been crucial to the design of real and imagined technologies in the post war period. Atoms are not deterministic planetary systems, with absolute containment, they are something we do not fully understand, kept stable by strong but not absolute constraints.

Advances in the miniaturization and increases in transmission speeds of data now force us to confront the quantum nature of physics that previously had little impact on human time scales. This means that statistics and probability must play a role in our models of the way the world works. Discreteness, representing units of information, whether on the smallest scales or the largest, is an essential trait of both physical reality and of the artificial systems we build. We have to understand it, model it, and tolerate the way it interacts with important scales in order to exercise a sense of technological control over the world. As scientists, it allows us to know nature's secrets; as technologists, it offers us the stability on which to build for survival.

Whether by analogy or by 'digilogy', we employ the phenomena of stability to creative purpose.

4

All the Roads to Nowhere

How keeping things in balance is the essence of control.

"Plus ça change, plus c'est la même chose."
(The more everything changes, the more it all stays the same)
– Jean-Baptiste Alphonse Karr

Don't move! Stay where you are! Don't leave town! Don't go anywhere!

Let's hope these are not phrases you have had occasion to hear very often, at least outside of fiction. They are arresting exclamations, challenging someone to stay put, i.e. maintain a stable location, with varying degrees of accuracy—which is a turgid way of saying that they describe a status quo. One could also say that they are different ways of expressing an absence of change, at different scales: they represent different approximations to staying put. The sequence starts with millimetre movements of your muscles, then relaxes to your immediate surroundings, falls back to a geographic region, and finally gives up altogether being specific about location.

We understand these vague concepts intuitively. Our brains' semantic analyzers regularly decode such patterns of words, and attach meaning to them in the context of a scenario. That is the power of the human mind. If someone says, "I didn't move for 20 years", this does not mean that they were frozen in liquid nitrogen for two decades. It probably means that they settled in the same home, in the same town, i.e. that their average position remained within some general threshold radius, even allowing for one or two excursions to holiday destinations.

We are so used to using such concepts that we don't think much about what they actually mean, and there is good reason for that. Roughness and approximation play an important role in keeping logic and reasoning manageable and cheap to process. Even if someone moves around quite a bit, we can feel happy that they are basically in the same place. A hierarchy of approximation is a useful tool for both understanding and making use of scale as we build things. As we'll see in part II of the book, we handle approximation effortlessly when we model the world, in order to avoid overloading our brains with pointless detail. In the context of stability, however, this semantic interpretation probably emerges from a key survival need: to comprehend shifts in average behaviour.

This chapter is about what change means to stability, on a *macroscopic* scale—which is the scale we humans experience. It will introduce new concepts of dynamical stability and statistical stability, which form the principles on which a public infrastructure can prosper. It takes us from the realm of singular, atomic things and asks how we build up from these atoms to perceive the broader material of stuff. In the last chapter, we examined the world from the bottom up and discovered patterns of isolated microscopic behaviour; here, those patterns of behaviour will combine into a *less* detailed picture of a world that we can actually comprehend. This is the key principle behind most of modern technology.

The four exclamations in the opening of this chapter may all be viewed as expressions about required stability. If we are willing to overlook some inexactness, then we can characterize the location of a person as being sufficiently similar over some interval of time to be able to ignore a little local variation for all intents and purposes. This then begs the question we've met earlier: at exactly what threshold is something sufficiently similar for these intents and purposes.

By now, you will surely get the picture—of course, it's all about scale again, and there are no doubt some dimensionless ratios that govern the determination of that essential threshold. We understand the difference between 'don't move' and 'stay in town' because it is easy to separate the scales of an individual human being from a town. The ratio of length of my arm to the radius of the city gives a pretty clean measure of the certainty with which I can be located within the city. Had we all been giant blobs from outer space, this might not have been such an obvious distinction. I, at least, am not a giant blob (from outer space), so I can easily tell the difference between the boundaries of my city and the end of my fingertips. Similarly, if my average journey to and from work each day is much less than the radius of the city, then it is fair to say that my movements do not challenge the concept of the city as a coarse grain to which I belong.

Separability of scale is again an important issue. However, there is another aspect of stability present in this discussion that has fallen through the cracks so far. It is the idea of dynamical activity, i.e. that there can be continual movement, e.g. within the cells of our bodies that doesn't matter at all. This simple observation leads us to step away from the idea of exactness and consider the idea of *average* patterns of behaviour[72].

  Suppose we return to the concept of information, from the previous chapter, for a moment, and insert it into the description of behavioural patterns at different scales. A new twist then becomes apparent in the way we interpret scale. As we tune in and out of different scales, by adjusting the zoom on our imaginary microscope, we see different categories of information, some of which are interested to us, and others that are uninteresting. We elevate trends and we gloss over details; we listen for signals and we reject noise. We focus and we avoid distractions.

  This focus is an artifact of our human concerns. Nature itself does not care about these distinctions[73], but they are useful to us. This is perhaps the first time in the book that we meet the idea of a *policy* for categorizing what is important. We are explicitly saying that part of the story (the large scale trend) is more interesting than another part (the fluctuation). In technology, we use this ability to separate out effects from one another to identify those that can be used to make tools. For example, I consider (*ad hoc*) the up-and-down movement of keys on my keyboard when I type is significant, but the side to side wobble by a fraction of a millimetre isn't, because one triggers a useful result and the other doesn't. But that is a human prejudice: the universe is not particularly affected by my typing (regardless of what my deflated ego might yearn for). There is nothing natural or intrinsic in the world that separates out these scales. On the other hand, there is a fairly clear separation, from the existing structure of matter, between the movement of the few atoms in a key on my keyboard and the separation of planets and stars in the galaxy.

  Sometimes policies about the significance of information are *ad hoc*: for example, a journey may be considered local to the city if it is of no more than three blocks, but four blocks is too far to overlook. This judgement has no immediate basis in the scale of the city. Other times, policies are directly related to the impact of the information on a process we have selected as important to our purposes. For making technology, we often choose effects that *persist* for long enough to be useful, or show greater average stability so that we can rely on their existence.

  We can visualize the importance of 'persistence stability' with the help of an analogy. Before digital television, television pictures were transmitted as 'analogue', pseudo-continuous signals by modulating high frequency radio waves. When there was no signal, the radio receiver would pick up all of the stray radiation flying around the universe and show it as a pattern of fuzzy dots, like the background in Figure 4.1. This was accompanied by the rushing sound of

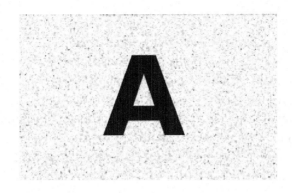

Fig. 4.1. Analogue noise on a television set contains a large amount of information.

the sea on the audio channel (from which the concept of noise comes). The persistent pattern in between the random dots was an example of a stable pattern from which one could perceive information. After digital signals, loss of signal results in nothing at all, or sometimes missing frames or partial frames, which one of the advantages of digital.

Years ago, when I used to teach basic information theory to students at the University, I would switch on the old pre-digital television without the antenna and show the fuzzy dots[74]. Then I would plug in the antenna and show them a simple channel logo BBC or NRK, like the letter 'A' in Figure 4.1. Then I would ask the students which of the two images they thought contained the most information. Of course, everyone said that the letter 'A' contained more information than the fuzzy dots. Then I would tell them: imagine now that you have to write a letter to a friend to describe the exact image you see, so that they could reproduce every details of the picture at their end. Think about the length of the letter you would need to write. Now, tell me, which of the two pictures do you think contains more information?

The point was then clear. Noise is not too little information, it is so much that we don't find any persistent pattern in it. The simple letter 'A' has large areas (large compared to the dots) all of the same colour, so the total amount of information can be reduced, by factoring out all the similar pixels. In a digital encoding of the picture, the letter 'A' is just a single alphabetic character (one symbol), but in an old analogue encoding, we have to send all the variations of light and dark broken down into lines in a raster display, and this is much more sensitive to noise. To write down a description of every fuzzy dot and every change in every split second, would require a very long letter, not to mention a very boring one that might make writing to relatives seem gleeful by comparison.

Despite the presence of noise, we can find a signal, like the letter 'A', by choosing to ignore variations in the data smaller than a certain scale threshold. Recall the discussion of thresholds in Chapter 2. Try half-closing your eyes when looking at Figure 4.1, and watch the noise disappear as you impair the ability of your eyes to see detail. This same principle of separating transmission as part signal and part noise can be applied to any kind of system in which there is variation[75]. It doesn't matter whether the variation is in time (as in Figure 4.2) or whether it is pattern in space, like the letter 'A' (as in Figure 4.1).

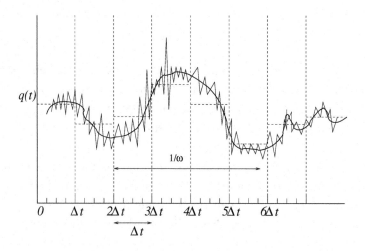

Fig. 4.2. Coarse graining of different representations of a pattern changing in time: the actual detailed signal (jagged line), smoothed into a trend (smooth curve), and then re-digitized into coarse blocks of width Δt.

This idea of separating out noise, is not really different from the way we handle any kind of detail, whether perceiving or building something. Imagine how you would depict a scene for someone: if you visually sketched or otherwise described the object, you would probably begin by drawing the main lines, the broad strokes of the image, and only then start to fill in details at lower levels. You would start from the top down in the scale hierarchy. However, if you tried to draw something like a lawn of grass, with thousands of detailed parts all the same, you would probably just start drawing the details one by one, because there would be no trend to identify. There would be nothing to gain from starting anywhere else, because there is not identifiable trend to extract. The half-closed eye test allows us to see major trends and features in an image.

Trends are part of the way we perceive change, whether it is change in time or in space. It is common to decompose variation into something that is *slowly varying* that we want to see, and something else that is *fluctuating* on top of it that we don't (see Figure 4.2). It is a common technique in mathematics, for instance: it is the basis of Fourier analysis, and it is the basic method of *perturbation theory*. It is a property of weakly coupled (linear) systems that this decomposition of scales leads to a clear description of trends. In fact it is a property of the interference of waves. We can express it in a number of suggestive ways:

Change = Stable Variation + Perturbation

Variable data = Trend + Variation

Transmission = Signal + Noise

In each case, the aim is to make the contributions on the right of the plus sign as small as possible.

Recall, for example, our love boat from chapter 1, sailing on the calm ocean. At any particular zoom level, the picture of this boat had some general structural lines and some details that we would consider superfluous to the description. Viewed from the air, the picture was dominated by a giant storm, and then the ship was but a blip on the ocean. At the level of the giant waves, the ripples close to the ship were irrelevant details. At the level of the ripples, the atomic structure of the water was irrelevant, and so on.

Remember too that a small perturbation can unleash a self-amplifying effect in a non-linear system—the *butterfly effect*, from Chapter 1. If the small variations in Figure 4.2 did not average out to keep the smooth trend, but in fact sent it spinning out of control, then we would be looking at useless instability.

That is not to say that details are always unwelcome in our minds. Occasionally we are willing to invest the brute force to try to be King Canute in the face of an onslaught of detail. Perhaps the most pervasive trend in modern times is that we are including faster and faster processes, i.e. shorter and shorter timescales, in our reckoning of systems. We used to let those timescales wash over us as noise, but now we are trying to engage with them, and control them, because the modern world has put meaning there.

The fighter jet's aerodynamic stability was one such example. Stock market trading prices are another where people actually care about the detailed fluctuations in the data. Traders on the markets make (and lose) millions of dollars in a split second by predicting (or failing to predict) the detailed movements of markets a split second ahead of time. Complex trading software carries out automated trading. This is analogous to the tactics of the fighter jet, to live on the brink of stability, assisted by very fast computers that keep it just about in the air, in a fine detailed balance at all times, modulo weekly variations. In most cases, however, we are not trying to surf on the turbulence of risk, we are looking for a safe and predictable outcome: something we can rely on to be our trusted infrastructure.

We now have a representation of change based on scales in space and time, and of rates of change in space and time. This is going to be important for understanding something as dynamic as information infrastructure. These two aspects (position and rate of change) are known as the canonical variables of a dynamical system. Let's pursue them further.

As we zoom into any picture, we may divide it up into grains[76], as in figure 4.2, and imagine that the trend is approximately constant, at least on average, over each granular interval. The variations within the grain can thus be replaced by the flat line average of the values in the interval, for most purposes. If the grains are small enough (so that the size of $\Delta t \to 0$), the result is that one smooths out the jagged fluctuations, leaving the smooth curve in the figure.

One may also do the same thing with the difference between the actual value and the average value. This gives us the average size of fluctuations, relative to that average base value in the grain. We can separate clarity and fuzz. The method does not work unless there is a separation of scale, however. If fluctuations are no smaller than the variations of a trend, then we can't tell the difference between them, and the line is simply irreducibly jagged at all scales. This is called *scale-free*, *self-similar*, or even *fractal* behaviour. Dividing up a model into grains is also a strategy for computational modelling, but it does not work very well in non-linear systems, which is why it is hard to predict the weather (see chapter 1).

Now back to information. Smoothing out fluctuations into a continuous curve is one approach to finding a stable representation of a process, but it is still varying continuously (or pseudo-continuously). What if we don't make the grain size vanishingly small, but keep discrete grains or 'buckets'? Then the value of the variation stays at the same fixed value for longer. This is a kind of quantization of the horizontal time axis. By removing detail, removing information, we actually find more meaning.

This idea can be used to exploit another approach called re-digitizing the signal. This is a way of sorting a signal into fixed symbol categories on the vertical axis (see Figure 4.3). This is where digital signal transmission comes back to us as a technology rather than as a discovery.

Recall that the telegraph used the clarity of digital Morse code to avoid the noisy transmission lines of the electrical wiring. By standardizing discrete units of time for dots and dashes, i.e. by digitizing the time for a dot, we can distinguish a dot from a dash in terms of a simple digital time scale. By setting a threshold between signal and no signal, a message of dots and the dashes could be distinguished as symbols from no message at all.

This same principle was applied both to the time axis and to the signal value, to digitize many other kinds of signal, starting from around the 1980s. What had previously been treated as continuous was cut up into a discrete template, or *sampled* (see Figure 4.3) so that it could be encoded as digits or symbols. Digital music resulted in the MiniDisc in Japan, and the Compact Disc (CD) all over the world. Video discs, DVDs and Blue-Ray followed. Now digital television and radio are the norm.

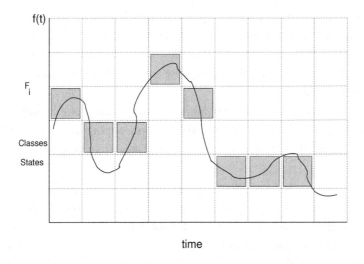

Fig. 4.3. Re-digitization of the vertical axis an analogue signal is called A/D conversion. The rendition is not 'perfect', but we can make the symbol sensitivity as large or small as we like, so that variations within a digit do not matter.

Re-digitization brings stability to our perception of location on these maps of sound and picture: as long as a signal stays within the bounds of certain thresholds we have assigned, the digital representation records a specific symbol. Thus, if we divide up the 'continuous' signal values into coarse enough ranges, then the effect of noise will be almost unnoticeable, because it will be like moving a couple of blocks within the radius of the city. Our ears are not sensitive enough to detect the difference. A perturbation of the average signal will still be within the bounds of a category. This is the method of analogue to digital (A/D) conversion.

Harry Nyquist (1889-1976) made famous a theorem which tells us that, in order to capture the detail of a change in time, we have to sample the signal into buckets at least twice as fast as the fastest expected change. That is why digital music is represented in sampling rates of 44kHz (16 bits) and 48-192kHz (24 bits), as the highest frequencies available to human hearing are reckoned to be at most 20kHz. The higher quality sampling used by audiophiles is designed to capture more of the harmonics and interactions that happen during the reproduction of the music, even if the actual frequencies cannot be perceived directly.

Average behaviour seems to be a key to the way humans perceive change. I'll return to this topic in the second part of the book. We can grasp trends over a limited range, and we ignore the fluctuations on a smaller scale. Thus our interaction and comprehension of a scene depends completely on how we set our scope. These matters are important when designing technology for human interaction, and they tell us about the sensitivity of machinery we build to environmental noise.

So let's delve deeper into the balance of fluctuations, and consider what this new notion of stability means, based on the more sophisticated concept of averages and statistical measures. A change of setting might help.

Global warming and climate change are two topics that rose swiftly into public consciousness a few years ago, to remind us of the more tawdry concept of accounting and balancing the books. It took what had previously been a relatively abstract issue for meteorologists about the feedback in the global weather systems and turned it into a more tangible threat to human society. The alleged symptoms became daily news items, and pictures of floods, storms, and drowning polar bears became closely associated with the idea. Climate change is a new slogan, but it all boils down to yet another example of scaling and stability, but this time of the average, statistical variety.

The weather system of our planet is a motor that is fuelled primarily by sunlight. During the daytime, the Earth is blasted continuously by radiation from the Sun. The pressure of that radiation bends the magnetic field of the planet and even exerts a pressure on the Earth, pushing it slightly outwards into space. Much of that radiation is absorbed by the planet and gets turned into heat. Some of it, however, gets reflected back into space by snow and cloud cover. During the night, i.e. on the dark side of the globe, the heat is radiated back into space, cooling one half of the planet. All of these effects perturb the dynamical system that is the Earth's climate.

As chemical changes occur in the atmosphere, due to pollution and particles in the atmosphere, the rates of absorption and reflection of light and heat change too. This leads to changes in the details that drive the motor, but these changes are typically local variations. They happen on the scales of continents and days.

Usually, there is some sense in which the average weather on the planet is more or less constant, or is at least slowly varying. We call the slow variation of the average patterns the *climate* and we call the local fluctuations the *weather*. By analogy with the other cases above, we could imagine writing:

$$\text{Atmospheric evolution} = \text{Climate} + \text{Weather}$$

and, even though the weather is far from being a linear thing, we might even hope that there is a sufficient stability in the average patterns to allow us to separate the daily weather from the climate's long term variation.

It makes sense then that, in the debates of global warming, the average temperature of the planet is often referred to. This is a slightly bizarre idea. We all know that the temperature in Hawaii and the temperature in Alaska are very different most of the time, so temperature is not a uniform thing. Moreover, the retention of heat in the atmosphere is non-linear, with weather systems creating all manner of feedback loops and transport mechanisms to move heat around, store it and release it. Ocean currents, like the gulf stream, transport heat from a hot place to a cold place. The planetary climate system is as intricate as biology itself.

The average temperature somewhere on the planet is thus in a continuous state of re-evaluation. It changes, on the fly, on a timescale that depends on the scale of the region we look at. For the average temperature of the whole Earth to be unchanging, the various absorptions, reflections, and re-radiations would have to balance out, in a truly Byzantine feat of cosmic accounting. A net effect of zero means that for all the energy that comes in from the Sun, or is generated on the planet, the same amount of heat must leak away. Such a balance is called a state of *equilibrium*.

The word equilibrium (plural equilibria) is from the Latin *aequilibrium*, from aequus 'equal', and *libra* meaning a scale or balance (as in the zodiac sign). Its meaning is quite self-explanatory, at least in intent. However, as a phenomenon, the number of different ways that exist in the world for weighing measures is vast, and it is this that makes equilibrium perhaps the most important concept in science.

Once again, equilibrium is about scale in a number of ways. As any accountant knows, yearly profits and monthly cashflow are two very different things.

You might make a profit over the year, and still not be able to pay your bills on a monthly basis. Similarly, planetary heat input and dissipation both on the short term and in the long term are two very different issues. Of global warming, one sometimes hears the argument that all the fuel that is burned on the Earth is really energy from the Sun, because, over centuries, it is the conversion of raw materials into living systems that make trees and oil and combustible hydrocarbons. Thus nothing Man does with hydrocarbons can affect the long-term warming of the planet, since all the energy that went into them came from the Sun. On the short term, however, this makes little sense, since the energy stored in these vast memory bank oil reserves can be released in just a few years by little men, just as the chemical energy it took to make a stick of dynamite can be released in a split second. The balance of energy in and out thus depends on your bank account's savings and your spending. Timescales matter.

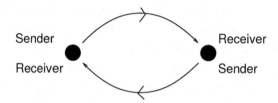

Fig. 4.4.   The detailed balance between two parts of a system showing the flows that maintain equilibrium. The balance sheet always shows zero at equilibrium, but if we look on shorter timescales, we must see small imbalances arise and be corrected.

The basic idea of an equilibrium can be depicted as an interaction between two parties, as in Figure 4.4. The sender on the left sends some transaction of something (energy, data, money) to the receiver on the right at some kind of predictable average rate, and the receiver absorbs these transactions. Then, to maintain the balance, the roles are also reversed and the sender on the right transmits at an equivalent rate to the receiver on the left. The net result is that there is no build up of this transacted stuff on either side. It is like a ball game, throwing catch back and forth, except that there are usually far more transactions to deal with. In the case of global climate patterns there are staggering numbers of molecules flying back and forth in the atmospheric gases, transferring heat and energy in a variety of forms, and there are clouds and ocean currents transporting hot and cold water.

Equilibrium is what we observe when the slowly varying part of information grinds to a halt and becomes basically constant, so that one may see balance in the fluctuations. Equilibrium can be mechanical or seemingly *static*[77], like when a lamp hangs from the ceiling, held in balance between the cord it is attached to and the force of gravity, or it can be more *dynamic*, such as the heating of the Earth, or a monthly cashflow, with a continuous input and output of income and expenses. (Imagine putting a group of people on a very large balance and weighing them first standing still, and then jumping up and down.) When an equilibrium is disturbed, the shift perturbs a system and this can lead to instability. Sudden destabilization catastrophes can occur, leading to new metastable regimes, like ice ages, microclimates, and other things. Equilibrium of discrete informatic values is often called the *consensus* problem in information science[78].

Equilibrium might be the single most important idea in science. It plays a role everywhere in 'the accounting of things'. It is crucial to our understanding of heat, chemistry, and economics—and to the Internet.

Although the simple depiction of equilibrium in Figure 4.4 shows only two parties, equilibrium usually involves vast numbers of atomic parts, taken in bulk. That is because equilibrium is a statistical phenomenon—it is about averages, taken over millions of atoms, molecules, data, money, or whatever currency of transaction we are observing. Staying in town, or quivering in your shoes are also statistical equilibria.

The accounting that leads to equilibrium is called a situation of *detailed balance*. It is detailed, because we can, if we insist, burrow down into the details of each individual exchange of atoms or data or money, but it is the balance over a much larger scale that is the key. The principle of detailed balance was introduced explicitly for collisions by Boltzmann. In 1872, he proved his H-theorem using this principle. The notion of temperature itself comes from a detailed balance condition.

A simple example of detailed balance is what happens in a queue. Recall the supermarket checkout example in chapter 2. Customers arrive at a store, and they have to leave again, passing through the checkout. It seems reasonable to expect that this would lead to an equilibrium. But what if it doesn't? What if more customers arrive than leave? When a sudden change in this equilibrium happens, the balance of flows is affected and the detailed balance goes awry until a new stable state is reached. This is a problem for non-equilibrium dynamics. However, often we can get away without understanding those details, by dealing only with the local epochs of equilibrium, in the pseudo-constant grains of Figure 4.2.

Queueing theory begins with a simple model of this equilibrium that repre-

sents the arrival and processing of customers to a service handling entity, like a
store, a call centre, or form-processing software on the Internet. In the simplest
queueing theory, one imagines that customers arrive at random. At any moment,
the arrival of a new customer is an independent happening, i.e. it has nothing to
do with what customers are already in the queue. We say that the arrival process has no *memory* of what happened before. This kind of process is called a
Markov process after Russian mathematician Andrey Markov (1856-1922), and
it is a characteristic signature of statistical equilibrium. An equilibrium has no
memory of the past, and no concept of time. It is a *steady state*.

Queueing theory can be applied by setting up the detailed balance condition
and solving the mathematics. In normal terminology, we say that there is a rate
of customers arriving, written λ requests per unit time, and there is a rate at
which customers are served, called μ requests per unit time. From dimensional
analysis, we would expect the behaviour of the queue to depend on the dimensionless ratio called the *traffic intensity*,

$$\rho = \frac{\lambda}{\mu}.$$

as indeed it does. To see that, we write the detailed balance as follows. A queue
of length n persons will not be expected to grow or shrink if:

Expected arrivals = Expected departures

Or, as flow rates:

$\lambda\times$ (Probability of $n - 1$ in queue) = $\mu\times$ (Probability of n in queue)

This says that, if a new person arrives when there are already $n - 1$ persons in
line, it had better balance the rate at which someone leaves once there are now
n persons in line. This detailed balance condition can be solved to work out an
average queue length that can be supported, based on the dimensionless ratio ρ:

$$n_{\text{average}} = \frac{\rho}{1 - \rho}.$$

A picture of the results of this average length can be seen in Figure 4.5, and
they are quite intuitive. As long as the arrival rate of customers is a bit less than
the rate at which customers can be processed, ρ is less than the dimensionless
number 1 and the queue length is small and under control. However, there is
a very critical turnaround as one scale approaches the other, sending the queue
into an unstable mode of growth. The suddenness of the turning point is perhaps
surprising. The queue has a major instability, indicating that we should try to
keep queues small at all times to avoid a total breakdown. Indeed, after a half

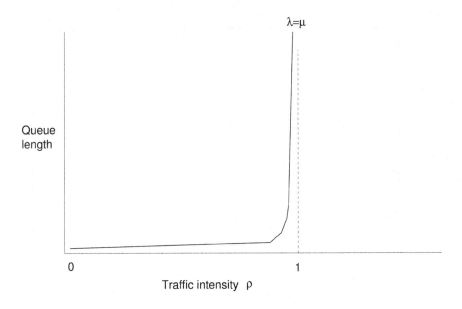

Fig. 4.5.   The behaviour of the average queue length predicted by a detailed balance relation in queueing theory. The queue goes unstable and grows out of control when $\rho \to 1$. theory

century of queueing theory, the crux of what we know is very simple. A queue has basically two modes of operation. Either the expected queue length is small and stable, or it is growing wildly out of control—and the distance between these two modes is very small.

The model above is completely theoretical, but since it is based mainly on simple scaling assumptions, we would expect it to represent reality at least qualitatively, if not quantitatively. For computer processing, queueing is a serious issue, that affects companies financially when they make legal agreements called Service Level Agreements, claiming how fast they can process data requests. Companies need to invest in a sufficient number of servers at the 'data checkout' of their infrastructure to process arrivals in time.

In 2007, together with students Jon Henrik Bjørnstad, Sven Ulland and Gard Undheim, I studied how well this very real issue is represented by the simple model above, using real computer servers. For all the wonders of mathematics and modelling, simplicity is an asset when building technology, so we wanted to know if a simplest of arguments would provide good-enough guidance to datacentre infrastructure designers. The results can be seen in Figures 4.6 and 4.7.

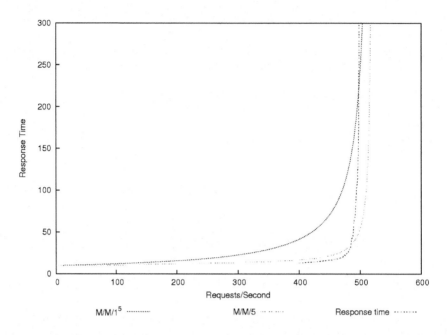

Fig. 4.6.   Queue behaviour of five servers in different configurations, comparing the two models with measurements.

The different lines in Figure 4.6 show the same basic form as the theoretical graph in Figure 4.5, indicating that the basic qualitative form of the behaviour is quite well described by the simple model, in spite of many specific details that differ[79]. This is an excellent proof of the universality of dimensional arguments based on scaling arguments.

Figure 4.6 also shows the different ways of handling requests. The experiment was set up with five servers to process incoming online requests. Queueing theory predicts that it makes a difference how you organize your queue. The optimum way is to make all customers stand in one line and take the first available server from a battery of five as they become available (written M/M/5). This is the approach you will see at airports and other busy centres for this reason. The alternative, is to have a separate line for each sever (written $M/M/1^5$). This approach performs worse, because if the lines are not balanced, more customers can end up in a busy line, while another line stands empty. So we see, from the graph, that the single line keeps faster response times much closer to the critical turning point than the multiple-line queue, which starts going bad earlier—but both queue types fail at the same limit.

Unlike the simple theory, we can also see how the finite capacity of the com-

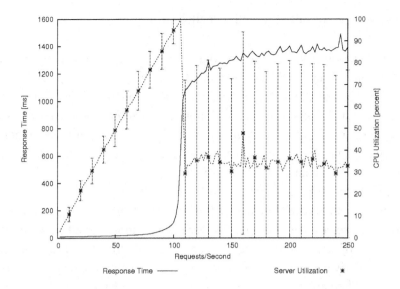

Fig. 4.7. Two overlaid graphs showing the CPU utilization and the response time of a server depending on the arrival rate of requests. The utilization is a straight line up to saturation at $\rho = 1$ and then it actually falls as the system goes chaotic. The response time rises to a maximum value at around 1300 ms and stabilizes due to the finite scale of resources in the computers.

puter eventually throttles the growth of a queue (another dimensionless ratio), illustrating where the simple model of scale and balance breaks down. Compare Figure 4.5 with Figure 4.7. When the response time was modelled in detail to find the limit, we see that the response time does not actually become infinite, because the computer cannot work that hard. In fact what happens (compare the two overlaid lines in Figure 4.7) is that when the queue length is so long that the CPU cannot process the requests any faster ($\rho \to 1$), the computer becomes immobilized by its own inundation with work and it begins to drop jobs. This situation is called *thrashing*. The computer loses the ability to focus on processing jobs and so its average CPU utilization actually falls, as the jobs are still building up. The vertical bars, showing the statistical variation in repeated experiments, show how the processor becomes very unpredictable. It copes about half of the time to do useful work, and the response time of the few jobs that get done reaches a maximum limit.

The simple M/M/5 model did not take into account the characteristic limiting scales of the computers so it was always ready to fail once that assumption was violated. Before this point was reached, on the other hand, the main features of the behaviour were still very well modelled by it.

The expectation that equilibrium would be important to computer behaviour had been one of my chief lines of reasoning in the paper, Computer Immunology, when I wrote about self-healing computer systems even as early as 1998, because it is such a universal phenomenon, but I had not then had time to think in detail about what kind of equilibria might be important. It seemed therefore important to gain a broad understanding of the kinds of phenomena taking place in the world of computer based infrastructure.

Beginning in 1999, and working with colleagues Hårek Haugerud, Sigmund Straumsness, and Trond Reitan at Oslo University College, I began to apply the technique of separating slow and fast variables to look at the behaviour of different kinds of service traffic (queues) on computers that were available to us. I was particularly interested in whether the standard methods of statistical physics could be applied effectively to describe the pieces of technological wizardry being used at a different scale. Dynamical similarity suggested that this must be the case, but idealizations can sometimes go too far. To what extent would it be possible to make simple idealized models as in Newtonian physics?

We began by measuring as many of the facets of computer behaviour as we could, over many months, to see what kinds to phenomena could be identified. Collecting numbers is easy, but piecing together an understanding of what they mean is another matter altogether. This is the first stage of any scientific investigation: look and see[80].

The initial investigations were less than interesting. Merely collecting data is no guarantee of striking gold, of course. We began by looking at a group of computers used by the staff at the university on their desktops. They were readily available and so setting up the experiment was quite easy. However, the data returned were both sparse and hard to fathom. If you imagine, for a moment, the life of a typical desktop computer, it is more like a cat than a ballet dancer: it sleeps for a lot of the time, we feed it now and then, but there are no sweeping patterns of regular activity that could be used to infer some larger theme, worthy of even the most paranoid scrutiny.

Desktop and laptop computers, it turns out, are very wasteful of the quite generous resources they sport. We almost never utilize their potential for more than a small percentage of the time they are switched on. We shouldn't expect to see any fathomable pattern from a single computer, over a timescale of its usage. Most of that time they merely sit idle, waiting for something to do.

A negative result is still a result, though. Knowing what can cannot be known is an important part of science: fundamental uncertainty, somewhat analogous to the quantum world, where the behaviour of individual quanta is truly uncertain, but where patterns emerge on average at much larger scales. Indeed, as we moved on to explore 'servers' (these are the computers that handle what happens when you look up something online, for example, like web pages and database items), basic patterns of behaviour revealed themselves quite quickly. In fact, we could see two kinds of system: those where very little happened and dominated by random noise, and those with clear patterns of periodic activity. Computers that were used by just a single user from time to time, like workstations and PCs were dominated by noise, because when so little actually happens, everything the user did was new and apparently random. Busy servers, on the other hand, servicing hundreds or thousands of users, showed clear statistical patterns of repeated behaviour.

Classical computer science would have us believe that computers are just machines and therefore they can only do what they have been told to do, slavishly following a particular path. However, this is manifestly not the case. It's a bit like saying that if the Sun is shining, it must be sunny—that is too simplistic (clouds still get in the way, even if the sun is shining, for instance). Even when we had found enough data from busy servers to see recognizable patterns, there were things that defied the classical explanation of a deterministic system.

Overlapping timescales were one such mystery. When you know that a certain task is executed at a certain moment by a computer, you might expect to see a clear signature from this task, but that is also too simplistic. The more we looked for signs of specific deterministic behaviour in the measurements, the less of a pattern we actually saw. It was almost as if the computer's response to individual behaviour was doing the exact opposite of what one would expect. It was surprisingly stable and seemed to be more of a mirror for our circadian rhythms than our intentions. Immediate human intent was the farthest thing from what we were seeing.

The mystery deepened when the 'auto-correlation' time of signals was longer than the variations in the trends we were observing. A correlation is a similarity in a pattern of measurement at two different places (in space). An auto-correlation is a correlation at two different times (in time). It represents the appearance of a memory in what otherwise looked like quite random data. Computers were not Markov processes.

But in fact the problem was neither paradoxical nor counter-intuitive. The problem lay in trying to look for channels of determinism in measurements that were overlapping to such a high degree that the signals of individual contributions were averaged out—or *coarse grained* away (as in Figure 4.2). All that remained of the signal was the slowly varying trend. What we were looking at was no longer a deterministic machine, but a non-equilibrium body immersed in a bath of environmental chatter. We were seeing clear patterns that were dominated by the human working week (see Figure 4.8).

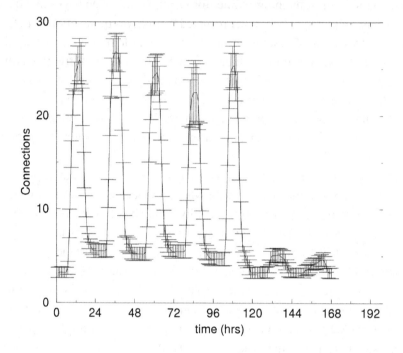

Fig. 4.8.   Measured data from a Samba file access services, measured over many weeks, plotted overlapping onto a single week. Vertical bars represent the variation of the measurements. The fact that the error bars are small compared to the scale of variation, shows this to be a strong signal with little noise.

On single-user machines, users' behaviours became the loudest message in the flood of environmental signals. The behaviour looked unpredictable, because user behaviour is basically unpredictable when viewed on a one by one basis. First you type some letters, then you make a cup of coffee, then you type some more into a different application, then you are interrupted by a colleague. On this individual basis, there is a strong coupling between user and machine, making it difficult to see any long term behaviour at a separate scale; but, once a machine is exposed to many users (the more the better, in fact) all of those specific details interfere and details smudge out the fluctuations leaving only the trend.

Once we saw how the dynamics were being generated, it led to some obvious ways to unite theory and practice. The strong periodic behaviour first suggested that we should model the system using periodic variables. The mathematics of Fourier analysis then make the prediction that the effective contributions to system behaviour will be quantized in integer multiples, just like the energy levels in quantum blackbody radiation.

Moreover, the strong periodicity suggested that, if we subtracted the emergent trend from the rest of the signal, by separating fast and slow variables, what would be left should look like an equilibrium distribution, with periodic boundary conditions, much like Planck radiation. Sure enough, when we did this, out popped a beautiful picture of the Planck spectrum[81].

It is important to understand why the spectrum of fluctuations in our computer systems matched the quantum radiation signature of blackbody radiation. There is nothing quantum mechanical about computer behaviour at the scale of desktops and servers. However, the periodicity of the environmental driving factors effectively led to a system that was *dynamically similar*, and similar systems have similar behaviour. The conclusion is that computers are, in fact, in effective equilibrium with their surroundings at all times, with regard to their network connections, just as the Earth is in equilibrium with outer space.

What was perhaps more important than the dynamical similarity was that one could immediately see that computers were not to be understood as something operating independently of humans. They are not just machines that do what they are told: it is all about understanding a human-computer system[82]. The message visible in the non-equilibrium pattern gave us strong information about the *source* that drives the trends of change.

This is not mysterious either. Computers do indeed do more or less what we tell them, but what we tell them is only one message amongst many being received and processed by a modern computer. There are multiple overlapping messages from software, from the keyboard, the mouse, the network, and all of these are overlapping and interfering with one another. The difference is quite analogous to the transition from the picture of a Newtonian particle as a point-like ball moving in a straight line, to a spritely quantum cloud of interfering pathways, as revealed by Feynman's diagrams.

In looking at a small web server, we observed that we needed to have a minimum amount of traffic to the server in order to be able to see any pattern on the time scale of weeks. This revealed a periodic pattern on the scale of a week. My team was unable to go beyond this stage, but online retailer Amazon took this to the next level in the early years of the 21st century. Amazon web traffic is vast.

With traffic intensity and levels tens of millions of times greater than our lowly web server, and data collection over years, it was possible to see a pattern on an even greater scale of yearly patterns.

Amazon's sales are fairly steady throughout the year, except at the time lead-ing up to Christmas, when sales suddenly rise massively. Extra information processing capacity is needed to cope during these months. This is no different to the need to hire extra sales personnel for the Christmas period, in more tradi-tional store, just on a much greater scale. Amazon builds extra capacity to cope with this sudden demand each year, and rents out the surplus during the rest of the year.

The growth of Amazon's traffic is so large that there no sense in which we can think of it as an equilibrium system over several years. What is interesting however is that the identification of the trend pattern has similarities that still make it somewhat predictable. This kind of knowledge enables Amazon to buy datacentre capacity at the level needed for the Christmas peak, but then rent it out to other users throughout the year. This was the start of 'cloud computing', using scale and detailed balance as a tool to spread the balance of costs.

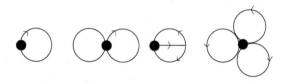

Fig. 4.9.   The quantum loop expansion—all the ways of staying in the same place

To predict the emergence of a Planck spectrum in weekly computer behaviour, I used the same trick that Feynman and Schwinger had used of summing up contributions of cause and effect in the development of QED. Closing the loop on the QED story illustrates yet again the generic structure of information trans-fer that underpins disparate phenomena. Based on the methods developed by Schwinger and students after the seminal work on QED, it is possible to see the signature of equilibrium visually, in a much broader context with the help of Feynman diagrams. The juxtaposition is fitting, as the work of Feynman and Schwinger have reached a kind of equilibrium of their own in modern times. The so-called *effective action* in quantum field theory is the generator of equilibrium processes in quantum field theory. Schwinger referred to this as merely a 'gen-erating functional' for calculating particle processes. Feynman's interpretation might have been more visual. Today, the effective action summarizes what is known as the quantum loop expansion, and it is known to be related to the free energy for equilibrium thermodynamics.

The significance of the effective action is that it generates all closed-loop diagrams and hence it represents the sum of all processes during which a 'particle', 'message', or 'transaction' (take your pick) is in balance with a counter-process so that the system goes nowhere at all. It sums up all the roads to nowhere. At equilibrium, for every message forwards, there is one backwards. These are the basic diagrams of an equilibrium, generalizing Figure 4.4.

In complete equilibrium there is no notion of time in a system, because we cannot observe any change of state. In fact, the notion of time disappears altogether.

Discovering the well-known science of equilibria in the statistical behaviour of information technology was a welcome opportunity to see modern infrastructure in a new light. For the first time, one could begin to develop a physics of the technology itself, to really begin to understand it behaviourally, in all its complexity, without oversimplifying or suppressing inconvenient issues.

Equilibrium presents itself in many flavours, important to technology, and this chapter could not call itself complete without mentioning more of the practical applications of equilibria. What one learns from the loops above is that a state of equilibrium is always a place from which to begin generating an understanding of dynamics, because it represents a state in which nothing actually happens on average, but which is poised to unleash anything that is possible by perturbing.

Consider the climate analogy again. The net warming of the planet is not the only manifestation of disequilibrium in climate change. The increased energy from warming causes more water to evaporate from the oceans and then more precipitation to fall over land. This is a sub-part equilibrium around water. Rain and snow pour greater and greater amounts of water onto land, causing flooding in many areas. Why flooding? Flooding occurs because drainage systems cannot cope with the amount of water falling, so rivers burst their banks and irrigation/drainage channels become super-saturated in their attempt to return water to the sea: a broken equilibrium. The same effect happens with Internet traffic, but it is harder to visualize.

Flooding seems to be worse in recent years, and it has been speculated whether this is due to poor drainage in farmland. Drainage, of course, is not a natural phenomenon; it is one of our human infrastructure technologies for maintaining an artificial equilibrium. If drainage is designed during a time of little precipitation, it is tempting for the engineers to dimension their system for a capacity on the same scale as the average levels of rainfall over recent years. No one builds for the hundred year flood, because that does not make short term cashflow sense. Unlike Amazon, drain builders cannot monetize their peak load investments by renting out spare drainage capacity during the times of low rainfall. This makes the boundary between land and water unstable to rainfall, because it cannot be equilibrated.

We can understand the key features of this instability easily by looking at Figure 2.1 again, with a slightly different focus. The left hand picture, which was stable to the location of the ball, has a beneficial effect to perturbations like the wind that pushes it around; but it has a harmful effect if your perturbation is the arrival of new balls, like raindrops, for then we see that containing these causes the valley to fill up and flood. This has to happen on a timescale determined by the size of the valley and the rate of rainfall.

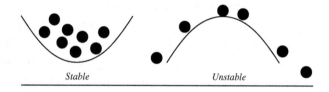

Fig. 4.10.   A valley is unstable to filling with raindrops, but a hill is stable.

The right hand picture, which is unstable to ball position and motion, now becomes the perfect drainage system, keeping it free of flooding. Thus the roles of the potential are reversed with respect to the two different kinds of perturbation.

This situation is very interesting from a technological perspective, because we have discovered something new to the discussion thus far, namely a *conflict of interest* in the design of a system. We need a mechanism to support two different goals, and we find that it cannot necessarily do so, at least without redesign.

Suppose you are a technology designer, or infrastructure engineer, with the responsibility to build a safe and practical solution to keep animals safe and contained. You might consider making a confining potential to keep the animals from wandering off, and you might not consider the possibility that flooding might have placed these animals in the perfect trap where they would drown. There is thus a design conflict between containment and filling up with water.

Now, if water is allowed to drain out of the potential valley above, by making a hole, say, one could try to change the unstable growth into a manageable equilibrium. Then we introduce a new scale into the problem: the size of the hole, or the rate at which water drains from the valley.

In fact, the very same conflict exists in many cities where insufficient planning is made for drainage. In some towns where there is rarely rain, there are no storm drains at all, and water has to flow across concrete and asphalt roads causing flooding. In my home city of Oslo, Norway, snow often builds up in winter and snow ploughs pile the snow on top of storm drains so that, when the snow begins to melt, the drains are blocked and the streets flood. Buildings with flat rooves with walls around them have a similar problem: water builds up on the roof and does not drain away properly, causing leakage through the ceiling below.

Conflicts of interest between design goals may be considered part of a more general problem of strategic decision-making, a topic that has been analyzed extensively by mathematicians during the 20th century. The subject is also known as *game theory*.

John von Neumann, whom we met in the previous chapter, was one of the earliest innovators in game theory. He discovered the solution to the now famous concept of *zero sum games*, a kind of game in which what one player loses, the other player gains. Game theory developed over the 20th century to be a key consideration in formulating problems of economics. Indeed, von Neumann's seminal book with economist Oskar Morgenstern (1902-1977) is considered by many to be the birth of modern economics[83].

A zero sum game is a game with conservation of rewards, i.e. where there is a fixed amount of benefit to share amongst everyone. This is like the accounting of energy in physics, or a scenario in which there is a fixed amount of money to go around. Although we can make games with any number of players, it is easiest to imagine two opposing players in a tug of war, each competing to maximize their share of the reward. The reward is referred to as the *payoff* in game theory.

Suppose, for example, we think of the water sharing problem again: only a fixed amount of rain falls on an oasis in the desert. It is captured in a tank and we want to use it for a variety of different and conflicting purposes. One competing player wants to use the water to drink, another wants to use it to grow food. The water here is itself the payoff, and the players pursue a tug of war to maximize their share of the water. If one player gets 2 litres, the other player loses those 2 litres, hence the sum of the payoffs is zero.

The idea in game theory is that both players, or stakeholders formulate their strategies, possibly several different ones, in order to maximize their use of the water. We can then evaluate which strategy would give each player a maximum payoff, given that the other player is trying to do the very same thing. It is a tug of war.

Von Neumann used the concept of an equilibrium to formulate a solution to this kind of game. He showed that one could make a detailed balance condition for the payoff known as the minimax condition, where one balances the combination of minimum payoff for an opponent with the maximum payoff for oneself. The minimax detailed balance looks deceptively simple:

$$\max_{1} \min_{2} (\text{payoff}) = \min_{2} \max_{1} (\text{payoff})$$

but it is not very illuminating without delving into the detailed mathematics. Importantly, von Neumann was able to show that every zero sum game could be solved to find the optimum compromise for both parties in the case of the zero sum game. If there was detailed balance, each player may choose a single pure strategy to maximize their payoff. If the balance was broken, they could still find compromise, but only by playing a mixture of different strategies. This was called his minimax theorem.

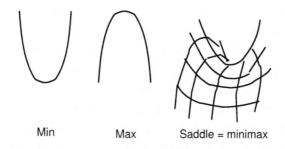

Min   Max   Saddle = minimax

Fig. 4.11. A minimax or saddle point is a maximum in one direction and a minimum in the orthogonal direction. The saddle point represents the compromise between the desire to maximize one variable and minimize another.

The minimax theorem was hailed as a triumph of rational thought, and encouraged strategists, especially during the Cold War, to spend time on optimal strategy computation. It applied equilibrium thinking to human motivated compromise, using only numbers for payoffs obtained from, at least in principle, a rational or impartial source. The limitation of zero sum was restrictive however. Not all situations are so clear cut about who wins and who loses. A more general scenario is the non-cooperative game, in which players each seek to maximize their own value, but the game is not necessarily zero sum anymore.

For example, suppose you are watching the television with your family, and everyone in the family has their own remote control (perhaps as an application on their smart phones). This might sometimes work in everyone's favour. You might choose to work together, but you might also choose open conflict, changing the channel back and forth. Non-cooperative game theory asks: are there any solutions to this kind of scenario, in which everyone in the family maximizes their winnings? If this example sounds frivolous, consider an analogous scenario that is more serious.

Many of our technologies rely on sharing common resources amongst several parties, such as agricultural and grazing land, phone lines, electricity, water supplies, and computer networks, to mention just a handful. When we do this, we are aware that there will be contention for those resources—a tug of war, but not necessarily a zero sum game. Consider two examples that have a similar character. Imagine first that you are staying in a hotel. The hotel has limited space and can choose to give every customer either a tiny private bathroom with a ration of hot water, or a common bathroom with the same total amount of water and more space. The common bathroom would be much more luxurious and the experience would be superior, with more hot water available and more space, provided not many customers tried to use it at the same time. We could say that, as long as bathroom traffic was low, the common bathroom would be superior. However, when traffic becomes high, the private bathroom is preferred because customers then know that they will always get their fair share, even when that fair share is very small.

The same scenario could be applied to sharing of drains and sewers that might be blocked in a developing community. It also applies to the data networks that are spreading all over the planet. Two kinds of technology for network sharing exist: free-for-all sharing technologies like Ethernet and WiFi, which correspond to the common bathroom, and private line technologies like ATM, MPLS or cable modems, which correspond to the private bathroom[84]. If you are lucky and you are using a common wireless, the experience can be very good and easy, but when many users try to use it at the same time, you no longer have the experience of a fair share. Indeed, when the more users try to share, fewer actually get a share because a lot of time is wasted in just colliding with one another. Thus what is lost by one is not necessarily gained by another. This is not a zero sum game: it is worse.

The scenario was called the Tragedy of the Commons by ecologist Garrett James Hardin (1915-2003)[85], and is often cited as an example of contention for shared resources. In economics, and indeed politics, the same situation occurs in bargaining for something, and it had long been recognized that the work of Morgenstern and von Neumann did not adequately address this issue.

A formulation of this problem was found by mathematician John Nash (1928-), when he was still an undergraduate at Princeton in 1949[86]. Nash was eager to work with von Neumann on the issues of game theory, and went to some

lengths to show him a proposed solution, but von Neumann was dismissive of
the idea, busy with his many projects and consulting engagements and had little
time for undergraduates. Nash was encouraged nevertheless by another mathematician and economist David Gale (1921-2008) and his work was published
in the monthly proceedings of the National Academy of Sciences. Nash used
a similar notion of equilibrium, called the Kakutani fixed point theorem, based
not on single solutions but on mixtures of solutions (see Figure 4.12).

He showed that it was possible to find sets of strategies, in all cases, that
would lead to an optimum outcome for mixed strategies. A Nash equilibrium

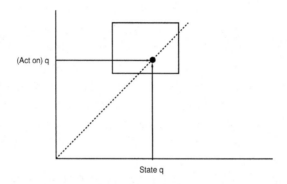

Fig. 4.12.   Fixed points are equilibria between the input and output of an operation that
acts on input (horizontal axis) and produces an output (vertical axis). An equilibrium
where (Act on) $q = q$ must lie on the dotted line. In minimax a single match can be
found. In the Nash equilibrium, sets of solutions that intersect the diagonal can satisfy
the fixed point condition.

is simply a stalemate in which no player can improve his or her position by
changing strategy—the detailed balance of trying to maximize individual payoff
could be solved. Nash showed that, for a very large category of games, such a
solution had to exist. Since it was a generalization of the minimax theorem, it
has largely superceded it today, and has become the de facto approach to looking
for solutions in game theory [87].

The Nash Equilibrium, as it is now known, has had an enormous impact on
our understanding of subjects as wide as economics, evolutionary biology, computation and even international affairs[88]. It can be applied to policy selection in
the continuum approximation, but not necessarily in a discrete system.

Fixed points are equilibria, and thus they are starting points for building stable
systems. If we could construct technologies whose basic atoms only consisted

of such fixed points, it would be a strong basis for reliability. No matter how many times the operation was applied, it would always stabilize. It turns out that we can, in many cases.

It is possibly ironic that an understanding that powered the dirty industrial age of steam should share so much with that which is powering the pristine information age. Harnessing equilibrium for constructive, predictable control of change, we can conquer many frontiers of interaction, from machinery to chemistry, biology, decision making, maintenance and even information. Dynamical similarity works in mysterious ways, yet it is the nature of this form of dynamic stability that brings a universality to our understanding of it. It means we can be confident that such simple minded arguments are still at the heart of phenomena across all areas of technology.

5

Zero and the Building Blocks of Babel

How to forge the atoms of reliable infrastructure.

London Bridge is falling down,
Falling down, falling down.
London Bridge is falling down,
My fair lady.

Build it up with bricks and mortar,
Bricks and mortar, bricks and mortar,
Build it up with bricks and mortar,
My fair lady.

Set a man to watch all night,
Watch all night, watch all night,
Set a man to watch all night,
My fair lady.

Suppose the man should fall asleep,
Fall asleep, fall asleep,
Suppose the man should fall asleep?
My fair lady.

– Traditional nursery rhyme, excerpt

Until the early 2000s, the fact that computer software was riddled with potential instabilities was of little practical consequence. Software would crash, computers would be rebooted, and life would go on. Users learned to work defensively around the problems with their personal workstations, by making backups and regularly saving data. Even when networking became common, and there were services like email and file sharing, a reasonable equilibrium

108

could be maintained between 'downtime' caused by perturbations from a noisy environment, and human repairs to the system (by custodians known as system administrators), to satisfy most requirements with only minor inconvenience, just by tending computers by hand. The approach used was much like an emergency services model, e.g. like fire-fighting or ambulance. You wait until a problem is reported, then you sound an alarm; technicians rush to the rescue and try to diagnose and solve the problem.

In the early 2000s, Internet commerce became much more widespread, no longer limited to a small number of expert organizations, and the total amount of money involved started to become significant. This was when interest in automation began to grow. That is not to say that some users were not already using state of the art management techniques. High Performance Computing labs such as those used in oil companies, banks, and other early datacentre builders were operating on a different level than most. The computer immune system, CFEngine, that I had worked on was already being used by many of these larger and more forward looking organizations[89],

The pain point hit for everyone else, however, when online services started to become successful, and companies suddenly needed large numbers of computers to service the transactions in their businesses. Datacentres grew from hosting hundreds to thousands, and then tens of thousands of computers—growth by orders of magnitude, according to a classic network accretion power law[90]. This continues today, and some companies are at a hundred thousand and even a million servers in their businesses. At that point, repair by hand was no longer an option: it would be like trying to work a modern farm of hundreds of hectares with only a hand hoe.

It's only when humans build on a sufficiently large scale that the economics of size, or the risk of failure, force us to think more carefully about methodology. Internet commerce was probably the tipping point for a move away from the small *ad hoc* datacentre building towards true infrastructure engineering for the information age. A level of resilience is needed to support any infrastructure development that will support a mainstream of society. That can only happen if the economics are right, applying the right level of engineering resilience to ensure necessary permanence, but sufficient adaptive agility to support its users.

In history, the pyramids are surely the supreme example of over-engineering on a massive scale, at least viewed according to the values of the modern world. They were structures designed to protect pharoes' mummified remains for eternity, while their spirits fulfilled their rites of ascension to the afterlife. Viewed on those terms, their design concept seems to have been pretty resilient. What the pyramids exhibit both symbolically and physically is the idea that a sturdy summit requires a broad and solid base of layered infrastructure to survive.

This chapter is about how we apply what we know about stability to prevent information systems from falling apart.

Both in nature and in technology, there are mechanisms to perform maintenance on information at the smallest 'atomic' levels. Mechanisms work behind the scenes in our cells, computer disks, memory chips and network devices to maintain data integrity.

Recall Bell Labs scientist Claude Shannon and his Theory Of Communication from chapter 3: Shannon looked at digital errors that occur when messages are transmitted over a noisy channel. Noise can come from any source and corrupt an existing structure; indeed, we define it simply to mean anything that corrupts a pattern of information, causing it to be transmitted incorrectly through time or distance.

One of Shannon's achievements was to show that it is possible to provide error correction channels for keeping information correct to an arbitrary level of accuracy. In his error correction theorem he said the following: suppose we have a communications channel that is not overloaded, i.e. it has some spare capacity; in that case, it is possible to find a way of transmitting information essentially error-free over that channel, using a part of the channel to check and correct errors[91]. Shannon did not say exactly how this would be done – by clever reasoning, based on theoretical limits, he didn't have to, but he did prove that that there was no impediment to doing so. In showing this, he provided one of the most important results of our Information Revolution. It forms the basis on which all our digital communication and storage are built.

Shannon went even further and showed that it is possible to take a small part of a single channel in order to embed the error correction within it. An example is the so-called parity bits used in early signalling. The original ASCII code for teletype text used 7 out of 8 bits, coding 1s and 0s to represent the letters of the alphabet and associated symbols. The eighth bit was used as a check. If the first seven contained an odd number of bits, the eighth would be set to 1, if even it would be set to 0. When the byte was transmitted or read somewhere else, the receiver would check that the parity bit was still consistent with the number of 1s and 0s after transmission. If any single bit changed, the parity bit would show an error, and the byte could be retransmitted.

This was the simplest kind of error detection 'protocol', i.e. a pattern coded into the data for quality assurance. If there were an odd number of transmission errors, we could detect them. If for some reason two bits were changed, however, this would go unnoticed. The strategy was a gamble: it wasn't guaranteed to detect errors, but because the technology was quite slow and relatively robust in size, the chance of getting more than a single bit error was very small, and the gamble paid off in most cases. It worked *probabilistically*, not deterministically.

Over time, as data speeds increased, and device sizes shrank, the density of data grew higher relative to the density of interfering signals (a dimensionless ratio of densities), and the effects of thermal and electrical noise became worse. More sophisticated mechanisms called checksums were then needed to detect errors, with more complicated transmission protocols to embed them.

Detecting errors is not enough, however. More clever coding schemes like Hamming codes could not only detect errors but actually be self-correcting too, by exploiting two dimensional patterns in bit streams. They work by extending the idea of parity in two dimensions, so that using a small number of $2n$ bits, one can cross check a large number n^2 cheaply. Once again, it is sufficient to detect an error to know how to fix it, since a bit has only two possibilities.

Such mechanisms as these are built into every piece of information technology we use today, but if this sounds reassuring, you'll have to think again. When current technologies were designed, the amounts of data stored and transmitted by a typical system were about 200,000 times smaller than they are today. In other words, data densities have grown by five orders of magnitude, and the assumptions used to gamble on bit errors in parity methods have been swept away by the storm of progress.

The argument is easy to see. If there is only a small chance per unit volume $\epsilon \simeq 0$ of a bit symbol being corrupted in a medium, within a small amount of data D, then the amount of data corrupted will be about $\epsilon \times D \simeq 0$. However, if we increase D by five orders of magnitude, the amount of error becomes correspondingly higher. Then this number is no longer negligible, and we need to pay special attention to errors. Simple parity mechanisms will not suffice any longer. Modern checksum algorithms like MD5, SHA, and HMAC can detect errors with a high degree of precision but they are much more expensive to compute than parity methods, and they do not help in reconstructing corrupted data so they are only a partial solution.

This turns out to have an important effect on the kind of disk storage used in datacentres. Towards the end of the 1980s, researchers from the University of California, Berkeley, David Patterson, Garth Gibson, and Randy Katz, applied the method of Hamming codes to computer disk storage to develop a set of hardening technologies against error known as RAID. They combined multiple disks into a redundant array so that the failure of a disk would not mean the loss of data. It was not a backup, in the traditional sense, but something that would prevent loss by hardware corruption.

RAID now stands for Redundant Array of Independent Disks (originally the I stood for Inexpensive). Different RAID levels would correspond to different ways of ensuring multiple copies of data for error correction. The simplest approach is to duplicate disks so that there are two copies of everything at all times. The most commonly mentioned example, that employed the Hamming code parity blocks is called RAID 5. In the original specification, the idea was that instead of a having exactly the number of disks needed, one would add extra disks, and parity information would be spread around these disks in a redundant manner. If an error occurred on any disk, there would be a very high probability of finding parity data somewhere else to automatically reconstruct the data on the fly. Even if an entire disk failed, its contents could be reconstructed from the information on the other disks.

Fast forwarding to the present, the probabilities for RAID no longer add up either. Whereas RAID 5 was previously felt to provide a strong level of assurance for data integrity, today RAID 5 now has something like a 39% chance of loss during reconstruction of a bad disk. This is obviously quite useless as an insurance policy[92]. If data storage size gets smaller, a small error is a lot of data.

Parity technologies work by assuming that data are basically immutable to a high degree. Storage manufacturers today are having to resort to somewhat different methods for maintaining the state of data, much more akin to the methods used to maintain other dynamical systems. An arms race has thus begun between the forces of environmental noise and those technologies of repair, a kind of Nash equilibrium, where the player of storage miniaturization and the player of data maintenance thrash it out for supremacy. Although the numbers of storage are easier to relate, a similar problem arises for network transmission at increasing speed.

Today, higher level feedback techniques of a different kind are used, like the concept of disk scrubbing, which refers to periodic maintenance sweeps that read and check every byte of storage on a regular basis. This is a process much like the detection mechanisms of an immune system, and not unlike pulling weeds out of the flower beds in your garden.

In work done with Trond Reitan on studying backup coverage in storage arrays, I called this the windshield wiper model[93], because it uses a periodic sweep of everything, like clearing raindrops from a windshield, clearing snow, or repainting the garden fence, to maintain an intended, or desired state. These were the exact properties required by Computer Immunology, as we'll see next.

Not every data correction problem can be handled in the simple manner of parity codes anyway. Once we approach high levels of information, with more sophisticated patterns than just 1s and 0s, the processes required to deal with errors are much more complex.

In fact, this has both good and bad sides. It allows for a new possibility: data compression. It might not actually be necessary to maintain copies of absolutely every detail in information in order to maintain it. At a high level, we might be able to find a description of the pattern of data that is smaller than the actual data. It is possible because a lot of information contains redundant patterns. Consider the following:

> 'There, there', said the therapeutic mother.

The pattern 'the' uses 3 symbols, but it is repeated many times as a unit. The atomic symbols thus form a small 'molecule' that can be replaced by a single symbol to shorten the message:

> '?re, ?re', said ? ?rapeutic mo?r.

These redundancies only occur at a larger scale of data than the atomic bits or even ASCII symbols. That presents the possibility of maintaining a smaller amount of information at a high level, without sacrificing any integrity.

This is essentially the idea of a *policy* based system: we might not need to micro-manage state, if a few more generic guidelines will suffice to do the job. As long as we know how to build replacement parts of an information system, we don't need a exact copy, because we can reuse information at a high level, like having a library or warehouse of standard patterns.

This is also the approach used in biological evolution. DNA contains a compressed form of instructions for making replacement parts, much smaller in size than even a single cell, yet it can build many complete cells, given the right machinery around it.

Shannon's error correction describes correctness of *state*, which is an important part of maintaining a stable equilibrium of a message, or put differently, the message's integrity. High-level immunity allows us to maintain correctness of patterns. As already mentioned, there is a third issue with information systems, namely correctness of interpretation.

The principal difference between smart materials, like plastics or wood, and the servers for your online shopping, is just how *programmable* they are.

Mechanical constructions are relatively simple: they are easily built with a notion of intrinsic stability.   They do one thing well, and their entire form and function can be designed around that purpose. Programmable devices, on the other hand, are unfinished: they need to be told how to behave, and there are usually no limiting constraints or safeguards to govern them by a sense of stability. That makes them vulnerable to failures of decision making that are based upon how we use them. It places all the responsibility of correctness in the hands of a programmer, who does not have all the information up front.

Computers, as programmable devices, do not merely follow a mechanical conveyer-belt process. Computer programs, exceeding the mere weaving patterns they evolved from, string together chains of dependent patterns, with decisions that rely on contextual information sucked in from the environments where we employ them. Such information is unpredictable, else we wouldn't need it. Computers cascade through a tree-like network of branching points, that consumes the input and turns it into dependent actions, in what can be called automated decision-making (recall chapter 2). That implies a total decision structure with a 'single point of failure' at every branch point.

For this reason, programmable computers have an inherent fragility about them. Indeed, we build them to be precisely so unstable that we can mold them to any purpose, like the fighter jets discussed earlier, operating just on the edge of stability all the time. That is the price one pays for flexibility. The danger of wielding such power comes when we then place the entire burden of this risk in the hands of human monitors, without intrinsic stabilities as failsafes. This means that humans are forced to find ways to avoid their customary inconsistencies and lapses of reason.

The same fragility is true of our biology, so this is not a purely man-made. The fact that our cellular biology can be controlled by DNA, RNA, and proteins allows our cells to be adapted to a huge variety of different tasks in our bodies, and it also allows viruses to hijack the cells for their own purpose. A virus is simply a message, after all, written in DNA or RNA that changes the operational programming of a cell to replicate itself. Protein channels like prions also allow reprogramming through protein manipulation. Biology provides automated immune responses however, to keep this programmable instability in check. It does so with a highly data-compressed policy for health, coded into its molecular chemistry.

The key to building a robust technology lies in finding the right compromise between adaptability and robustness. We thus need to understand not just how to make strong materials for physical construction, but also how to make programmable information-enabled systems analogously tough-but-flexible, or strong-but-not-brittle. So, let's now consider how information systems can be built to mimic these properties, and avoid defects that lead to failure.

We build by putting together atomic pieces into a larger whole. The structure of relationships between the parts (essentially the promises they keep to one another) then determines whether they work together as a unit, or remain as separate entities: a building or a pile of stones. Strength and utility thus lie both in the raw materials and in the way they bond together. When infrastructure and information combine, we need to understand both aspects of the edifice.

A critical breaking point for a system can often be initiated by the smallest defect in construction. Every time I open a banana, I am reminded of this, because of the basic material physics of stress concentrations. Banana skins are quite tough, and can be almost impossible to break unless you first nick them with a knife. If you do that, and apply a bending force to the stem, this concentrates the force around the tip of the nick and causes a cascade failure, making it much easier to open. This happens because the crack or nick acts as a lever, focusing all of the force onto a single point at the tip, offering a 'double whammy'— amplified effect over a smaller region. This is essentially the reason why glass shatters under sudden forces: untreated glass is full of small cracks and sound waves or shocks get concentrated by these cracks causing multiple failures[94]. Analogous stress points exist in computer and other information systems, because of program 'logic', which creates decision branching points that have a similar role in concentrating information impact. We'll return to this topic in chapter 12.

The trick is to remind ourselves that even the physics of forces can be viewed as the transmission of messages, like digital information. The effect of a perturbation on a weak point can be large, if just the right perturbation message comes along to prise open the appropriate chink in its armour. Special types of perturbation are needed to unleash an instability in nearly all cases. Some materials, for instance, withstand being crushed (compression), others withstand pulling apart (strain). Some are stable to slow change, others resist even sudden impacts. Try to move your hand slowly through water and it meets little resistance, but try to move it rapidly and the resistance is much greater, because there are key scales that come into play.

There is usually a key to unlock every door to instability, if one can only find it. Information-rich environments are dangerous because they usually do find it, by picking the lock through random selection.

Suppose we translate this idea with the information viewpoint discussed in Chapter 3. We begin by thinking of any piece of hardware or software as a partial 'system' that is exposed to an environment of perturbations. For software, the perturbations include user input, network transmissions, communications with storage, and a variety of other in-out messages perhaps from other pieces of software. That environment is information rich, we might even say it is noisy, meaning it is being perturbed by a complex variety of message symbols that could mean a variety of different things to the software in different contexts.

In fact, it gets worse when you consider that there are perturbation messages coming in on several different channels. A computer receives information from a keyboard, a mouse, a network, but also from unintended sources like background radiation and 'cosmic rays'[95], responsible for corrupted media and memory errors.

Now recall the idea of a semantic instability from Chapter 2, that is to say an instability of possible interpretation. If we cannot isolate a partial system, like software or a piece of glass, from the noisy environmental chatter of perturbations, or alternatively answer every message or force with a counter-message or counter-force to negate it (as with the aerodynamic challenges of the fighter jet), then eventually we will provoke an instability that could lead to failure.

In a mechanical systems, we often test resistance to perturbations by throwing a controlled force at them. This can be a useful way of stress testing the system to see how it holds up. This method fails in information systems, however, because the problem is not merely one of force, but one of interpretation and 'logic'. The channels for semantic instability and simple message instability are difficult to separate in computers. The semantics of a message depend on the message, and possibly its history, and go on to lead to branching channels of behaviour that further add complexity.

Semantic interpretation usually involves logical reasoning, which is a sequential, bifurcating (branching) process, like when we tell a story about something or make an argument[96]. It has the structure of a chain of questions, or a tree of decisions. As a system makes decisions, it steps through a process and makes choices, such as go left or right, choosing one branch or another. What we end up with is a kind of pathway through a complicated graph.

It is worth exploring this with a specific example. As mentioned earlier, a computer system is built essentially from a large number of messages being passed back and forth over different media and channels, ultimately based on electrical signals. Suppose a computer program waits to receive a single symbol X from a user, and uses this input to create another message, which is based on X, and which we may call Message-from-X. Suppose further that it then sends Message-from-X to a peripheral device like its harddisk, as a way of querying for some data it has. Then suppose the harddisk responds with its own message which is based on that query, the reply Reply-to-Message-from-X.

$X \rightarrow$ Message-from-$X \rightarrow$ Reply-to-Message-from-X.

This kind of message passing could go on, increasing in complexity:

$\rightarrow$ Message-about-Reply-to-Message-from-X.

What sounds like the proper names of ancient warriors (Tildor, son of Antiger who was born of the keeper of the message X), becomes more like a game of Chinese whispers. Every step in the chain is sensitive to the presence of an error in the original message X.

On each new development, more history gets added to the message, and a growing number of consequences can be traced back to an initial transmission of information. A cascade of consequences comes from a single point of invocation, yet each transformation of the original message adds new information, so we accumulate both cause and effect at each juncture.

What might go wrong with this? The answer is many things! First of all, the symbol X has to be received correctly by some receiver from the source without error. Then it has to be recognized correctly and its meaning interpreted correctly. It should not be confused with any other symbol, or the meaning will be changed. Next, the message based on it has to be formulated in a specific way and transmitted correctly to the disk, which must then receive it correctly and recognize the symbols in the message, interpret its meaning, and act upon it, and so on. Then the disk must transmit its own message back, and so it goes on[97].

The longer the chain of dependences, the greater the number of places where an error could spoil the whole process. We say the process is fragile. Each decision point is like a crack in a piece of glass (or a banana skin). All of the power of the messages from the environment to provoke faults is focused on these gatekeepers of correctness (what we called 'single points of failure'), and risk unlocking pathways through the system that are best kept locked up.

Information systems have more than just one dimension of possible error to compound the issue. The lengths of the messages have not been mentioned at all yet, but the length of a message is intimately connected to its possible meanings; so, let's suppose that X can only be one symbol, but the disk controller expects the message M to be four symbols long, and the reply R from the disk to be of indeterminate length, but less than 10 symbols in order for the program to have room for it:

$$X_1 \rightarrow M_4 \rightarrow R_{<10}.$$

This chain of messages is not a robust Markov process, like catching customers in a queue, with arrivals that have no need of any memory of what came before: the order of things matters, and each part of the sequence depends on data that emerged from the previous step, so it cannot be kept stable by a simple symbol-by-symbol processing equilibrium. Instead, it forms a dependency chain in which each message depends on the previous message with some precise constraints, like a security code or password: the lengths of the messages, their format, and their detailed content all matter. The whole house of cards is worryingly fragile.

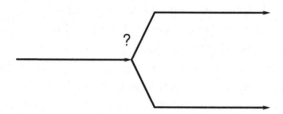

Fig. 5.1.   A branch point or bifurcation in a process is a forking of possibility.

What I'm saying is that, at each phase of a chain of reasoning (highly typical of what goes on in information infrastructure), there are potential 'fault pathways', or modes of failure. These come about because the next thing depends on the last thing, and every stage can introduce a new error. The possibilities may be mapped out by the many questions we might ask about the behaviour of the system: what will happen if the symbol X is not recognized? Will the software generate the message based on X, or will nothing happen? What happens if X is not a single symbol but several? Will the first symbol win, or the last? Or will is blow up? Will it take each symbol in turn? Will it insert more than one symbol into the message, making it more than 4 symbols long? We simply don't know in general.

In a mechanical system, one generally has Newton's laws, or the rules of mechanics to give us some idea of how the system will behave at each juncture. In an information system, we have only pathways in a story network, with the route selected on the basis of logical choices. How we make those choices becomes absolutely crucial to the outcome.

We may put question after question, laying out all the possible outcomes of what happens to the symbol X on its journey of Chinese whispers, until all of the possible branches of the scenario are manifest. We would then see the complete graph or network of the system, as discussed in Chapter 2. This is an example of what is called a 'many worlds' scenario[98], because each decision effectively places the system into a state that it cannot retreat from. A system can end up in a state that depends on a history of all the branching alternatives it has passed through, i.e. the history of everything that happened to it (see Figure 5.2). The explosion of possible outcomes is the result of a very large branching process. If a system relies heavily on a very particular outcome, then the chances are slim

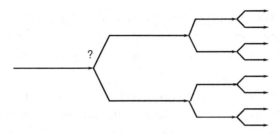

Fig. 5.2.   A many worlds process, with bifurcations bringing exponential complexity.

that it will reach it, the more branching points there are along the way. As the number of branches multiplies from a trigger event, the likelihood of being in the right branch becomes a smaller and smaller number. The answer is to either reduce the number of alternatives or make the right choices somehow inevitable.

This story tells of a low level view of what we now lovingly refer to as 'bugs' in software. Many righteous remarks are made about the number of bugs that exist in modern software, and many harp on about the terrible state of quality assurance in software systems. Those criticisms are perhaps fair in the sense that there is indeed a high potential for bugs to exist in decision making systems. They are less fair in the sense that software systems are designed deliberately to use this basic instability. If you flirt with danger, you will eventually end up dating it and even having its children.

Computer software is much more complex by design than any other kind of machine that we build, because it tries to get all the benefits of flexibility and none of the dangers. Computers are purposely built to exhibit combinatoric complexity, and the number of possible worlds that come out of using software is large compared to the number that might actually be useful. We are essentially like King Canute trying to hold back a sea of bugs.

It is a curious anachronism that, to keep vulnerability at bay, we still use different forms of human monitoring. Just as sick patients' vital signs are monitored for nurses, and we use smoke detectors in buildings to summon a human response, and so on, visual monitoring is still the main approach used to manage information systems. Human guards are typically in front of the feedback to wait for a significant event or alert, again like Canute, hoping they can catch whatever problems occur[99].

Biology, by contrast, has developed autonomic systems for this, to provide *homeostasis* or self-regulation. It doesn't have to make decisions every time something happens: simple, dumb, pre-determined policies trigger automated feedback responses that bring self-repair. If we want to prevent trouble from occurring, we can look for ways to assure quality or safety in advance.

To make information-responsive systems safe, we need to look for ways to constrain their freedoms and to bring them back to the level of simpler purpose-built devices, where intrinsic outcomes can be assured. Some software systems are being hardcoded into specialized chips, which suffer from the same problems and are even harder to correct. We'll need design engineering to either filter out certain messages before they can be heard from the inputs of software, (as one filters out noise in audio), or to respond to every possible message that arrives with a suitably stable response – and on a timescale commensurate with their appearance. For this, we have discussed two possibilities: intrinsic and extrinsic stability, using either direct feedback or statistical equilibrium.

Finding a universal way to approach this in the context of information infrastructure has been the work of the Computer Immunology project, mentioned in the introduction, and it led to the notion of statistical equilibrium that I called *convergence* towards a desired state. Convergence is basically the application of a kernel of internal and external stability in the decision graph: a fixed point in the software that maintains software's configuration state, which in turn governs desired pathways of behaviour.

Shannon's work on error correction was simple because there are no semantics at the level of symbol transmission: if a bit gets corrupted, you replace it with the right one. A bit can be corrected without any logic, like topping up a bucket: if 1 is wrong, you know the answer must be 0, and if 0 is wrong, you know the answer must be 1. It is an atomic operation, and the operation always takes you back to a known desired state, determined by keeping some kind of copy of the original message.

The CFEngine project came up with a simple language to describe the policy for what was an acceptable alphabet of system correctness. It would later become known as 'promises'. A special software agent compares the current state of an information system with the policy and decides whether something needs repairing, much like the immune system's lymphocytes in our bodies – a promise of a healthy state. The language description was and still is based on *desired states*, and uses operators that have fixed points at the exact configurations promised in policy. Like the immune system, it provides extrinsic stability to the system through the intrinsic stability of the agents.

The solution required two parts: equilibrium between change and repair, by repetition of the policy message at the correct timescale, and semantic stability of the policy operators with no logical branching.

Achieving statistical equilibrium requires only repeatability, like Shannon's error correction, or immune system tolerance, but to accomplish semantic stability also, there is an additional requirement: as little logic as possible, and only one possible outcome of each operation. With these two properties, we should be able to go on mindlessly applying the stable message of policy forever in a harmless manner.

The two properties later became discussed as *convergence* and *idempotence*, the latter being a mathematical word, which means that repeated operations are the same as a single operation. Drinking a glass of water is idempotent, because once it is done, doing it again has no effect. A convergent operator is like replacing a faulty part with a working one: replacing a working part with another has no effect. Thus what is convergent is also idempotent.

1. Equilibrium by negative feedback towards desired state (convergence),

2. No logic or bifurcations (idempotence).

Idempotence is not enough, because you also need to know you are doing the right thing, not just any old thing that is only effective once. I showed that an operator that was convergent was also automatically idempotent. It was not just about repeatability, but correctness[100]. Recall the transitions in chapter 3:

$$(\text{Act on}) \text{ state} \rightarrow \text{new state}$$

A convergent 'repair' operator would have to satisfy two constraints:

$$(\text{Repair}) \text{ any state} \rightarrow \text{desired state}$$
$$(\text{Repair}) \text{ desired state} \rightarrow \text{desired state}$$

The second line in the repair operations is exactly idempotence, so convergence embodied idempotence. This answer could not be simpler.

The specification of the desired state would be a policy decision, written in the alphabet of states that had been pre-tailored to whatever the system's purpose required. However, it would work best if the repair operations were independent, or atomic. If they depended on one another, it might take more than one iteration to complete convergence, because then there would be self-organizing waiting.

The original proposal of convergence met with mixed reactions in the world of computers. A few understood the importance of convergence immediately, but many riled against it. It flew in the face of everything taught to programmers, about flowcharts and step-by-step logic to absolute atomic replacement. It was a shift from relative change to absolute change, more akin to abstruse academic logic programming than the step by step flowcharts of software engineering.

In the operations above, we start from any state at all and we fixed the end state, like a fixed star in the heavens to navigate by, or the destination on your GPS navigator. How you arrive at the destination or where you started from is of no real interest, as long as you get there. Programmers are taught the opposite, however: start from the origin, a known state, and work relative to that to see where you end up.

The application of simple dumb symbolism, was like taking a semantic problem back to the level of a hammer and a nail. If the nail pops up, you hit it again. In fact, if you hit the nail every five minutes to be sure, no harm is done. Once it's in place, no harm will come. It's stable. The traditional programming approach of 'scripting' had been to start from a known initial 'blank slate' and work, relative to this, to hammer in all the nails from scratch: to actually rebuild the whole tower at regular intervals.

The fact that all of these requirements could be solved with just one simple construction, however, made system maintenance very cheap and reliable. It effectively allowed policy to be enforced by reiterating the same message over and over, like a mantra.

A possibly surprising twist in the tail of the story came a decade later when a new way to understand the idea of digital stability popped out of a different and somewhat unexpected source: the number zero.

Some time around 2008, Dutch computer scientist Jan Bergstra and I were walking through the streets of Utrecht on a rainy afternoon, seeking the enlightenment of a perfect cappuccino, when he began telling me of his interest in revisiting the issue of division by zero, with his friend and colleague John Tucker. What happens when you try to divide a number by zero is a source of many problems in computation. Sometimes it happens by accident, sometimes due to an unfortuitous ordering of tasks, but either way you need to handle the matter.

Computers have already developed so far from the punch card looms of the 19th century, and mechanical engines that spawned them, that it is easy to forget that what lies behind today's multimedia gloss is a simple electronic mechanism to add and subtract numbers. Layers of progressive ingenuity lie atop those simple calculations, to bring about the illusions we take for granted, but the basic algorithms or recipes of computation are nonetheless based on simple number crunching and message transmission. It occurred to me that there was a direct link between the indeterminism of dividing by zero and the lack of certainty in the state of information in computers.

Arithmetic is a form of digital building. If we pile three bricks on top of 2 bricks, the result is five bricks. Chapter 3 discussed how almost any physical process can take on the character of a computation, and vice versa. Creating and computing are closely related to one another. Just by using addition we can get subtraction and multiplication, then division, using patterns of digits. The symbolic representation of numbers is the key to digital calculation.

As a physicist, it turns out that I had had long experience of dividing by zero in complex analysis, making sense of calculations where such problems can occur. We are all taught in school that you simply can't divide by zero. Then, later, some are taught that the answer is infinity. Then even fewer are taught the answer is 'indeterminate' or 'not a number', then fewer still that dividing by zero is absolutely essential to compute certain calculus problems where the sum of the residues is actually the legitimate answer[101]. The story continues in modern physics with methods for 'regularization' and 'renormalization'. But as far as I knew, no one had recently looked at this issue from the viewpoint of maintenance.

The invention of the number zero is an interesting story in its own right, going back to Brahmagupta in India, 628 AD, but not one we'll pursue here[102]. Zero is a unique and important object in mathematics, because it has special properties under addition and multiplication. It is an 'identity' or empty operation under addition:

$$x + 0 = x,$$

for any number x, i.e. it has no effect. It is a fixed point under multiplication:

$$x \times 0 = 0,$$

for any number x. Thus, as a multiplication operator, it takes any input value and transforms it into the same zero value always. It has maximal effect!

Zero is a fixed point under multiplication. It has the same property as the fixed points discussed in chapter 2. If we make the '(Act on)' operator represent multiplication by zero, in the operational description of states, and 0 be the desired state, then there is an immediate representation of this ideas as numbers[103]:

$$(0\times)\text{anything} = 0$$

$$(0\times)0 = 0$$

or

$$(\text{Zero}) \text{ anything} = 0$$
$$(\text{Zero}) \ 0 = 0$$

Zero thus has a remarkable property. It brings complete certainty of outcome: no matter what we give it, it gives us a reliable and predictable answer: 0. It is a patron saint of certainty!

A zero operation can therefore be used as a representation of a convergent operation. This is a useful discovery, as zero is an easy object to construct in many scenarios. To make a policy about the state of repair, as a decisionless convergent operator, just calibrate the value of zero to desired state and any initial condition can be transformed easily and repeatably, in a single step, to the desired state zero. It is like a GPS teleportation device: no matter where you start, it will get you to your destination in a single hop, admittedly the same destination always. There are more details to be told in the next chapter about the patron saint of certainty.

It is the atomic nature of symbols that makes them easy to correct; their lack of dependence on something else. But not all structures can be understood in such simple terms. If you are building a house, for example, you could try to build it from raw materials like sand and water, but this is an effective way to build at larger scale.

To make the process repeatable, it makes sense to have certain off-the-shelf items as your 'effective atoms' of construction: bricks, doors and windows, for example. Bricks and windows belong to different scales. A window is typically an order of magnitude larger than a brick, so we have to interrupt a brick pattern to put in a window, then resume (see Figure 5.3) the pattern again on the other side.

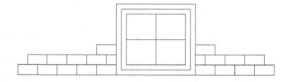

Fig. 5.3. A pattern with a parenthetic remark (a window).

The order of things starts to matter now. A brick laying pattern is regular, but a window is an interruption that correlates several rows of bricks: it spans a different scale.

In fact, there is science behind such patterns too, and how we generate them. It begins in the work of Alan Turing and was immortalized in the work of MIT researcher Noam Chomsky in the 1960s. As a linguist, Chomsky was interested in patterns of natural language, and showed that patterns could be defined quite mechanically as formal *grammars*. A grammar, according to Chomsky's work, is a pattern of symbols that has a particular structure, and can be computed by a machine with a certain level of sophistication. Reading a stream of symbols and digesting them is called *parsing*. What Chomsky showed was that symbolic patterns formed languages that could be classified by different types of computing device.

A regular language, for example, is a simple stream of symbols with no complicated structures, such as:

There was an old lady who swallowed a fly.

It can be parsed by the simplest kind of finite state machine (recall Chapter 3). However a stream of symbols with a possibly unlimited set of parentheses cannot be parsed by a finite state machine, it needs to have some memory to remember where it is while deciphering parentheses. So:

The old lady, who swallowed a horse, died of course.

requires some memory to be able to put 'who swallowed a horse' into a different level of meaning than 'The old lady died of course'. This is on a different level of sophistication than the simple regular language.

Subroutines in computer programming face the same issue, which is why there is a connection between computation and grammatical patterns. Software engineers are taught to think in sequences and flows for a good reason: many problems may be solved easily by thinking in this way, like building a tower from some assumptions to a conclusion.

What kind of process would you need to follow, i.e. what algorithm would you follow to determine if a word was a palindrome? A palindrome, for example, is a sequence of symbols that may be read forwards or backwards with the same effect. Thus:

wasitacaroracatisaw

is a palindrome from: 'Was it a car or a cat I saw?'. It is not too hard to imagine that verifying a string of symbols as a symmetrical palindrome requires some memory, and hence is not merely a regular grammatical phenomenon. If we don't care that a string is a palindrome, then we could naturally treat it just like any other string. In the general case, an unlimited structure requires an automaton called a Turing Machine to model and build it.

This matter of computation has a practical consequence, if we are trying not only to parse and understand the structure, but to build and maintain it. It doesn't matter whether you are a human or a robot brick layer. If a single brick in the wall should drop out (perhaps in response to a Pink Floyd recital), this is easily repaired by Shannon error correction as long as there are replacement bricks. But what if the entire wall with window and all were to be destroyed? Then we would want to reconstruct it from a pattern that has a more complex grammar, going beyond single symbols.

A traditional software engineer would probably think: start with a blank slate, then add one brick and another and another, then leave a space, and so on, building from a step-by-step recipe, from a known initial state. Assuming that the recipe is complete, and the structure is stable in its environment, during the building process, this will succeed in building the desired state of a wall with a window in it. But what if the process does not start from a known state, and the environment is not stable? We might arrive to find half the wall completed, then the recipe would fail. If an earthquake shook down parts of the wall during building, the recipe would fail to complete adequately, because each step assumes the integrity of the last. A sequential process is like a tower of dependencies. Moreover, once the wall is built, the recipe cannot be simply repeated to repair the wall, that requires an entirely separate kind of machine.

The idea of a convergent building process is to roll all of this into a single idea that is not sensitive to the starting state, but which can be continuously left running to build, rebuild, and maintain the wall, no matter what the environment throws at us. We focus on the desired outcome, computing it from whatever the initial state is. This requires negative feedback, idempotence and dumb simplicity. The wall would heal, all by itself, like skin after a cut.

Modern software engineers, especially in the functional programming community have now begun to realize the importance of convergence. Instead of imperative interactions, they now discuss declarative data and distributed evaluation. The language used by functional programmers is somewhat different to the one I use here. Their terminology borrows from category theory and algebra, and is naturally focused around data structures and computation. Rather than convergence, they will speak of semi-lattices and magmas. Instead of talking about policy patterns, they will talk about requests as 'data'. The important revelations are the same[104].

So we may ask, what is the corresponding zero operation for such a pattern? The answer can be written simply enough, as the pattern that satisfies the same algebra as the convergent operations on symbols:

$$\text{(Zero-Pattern) anything} = \text{zero-pattern}$$
$$\text{(Zero-Pattern) zero-pattern} = \text{zero-pattern}$$

The difficult lies in constructing the operator (Zero-Pattern), when there are strongly coupled patterns that transcend a particular scale. Then we step up a level on the ladder of *computational complexity* and have to deal with additional coordinating messages. Remarkably, this does not always require a complex bifurcating logic: it is still possible to make zero patterns using the techniques described above, as we might expect from the fantastically creative processes we observe in cellular biology. We must return to this issue in the next chapter.

Patterns mix symbolic sequences at different scales, so let's return awhile to the topic of scale, and see how digital scale relates to the continuum picture we perceive as humans.

As we described above, software is a recipe with a labyrinth of potential pathways that depend on the answers to certain questions we ask along the way. During the 1980s it was popular to write fiction in which the reader could write the story themselves, by choosing the outcome of a particular altercation. They would jump to page 30 if the lead character lived, or to page 102 if he died, and continue reading up to the next branch point. This is software too.

In all cases, we can think of software as a web of messages, at the information level. The network of cooperating senders and receivers, such as we find in modern software, is very large, making finding bugs a highly non-trivial problem. Some bugs only occur when a certain threshold is reached, i.e. when a certain set of conditions is triggered by the interactions of scales in the system. Then we should ask: what are the dimensionless variables? Other bugs occur when a certain equilibrium fails to be maintained. Then we should ask, what governs the detailed balance rates? The interacting scales:

- The *environment*,

- The *software*, and

- The *hardware*,

make a three-part system that has to be understood together. They are inseparable, and that is no simple problem. We are therefore likely to struggle with the issue of latent bugs for some time to come, until a deeper understanding of software instabilities emerges[105].

Regrettably, few software engineers know about the concepts of dynamical similarity, or are familiar with techniques for testing all three parts of the software interaction. It is normal to test only the semantic stability of the software, and leave everything else to watchful providence.

One could imagine building a kind of wind tunnel for testing software, as one tests scaled models of planes and ships under controlled conditions, with a sufficient understanding of scales. These are not skills taught in software engineering (or for that matter computer science) courses, but they are an important aspect of understanding software systems.

The paradox of modern computing is that we have opened Pandora's box on the world of flexibility, and winning back control is not always as simple as it seems, had computers never been invented. We throw computation at problems of considerable enormity, not always with adequate preparation.

Freedom of expression is a seductive siren, but it has to be balanced by restraint. This is why we forego certain behaviours in civil society, why specialists develop standards and regulations to govern, and even why the physical laws of Newton can be seen as a balance between freedom of space and time, limited to stable trajectories by a balance of forces. The concept of a safeguard is familiar to us in the physical world, but often seems relatively unfamiliar to software engineers.

The converse is also true: constraining freedom also has a cost. Our relationship to tools and technology does not free us from the basic physical realities. For example, suppose you want to work with animals: first, you need to locate them. Because they tend to run off, this is a rather unstable arrangement. You thus confine them with the technology of a cage, improving the stability of the location situation. This is beneficial, except that now you've inherited a cost, namely the management problem of feeding them and watering them, not to mention keeping the cages strong and locked. The bottom line is that, if we want to harness tools, there is usually a tradeoff to be made about maintaining them.

In 1999, building on the assumption that information systems could be maintained convergently close to an equilibrium state, I began to examine the problem of trading back flexibility for stability in those computer systems that run our commercial and governmental infrastructure. Society needs such systems to be dependable, and on a timescale of minutes rather than weeks.

I pursued an approach of applying the simple ideas of detailed balance from the continuous physics of equilibrium, translated into a digital language of computer science, and developed a 'Maintenance Theorem' which proved that it was indeed possible to maintain systems if you were willing to put in the necessary work. In fact, it was closely related to Shannon's error correction theorem. The gist of it went something like the following[106].

> A computer can never be guaranteed to be in a perfect state of operation,
> because there is an environment of changes and signals coming from users,
> locally and across the network. But if you want to be sure that the system is

operating basically correctly minute by minute, then you need to be willing to observe and repair the system on the same timescale of at least every few minutes.

Reading this, computer scientists and engineers had difficulty in seeing that the issue could apply to computers. What if we translate:

A keeper of animals can never guarantee that a bucket of drinking water will always be exactly full, because the animals drink, there is spillage, evaporation, leakage, and so on; but if you want to be sure that it is approximately full on average every hour, then the zookeeper needs to check the bucket and be willing to refill it on about the same timescale of at least every hour.

The common reaction from computer engineers was always: 'This doesn't apply to us. Computers do what we program them to do – there are no random signals, computers are deterministic!'

Alas, neither of those assertions is true, no matter how nice it would be to imagine. Whenever someone says: 'what could possibly go wrong?', then you know the surprise is just around the corner. Thus, it took some years before the idea of maintenance was allowed to intrude on the common consciousness of IT infrastructure. In fact, the idea is very similar to Nyquist's theorem, mentioned in Chapter 4. The details required to make it mathematically plausible cost rather more lines than I have expended on it above, but the gist is the same.

Claude Shannon had already discussed the idea of fast correction of digital symbols during message transmission. The idea of keeping a system in a fit state is very much like transmitting the message with integrity. When you send a message over a noisy channel, certain symbols can become altered, and need to be corrected if the integrity of the message is to be maintained. The integrity of a computer system over time is essentially the same: instead of sending a message over distance, you are just transmitting a message about the state of the system into the future, at the same location. There is still noise, and the signal still degrades. Sometimes this is called 'entropy'[107].

The Maintenance Theorem was a general result that combined the notion of timescales with the idea of error correction, and showed how to separate fast and slow variables to understand the trends and patterns from Chapter 4. It thus made the connection between the timescales of user interaction where changes seem continuous, and the digital discrete nature of the computer's underlying mechanisms. In a sense, it put meat on the skeleton I'd exposed in the closet, in the Computer Immunology paper, turning speculation into concrete result.

CFEngine addressed the issue of zero patterns, in order to stabilize computers running in noisy environments. Rather than filling up buckets with water, it was about resetting the states to their correct settings. Injecting digital repairs directly into computers is a simple matter (as long as one doesn't make it complicated), but to bring about a dynamic equilibrium, there also had to be a cyclic process, because you have to refill the bucket every hour.

Computer state had to be repeatedly corrected every few minutes because it was being spoiled by other processes happening on that timescale. This was, in fact, what CFEngine did. Its key innovation was in finding a way to make the process reliable. What caused a stir was the fact that the solution would fly in the face of everything programmers had come to believe in.

The problem we face in putting together a reliable technological infrastructure is depressingly reminiscent of the legend of the tower of Babel. Technological infrastructure, is built layer by layer, to stand on the shoulders of past accomplishments, breaking up a huge tower of imagination into pieces that are put together block by block. It begins as a story of human hubris, and ends with the forces of nature showing who is boss.

Each piece of the tower was designed and assembled thanks to communication with the mythical universal language of Mankind, both to describe its structural composition and its plan of execution. The environment provided the watchful providence, alas seldom benign, that confounded that perfect language of cooperation and provoked errors and misunderstandings, leading to its collapse. A woeful tale of structural and semantic instability. In the worst case, any tower of dependencies can come crashing down, like the tower of Babel[108].

The cracks in the skin are the points of bifurcation, concentrating the semantic leverage of decisions and amplifying mistakes. Avoiding logic and decision-making, wherever possible, can make the outcomes of processes more stable. For example, one can pre-decide outcomes through some kind of *policy*, restricting the amount of new information that can enter the system. This is a retreat from flexibility, back towards the simple mechanical reliability we used to build with.

By reducing flexibility we can reduce the explosion of possible outcomes, thus reducing the corresponding explosion of complexity. However, this is somewhat contrary to the current fiesta of creative opportunity celebrated by modern software development, which strives to 'leverage' information and services for convenience rather than stability.

The message seems to be this: if we focus too much on the semantic stability, we could be in danger of merely trading the earlier insight about scales for another about branch points of failure. Common sense suggests that there has to be a way to deal with both issues at the same time. Flexibility versus stability is the strategic game we are playing, and we need a Nash equilibrium for picking the right level of semantic and intrinsic stability.

If you need flexibility to move around chairs in an office, you put wheels on the chairs. If you want stability on an aircraft, you bolt the chairs to the floor. Bolting chairs to the floor in a restaurant makes it difficult to re-organize for parties of different sizes that arrive. That makes the restaurant's service brittle and inflexible. To make them more flexible, you could make the chairs out of jelly, which has flexibility at the atomic level, but that would make structures too flexible, and unstable to perturbations by heavy guests.

The scale at which we make the trade-off between stability and flexibility is therefore the key to finding a solution. Scale must form part of the language of design between sub-system and environment.

Only during intervals of sufficient stability do structures have any meaning or purpose in the grand scheme of the world. We piece together buildings in fair weather, and they fall down under hurricanes and earthquakes. Life begins under shelter and protection and is taken by predatory chance. Stars and planets congeal during uneventful eons and are then broken up under tumultuous collisions and celestial encounters. There is an on-going cycle of construction, destruction and repair.

Unsurprisingly, human culture reveres fragile stability. We build, we settle, we even try to capture impermanence and the fleeting images we experience with longer-lasting photographs, paintings, and statues. We keep diaries and write books for posterity. Human creativity, be it art, engineering or literature is expressed through things we consider to be more or less permanent. Nature 'creates' by using the tendency for randomly assembled things to survive against the odds of destructive forces. Many species of life build survival structures, and stand up against the forces of chaos and destruction.

In the foregoing chapters, stability and its meaning has a been a theme, because it is the prerequisite for infrastructure. The robust building blocks can be self-healing cells, or strong, dumb bricks. We can try to match the change make in a dynamical system by repairing it in real time, but what happens if the system is chaotic? Then we know we cannot hope to match changes exactly. We would need either an overwhelming force to shut down all activity, or avoid getting to the chaotic region in the first place.

Looking down on our planet, we are confronted with the end result of eons of change brought about by myriads of microscopic agents seething with activity. Sometimes nature's antics lavished vistas of tender calm and bountiful resources, and sometimes they wracked the surface of our world with episodes of spectacular violence and even chaos. As minor participants in these machinations, we are fascinated by the spectacles, but what is most important to us is the moments of stability. It is that stability that provides the opportunity for building the infrastructure on which all life depends.

Humans often confuse aesthetics with robustness. We base our ideas of simplicity on the way we think. Tidiness does not imply stability. The Amazon jungle is a mess on a small scale, but it has survived millions of years. Compare this to city planning anywhere in the world: cities seem tidier on small and short scales, but the order is unstable and prone to decay: we find that cities tend to become more jungle-like than vice versa over time[109].

We would all like to be able to tell the world 'Be this! Do that!', but we can't. The world does not respond to obligations or commands. We merely influence it somewhat, through our choices of interactions.

Society lives at the mercy of its infrastructure, the stable platform and canvas on which to paint its vision. Computers have become a special part of that weave, intruding into almost every area of our infrastructure. They tease us with that feeling of control, a sense that we might do anything at all, but that is a risky assumption, and we need to go deeper to understand why they can play such a ubiquitous role in our lives, and what makes them behave well or badly in the context of infrastructure.

The future will surprise us yet, in what we think of as computers. If we have been willing to recognize biological living tissue an analogue computer (recalling the discussion in Chapter 3), as today we make computers from DNA, then we can also imagine other kinds of construction materials that behave as computers: smart building blocks computing repairs on the fly, or adapting their behaviour to changing environments, cleaning windows, regulating the flow of heat for internal climate control autonomically, and so on. The foregoing chapters should have made it clear by now that computers have basic limiting scales of speed and size, like any other physical system.

We end this chapter, the section of the book, armed with certain knowledge of an absence of certainty, stifled by the forces of information, and with only the tool of an empty digit to stave off entropy. The world of mixed up scales in an ocean we cannot hold back. How can we live in such a world? How do we make the best of it? Put simply, to have a fighting chance, we must observe deference to the reality of unpredictable error, and then make the best of imperfect information.

Part II
Certainty

Living with incomplete information

6

Keeping It Together by Pulling It Apart

How weak coupling strengthened human infrastructure

"The most powerful dehumanizing machine is not technology but the social machine, i.e. The formation of command structures to make humans emulate technology in order to build pyramids and skyscrapers..."
–Lewis Mumford (1967)

The story of certainty in technology isn't the story of brilliant engineers who brought skill and wisdom to bear in building their systems. It is a story of how society experiences systems from the hard edge of everyday life. To discuss what certainty means for information technology, we need to place ourselves at the heart of the changes that took place.

In the autumn of 2002, I was asked to hold the keynote at the NordU computer infrastructure conference, which was to be held in Västerås, Sweden, in February of the following year. The early 2000s were a time during which the whole world of information technology seemed to be raging: mobile computing, online commerce, and the World Wide Web were maturing into something mainstream, and it was the wake of the 'dot com' boom, where many expectations had been inflated and popped. As I planned the talk, I recall being haunted by an image from an episode I had experienced a few years earlier.

I'd been walking through a part of downtown Oslo called Grensen (literally "The Edge") with a visiting colleague, fleeing snow pellets that were blustering through the streets. In those days, Grensen was the hangout for a tribe of solvent sniffers and down-and-outs, who limped about the streets, often mumbling to themselves, tragically like a scene from a zombie movie. However, the harsh weather meant that they were sheltering around the entrance to the Ibsen parking lot, where we were headed. One of them had found a mobile phone casing and was pretending to talk to a friend to show to his audience that he too was part of

135

the mobile phone revolution.

As we entered the high tech lobby to the car park, I heard another voice talking frantically. There stood a figure, in an expensive black suit, with an equally expensive attache case in one hand, while gesticulating wildly with the other. He was standing completely alone, next to the payment machines, stepping back and forth impatiently, with his face to the wall, and there was no one else there. My first thought was that perhaps he too was an unlikely substance abuser, or perhaps mentally ill, but I also recall seeing a wire hanging from his ear. At the time I didn't understand the significance of it: hands-free ear pieces were brand-new then and I didn't know what I was looking at. It just seemed that he was ranting to himself.

As he sensed us enter, the man turned and seemed shocked, as if we had ripped him out of a personal reality bubble. Right there in the most public place imaginable, he had rewritten the boundaries of what was public and what was private, and had lost himself in the illusion. He wasn't talking to the wall, or to a ghost, but he was talking to a voice in his head—a kind of telepathy brought about by technology.

Here was wealth and poverty, within just an arm's reach of one another, both trying to block out the present and replace it by a conversation with the void. This really was The Edge: the cutting edge of technology, bordering on the edges of society, and the also boundary between public and private. Could we even tell the difference between this technology and delusion?

It struck me at that instant that the new mobile communications infrastructure had changed something of the utmost importance to society: the nature of the relationships between individuals, and their relationships with the spaces around them. The technology of mobile communications had ripped away the interaction with his surroundings and replace it with a targeted communication from far away. It was promoting semantics over dynamics, meaning over locality. There was an immediate and tangible conflict of interest: the mobile communication was more valuable to the man's mental model of the world, but a local communication would always win if it came to blows.

I entitled my keynote 'Talking to the Walls', and used it to explore the way that modern information-enabled infrastructure, embedded so pervasively in our walls, not only supports society, but also feeds back on it, and changes us in the process[110]. It was like a vision from *Star Trek*, with humans talking directly to their televisions and cookers.

A decade later, however, it turns out that we didn't end up talking to our walls directly. Rather, we still call them up with our phones.

Mobile information technology has brought the world closer together, by letting its pieces drift more freely apart. There is something counter-intuitive about bringing unity by relaxing control, yet this is an important notion in the construction of a model to understand information systems distributed over time and space.

Mobile devices, smart-phones and tablets, are a visible shift in our way of thinking about interacting with the world. They have become a kind of skeleton key to unlock the information-rich interfaces springing up around us. All of us are now poised at the tip of an iceberg of technological infrastructure that gives them life. We pour extensive resources into the building of that infrastructure, so that ordinary people can exploit a growing personal freedom with the aid of mobile devices. The cost, in carbon emissions, to support this freedom, is set to exceed that of the airline industry quite soon. That should be a wake-up call to anyone wondering whether managing our information infrastructure is an important topic.

For most of human history we lived very simply and autonomously, sharing resources for efficiency and protection. For a human to live for a year, required about quarter of a ton of food, half a ton of water, and small amounts of animal hide, sticks, mud, and stones: these were a few things taken from the local environment. Today, we equip our environment with tools and artificial services in an elaborate life support system that is Byzantine by comparison. We consume minerals, ores, fossil fuels, and biomass not only in what we eat and wear, but also to make houses, cars, and refrigerators, and of course a plethora of electronic gadgetry etc. Currently developed countries' citizens consume an average of 16 tons of those four key resources per capita ranging up to 40 or more tons per person in some countries. By comparison, the average person in India today consumes four tons per year.

According to the report by UNEPs International Resource Panel, by 2050, human beings could devour an estimated 140 billion tons of minerals, ores, fossil fuels and biomass per year—three times the current consumption rate—unless economic growth is decoupled from natural resource use[111]. This could not happen without an extensive network of infrastructure around our planet.

The way we've consumed these resources, in the so-called developed world, has been through a welter of supply and service points. They were manned interfaces, counters and shops. We learned to *know* these, *interact* with these, and *consume* their resources as part of a regular relationship with our environments. As information technology integrates with these service points, they disappear from immediate view and become part of the backdrop of smart infrastructure.

Think of shops, petrol or gas stations, electrical power, telephone service, and so on. The environment of an average person in a city is a seamless collage of service offerings we barely notice, yet we depend on them, and, in the process, interact with a massive amount of visible and invisible technology. Think:

> Buildings, structures, roads, paths, moving walkways, escalators, elevators, shops, hospitals, airports, sea ports, transportation, pipelines for oil, gas, water, drains, power networks, fuel supplies, communications networks, satellites, defence early warning systems, weather forecasting, hospitals and healthcare, government institutions, law enforcement, snow clearing arrangements, cleaning services, waste removal, forestry, irrigation, beaches, wildlife preserves, security monitoring, surveillance, supply logistics, money.

The list includes infrastructure for supply, for protection, for repair, and for assurance, to mention just a few of the areas we rely on for our lifestyles.

As an exercise, imagine something as prosaic as a trip to your favourite local coffee shop (an increasingly universal experience across the planet) and try to identify how many of the items in the list above had to be in place in order for you to enjoy the experience of that cup of coffee, with the music playing in the background and your wireless Internet connection.

Without irrigation, there might be no coffee plantations, without transportation there would be no beans in your country, without fuel there would be no transportation, without security the transportation would not arrive, without electricity there would be no hot water or music playing. This web of interdependency is every bit as complex as a biological ecosystem today.

Society takes infrastructure for granted, and for good reason. Many key technologies are truly invisible to us[112]. Most of the concepts of infrastructure have been familiar to us for a century or more, but the utilization of information systems to yield what we dare to call smart behaviour is a significant new trajectory that bears examination. Changing the nature of infrastructure, by embedding computational and communication systems within it, allows it to adapt to us, instead of us adapting to it. Is this a good thing?

Information has encroached on our management of systems all along, in more primitive forms, using pen and paper, bureaucracy, word of mouth, duty officers, and even as stories told around camp-fires to provide services to passing humans. It is not a new development to want to exploit information. The difference today is the use of computers and fast digital communications to embed many aspects of this information experience automatically, just as biology embeds many adaptive systems that enhance survival characteristics in life. We use information technology to extend the reach of technology into the world of human meaning.

The services we engineer to do this, in turn, feed back onto our social behaviour, as I noted in the introductory anecdote to this chapter. It has lead to phenomena like 'smart mobs', and 'swarm intelligence'[113]. If you don't think that technology and tools affect our behaviour, just look at the effect of smart-phones and tablets on individual social habits over the course of just a few years. The ghost of Thomas Hobbes, mentioned in chapter 1, is surely rattling his chains to society's emergent behaviour. In his 1651 book *Leviathan*, he described the effect on governance of the whole, by individual contract and independent decision, even if he did not quite anticipate this indirect cooperative interaction via new media channels.

What is the lure of these information-rich services? The answer seems clear enough. It enables the world to accelerate. Thinking about a rapidly changing world is a longwinded and expensive task for the human brain. In a slower world, we have coped by learning programmed responses and running on a kind of personal autopilot. Coping today is a strain because change has become the norm. We still want to 'cache' preprogrammed responses into our instinctive systems, i.e. those reactions that can act quickly when you almost knock over a glass of water. Tapping on a smart tablet can be the new instinctive way of acting. We rely more on following these simple repetitive patterns than we do on thinking very hard about common things, and hence we seek to simplify as many of our common interactions as possible.

Sewing computational reasoning into the lining of everyday experiences removes the burden of having to think very hard about everyday interactions. It is a way of turning what once required reasoning into a completely instinctive behaviour[114]. Every time we do this, we win more time to focus on creative pursuits, and we give up resilience and self-sufficiency as the price. Society becomes hostage to those support systems, irreversibly accepting the numb *trust* that they will support us forever.

How did infrastructure become smart? Historically, the first electronic control enhancements to mechanical systems were spin-offs from the telemetry and control systems of the space programme. They were rather simple. They performed no reasoning. They were about being the eyes and ears of humans who had perhaps over-extended themselves in what they had built. Instead of hiring a small human army to patrol an industrial installation, it was simpler to extend the sensing capabilities of a single person to see more from a fixed location. Closed circuit television was the most pervasive example, still used today for human surveillance. A variety of mainly proprietary technologies, that fall under the banner of Supervisory Control And Data Acquisition (SCADA) were built to manage industrial control system, where human presence was either expensive or hazardous. Oil wells, water-pumping stations, and factory processes could all be handled remotely[115]. A significant clue to their importance lies in the way they can take over the maintenance of many relationships that we would traditionally expect to have with our surroundings. This is most powerful when they use information based on carefully designed messages, with clear intent, i.e. where the meaning of a transmitted message has an immediate and clear interpretation. Information technology thus brings automatic semantics to our environments, and we call this 'smart behaviour'.

Regulation is one of the classic forms of relationship management in which automation replaces a human observer: fault maintenance, speed limiters, even drainage systems, water flows, electricity flows, and traffic flows. Knowledge about a non-local part of a supply network can be used to optimize the behaviour in a local region: buyers can locate and order from a supplier with a surplus at a cheaper rate. If we know of a traffic jam, or a blockage in a transport network, other traffic can be routed around it, assuming there is a network with sufficient reachability (see Figure 2.6).

Smart interfaces help us to see the world through different lenses and work around our cognitive limitations. Another important use of such an interaction-ready environment is to track objects as they move around, by receiving messages from them on a continuous basis. Children, cars, books, and transport containers are all valuable and all move around and we want to be able to track them to foster a feeling of certainty in a world we basically can't control. Some cities in Europe provide essentially free bicycles in exchange for consuming a little advertising, or car pools for hire; the idea is that you can pick up a bike at any one of a number of caches around the city, and return it to any other. This is very flexible, but only if you know where the pick-up and drop-off points are, and how many bikes are available. A local resident might be able to know these things in their home town, after learning about them, or you might even be able to hire a guide in a foreign city to know it for you. Today, the burden of that trivial relationship can be relieved and you can download a more omniscient friend to your phone and rely on its knowledge.

The invisible infrastructure to make all this happen is extensive, and builds on generic patterns of information usage. Since 1978, the navigation system known as the Global Positioning System (GPS) has had operational satellites in orbital operation to locate positions on the surface of the Earth. GPS devices send out digital messages on a continuous basis to remove the need to constantly ask the question: where am I now? Navigators no longer need to look for landmarks and sign posts (artificial landmarks), the computer does this for us, using a satellite coding system and a map.

This pattern is generic: we replace a trivial human repetitive task with an automated one, based on a universal standard, i.e. we give up control to bring unity. Having a common standard of reference for labelling places, like the GPS, enables us to form a common *model* of reality and sense of certainty about what we believe we know. It adds universal semantics (a simple model) to the notion of resource finding, and removes the immediate need for us to actually see something, by being there at the same location. Labelling items with bar-codes and QR codes is somewhat analogous to having GPS coordinates. It provides interpretable meaning to the thing you are holding, allowing you to track it and ask it questions. This idea is now almost universal: it is used for everything from library books and warehouse items to meat and other perishables, and of course for our own movements around the world, with passports and credit cards.

Translation between different message formats and languages is another use for information systems, and not only human language. Computation is now used universally to turn physical motion into commands, through *transducers* like the mouse, touchscreens, motion sensors, and so on. Automated human language translation is, of course, embedded into a sizable fraction of the software we use on a daily basis.

This brings us to a third aspect of information associated with infrastructure, which is *learning*. Learning offers the possibility of escaping the constraints of scale, i.e. the ability to zoom in and out of different levels of detail. By equipping infrastructure with long-term data collection facilities, information can be gathered and studied to look for patterns that we simply cannot see from the limitations of the here and now. One can enquire about patterns of activity, such as the movement of bicycles, that only an oracle would know about.

This is how science studies phenomena: first one collects as much data about general dynamical behaviour as possible to see the broad trends, and then the pattern is divided up into appropriate scales and the phenomena that apply to each. The weather can be analyzed in this way, as can market trends. The information systems implicitly allow us to navigate up and down scales, not merely sideways.

The same learning technique can be applied to interaction semantics: retailers like to give you recommendations: 'customers who bought this item also bought brand X'. This hint about like-minded behaviour suggests that there is no need to think about this matter yourself, or expend any time researching, you can take the information on trust, just assume it is just as good as any recommendation from a friend. Do we have your item in our store, no? If not, which other stores or suppliers might have it? Shops use data from sales to analyze what customers actually do, and airlines and train companies learn the behaviours of travellers to better adapt to their needs: infrastructure adapting to us.

Medical databases associate symptoms with known diseases so that rapid assistance can be presented to an expert medical practitioner; symptoms of problems with engineering installations such as the appearance of certain cracks or sounds, can shorten the time to diagnosis of a potential problem. Even catalogues of known signals from the galaxy that do not represent intelligent life are easily correlated by brute force searches with information technology.

We are talking about the capability to learn from the recorded experiences of users passively experiencing their environment. This is tantalizing, but also risky. It would not be sufficient to merely store information for ever. Information grows with time and would eventually become so cumbersome as to be useless, regardless of whether we have the space for it. How we forget information is at least as important as how we recall it and learn from it.

In the cases just outlined, the infrastructure was constant, while the applications adapted on top of it. There are some cases, however, where the infrastructure itself can offer beneficial adaptations to the environment. It usually makes more sense for infrastructure to vary from place to place than significantly from time to time, but 'smart' means that we may always draw the line between infrastructure and application differently to suit the circumstances.

On a bus route or taxi rank, more buses or cars can be arranged if we know that there is a surge of passengers. That most ancient and iconic infrastructure item, the road, is best known as a completely static technology with no adaptations. We do not imagine that roads need to have an extensive dialogue with either users or environment, because their pattern of usage is fairly constant. Nevertheless, roads can be built with embedded temperature regulation to melt ice in winter and cool tyres in summer. They could even be built to have self-repairing systems for potholes and cracks, even debris left on the roads. These features would be offered autonomously by the road itself, but would it also make sense to have on-demand services for roads?

Should car drivers be able to switch snow-clearing heating elements on and off themselves, with a remote control inside their vehicles? It would probably be a disaster. This kind of 'remote-control' push-button thinking is how many users think of technology, thanks to years in front of the television. However, to manage shared resources responsibly (which includes most public services), there has to be an impartial arbiter. What one user wants is not usually what another user wants. So even if each user were authorized to switch on the heating (and spend the money it costs to run it), different users might disagree about the best course of action. One would end up with a war for control of 'the remote'.

In such cases, the road itself has to be the one to arbitrate the decision. The road needs autonomy. It needs to be unshackled from strong coupling to its users. Indeed, no matter what the users think they want, it must basically provide its service on an *autonomous* or *voluntary* basis, to make decisions fairly and effectively. Anything else would lead to an inconsistent set of expectations to all the individual users of the road who tried to control it.

Infrastructure should not change at the whim of its users. If it changes at all, there has to be hysteresis, inertia that keeps it stable. There is little advantage to making infrastructure so adaptive that it is unpredictable, but one can speed up the laws of supply and demand, passively accelerating the rate of information acquisition, and learning patterns that could enable beneficial behavioural semantics. Smart behaviour comes with the warning of the previous chapter however: what was originally dumb and weakly coupled, inevitably becomes initially more tightly woven and dependent as we try to make it smarter. Thinking like this, the smarter something is, the greater the chance for instability.

Smart does not have to mean controlled by humans. *"Autonomous and voluntary behaviour."* These words, hewn from the discussion about avoiding conflicting interests, strike fear in the hearts of technologists. "Control and determinism" are the words they want to hear — those over-sold consorts of certainty. Yet, paradoxically, these freedoms are quite possibly the magic cure for uncertainty. Loosening our grip to get a better grasp is a theme of this chapter, and the idea is as important as it is counter-intuitive.

The idea is hardly a new one. In fact, from a dynamical perspective, it goes back to the idea of atomicity and stability, discussed at length in the first part of the book. But, in the human world of technology, the counterpoint of dynamics is always semantics. The twin deities of instability are:

- Dynamical vulnerabilities: thresholds and intrinsic scales.

- Semantic vulnerabilities: misinterpreted or misintentioned messages.

In both cases, the most stable and least vulnerable system is an autonomous one: one that is immune to outside scales, and one that receives no messages.

There is a pattern here, which the history of tool-making has explored repeatedly. In the quest for successful resource management approaches, designers have allowed the pendulum of doubt to swing between the opposing poles of 'holding tight' and 'letting go'. The pattern, in its basic form, goes something like this:

$$\text{Monolithic} \rightarrow \text{Atomized} \rightarrow \text{Distributed}$$

It begins with structural unity and perceived simplicity of form: a single, self-contained construction, held together strongly by the internal coupling of its parts (a television). The next phase is to decouple the dynamics by atomizing into modules or components, weakly coupling them for greater dynamical stability (re-usable electronic components, screen separate from the receiver, etc). This encourages diversification, adds indirection and give us more things to think about, which tends to reduce our level of insight and affects trust. When this atomization goes too far, and fear of its uncertainty kicks in, there is often a swing back to towards unification.

The telephone system began as a single mass of wires, then it was broken up into different companies, technologies, mobile cells, and finally these were forced to work together to reunify the experience for users. The pattern repeats, with evolutionary improvements, like Bach's endlessly rising Canon, or Escher's endlessly rising staircase, as immortalized by Douglas Hofstadter[116].

This can be interpreted in several other ways:

$$\text{Keep it simple} \rightarrow \text{Manage resources} \rightarrow \text{Relax control}$$

$$\text{Contiguous} \rightarrow \text{Discrete} \rightarrow \text{Autonomous}$$

In dynamical terms, this is a transition from fragile to robust, but in semantic terms, it moves from conceptually simple to conceptually complex, from monolithic to distributed. These two forces seem to be in confusing opposition, which perhaps helps to explain why technology designers struggle to eliminate all the perceived 'bugs' from the systems we rely on.

It is as though simplicity of behaviour is traded for complexity and lack of comprehension. Human designers often imagine that what is easy to understand guarantees the best behaviour too, but this is not always the case. It leaves us with a feeling of uncertainty. Indeed, biology offers evidence that this is not the case. The most successful organisms are multi-celled, a highly intricate balance between simplicity and complexity over multiple scales.

In technology itself, the analogous pattern has repeated many times.

$$\text{Central services} \rightarrow \text{Specialized departments} \rightarrow \text{Local offices}$$

$$\text{Public transport} \rightarrow \text{Rentable transport} \rightarrow \text{Private transport}$$

$$\text{Shared tape stream devices} \rightarrow \text{Local disks} \rightarrow \text{Block devices}$$

$$\text{Shared circuits} \rightarrow \text{Dedicated circuits} \rightarrow \text{Packet networks}$$

Integrated mainframes → Virtual machines → Embedded virtual containers

The upward staircase is this non-cooperative game between dynamics and semantics, which seems to prevent us from reaching a final Nash equilibrium. The players struggle with finding ways to keep the benefits of one viewpoint, while exploiting the cost effectiveness of the other. The ascent steers the path of evolution away from the tethers of human comprehension and direct control. Economics drive these changes, as economics drive selection in all forms of evolution.

From the 1980s to the present, the world of technology evolved to cope with demand, by breaking into pieces. As the Internet grew, the same thing was happening to society as a whole. Information infrastructure followed a path reminiscent of that seen during other major industrial shifts. The introduction of simple machines of increased power, that could enact change by brute force got us started. Classical ideas of centralized command and control enabled humans to guide systems manually. Later, the employment of simple machinery, that mimicked the manual labour, provided an easily comprehensible starting point for engineers to progress to the next level. This basic infrastructure acted as a kind of seed around which society could grow into the changes. As these achievements were won, there was the formation of a class division between 'land-owners' and 'workers', i.e. between those who could afford the infrastructure and those who would use it and maintain it.

During the decade of the 1970s, American futurist and writer Alvin Toffler described the nature of this evolution in terms of three waves of societal development, starting with the manufacturing industry, and moving on to the information age. The First Wave was the age of manual labour: a poverty trap of endurance, where humans worked reactively to cope with crisis after crisis, sometimes in self-cancelling ways, and without a clear direction or goal[117].

Then came the Second Wave, an industrial era of mass production, where choice was controlled in order to scale up production. Simple tools amplified human effort to lift businesses out of the poverty of firefighting. In the Second Wave, things become simplistic. The simplistic mass production forces everything to be the same, which in turn forces consumers of those patterns to make do with 'one size for all', or as Henry Ford said 'any colour as long as it's black'.

The Industrial Revolution in the 1800s had been the way out of the First Wave for the manufacturing industry, spurred on by essential innovation. In the Second Wave, industrialization and its machinery allowed society to scale up production to escape literal poverty, but the distribution of resources was uneven: a classic division grew up in information systems between the network providers (the landowners) and the computer maintainers (the users of the network).

The Third Wave, in Toffler's model, is when a society gets interesting. Once production surpluses lift consumers out of the trap of poverty, they begin to demand more from the world than 'one size for all'. This demand drives diversity and we begin to feel that we are no longer in control of what we are doing. In the Third Wave, power shifts from the producers (who want to control what they give to consumers) to the consumers (who demand novelty and force providers into increasing competition). Instead of a simple centralized mass production, demand drives decentralized variety: an information rich variety of goods and services. The pendulum swings to the right, and production is pulled apart in order to keep society together.

Although the Third Wave of manufacturing is about increased and better use of information, the management of its information technology has been through three waves of its own. For the information technology, the First Wave was the manual management of computers that led up to the 1990s. The innovations for Second Wave 'one size for all' scaling began during the 1980s and are only now beginning to be surpassed. A Third Wave of information technology has to support rich variety in a scalable way: it is decentralized and diverse.

The ability to mass produce everything the same, with expensive technology, also led to a classic owner-worker distinction between network and machine, that stemmed from the sense of ownership major corporations felt for the enabling network infrastructure. Network providers were typically part of the already-rich telecommunications industry, and viewed networking as a high ranking form of engineering, with certified qualifications, graduates from colleges and vendors. Their wealth and status grew because they controlled to machinery that made the revolution possible. Computer maintainers, called system administrators, on the other hand, were viewed as mere blue collar workers (or IT workers in more modern parlance), seen as low-status individuals merely performing factory work that could be learnt at a community college.

The emancipation of system administrators to the level of engineers was a vision that was held and nurtured by special interest groups during the 1990s, and became a long process involving highly motivated individuals, that continues to this day. As town planner Lewis Mumford remarked of the industrial relationship between man and machine, industrialization grew from making humans imitate the work of machines: it could be deeply de-humanizing, making humans work for the machinery, as machinery, emulating it, and even competing with it, to create an engine for manufacturing[118].

In the Third Wave of Toffler's vision, human freedoms become the driving force for technology: freedom, commerce and mobility demand diversity from the infrastructure. Technology becomes an enabler of human freedom rather than suppressing it by forcing humans to work on its behalf. Whereas the first and second waves are dynamical in nature, the Third Wave is really a semantic transition. It goes from approaching certainty as the need control simple mass replication and maintain artificial uniformity, to replacing it with a tolerance of diversity, and a more effective exploitation of robust growth, through mobilization of responsibility and contextualization knowledge. The Third Wave is a business man talking into thin air on a mobile phone.

History shows, nevertheless, that humans are quite predictable in approaching new phenomena. We start from a First Wave each time. Our answer to governance is to seek control through mastery: we put a human in charge, make someone responsible and liable, and tame the beast with our bare hands. The words 'manage' and 'management' come themselves from the Italian word for putting a horse through the paces, *maneggiare*, which has the same root as 'manual': *manus*, the Latin for hand. We want to break in the phenomenon and ride it. We want to conquer by hand. If things don't work out, then at least there is someone to blame.

As information technology began to gather momentum, around the mid-1990s, the First Wave pattern played out in many organizations: overwhelmed by crises, ad hoc system administrators fought to keep their heads above water, so busy that they never won enough time to escape from this condition. Between 1990-2000, the Second Wave began to kick in, with the development of factory-based mass-production technologies for pumping out new computers and software into active use. Finally, a Third Wave of highly customized, context-specific systems, is now beginning to transform engineering before our eyes, and on a scale that is several orders of magnitude greater than anything we have seen before.

At this level, science and engineering become not only crucial to our understanding, but come under pressure to deliver new answers. One of those answers, for information technology, would involve the revival of Computer Immunology, of autonomy and voluntary behaviour.

Computer Immunology, with its self-healing characteristics, had been proposed at just the wrong time to prosper immediately, and it was known only to a small part of the IT world, those using the CFEngine software. Thus it was quickly overwhelmed by other forces at work during the 1990s, and left as a manifesto for future work as part of CFEngine. The Second Wave 'sandblasting' approaches to managing information infrastructure began to take on board aspects of scripted programmability, allowing the industry to cling onto manual methods for a while longer.

Although the automation the CFEngine project introduced, in 1993, was relatively unique in its concept, and became popular by the end of the 1990s, it was not alone and was still controversial. Others were having similar and alternative ideas, along the points of the pendulum swing between centralization and autonomy. Paul Anderson of the University of Edinburgh had described the need for a better approach managing computers in 1994, and implemented a system called LCFG at about the same time as CFEngine. Remy Evard of the Argonne National Laboratory, and Alva Couch of Tufts University had begun to espouse similar ideas in 1997[119]. Steve Traugott, a consultant at NASA Ames Laboratory, coined the term infrastructure and would eventually argue both for and against aspects of the Computer Immunology idea.

There were other distractions to consider too. The 1990s were obsessed with the burgeoning problem of computer security, following the events of the Morris Internet Worm of 1988, which had spread virulently across the Internet, shutting down business and government systems. A large number of viruses aimed at personal computers also grabbed their share of attention. These demonstrated the vulnerabilities in the software of the day, which had mostly been written to assume trusted environments.

Security drew attention away from the need to handle growing complexity of the service composition, by focusing on detecting hostile behaviour. Other aspects became secondary. Interestingly, there was a parallel to CFEngine's approach in the work of Moffet and Sloman for describing Policy Based Management of security controls[120], which also appeared in 1993, showing at least that the time was ripe for declarative thinking. Instead of looking at the maintenance of computers, these authors used ideas about logic to design desired-state security.

The changes in thinking that began in the 1990s, with Computer Immunology, were a seed for a Third Wave, but there is no clean transition between the epochs. Other approaches for computer management had been conceived within the business world.

The IT Infrastructure Library (ITIL), for example, was a wrapping of basic white collar management techniques around the processes for managing computing and networking equipment was compiled in the 1980's by the UK governments Central Computer and Telecommunications Agency. ITIL was developed mainly out of human management processes, including continuous delivery and continuous improvement, and it borrowed some of the ideas of W.E. Deming, the American physicist who travelled to Japan in the wake of the second world war to rekindle its manufacturing industry[121]. Similar stories, like COBIT and eTOM came from the telecommunications industry, but never became widely used.

Earlier in the 1980s, standardization had been used by the dominant vendors to try to freeze the market with 'one size for all', and sell their own standard solutions to resource management and configuration. The effort resulted in an era of closed proprietary thinking that was soon to be blasted apart during the 1990s. It was yet another symptom of the division between landowners and workers that was taking place. The segregation between the infrastructure providers and its consumers, led to an industry split into: *network management* and *system administration*. The latter represented computer 'server' management (a server being a computer or task which delivered a service to end users). These two branches of the tree were almost completely disconnected, with different models and very different ideas, in spite of facing essentially identical problems. One reason for this was that networks were owned and locked in by the major hardware and software manufacturers, whose devices were simpler to operate because they were tied to a particular job, while the computers quickly became open to a wider range of contributions and could not be handled by the same models.

The idea went something like this: if information technology was a bunch of databases and networks, then those same things were surely also the solution to the problem. It was even more convenient that the companies happened to sell databases too. The major vendors thus came together to codify standards that would guarantee them a cut of the commercial action and allow them to sell their own products to manage the problems users experienced. These were all based around the idea of data modelling, using state of the art Structured Databases[122].

The first standards began in the 1980s and many survive all the way up to the present day. A plethora of management protocols, including the Simple Network Management Protocol (SNMP), the OSI network management model, TMN, and others, all used the network like a command and control system, pushing commands over a transport layer from a static database of resources[123]. The protocols were designed for the kind of purpose built hardware one finds in network equipment. They could use classical computer science concepts like 'managed objects'. However, they coped poorly with the infinitely variable and infinitely programmable operating systems of the 1990s.

Major changes were thus afoot in the world of computers in the 1980s and 1990s. The appearance of personal computers and workstations in place of terminal access to mainframes went hand in hand with the availability of cheap networking: Ethernet and TCP/IP networking, or what we now understand as the technology of the Internet.

The dominance of distributed workstations with flexible operating systems, like Unix, led to a hotbed of innovation in software, as they began to be used widely in business. The break up of a monopoly on ideas was about to become the beginning of the Third Wave for software. Openness is a treasured attribute in research. It is the way that ideas spread and mingle and mutate. It allows the formation of a primordial soup for ideas to come into contact and evolve. The research efforts from projects like the Internet were also starting to be noticed. IBM had failed to commercialize an early network technology called Systems Network Architecture in the 1980s, by keeping it under a tight rein. The open Internet standards quickly dominated in its place.

The Unix operating system itself had grown out of the remnants of a closed computer project called MULTICS, a monolithic visionary computer operating system design with an impressive computing architecture. Although MULTICS itself was ahead of its time and later got bogged down in management complexity, many of the innovations for MULTICS have since reemerged in other software. Two of its former programmers, Ken Thompson and Dennis Ritchie, were not willing to wait however, and put together Unix as a best-of but stripped down version of it designed as flexible and open alternative to the highly regulated MULTICS to make developers productive[124]. They had to break it up in order to keep it together. Unix and its increasingly open variants became the player of choice as the platform of Internet services due to its open implementation of TCP/IP Internet protocols, and its status as the platform for innovation changed radically with the emergence of Free and Open Source Software[125].

The watershed for computer innovation happened when MIT graduate student Richard Stallman formed the Free Software Foundation, from a community of hackers at the MIT labs. It was a kind of Berlin Wall moment for the computer industry, tearing down the barriers to innovation that had been erected by proprietary interests and restrictive licensing of major vendors. Stallman believed that software should not be locked down by licenses that placed so many restrictions on users as to render it useless. He began a campaign to rewrite most of Unix under a free 'copyleft' license called GNU (GNU's Not Unix), recruiting software developers from anywhere in a spirit of freedom. Sharing and modification of the software was encouraged. The approach appealed to the scientific ideals of universities, in particular.

Thanks to Stallman, software innovation was no longer limited to large companies, moreover, the availability of bulletin boards and the Internet meant that software could change hands, freely. This new open software thus became the primordial soup of innovation for a quarter century. The CFEngine project came out of that soup, and so did the GNU/Linux operating system which accounts for a large part of Internet services today.

As with most political movements, ideology eventually gave way to commerce and the original goals of the Free Software Foundation were subordinated in favour of the free trade in ideas. Dynamics always trump semantics. These developments undoubtedly accelerated the rate of growth of both the Internet and software. The 'dot com bubble' of investment in Internet companies was enabled in large part by this shift.

The freely available tools of Unix and its free clones allowed Unix system administrators to ignore the proprietary databases of the network management world and program their way out of the complexity exhibited by computer management. By applying logic, there was no problem they couldn't solve. At least that was the theory. Unix offered a rich command and control language, which could be harnessed effectively by 'scripting' them into complex litanies of step by step instructions. This worked well in small environments, but quickly led to inflation in the logical complexity, especially where several computer manufacturers' equipment had to co-exist. Another side effect of proprietary interests was that there were significant differences between different versions of Unix. This obfuscated attempts to script in a simple way. Indeed, concealing such differences was a large part of the motivation for the CFEngine project in 1993, as a declarative interface for describing desired state (see Chapter 5).

The lesson from the security incidents of the 1990s was relatively simple to state: when information systems gather input, as messages from an external source, they are vulnerable to misinterpretation, and even to malicious intentions in those messages. To protect against instability, software has to properly validate the input against its own expectations. Successful intrusions and attacks are usually cases where lazy assumptions about input messages can be exploited by smart attackers, due to the presence of semantic instability. These semantic attacks work equally well on the human operators (known as social engineering), and on any channel of input the software used to read data (called cracking systems), which includes globally variable data like databases[126].

Although interest in the subject peaked, the presence of security issues did not end with the 1990s. Rather than scaring developers off, the programmability of systems, which had been responsible for both the innovation and vulnerability in the 1990s, was embraced and extended even further. The need for change, cost reduction, and competitive advantage in online services drove the strategy pendulum towards massive growth and simultaneous atomization of computing resources. Rentable virtual machines became the start of a new wave resource called 'The Cloud', named after the usual way the Internet was represented as a kind of 'nebulous outer space' in networking diagrams.

Amazon Web Services was the first company to successfully allow users to rent and deploy computing resources around 2006, using programmable interfaces. Today, it is not only allowed, but encouraged to script and program freely around rentable infrastructure. Formalized 'APIs' or Application Programmer Interfaces provide open command channels into remote systems, offering a level of programmability that would send chills down the spine of 1990s security officers. Hopefully, better protections are now in place against malicious use of these command pipelines. What remains to be decided is how 'smart' they should be, and what this means. We must return to this issue later in the book to understand what its implications might be.

Whatever the level of semantic stability in cloud computing, there seems to be no way back from the flexibility it offers. If Free and Open Source Software was the primordial soup for software innovation, then cloud computing plays the same role for businesses. It is the arena in which random ideas play out and mutate, then grow when the niche for success has been identified.

The seeds of reliability and certainty could begin to form in the experiences of the past 25 years, but a looming conflict of interest, between stability and flexibility, is still clearly apparent.

An increasingly programmable infrastructure, accessible with the remote controls of an increasing number of consumers, makes a conflicts of interest. This does not require sinister intent to become a threat, only a difference of opinion. If the pendulum swing continues on its ever rising canon, the logical outcome would be for the pattern to repeat again, for cloud computing to leave its dedicated datacentres and become embedded in the urban infrastructure, along with the electricity substations and the smart roads. Everything has to be pulled apart and made pervasive in order to bind it more permanently to society.

Second wave models for managing technological infrastructure will be superceded soon enough, as they become overwhelmed by scale and complexity. The question is: what will replace them? If this chapter's lightning sweep of history offers any lesson, it must be that answers lie in distributed autonomy, in embedding self-stabilizing infrastructure everywhere. The CFEngine project was my own strategy for addressing this, and only time will tell if it can be successful.

Could this work? Is it science fiction? How smart would it need to be? Could a smart interface outsmart us? Can we know or, better still, ensure that the interactive feedback is safe feedback that will result in a stable outcome, or could our tampering with a reasoning environment lead to dangerous instability? The answers lie not in suppressing uncertainties, but in facing them and dealing with them. We are not merely talking about web services and online hotel bookings, but the life support systems of human beings in the balance. Perhaps this sounds sensational, but who hasn't cursed some piece of software for trying to be too smart on our behalf, or for making default decisions that were felt inappropriate? Is the capacity to reason on society's behalf a good thing, or a ticking time bomb?

The uncertainties we face are of two kinds. If we deconstruct the journey so far, two facets of technology have left their signature on the past, and continue to duel for attention: *dynamics* (how things change) and *semantics* (how we interpret behaviour). The answers we pursue will inevitably pit these two interests against one another, and thus is useful to frame their roles.

	DYNAMICS	SEMANTICS
INDIVIDUAL	KINEMATICS	INTENT
COLLECTIVE	MECHANICS	COOPERATION

Each can be divided into a part which describes the behaviour of singular parts of a system during change, and a part which describes how pieces work in concert. Mechanics are how parts of a system interact, kinematics are how they move independently. Cooperation is how parts interact, and intent is how they behave independently. Both aspects must be understood to pull technology apart in order to keep it together.

Meanwhile, another creative pendulum also swings back and forth between the poles of simplicity and flexibility.

SIMPLICITY	FLEXIBILITY
FEW PARTS	FUNCTIONAL
SPECIALIZED	GENERALIZED
CENTRALIZED	DECENTRALIZED
MONOLITHIC	PROGRAMMABLE/MOBILE
CONTROLLED	AUTONOMOUS
COMMON	PERSONAL
DISCONNECTED	CONNECTED
OUT OF THE BOX	DO IT YOURSELF

We go from 'do it yourself' to 'out of the box' and back, or from mainframe to personal workstation, from datacentre to embedded system, from dedicated dumb phone to programmable smart sleeve, and then back again. As complexity of customization grows cumbersome, we fall back on simplified and specialized devices, then as these become restrictive we add more customizable parameters again. The effect is an upward spiral of development that oscillates between the domains of experts and mainstream users.

A simple rule of thumb is this: when the complexity of an environment exceeds the complexity of a sub-system embedded within it, that sub-system will be unpredictable. So, if the information-rich technology we are committing to depends increasingly on programmable reasoning, and if that reasoning is only as good as the evidence put into it, then we need to ask tough questions about the gathering of such evidence. We should examine how messages are read by the receivers, and decide whether there really is an objective notion of certainty on which to build a stable infrastructure.

7

Seeing Is Disbelieving

How to explain what we see and make use of it

"What you see is what you get." (WYSIWYG)
– Design principle for word processing

Western culture is obsessed with notions of right and wrong, true or false, black and white. We want answers to questions, and we want those answers as clear, contrasting absolutes. We criticize vagaries and muddle, imprecision and nebulousness, at the very same time as we are all guilty of all of these things at a fundamental level, and even depend on them for survival. As every writer, teacher and editor knows, clarity and simplicity are no mean feats; and as every engineer or designer knows, 'good enough' is the only way to build for survival in a noisy environment. Clarity and robustness are conflicting interests.

Still we strive for such clarity, because it seems to lead to certainty, and that is a valued commodity. Perhaps we are afraid of the future, perhaps we are merely spoilt in an information-rich age; whatever the reason, we are apt to draw a line and paradoxically demand: don't give me details, just tell me yes or no! Certainty is about a desire for predictability, about a desire to *know*.

These tendencies all bear further inspection. The natural world does not want to be shoe-horned into bi-polar categories of this kind, at least not at the scales of human interaction. There are few, if any, questions to which the honest answer is "yes" or "no", or "true" or "false", and those questions which can be answered in such a simple manner are usually contrived and of limited value: such precision exacts a price. We want to take complex issues and reduce them to simple sound-bites but this is not always possible.

Fair enough, sometimes we take simple ideas and complicate them artificially. This kind of complexity could be eliminated by careful editing, but other times issues cannot be reduced to something simpler, they simply are complex and can be reduced no further without sacrificing something (such as the shortest route to a destination). Like it or not, this is the nature of the world. So what can be really expect? How should we learn to manage without knowing absolutely?

In the first part of this book, I held stability up as a key principle for designing technology, because it is the fundamental and objective idea behind predictability. The conclusion was that we may unify all the disparate ideas about stability with a simple picture of consistent messages, transmitted either by humans or by nature, from place to place and from time to time. The semantics of those messages play a major role in our understanding of interactions with everything around us, natural and man-made. In fact, we take our semantics so much for granted that we usually speak of *intuition* instead. Intuition is a vague idea, whereas semantics can be made precise, so the quest for certainty will undoubtedly bring us closer to this issue.

The perspectives of history suggest that information-richness goes hand in hand with decentralization. Atomizing systems allows them to become more responsive to their environments, but only if they can still receive messages from it. This motivates an exploration of what qualities a message might have to enable it to bring certainty. The basics of how the messages are perceived and understood, must be unravelled. We should therefore expend a minimum of effort to review the science of measurement and observation to see how it must be incorporated into a new science of infrastructure.

We sample and measure data all the time, as part of our most basic interactions with the infrastructure around us, often without even knowing it. The decisions made by computers are based on the contents of variables that were determined by observing or reading input from users in the unpredictable world outside them. In an information-rich world, any such interaction has the character of a measurement. Data are exchanged by Shannon messaging when changing the channel on the television, when checking your bank account, swiping cards and opening code locks, online purchasing, and especially when aligning smartphones with network stations and global positioning satellites.

To fully understand the implications of using information for decision making, we need to examine what the receiver of a message experiences and believes about a signal it receives, regardless of whether it asked for the information, or if it arrives unsolicited. Observation is the front line of information acquisition, it underpins every interaction with the world, man-made or natural.

What is an observation? To observe, there must be interaction. Shannon's model of communication over a noisy channel is exactly what we need to understand these interactions. Every interaction with an object involves a message. A message transmits some aspect of a source object to a receiver. The receiver records the essence it decodes from the message, and this essence may be called an observation.

Receiving a signal from a transmitting source does not guarantee that we can explain or interpret what we receive, however. Recall that communication over a (noisy) channel can only work if:

1. There is an agreed alphabet of 'symbols' for representing the message.

2. The receiver decodes symbols accurately.

3. The symbols are not subject to distortion or noise.

4. The symbols are correctly recognized by the receiver.

5. The message is interpreted with agreed semantics.

These points are stylized for a symbolic message, but we know that even a pseudo-continuous signal like a radio or light wave can be handled in the same way, by adjusting the scales of definition appropriately (see figure 4.3). This simple model can be a framework in which to discuss observation.

The receipt of a message is a unique and individual experience that cannot be reproduced exactly. One may then go beyond mere observation and try to formalize the idea, in order to strip away as many individual subjectivities as possible in message reception. This is done by replacing the observation, as coded in the original message alphabet, with a new message in a standard alphabet and format, based on an agreed set of dimensional *scales* for measurement.

Measurements are thus observations made using some kind of measuring instrument. An instrument is a device which converts or *transduces* one kind of message into another. We use instruments to compare observations made at different times, and at different places, to a standard measuring scale, because our own senses are not equipped with standardized, objective scales. Instruments can be simple tools like sun dials, measuring sticks, weight balances, or they can be sophisticated tools like magnetic imaging detectors, whose signals are processed by computation.

The process of obtaining a second opinion, by making a comparison with a third party, is called *calibration*. Human perception is subjective and works by comparing things. Thus, for more than one person to agree on a measurement, or even for the same person to agree with themselves at different times, we need this kind of external standard. In the past, standard measures have been represented by actual singular physical objects with fixed length and weight, such as the platinum-iridium bar measuring a standard metre, which was kept at the French *Bureau International des Poids et Mesures* (The International Bureau of Weights and Measures), at the constant temperature of melting ice. Copies of these objects were then calibrated to the best of technology's ability against the original, and distributed as tools for everyone. Today, standard dimensional units are defined in terms of the properties of light that are more easily available.

Measurements fall into two main types. Some are numerical or 'ordinal', based on counting. These include distances and times, which may be viewed as counting a number of standard length or duration intervals from start to finish. Others are qualitative or 'nominal', such as the naming of colours. Imagine, for example, how to decide whether a horse is red or brown, and what shade of these? Such matters represent naming conventions, and standard references are used to give approved names or labels to these observed measures too. The colour charts one uses to buy domestic paint use codes that explain how to mix the shades from standard pigments. Thus each unique shade is assigned a unique name, and visual inspection of closest match can be used to identify a paint on a scale of comparison.

Where possible measurers try to convert observations into ordinal numbers, as such numbers have simple arithmetic properties, and mathematics has developed more tools for dealing with numbers than for the names. However, merely using a number for a name does not help to make sense of it. Referring to Alice and Bob as subjects 1 and 2 does not allow us to add their numbers with any meaning. We could not say that Bob was 'greater than' Alice, simply because he was represented by a higher number. Counting the number of people called Alice and Bob, on the other hand, does offer a different kind of information that is amenable to arithmetic analysis. It does make sense to say that the number of people called Bob is greater than the number of people called Alice.

Our senses are themselves simple measuring instruments, even without the assistance of scales, and we use them every day to compare experiences to a model of the world that we have built up in our brains. This is why humans are involved in managing systems (and steering horses). Each message that is sent from a happening event to our brains may be called an observation. However, we reserve the word measurement for those observations that can be verified by independent 'third parties', using an agreed upon standard scale.

Measurements are thus observations involving intermediaries. For each measurement there is a measuring instrument that plays the role of a signal transducer, i.e. something that converts one message into another.

Event $\longrightarrow$ Instrument / transducer $\longrightarrow$ Observer

We make two assumptions about measurements, that allow us to interpret the results consistently, in spite of the uncertainty. First, the conditions under which measurements are made should be constant. If they are not, we cannot know whether the measurements are really comparable to one another, i.e. if they are truly calibrated on the same scale of measurement.

Uncertainties in measurement strike doubt at the heart of these assumptions; they come from both random and systematic errors[127]. A random error is a fluctuation of noise around a more or less constant signal. Different measurements could be affected by noise by different amounts if the environment is changing at random, such as the fast variations in the separable signals of chapter 4. Then there is systematic error, which is an inaccuracy caused by a constant shift of all the results, as if the placement of a measuring stick was gradually slipping during the data collection. These correspond to the slow variations of chapter 4.

The second assumption about measurements is that the act of measuring a system does not affect the measurement itself. We want to know that what we observe is what would have happened had we not interfered with the system at all. This is somewhat wishful thinking, however. Newton's third law tells us that any interaction we use to probe a system will lead to a reaction on the system itself. The goal is to make that interaction negligible. Imagine measuring the pressure in a tyre over and over again, each time letting out a little more of the air inside. Each act of measurement reduces the pressure. Eventually it would be significantly reduced.

These two conditions protect the semantic stability of measurements. Without them, we would have only one chance to view any change happening in the world. We would never be sure we had measured something correctly, or be able to meaningfully compare one observation with another. We would never identify repeated patterns, or build a body of equivalent evidence. More importantly, technology would not help us to improve the certainty of the results.

This presents a dilemma for any sensor that equips a part of society's technological life support systems with interactive behaviour. The gathering of data, on which to form reliable conclusions, is a very difficult challenge to satisfy. That is why, in the past, technology has not been warranted to make decisions alone, only to pass on data in some kind of graphical representation, meter or alarm for a human to take responsibility.

Consider the measurement of temperature, as an example. With a traditional thermometer, heat from an environment is transmitted through the air to a bulb of Mercury, which expands to a certain length. We try not to touch the mercury column, transferring body heat and hence distorting the result, but, if we inadvertently do so, there is no way to determine that the error happened. The column of Mercury does not understand the concept of temperature, rather we use the physical property that metals expand as temperature increases to make a transducer. By observing the behaviour of Mercury over time, a human has calibrated the markings to temperature, using some assumptions and agreed standards. A graduated scale is thus marked along the side of the Mercury column, which transduces the length of Mercury into a temperature that is readable by anyone. The Mercury column is difficult to see, so reading it is subject to some error, also lights and other nearby heat sources can affect the reading.

The Mercury thermometer perhaps seems a little old-fashioned in today's computerized world. So, imagine a more modern version: a temperature sensor which generates a stream of electrical signals based on a sampling of electricity. The technology is different, but the concepts are essentially the same. Again, the sensor does not actually understand the concept of temperature. It is based on the electrical properties of a certain kind of semiconducting metal, which does not read a temperature directly but a generates a voltage that changes with temperature. The voltage signal reaches an electronic transducer, which converts it into a number, calibrated in degrees Celsius, by employing a simple look-up and computation, and transmits this digitally encoded number to a register where it is accessible to users of the computer (see fig. 4.3). This sounds quite reliable, but if there is a random electrical error in any part of the chain, we would not be able to detect that it had happened. The final result is quite similar to the Mercury thermometer. Using a computer does not make the process any more reliable, only more convenient.

In each of these cases, the stability of the result is quite *ad hoc*. Unless we can repeat the measurement to verify its integrity somehow, there is no real way to trust it. Also, in both cases, transduction of one scale into another is very much like a code book or foreign phrase translation: a message is looked up in a translation table and the decoded message is read off, symbol by symbol (see figure 7.1).

This measurement problem is highly relevant when we try to build observational models of computer software systems. Software systems run all of modern computers so there is little we can know about a computer without using software to measure software. This presents a dilemma: we have to violate the second assumption of measurement and change the state of the computer in order to measure the state of the computer. In practice, one typically executes some kind of software agent which looks at the resources held by other processes. This agent is itself a process which consumes resources, so its very existence will affect the measurements on about the same scale as the things one is trying to measure. Today, much of computing infrastructure is moving to so-called virtual machines, which are simulated computers that can be physically

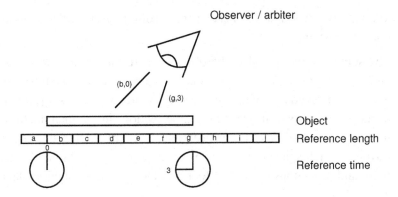

Fig. 7.1. Measuring involves observing an object's effect on a measuring instrument or transducer. To measure an interval requires two messages, one at the start and one at the end.

moved to different hardware without interrupting the flow of service to users. Each time a virtual machine is migrated to new hardware, perhaps to make the most efficient use of resources, we violate the first assumption of measurement about that machine. To address these problems, we need to understand how to make the best of what we can know, so let's explore this further.

It's clear from Shannon's model that every time we introduce a new message channel, there is the possibility of more noise and distortion of the message, leading to greater uncertainty about what to do with the information. Noise is a transmutation of one symbol into another. Thus every measuring instrument introduces additional noise and possible distortion into the signal. There is even a case to be made for saying that the transducer is an intended distortion to the standard scale: a helpful distorting translation that we hope is performed reliably. In using distortion as a tool, we now have a distinction between *intended* and *unintended* transitions.

We can appreciate the generality of the Shannon model by considering a few more examples. In each case, an object (a sender) is projected (transmitted) onto a standard measuring scale (transducer) for interpretation, and this passes on the message to the final receiver:

1. Measuring the length of an object with a ruler. By ruler, we mean, of course, a strip of material (as opposed to a king, queen, or other head of state, which are typically quite unsuitable as standards for measurement). It can be made of wood, plastic, metal, with a number of graduations marked on it, typically centimetres or inches. Since we are measuring an

interval, two messages are needed: one from the start of the interval and one from the end.

The source of the signal is the object we are measuring, or at least its ends (see Figure 7.1). The transducer is the ruler itself. The transmission channel is formed by laying the two side by side, which is subject to noise of misalignment and misreading. Imperfections in the manufacturing of the ruler can also affect the measurement. Light shining onto the ruler travels through space to the observer's eyes, which might be affected by noise and distortions through colour blindness, poor eyesight, a blackout, etc.

2. Measuring an interval of time with a clock.

   The interval is demarked by two events: the start and the end of the interval. At each event, the event triggers an observation of the clock (transducer), which we assume measures 'real time'. The receiver observes the value on the clock visually, as in the previous example.

3. DNA is measured and copied during cellular activity.

   When DNA is copied during cell reproduction, or when a strand of DNA is read as part of the command program of the cell, an array of helper molecules interact with the strand. During copying, an imprint is created that leads to the writing of a copy. During reading, helper molecules are matched to the configuration of the DNA, affecting the production of working parts in the cell. The sender is the original DNA strand, the transmission medium is chemical, and the transducer is the intermediary molecules that perform reading and made the template for copying, and the final receiver is the copied DNA strand. Noise and distortion can occur chemically or by radiation, and this is a cause of DNA mutation.

4. Digital sampling of music is a very practical application of computerized measurement. Sounds are transmitted through the air from musical instruments (sources), or copied from magnetic tape, and are received by a transducer which converts the acoustic waves into electrical signals. These signals are divided up into a symbol table that is encoded in binary numbers by the transducer and are transmitted to a computer memory, which receives a binary data stream.

5. Computer-assisted collection of vital signs, either for human health, or technology health. An example of this would be the measurements of computer systems described in Chapter 3.

The data sources are usually one or more registers in sensor hardware, whose values are transmitted to a transducer by a data bus, or a computer operation. This either converts a value or computes an answer based on several sources. The computation takes a finite amount of time. Then the result is is transmitted by another copy operation to another memory location where a user can parse it. The exact timing is highly unpredictable, since the operating system has to share its time between many tasks, and has to find the time to complete the measurement while doing many other things. That means that during multiple measurements, the conditions might be quite unequal.

This is an internal measurement where the measurer and the measuree are part of the same system, sharing the same resources. There can therefore be interference between the measurement instrument and the process being measured.

The capture of observational messages is the act of *data collection*. Acquisition of the data is the pre-requisite for obtaining information about the environment. It is no longer something we only do in pursuit of research or forensics; an increasingly intrusive amount of the public infrastructure depends on such measurements for its operation. Most of those observations pass directly to simple mechanical or electrical feedback regulators, like the bi-metallic strip mentioned in chapter 2 used in thermostats. However, the rising trend is to embed sophisticated control systems into our environments to do much more than keep the temperature constant.

Computers regulate when water flows at dams, when to move taxis into an area of the city, when to switch on street lighting, activate alarms, close or open blinds for temperature regulation in buildings, when to start cooking dinner, when to switch off the power, water pressure regulation, telemetry systems and all the examples in the previous chapter. Weather sensors help us to predict the weather by feeding data into prediction models, and hardware detection in your laptop allows the software to correctly interpret signals from the mouse and keyboard, and generate the correct colours and shapes on the screen.

The rich variety of different information systems deployed into the world means that a constant environment cannot be assumed by information technology. We have to compensate by probing it to understand what infrastructure we are dealing with. The wireless Internet access point closest to you right now might use any one of a handful of different technologies, with different capabilities. In order to be able to use this, the hardware you are using has to be able to measure its capabilities and adapt to them.

Probing modular systems to establish an inventory of their capabilities, is a part of the everyday life of technology in an open 'Third Wave' environment. It is one of the costs we incur in supporting variety. Increasingly, computational logic is at the receiving end of quick, off-the-cuff measurements of the world, and complex computer software is ready to use the data to make decisions on our behalf.

Making an incorrect observation could be a problem, but what about not being able to make an observation at all, when we need to? If a cashier-terminal at the supermarket is not able to observe that your bank account has sufficient money to let you walk away with the goods, or if it provides information that is out of date, this might spoil your weekend or cause you to miss a one-time opportunity. If the wiring falls off the patient in the intensive care unit, no signals can pass between source and receiver; however, drawing the conclusion that the patient were dead would be hasty.

The semantics of responding to unexpected or unavailable data are not merely a trivial case of alive or dead, yes or no, or true or false, as discussed in the introduction. The fact that we are unable to receive an observational message does not mean we can conclude anything at all about the sender's condition. As the old adage says:

"Absence of knowledge is not knowledge of absence".

In communications, when no response is obtained from another party, there are three possibilities: no message was received by the other party, they were unable to respond, or they were unwilling to respond. The loss of communications between sender and receiver plunges us into complete uncertainty. This is not a modern development. Philosophers of science have encountered and pondered these issues for centuries.

In the 17th century, René Descartes (1596-1650) studied human sensory perception. He noted that matters were worse than the adage: knowledge of absence did not even guarantee absence of knowledge[128]. He wrote:

"I have been assured by men whose arm or leg has been amputated that it still seemed to them that they occasionally felt pain in the limb they had lost – thus giving me grounds to think that I could not be quite certain that a pain I endured was indeed due to the limb in which I seemed to feel it."

Descartes also observed that:

"Because it is the soul that sees, and not the eye, and because the soul sees immediately only by the intervention of the brain, ... it happens that madmen, and sleepers often see, or think that they see, diverse objects that are not before their eyes."

He notes that we can be fooled by hallucinations, or signals that are false. False readings on the sensors of flight systems are an extremely dangerous situation, which has resulted in a number of air disasters.

Descartes concluded that since he could experience only what the nerves from his sense organs transmitted to his brain, he had no direct knowledge of the world. Today, information technology has become our eyes and ears in many cases, and because we trust machines to be reliable, we tend to think that computer measurements must be trustworthy. Descartes' caution applies of electronic sensors too.

Of course, illusions can trick humans as well as technology. There are no simple answers for the avoidance of doubt, which is one reason why legal contracts expend a considerable amount of text to avoid liability for unknown potentialities. Our brains are extremely good at seeing what we want to see by justifying a model to scant evidence. We see faces in clouds, on cars, and interpret patterns on behaviour in people around us on the basis of incomplete information.

At the end of the 19th century, Italian astronomer Giovanni Schiaparelli (1835-1910) trained his telescope on Mars and was amazed to find a criss-cross pattern of lines which he called *canali*, meaning channels. Percival Lowell, misinterpreting his notes and enthused by the fanciful notion, mistranslated the word, and thus began the legend of the Canals of Mars, The War of the Worlds, The Martian Chronicles, and an extensive science fantasy around the red planet.

The *canali* were later discovered to be a trick of low resolution distortion in the optical system between Mars and the Earth: space, telescope, and eye, a loss of information, caused by random dark spots on the surface. A century later, another blurred picture of Mars apparently revealed a gigantic human face carved into the surface. On closer inspection, it was another trick of the light, fuelled by lack of resolution, much to the disappointment of UFO enthusiasts and indeed Hollywood, who went ahead and made the movie anyway[129].

Collection of data is a long way from being good enough a basis on which to draw conclusions. Once an observation has been made, the next question is: how can we be sure that the result is an adequate measure, what is its uncertainty, and does it have any kind of meaningful interpretation? Model fitting seems to be intrinsic to the way our cognition works, and we use that to good effect. When we look for meaning, we do so by attaching interpretive models to data we perceive. We then pass on this habit to the technologies we build. This makes the matter of certainty highly vulnerable to semantic instability.

Descartes' amputated limbs and Schiaparelli's illusory channels are not merely a diversion for morbid amusement. They illustrate general issues about observation, and they have urgent analogues in the technological present.

The Internet, as we now refer to the global network of information infrastructure, connects us together by cables and radio signals in a highly intricate way. If we want to get from point A to point B in this network, there is rarely a direct connection over a single wire to get us there, but there will be one or more routes, even if it means going through an intermediate point — like changing trains between different lines on the London underground or Paris Metro.

Sometimes, however, a route becomes blocked temporarily, or there is simply no connection between two parts of the network (see Figure 2.4). In that case, we say the networks are *partitioned* or disconnected. Sometimes, this is a deliberate act, e.g. security firewalls are actually designed to prevent certain kinds of messages from passing through a protective barrier. Other times it is due to a fault[130].

Today, messages that drive the world travel through a network of immense complexity and high reliability, and the sheer scale of many online services, and the distribution of their users across the world, has forced the technology to atomize service points from previously centralized delivery into 'local branches', as discussed in Chapter 6.

This is relatively new for information technology, but it is not new for other global services: chain stores and banks cover their highly distributed customer base with many local branches. The consequence of this decentralization, whatever technology it is based on, is that the experience users observe, when contacting an isolated branch of the service, may or may not be calibrated against any single common standard. Thus one can observe variations, inaccuracies with advertising and even semantic errors in the system. Is a branch of McDonald's or Starbucks exactly the same all over the planet?

There are three problems in scaling services, consistency, availability and proximity (CAP[131])—and there is a conflict of interest between them.

Availability to customers and users can be handled by distributing more and more branches around the world. This is only useful if the branches are all approximately the same, otherwise users still have to go to a specific branch to get what they want. We can express this more scientifically by saying that this requires consistency of the observed data, i.e. their goods and services need to be sufficiently similar. Consistency, on the other hand, requires there to be good enough accessibility to the stores, or close enough proximity, otherwise one could not send information between the branches to keep them sufficiently similar. If, for example, there were effectively a partition between branches, that would block such information and they would quickly become inconsistent, as different customers visited different branches and both account details and goods deviated away from a global consistency.

This is really a question of time scales and proximity (speed). There are two reasons why consistency-bringing messages will not reach their destination in time: the speed of communications between branches, and the unavailability of communications. The dimensionless ratio of interest is:

$$\frac{\text{Time between of changes to branch account}}{\text{Time to update other branches}}$$

If branches are far away from one another, messages will take longer to arrive. This shows that there is no way to avoid the possibility of inconsistency unless you control the entire world.

This is forcing an increasing number of technologists to confront an unfamiliar dimension to the uncertainty surrounding incomplete information: the need to deal with the *relativity of knowledge*[132]. Different users are going to see different things, have different experiences, depending on where they are relative to what they are looking at. In science, the analysis of this issue is called *relativity theory*, and many of the great minds of philosophy have struggled with versions of it, including Galileo, Einstein, and Kripke. What links these different ideas about relativity is simple: they are all about the incompleteness of information, due to limitations in the available channels of communication. Far from being an abstruse issue of mere academic interest, only for the Einsteins of our world, relativity is something that now affects us when we read our daily messages.

In the past, the slowness of the world made many of these limitations bearable, but that has now changed. Thanks to information technology, the speed with which users demand service means that it now takes only a temporary delay or the briefest outage in the flow of messages to place a user in the umbra of an amputation or a clot. Like the growing importance of storage errors in Chapter 5, the sheer scale of demand for observations of these services has amplified the impact of even the smallest error to a critical level.

In Einstein's theory of relativity, the controlling dimensionless ratio was the speed of a moving object relative to the speed of light. Because the speed of light is the generic rate at which all observable influences travel in nature, as any observer approaches the speed of light their experience of reality has to become limited by what light can manage to signal, as it races against other changes taking place. The same kind of effect is now hitting more information systems, because information technology has increased the rate at which changes take place, relative to the rate at which they can be communicated over distance.

Money management is a more mundane, and more long-standing example of the need to achieve consistency. Banks ensure a level of consistency in customer accounts by signalling messages to all their different branches and representatives. If they could not do this, people would either be unable to access their money when travelling, or would be able to spend more than they had. Banks try to provide a consistent experience about the contents of your bank account, as you travel around the world, even though the terminals you access could not possibly all be calling home to a single computer in your home town. So you are not likely to be able to call up different branches, or use different cash terminals and see different balances. However, to do this, they often make you wait something like three working days for a transaction to 'clear', or for the information to reach equilibrium with the rest of the world. The telegraph made this happen for international trade in the 19th century, by creating a mode of communications that was faster than goods could travel.

Today, due to the high speeds of demand and the enormous rates of usage, online social media services are trading away consistency in favour of availability. If you use some of the social messaging forums on the Internet[133], you might have experienced the following: when checking messages on your computer and then on your smartphone, you see different results. The information they retrieve is inconsistent. One of your devices shows a more up-to-date version of the world than the other. The reason for this is that different kinds of devices access the system through different channels, which are based at different locations, and these different locations have data that are not fully synchronized. The services feel that a responsive service is more important than the risk of a temporary inconsistency.

Databases are the backbone of shared memory in information systems, and they are behind all of these day to day messaging services. Alas, databases architectures were designed for an era when there were several orders of magnitude fewer users; they were designed to be monolithic stores. As the demand on services grew, the central database became a stress concentration, a bottleneck, and a single point of failure for information. To work around this problem, databases are now split into 'shards', or splintered fragments. Some users end up on one shard, others end up using another. If only the problem were that simple.

News channels actually profit from relativity. When information becomes available in some part of the world, each news channel wants to be the first to get the latest scoop. Because news travels by so many channels, the consumers of said news accept that not every channel reports consistent observations at all times.

In a Third Wave society, we are increasingly mobile both in terms of location and our preferences. There are thus two approaches to homogenizing information: either we have to do it immediately and make everyone wait for the changes to reach equilibrium (as banks used to close each night) or we refuse to guarantee consistency and promise only that there will be eventual consistency (like social media). Where do we draw the line?

Over short distances, we can continue to use parallel channels to increase throughput of information, and improve the rate of data equilibration. However, physical distance will most likely always be a barrier, due to the limitation of the speed of communications[134]. As we spread out into the solar system, we shall have to give up the idea of consistency and equilibrium.

If these examples are anything to go by, consistency of observation would seem to be about having a repeated relationship with the state of what we are observing. Thus, an answer to knowing the success of any measurement is to try to repeat the observation many times, before its underlying nature changes. That is the lesson of relativity and its time scales. There is a problem with this, however.

Each new observation adds its own uncertainty, so without a model for interpreting random and systematic errors, this just layers on more uncertainties. Measuring a static object multiple times can provide confirmation, but what if the thing we are looking at is changing? Measuring a river at a fixed point, for example, we are never measuring the same water twice, nor the same distribution of velocities, or fish. Repeated measurement would then lead to a lot of different values.

An observer does not always have the luxury of knowing that this is normal however. It is only because we know about rivers that we could interpret the changing measurements. But what if we measure something completely unknown and find an inconstant value, what could that mean? Perhaps the value is supposed to be changing and we are merely capturing reality. Perhaps the source is not changing, but our measuring instrument is changing. Perhaps the very act of measuring the source actually altered the value. Finally, what if the value is changing so fast that we cannot even measure it?

The extent to which repeated measurement improves certainty boils down to the relative rates of change, i.e. a dimensionless ratio of the rate of change of the observed object, and the rate at which we measure it. Even if we know this ratio at one moment in time, we cannot know that the rates of change will not change themselves. For example, a process that is accelerating might begin to decelerate. Thus what is true now, might not be true in a few moments.

All this is a potentially confusing situation to decipher. Measurement is not simple and straightforward. Can we not even know if a result we obtain is due to a faulty instrument or to an error in reading it? The point is that we can't. All we can do is to make lots of measurements and look for either a pattern, or a self-consistent answer, within the time window of the measurements. It then becomes a question of belief if we want to extrapolate the result to make a prediction about the future.

Repetition is the beginning of a basic relationship with an observable signal, allowing us to get to know the behaviour of the measurements, and perhaps eventually equilibrate the result. A relationship allows us to bolster belief and 'know' by experience, as we would say we 'know' a friend. We would not claim to know a person we had met (i.e. sampled) only once, so why would we claim to know the value of a measurement after a first date? The answer is clearly that we expect humans to be more complex than simple sensors, but this underestimates the complexity of the environment around the sensors.

We repeat a measurement even if we expect it to be constant. How many times? Most scientists would believe that as many measurements as possible would be the appropriate answer: there can never be too many confirmations of an explanation. On the other hand, it is pointless to go on measuring indefinitely. There will always be a residual uncertainty.

The 20th century Austrian-British philosopher Karl Popper (1902-1994) made famous the idea of falsification as a strategy for certainty. Popper maintained that we can never verify the truth of anything, because there is always one more measurement we could make that might falsify a result or its explanation. On the other hand, disproving a hypothesis is easy: it takes only a single piece of counter-evidence to topple a tower of belief. This is somewhat simplistically put, however. The flaw in this simple form of the argument is that the single piece of counter-evidence is also an observation that might is vulnerable to the same uncertainties as the positive values. Either way, we are looking for a body of evidence to believe in.

If measured values change, then we may either believe that variation is intrinsic, or that it comes from the environment itself, as noise. If we expect the data to change, then we only get one chance to collect each data point, and repetition serves to detect the approximate pattern of change. Intrinsic change complicates measurement there might be no way to separate noise from signal. This does not mean that the environment did not affect the measurement however, only that we are now unable to distinguish these sources from one another without basing an estimate of the uncertainty on some other analogous process which is believed constant.

Certainty thus suggests an accumulated redundancy of observation, and redundancy can be achieved both in series and in parallel. If serial repetition is out of the question, then multiple detectors could be employed in parallel to confirm or contradict one another. This is the approach used in flight computers and spacecraft, where human lives depend on split-second measurements in extreme and unpredictable environments.

Many other more mundane examples of technology also base their operation on this kind of reasoning. High quality audio cables, called balanced-line cables, use the idea, cleverly, to perform automatic Shannon error correction by duplicating the transmission channel. This requires no reasoning in operation, all the thinking is encapsulated into a simple convergent design whose operation makes the outcome inevitable. Each sound signal S is transmitted in dual messages, with positive and negative polarity (like mirror images) simultaneously. The signals are then subtracted from one another at the receiver. If there is environmental noise N, then both cables pick up the same noise from the environment with the same polarity. When the messages arrive, the mirror image is reflected again so that the original signal is now positive and the noise becomes a mirror image, by subtraction. When the signals are now combined, the signal is reinforced and the noise and its mirror image cancel out:

$$(S + N) - (-S + N) = 2S$$

This is called constructive and destructive interference, or interferometry: it is constructive (or additive) for the signal, and destructive (or subtracting) for the noise. The same idea is used to make sound-cancelling headphones for aircraft.

Repetitive observation, remembering and learning over time, acts as a form of self-imposed regulation on measurement. If we believe that earlier values have some weight on our belief about the present, then the act of remembering the past has a stabilizing effect, tempering the effect of noise on the present. It is a form of negative feedback. If we measure the values 10, 11, 10, 9, and so on, then suddenly we measure 56, this sudden change is a significant deviation from the past. However, if the response of a system to each impulse depends not only on what is new, but also on what happened over the past few measurements, the response will be some kind of average, as we saw in Figure 4.2.

The effect of remembering recent state, and having a stickiness or inertia to fluctuations, is known as hysteresis. This phenomenon exists in nature in certain materials, and accounts for their properties, but it can be used artificially to make systems persistent and hence increase our certainty of their behaviour. Conversely, forgetting the past immediately keeps data fresh and unencumbered, but without any ballast of learning, every new data point blows a measured value around like a leaf in the wind.

The knowledge relationship with data is an equilibrating process. One begins by observing the general patterns and discerning behaviour; only later do we go deeper and try to measure specifics. The goal of repeated measurement of equivalent observations is eliminate noise, and the goal of repeated measurement of inequivalent observations is to capture trends in the signal. The hope is (and it is only a hope) that there can be a detailed balance of fluctuations that will stabilize the measurement in a ways that makes sense.

As we peel back the layers of observation, what seemed at first to be a simple matter of taking a look or collecting some numbers, i.e. receiving a transmission from a sensor, becomes an increasingly precarious house of cards that can tumble at the smallest doubt.

We need to know how these matters influence our ability to know the state of information infrastructure, especially in cases where measurements affect critical functions in society. Shortly after Planck and Einstein discovered the quantum explanation of radiation, the problem of measurement in quantum systems led to one of the most extraordinary discussions in the history of science on the nature of measurement. Physicists were acutely aware that measuring quantum systems would always affect the state of the values being measured, because setting the system up for a measurement implied that a message would have to be passed from the system to measuring apparatus that was highly likely to change its state in the process, thus violating the principles of measurement.

In most human-scale experiences of the world, measurements are made by probing a system with a huge numbers of atoms (around 10^{23}) either quickly with something much much smaller, like a few photons or electrons, or over a long period of time with something slightly smaller, like with the thermometer. In order to represent a system properly, a measuring device needs to be stable with respect to the thing it is measuring. Both systems need to be in equilibrium with respect to the interaction that passes measurement messages from one to the other.

If we probe a large system with a small one, the large system usually dominates the small perturbation of the measurement and the small system comes quickly to equilibrium with the large one[135]. This leads to a stable value. If, we make a long-lasting measurement, then the time to equilibrate the two parts of the combined system costs more work, but there is time for it to take place. This is true of the thermometer. Successful measurements are thus made close to equilibrium. What might be the effect in a computer? Measuring from a sensor using a computer should be unproblematic, but measuring a computer using its own processes, as is normal in computer monitoring, could have varied results.

The fact that we are dealing with discrete transitions over an uncertain channel suggests we look to quantum mechanics for guidance.

In 2008, two of my graduate students Valeri Cheremetiev and Stian Østen, at the University College in Oslo, were embarking on an analysis of traffic from Opera Software's well-known Opera Mini service, in which mobile web traffic is optimized through a proxy service. They wanted to see if the patterns of growth could offer any insight into the way the cluster of servers should be run, for future capacity planning and optimization of resources. They began by looking for tools to measure the performance of the servers, and found some industry standard monitoring software. Initially working together on different aspects of analysing the service, they began to test the use of the software in an isolated environment with little traffic. There is a wealth of software available of monitoring computers, but not all of it has been written by people who know the science of measurement. What they found surprised them: when they measured the load on their servers, they saw a series of spikes at regular intervals that didn't seem to make any sense. They knew that the traffic they had was fairly continuous, so why the sudden anomalous activity from nowhere? After a brief discussion, we saw that what they were seeing was the effect of their monitoring software itself kicking in. The software was so resource intensive that it placed a much high load on the system than the traffic they were trying to measure. The software was merely looking at itself in the mirror. It was like using an elephant instead of a canary to measure lack of oxygen in a mine. The monitoring software itself was using up all the resources.

Two students might be excused for nearly making a mistake, saved by common sense, but the information technology industry as a whole does not have good credentials in this area. At a recent visit to one of the largest online trading sites on the planet, I saw humans being forced to stare at screens, watching measurements change in real time, hoping to see something important in a highly noisy signal environment. They had no controls that indicated what was the normal burden of running their monitoring software. They were merely trusting that the performance graphs were indicating something valuable and accurate. The physics of renormalization deals with the problem of measuring small effects that are masked by large ones. The statistical physics of information systems still has a long way to go to catch up with other sciences when it comes to measurement.

Without even a simple theoretical understanding of measurement, humans will waste enormous amounts of time in fruitless activities watching over machinery as if shepherds trying to diagnose stomach ache in a flock of sheep. This is one reason why we are reaching a crisis of incomprehension today. There are simple things we can do to change that.

In a quantum system, any measurement we make has to use an instrument that is at least as big as the thing we are measuring: there is nothing smaller or less intrusive we can use. Thus, quantum measurements must always cause a significant disturbance: there is no way for them to decouple, and there is no concept of equilibrium in a statistical sense. There are parallels here with what happens when we measure computers with computers. They are always far from any kind of statistical equilibrium. This much we can know, and yet the quantum world seems even stranger in disallowing certainty in measurement in a way that goes beyond our understanding[136].

Physicist Max Born (1882-1970) showed that, for whatever reason, the theoretical apparatus of quantum mechanics could, at best, yield *probabilities* of obtaining certain measured values, not the actual values one would obtain, as would be the case in Newtonian mechanics. In other words, it could not tell us precisely about the state of a quantum object, but it could characterize its statistical behaviour in a way that would be compatible with a process of repeated observation. For some scientists, this was a major setback. They believed that the world should be deterministic, and yet the best theory was not.

In spite of this philosophical blow, one could make good progress in understanding physical systems. Since the theory had no separable model for observation, it was impossible to know whether that uncertainty originated from the measurement process or something deeper, but the question was irrelevant because it was unanswerable[137]. One could still build sufficient certainty to manipulate atomic systems in practice.

In a similar way, if we are interested in understanding digital information systems both dynamically and semantically, we must also construct theoretical models to describe their dynamics using measurements obtained without a clear separation of scales, and lessons may be learnt from quantum mechanics and statistical mechanics to that end. This is not primarily because the technology is shrinking to quantum sizes (although that is also true), but rather because quantum and statistical physics are accomplished theories of *incomplete information*, where autonomous parts, composed of digital states, interact through message passing. Recall how these basic boundary conditions were baked into the formulations of Feynman and Schwinger. There is a dynamical similarity at work.

It was the essence of this idea that I had used to model the spectrum of fluctuations for online services in 2000, obtaining average results that could be used to make predictions (see Chapter 4). Quantum and statistical mechanics are about making the best of a bad situation; and they are, in fact, highly successful approaches to understanding systems where we *cannot* know details with sufficient resolution to allow determinism. Quantum measurement is truly both a black box and a flowing river at the same time. In that respect, it is a little like trying to see what goes on in the core of a computer relative to what outward manifestations we see. One has no real idea what is really inside the box before interacting with it, but every time one observes, we know that it is changed forever.

How can one know anything about a non-deterministic world, if every interaction possibly changes a state into something else? Part of the answer is that there is still the notion of *sufficient stability* due to 'confining potentials barriers', analogous to the hills and valleys in chapter 2. These set limits on what can happen. The fact that quantum mechanics is able to predict so much, so correctly is a testament to the cleverness of the theory in focusing on what an observer *can* know.

We should not take the analogy between quantum theory and computing too far, but there is good reason to be inspired by its successes in the face of incomplete information. If we cannot even infer the observed behaviour of infrastructure in the most mission-critical systems, with quantifiable certainty, then we have no right to trust human lives to it.

Perhaps the most important lesson one can take from quantum mechanics is that dynamics always win over semantics: in order to mean something at all, things first have to happen in a predictable way. Getting an answer that we can rely on is more important than understanding what it means about the inner workings of the system itself, because we are going to impose our own semantics on it anyway. As long as observers act as faithful transducers, converting observations into an effective model we can build from, it doesn't matter what the underlying semantics are, in the intermediate message channels or elsewhere in a place we cannot see. What we need to make progress is simply a way to remove the sensitivity of observations to the inevitable uncertainty they contain.

8

The Equilibrium of Knowing

Or how not to disagree with yourself

"Of all the principles that can be proposed for this purpose, I think there is none more general, more exact, or easier to apply than that we have used in this work; it consists of making the sum of the squares of the errors a minimum. By this method, a kind of equilibrium is established among the errors which, since it prevents the extremes from dominating, is appropriate for revealing the state of the system which most nearly approaches the truth."

– Adrien-Marie Legendre, 1805

Statistics is the name given to that mathematical discipline which concerns itself with characterizing measurements. It determines what we can know about what we have seen. Ludwig Boltzmann made impressive use of probability and statistics at a time when the ideas were still controversial. His analyses of the thermodynamic systems of the industrial revolution practically inferred the existence of atoms, before they were even observed. There is power in theoretical reasoning, provided it is based on a sound grasp of reality. Max Born later showed something similar was possible for the new quantum theory, an even stranger predictive framework. Today it is widely believed, in science, that we cannot really understand observational data without an understanding of the most basic concepts in statistics. Now, this applies to computers too.

The future is an unpredictable phenomenon. No matter what we might hope, it is not deterministic. We express beliefs and expectations about it, based on the reckoning of chance and probability, but of course we cannot ever know what the future will bring with complete certainty. To draw useful conclusions with statistics, we are entirely limited by what we know already about the origins and patterns of data we may analyze. The principal aim of statistics is to point out the plausible characteristics about data, with a quantifiable level of certainty. In colloquial terms, statistics is about making the best of imperfect information.

The history of statistics is closely allied with the concepts of probability, and stretches back into antiquity. The earliest ideas like the arithmetic mean (commonly known as the ordinary average) were known even to the ancient Greeks[138]. However, it was not until the mid-17th century that the concepts of randomness were developed more fully, by Pierre de Fermat (ca. 1607-1665), Blaise Pascal (1623-1662) and Christiaan Huygens (1629-1695), and were used by Galileo to deal with the uncertainties in their observations of the heavens.

Today, statistics has evolved into a complex field of study, with many aspects and dimensions to its approach[139]. We shall only be able to make the tiniest scratch on the surface of its methods here, to hint at a solution to the dilemmas of knowing in uncertain environments.

Chance and statistics are closely related. Chance is typically thought of as a way to predict the future, whereas statistics is a way to understand the past. If one believes that what happened in the past is a good guide to what will continue in the future, there is the possibility of making predictions, by turning the past into estimates about the future. This is what probability theory is about. Statistics therefore looks to the characterization of patterns and signatures in observed data: traces of regularity from which we might discern meaning or at least repetitive inference. The tools of statistics begin with analyzing and estimating the characteristics of observed data.

Francis Bacon (1561-1626), is often considered to be the father of the modern philosophy of science, particularly experimentation or *empirical* science. He proposed that one should always begin by categorizing a phenomenon, essentially creating a standard set of characteristics by which to compare similar phenomena. This is why zoologists spend time watching animals and their habits before trying to explain why they behave as they do. In statistics, this idea is formalized by placing data into categories. Some categories are easy to decide, like 'heads' and 'tails' for coins tossed; others are more arbitrary, such as age groups: 0—9, 10—19, 20—35, 36—50, and so on. Why these categories, and not some others?

Once certain categories have been agreed upon, one may then count how many measurements fall into these categories. The result is a histogram, or frequency distribution (see Figure 8.1).

Plotting the results graphically is a natural way to organize data for our perception. The histogram is a special case of a frequency distribution with discrete categories. Figure 8.1 shows an example, based on an imaginary experiment in which messages consisting of the alphabetic characters $A, B, C, D, E, \ldots$, are received by a receiver. For example, in an experiment with coins, we would

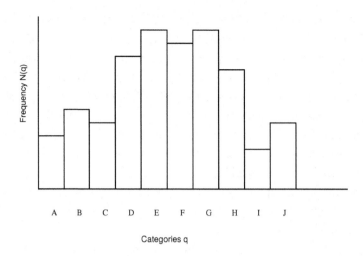

Fig. 8.1.   A histogram counts the number of observations $N(q)$ that fall into a given category q.

have just two symbols: one for heads and one for tails (A and B, or H and T, etc.).

A distribution is thus a pictorial representation of how many observations we see in each category. In physics, one sometimes calls this a spectrum, as in the case of the Planck spectrum, mentioned in chapter 3, because the composite light, received from a source like the sun, can be categorized into the relative strengths of its component parts using a prism to make an artificial rainbow. It's a way of attributing a pattern or 'signature' to a phenomenon, given by the shape of the histogram, that is sometimes particular to it. The usefulness of identifying a pattern is entirely dependent on choosing helpful categories. If one categorizes data into categories that do not reveal any contrasts, we learn nothing. For instance, if we categorized cups into 'tall' and 'taller' (as certain coffee franchises seem to do), the semantics of the results would not reveal useful analytical information. But if one categorizes by height in whole numbers of centimetres, it would offer a much higher resolution of insight.

Frequency analysis is one of the earliest uses for statistics, going back to the early Islamic Empire, where it was used for code breaking. Writings from the 9th century book entitled: "Manuscript on Deciphering Cryptographic Messages", written by Al-Kindi (801-873) gave a detailed description of how to use frequency analysis to decipher encrypted messages[140]. The idea was that certain letters in any language occur more often than others.

If one makes a histogram of all the occurrences of different character symbols, within a sufficiently large text, then one sees a signature pattern for the relative frequencies of the different letters. The letter 'e' is most common in English, for instance. If one encrypts English text by swapping the symbols for secret symbols, the code-equivalent of the letter 'e' would still be the most frequently occurring. Thus, one can begin to crack the code by using frequency analysis of this kind to reveal the true identities on certain symbols. This same kind of frequency analysis might possibly have spurred on the development of digital computers in the mechanical age of the industrial revolution too. Mathematician and inventor Charles Babbage (1791-1871) made use of the technique to decipher 'Le chiffre indéchiffrable ', or the indecipherable cipher, also known as the Vigenère cipher[141], during the 1800s.

In statistics, frequency refers to how frequently the occurrences of different observational categories occur—not to be confused with the frequency of radiation discussed in Chapter 3, which measures how frequently a wave rises and falls over a given time or distance[142].

Shape, symmetry, and characteristic values are the first things we look for in a statistical distribution. After that, we look for characteristic scales. Two quantities are particularly useful as characteristic scales in a system: the *mean*, written $E(q)$, and the *standard deviation*, written $\sigma(q)$. Let's try to get a feel for how the first steps work.

An average, known as the statistical mean value, is a characteristic value that removes common kinds of noise, somewhat analogous to the balanced-line cable we mentioned in Chapter 7. It is an easy and convenient way of computing a representative value from a body of data, given that the body of data satisfies the two assumptions of measurement.

The mean is found by adding the values together and then dividing by the number of them, so that any random noise cancels out[143]. Like the cable, it works well as long as it is used correctly. Suppose, in successive experiments, we measure the length of a book in centimetres, or the temperature of a piece of machinery. A set of measurements might be made by different experimenters, with different instruments, or at different times. The fact that there are different values implies that there is uncertainty about the length. Thus, we begin by collecting all of the measurements q. Suppose they look like these:

$$29.1, \quad 29.2, \quad 29.1, \quad 29.0, \quad 30$$

Now, an inexperienced experimentalist might begin by feeding these numbers into a formula, looking for a magical answer for the 'right value'; however, a smarter experimenter would realize there is no obvious right value, and rather look at the values and ask: do they make sense? Something immediately stands out: most of the results are very close together at about 29 centimetres, but one (30cm) is much larger.

Knowing that the data were made by humans, measuring with various rulers, we could immediately conclude that one of the measurements was made poorly, by someone who didn't care about the accuracy – they rounded the value up to the nearest half decimetre. This is actually not as terrible a crime as it might appear to be; indeed, the perpetrator was probably a physicist who had the following thought process: this book is an object on the scale of tens of centimetres, no particular accuracy is needed beyond a general order of magnitude, so I'll round this up to the nearest decimetre. When humans are involved, the difficulty of interpretation gets a lot more complicated, because different people think in different ways.

Depending on the context and intent of the measurement, a rounding up of numbers might be an entirely reasonable thing to do. However, the other experimenters all worked to the accuracy of a fraction of a centimetre, so mixing these two conventions in a single set of data is going to distort the results.

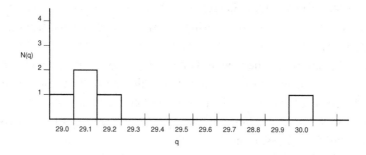

Fig. 8.2. A histogram of distribution of book measurements.

All is not lost, however, if we follow statistical method. We could begin by plotting a histogram of the data (see figure 8.2). This immediately reveals the peculiar measurement at 30. A value like this is sometimes called an outlier, or an anomaly, because it lies outside the range of the main body of results. Visual inspection is often enough to exclude it from the data, but we might not know enough to do that immediately. Suppose we now work out the mean value, with and without the outlying point. The mean value with the anomalous point would be :

$$E_{\text{contaminated}}(q) = \frac{29.1 + 29.2 + 29.1 + 29.0 + 30}{5} = 29.3$$

Notice that we round the value 29.28 to 29.3 to be consistent in the amount of uncertainty. The mean value is made artificially high by the anomalous entry. Calculating without the anomalous point gives:

$$E_{\text{clean}}(q) = \frac{29.1 + 29.2 + 29.1 + 29.0}{4} = 29.1$$

Now the result looks like what one would expect. It is not what the raw data tells us, but we have a model in our minds about what is reasonable, and the second version seems more reasonable.

To get an idea of how confident we are in the result for the mean, we have a simple measure of uncertainty in the standard deviation, which is the average distance between the mean-value and any of the actual data points. If the mean value is like the 'centre of gravity' of the data, then then standard deviation is like their approximate radius around it. The accuracy of this measure as a characteristic scale depends a lot on the shape of the distribution itself, but it is the simplest thing to start with.

The deviation of a data-point is its distance (i.e. difference) from the mean. We use the Greek symbol Δ (delta) to represent a difference:

$$\Delta_1 = 29.1 - 29.1 = 0$$
$$\Delta_2 = 29.2 - 29.1 = 0.1$$
$$\Delta_3 = 29.1 - 29.1 = 0$$
$$\Delta_4 = 29.0 - 29.1 = -0.1$$
$$\Delta_5 = 30.0 - 29.1 = 0.9.$$

Sometimes the distance is positive and sometimes it is negative, that is why it cancels out of the mean value.

To estimate the uncertainty, however, we use the theorem due to Pythagoras, which says that independent changes should be represented as geometrically orthogonal quantities, and added as a sum of squares: The average Pythagorean square distance is the square root of the sum of the squares, also called a root mean square. This is the standard deviation. It is always a positive number:

$$\sigma_{\text{contaminated}} = \sqrt{\frac{\Delta_1^2 + \Delta_2^2 + \Delta_3^2 + \Delta_4^2 + \Delta_5^2}{5}} = \sqrt{\frac{0.83}{5}} = 0.4$$

and

$$\sigma_{\text{clean}} = \sqrt{\frac{\Delta_1^2 + \Delta_2^2 + \Delta_3^2 + \Delta_4^2}{4}} = \sqrt{\frac{0.02}{4}} = 0.1$$

When quoting measured values from a body of data, it is standard practice to quote the mean value, plus or minus random error, characterized here by σ.

The theory of errors then tells us that we should write that our estimates of the measured size of the book are:

$$q_{\text{contaminated}} \simeq 29.3 \pm 0.4$$

and

$$q_{\text{clean}} \simeq 29.1 \pm 0.1$$

So what is the answer to the question, what is the size of the book? The first answer claims that the size is about 29.3 centimetres, but we only know to within a weak tolerance of plus or minus 0.4, so it could be as low as 28.9 or as high as 29.7. That does not look very precise. The second answer claims that the answer is about 29.1 centimetres, plus or minus 0.1. So it could be as low as 29.0 or as much as 29.2. This seems to be more precise (smaller uncertainty). Which do you think is most likely?

Even though the world is composed of whole numbers (integers) of discrete atoms, we need real numbers like the decimal fractions used here (e.g. 29.1), because the methods of averaging transform relative scales. If one book is twice the size of another, it is convenient to be able to say that the second one is 0.5 times the size of the first. We must be able to express fractions to describe this relativity of viewpoint.

The statistical mean works by adding all the observations together, so that the positive and negative deviations from the supposed value tend to cancel out; then it scales the total down to the original size by dividing by the number of measurements. The standard deviation $\sigma(q)$ tries to capture the approximate scale of the fluctuations—how much short, or over the line, the measurements are. It takes the mean as its reference point, assuming that the mean is the right characteristic value, and then it works out its own mean, using an average Pythagoras distance. These processes involve scaling numbers down, and this leads to the concept of fractional amounts, even though the real objects are still whole.

The fact that dividing a sum by a number does not give an exact whole number does not mean we have achieved a greater degree of accuracy in measurement by calculating an average (the standard deviation tells us how accurate we can claim to be). For example, think of the analogy of a digital camera which has a certain number of pixels, a density of dots that can be measured. Low resolution pictures look like old movies, grainy and blurred. High resolution pictures have more dots per square centimetre. Suppose we imitate the averaging procedure by taking four pictures, then laying them next to one another as one large picture. Then we scale them back down to the original size of one picture by taking a picture of the four pictures (see Figure 8.3).

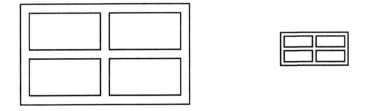

Fig. 8.3. Add together four pictures and divide by the number to scale back to the original size. Rescaling four pictures with low resolution does not lead to a higher resolution.

The picture we take of the other four pictures does not retain the resolution of each of the individual pictures, even though we divide each point by two in height and width. The limiting factor is the measuring final instrument that took all of the pictures: the camera. Each of the pictures get projected onto the same low resolution camera, and therefore ends up more blurred than before. No amount of rescaling can alter its limitations. Averaging does not improve the granularity of the image, it makes it worse. So it's important not to over-do the decimal places.

If we start out with a list of numbers measured to one decimal place accuracy, then average of those will also have about one decimal place of accuracy, not two or three, simply because the numbers do not divide exactly. This is what the standard deviation essentially points out, and it is the reason why we quote measurements:

$$\text{Characteristic value} = \text{mean} \pm \text{uncertainty}.$$

The simplest measure of the uncertainty would be to take the main scales of variation $E(\text{data}) \pm \sigma(\text{data})$, though more sophisticated estimates are routinely made, depending on the experimental setup. Notice that one does not quote the maximum possible error, but rather a more balanced estimate, as one has no more reason to trust the maximum than any one of the data points themselves. The admission of uncertainty applies to everything, thus we look for a kind of self-consistent account, not a 'right answer'. The uncertainty marked in graphs and plots by marking error bars on data points to highlight the limitations of resolution (see figure 8.4, and compare to figure 4.8).

Fractions arise from ratios (the so-called rational numbers), and they are the very basis of scaling. Recall the dimensionless ratios of Chapter 2. Real numbers don't exist in nature, but they allow incredibly beautiful, elegant models to be written down, which reveal deep relationships in ways that would be impos-

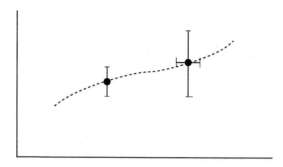

Fig. 8.4.   Data values are plotted with 'error bars' indicating the uncertainty in the axes on each data point, calculated from repetition.

sible if we had to worry about always using whole numbers.

In Chapter 7, I recalled an episode in which two graduate students noticed that the probes they used to measure computer performance were masking the actual measurements they wanted to make: their software made such a large impact on the system itself that they could not see the wood for the trees, so to speak. The idea of mean and standard deviation, even at the most elementary level, gives us a way to work around these challenges, with a little creativity.

If one is able to characterize what is typical or normal, or even what is locally stable about a measurement (see Figure 4.2), then it becomes possible to separate signals from one another by approximate subtraction. There is an inherent uncertainty in being able to do this, but it is possible to make progress and to come up with a quantitative estimate of the uncertainty involved. This is more or less how the discipline of statistics developed. The same basic skills need to be brought into the engineering of information systems too. Today, we treat information systems as if they were something apart from the real world, as if they are somehow exempt from common sense principles.

In the examples above, I deliberately chose cases where the pattern of data looked wrong, because this often happens during measurements, and I also deliberately kept two working models for the answer. This emphasizes that blind methods like statistics cannot replace common sense judgement, but can help us to reach decisions. If we try to collect data automatically for immediate use in a software system, there is a high chance that some erroneous conclusions could be formed and used. Recall the passenger flight disaster from Chapter 2, in which a sequence of events was initiated by a problem with a sensor.

Two interpretations of the data emerged from the example. With prior common sense, the second possibility seemed to be a more likely interpretation of the data, but only because we had some assumptions in mind, based on what we know about books, rulers, measurements, and measurers. Without those assumptions, one truly cannot be sure what the correct answer is, without going back and investigating further. Neither answer was incorrect, but the certainty of the conclusion was affected.

Do we have a right to exclude a funny looking data point? Maybe yes, maybe no. As the number of data values gets larger, our confidence in one or other model would doubtless change. Perhaps the book really is closer to 30cm and there were several faulty measurements with badly calibrated rulers. How can we be sure? Again, this is a difficult problem.

Automated collection of data values makes it all too easy to feed data into standard tools, without such considerations, and hope for the best. That might lead to real problems in a technological setting, if we intend to draw conclusions from the results.

Certain histogram shapes, i.e. certain statistical distributions crop up for repeatedly for good reasons. The 'normal distribution', for example, has a special importance in science, because it describes events that are causally independent. The normal distribution (often called the *bell curve* in popular media, because of its shape) was first derived by Abraham De Moivre in 1733 to analyse the tossing of coins, but it often goes by the name of the Gaussian, since Gauss analyzed it later in detail. The Boltzmann distribution is another important distribution. Both of these are examples of so-called 'maximum uncertainty' distributions, meaning that their shape can be explained by assuming that variations in measurements are completely random, i.e. we know basically nothing about them except the constraints in which they are measured.

The normal distribution is so useful for random independent errors that it is sometimes assumed to be lurking behind the answer, even when its use it not justified. The following quote summarizes the feelings many have about its universality[144]:

> "Everyone believes in the exponential law of errors; the experimenters because they think it can be proved by mathematics; and the mathematicians because they believe it has been established by observation."

Some phenomena we observe and measure have values that we never expect to change. The rest-mass of an electron, for example, is believed to be a universal constant at all times and in all places[145]. The speed of light in a vacuum, and Planck's constant are other examples. Other values, like the height of a four-year-old child, we do not expect to have fixed values, but can be characterized by a typical value and a description of how much variation there is.

Variations can occur because an instrument is too sensitive, and picks up every imperfection or variation, like scratches on an LP or mountains on the Moon, or because the instrument generates its own noise and the measurement process is unreliable. Separating out these issues is a matter for definitions as well as standard measures, i.e. semantics. So what is the correct answer? In each case, the bottom line is that we just don't know—and we shouldn't pretend to. We have incomplete information. There is no single 'correct answer'.

In fact this is a deeper issue: we prefer to believe in absolutes, when our senses are only designed to compare relative measurements. Absolutism is a cultural bias, that blossomed during Newton's model of clockwork certainty, but the mental models we use to perceive the world make heavy use of comparisons. This opens us to being fooled by simple illusions, as we see in the classic illusion (see Figure 8.5). To try to avoid these kinds of illusions, we make independent instruments that we trust to provide an objective sense of reality. We aim to capture a property without destroying it, but the inconstancy of the environment and the measuring apparatuses themselves infuses doubts at every level. The main task of empirical science is not to eliminate such doubts, but to get them under control.

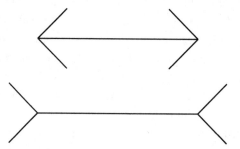

Fig. 8.5.   A classic illusion. The horizontal lines are the same length, but the one in the lower figure that has greatest total extent seems longer.

Statistics help us to gather repeated observation and fold it into experience, i.e. to 'know' the results of observations, as intimately as we know a friend, but this is not an infallible strategy. There are plenty of pitfalls and poor choices to be made when using statistics together with observation. We have to make sure we ask the kinds of questions that can be analyzed reasonably.

For example, suppose we wanted to answer the question: is statistics really science, mathematics, art, engineering, numerology? Then we might try to sample some data. There is no way of answering this except to measure the court of human opinion, so we might go out into the world and ask its users and practitioners what they think; please tell us which of these categories you believe statistics belongs in. The interviewees do their best to come up with a result, and we end up with a histogram of votes:

Science: 32 votes
Mathematics: 43 votes
Art: 98 votes
Engineering: 12 votes
Numerology: 1 vote

These results might be accurately measured or not, but they are basically flawed, either way. Why? Because, there is nothing more we can say about the numbers. How can we gauge how accurate they are? How do we explain them? What can we use them for? We could try to speculate about who gave the different answers and why, but that would be to embark upon supposition and speculation.

There is no way to go forward characterizing the uncertainty with which the measurements were made, nor what it may be attributable to. It is hard to say whether one category is right or wrong, or average, because it is an entirely subjective semantic result. The question was phrased in semantic choices, which are not easily understood, measured or assessed. The tool for analysing semantics is logic, not statistics.

Suppose, instead, we designed the experiment to use ordinals: what percentage of science do you believe statistics represents? Now the semantics are quite clear and universal, and we've created an ordered measuring scale:

0—24%: 1
25—49%: 40
50—74%: 60
75—100%: 85

It is possible to work out average values from the ordered scale, with characteristic scales and uncertainties quite easily.

If we ask semantically loaded questions, the result typically ends up being a belief about what other people believe about some artificially imposed categories, which might or might not fit their own mental model. In a sense, the uncertainty in such an answer is maximal, but we have no way to represent it, or own up to it.

The Scottish philosopher David Hume (1711-1776) made a crucial observation about uncertainty. He argued that there are really two kinds of knowledge (which we may loosely associate with statistics and semantics). We have direct observations of a world we know to be real, which are imperfect, limited, and perhaps even faulty. This implies uncertainty. Then we have idealized models about which we can reason perfectly, prove theorems, and calculate exact answers. However, we cannot know how well the models represent reality. This also implies uncertainty. Thus, Hume argued, we are trapped between the inability to generalize observations (upwards) from the specific to a general conclusion, and the inability to verify the details (downwards) from an embracing theory to actual observations. Certainty is thus held hostage by the physical and semantic scales of the world around us.

Statistical frequency analysis is about characterizing how the fractional parts of a system differ, based in information that is currently available. Probability is about using this assumed knowledge of the past and present to say something about the future.

Frequency analysis leads to an interpretation of probability as documentation of the past, known as the *frequentist* interpretation. Another definition is based on the idea of *belief* estimation, and it known as the Bayesian interpretation. The distinction between these viewpoints is significant.

In the frequentist view, data are measured and classified into categories, as in a histogram, so that we end up with a number N_i, measured in units of observations. This is the frequency for finding each category labelled by symbol q_i, with $i = 1, 2, 3, \ldots, C$. To turn this number into a probability, all we have to do is rescale or renormalize it so that the sum of all the possibilities adds up to 1. Probability is like percentages except the numbers add strictly up to 1 instead of 100.

A probability is another example of dimensionless ratio: a dimensionless ratio of frequencies, measured in units of 'observations per experimental trial'. That suggests that probability values will be important thresholds in behaviour. We say that the probability of being in category q_i is defined by

$$p_4 = \text{Prob}(q_4) = \frac{N_4}{N_{\text{total}}},$$

where $N_{\text{total}} = N_1 + N_2 + \ldots + N_C$, and the probabilities have been normalized so that they add up to 1:

$$p_1 + p_2 \ldots p_C = 1.$$

The assumption, in the frequentist view, is that what happened up to the present is an adequate predictor of what is going to be true in the future. One does not expect to get any new information in the future.

With this choice of scale, complete certainty represents a probability of 1 that something will happen, or a probability of 0 that it will not happen, and complete uncertainty represents the case when all the probability of all categories is exactly the same:

$$p_1 = p_2 \ldots = p_C = \frac{1}{C}.$$

This is called a maximum uncertainty distribution.

There is a little bit of semantic legerdemain in going from frequency measurement to probability: we flip suddenly from a measurement of the past to a prediction about the future. A probability is generally interpreted as a belief about what is quite likely to happen in the future. If something happened many times in the past, and the conditions of the experiment are still true, then it is reasonable to imagine that the same pattern might continue in the future. However, there are some obvious flaws in this thinking.

If we collect too little evidence, say just one or two measurements, we can still define a probability using the formula above, but the body of evidence would not be convincing. For example, if we toss a coin twice and get heads twice, the frequency analysis would say $N_{\text{heads}} = 2$, $N_{\text{tails}} = 0$, so Prob(heads) = 1 and Prob(tails) = 0. We know that, an unbiased coin has an equal probability of measuring heads and tails, but we might only see that equality as the number of coin tosses becomes very large or even infinite.

A solution to this issue was suggested by Thomas Bayes (1701-1761), who suggested that probabilities should be treated as beliefs from the beginning, and frequency analysis can be a starting point for a 'belief', or we might start from a different belief and use each new piece of evidence to modify it. Bayes was pointing out that there is no sense in which the past truly predicts the future, but it can surely affect our belief about it. In his interpretation, a knowledge of the past is like a boundary condition on the solution of an equation for the future: a point of certain knowledge from which to extrapolate forwards.

In the Bayesian interpretation, we can return to an operator view of evolving states: which now represents the state of our certainty about different outcomes:

(Update evidence) old probability distribution $\longrightarrow$ new distribution

If this process converges to a fixed point, we can say that we've learnt a stable set of expectations about the future. This model is obviously compatible with the operator view of systems and messaging, as well as the concepts of detailed balance and equilibrium, and it offers technologists a plausible way to learn the state of the world on the fly, without having to wait for a significant body of evidence.

The Bayesian view is a way to implement very cheap learning about the past, which is compatible with the perturbative view of stability discussed earlier in the book. If you recall, the first assumption of measurement is that the conditions are constant, and the second assumption is that the act of measuring will not affect the measurement itself. I pointed out, in the last chapter, that this is very difficult to achieve in a technology setting, because virtual computers are moved around leading to changing conditions, and measuring them is often a noticeable perturbation on their state. Moreover, waiting for multiple measurements under similar conditions might take so long that the system has changed before we arrive at a result, and (last but not least) we need to know how new observations compare to old ones, however calculating an arithmetic mean and standard deviation on the fly, from a body of evidence, is an expensive process that would certainty affect the system. It seems that we are doomed to violate the two assumptions of measurement in information technology.

Fortunately, the Bayesian view of statistics allows us to minimize the impact of these violations in both cases. The methods used under the name of Bayesian statistics are not always strictly according to the formulae of probabilities that Bayes inspired, but keep rather to the spirit of the interpretation[146].

The essence of Bayes insight, which he was too early to fully appreciate himself, was that we should not think of probabilities as estimators of prediction, but as dimensionless scaling ratios in the renormalization of uncertainty.

In 2002, based on the studies we had made at the University College about computer behaviour, I proposed a simple way of performing measurements with minimal damage to the two assumptions, for the Computer Immunology project.

To minimize the uncertainty and avoid unnecessary variation, we need a scale for estimating the uncertainty. One can use the only fact that the system does not change unpredictably, but has a very strong pattern that can be exploited, namely the regular pattern of the human working week (see Figure 4.8). By factoring out this pattern, the remainder of the problem became essentially an equilibrium at every equivalent time-slice during a week, with minimal uncertainty. In effect, the periodicity of the weekly pattern, meant that it was possible to factor time into two separate processes: what happened from minute to minute during a week, and what happened during the same minutes from week to week. Our measurements had shown that this was the way to get the smallest error bars on measurement, and hence the best signal to noise ratio on belief.

Atomizing the week into five-minute intervals allowed each interval to be treated as an independent system that was likely to reach equilibrium, and thus repeated measurements about it would also be near equilibrium. It was another case of pull things apart to keep them together, in this case atomizing the week, to keep predictability together.

The argument goes like this. Suppose we take a series of measurements $q_1, q_2, q_3, \ldots$ The mean value would be the sum divided by the number of points, but to calculate it we have to both remember all the points and update a growing calculation on every update. The calculation is as long as there are points, or we say it is order N, where N is the number of points. However, we can estimate an average estimator for these by using a convex combination iterated like an operator convergence process:

$$E_{\text{new}}(q) \to \alpha\, q_{\text{new}} + (1 - \alpha)E_{\text{previous}}(q).$$

where $1 - \alpha$ is the amount we remember on each iteration, and α is the fraction of novelty we allow in.

We can tune the value of α, between zero and one, it acts like a memory parameter. If α is zero, then the new value q_{new} is not used at all, and we are stuck in the past, always keeping the previous value, which therefore never changes. If α equals one, so that $1 - \alpha$ is zero, then we use only the latest measured value q and the past is immediately forgotten. Any value of α between these limits will balance remembering and forgetting.

This formula iterated leads to an interesting behaviour, which nicely balances the need to remember the recent past and forget the distant past. If we iterate, i.e. apply this formula again and again at regular time intervals, it doesn't just remember the previous value of the quantity q, but all of them, and it gradually forgets the older values in a controlled way over time. Mathematically, it generates a geometric series, as we met in Zeno's paradox in Chapter 3. Assuming that we start from memory state q_0, the first time:

$$E(q) = \alpha q_1 + (1 - \alpha)q_0.$$

We store this value until the next round of measurement, and then we measure q_2 and take the whole of the previous $E(q)$ and add it:

$$E(q) = \alpha q_2 + (1 - \alpha)\left(\alpha q_1 + (1 - \alpha)q_0\right)$$

Then we repeat this procedure on every new measurement, at regular intervals. Suppose $\alpha = \frac{1}{2}$, then after one iteration this looks like an arithmetic mean, with some small corrections:

$$E(q) \to \frac{1}{2}(q_1 + q_0)$$

After two more iterations, it becomes

$$E(q) \rightarrow \frac{1}{2}q_3 + \frac{1}{4}q_2 + \frac{1}{8}(q_1 + q_0)$$

If we prime the initial memory so that $q_0 = 0$, this is a simple geometric series[147]. In fact, as we iterate this more and more times, it behaves like an average in which older terms get smaller and smaller, by a factor of α. If the measurement q stops changing, then it converges to that value after some iterations.

Thus, although this is not a traditional mean value, it fulfils the criteria for an average measure, with the right dimensions and the right order of magnitude, and it can be used at almost no cost to track measurements to an order of magnitude running average. It is an expectation value, a plausible scale against which to measure expectation of new values.

The cost saving in using this algorithm versus a traditional computation of a mean value is substantial, somewhere between 10 and 100 times cheaper. For a traditional average, one would have to store about ten times as much data, with the overhead of retrieval plus the computation of a result of the order of tens of values every five minutes. Moreover, forgetting old values would require additional computation. For a system that needs to run in real time, this cost of computation is an important saving that makes measurement a viable tool.

In artificial intelligence, this kind of algorithm is called machine learning. Specifically, it is a process of *unsupervised learning*, because humans don't have to train and oversee the process and teach it how to recognize good from bad. The algorithm will adapt predictably to changes in the circumstances of the data automatically. Noise is eliminated in essentially the same way that fast and slow variables were separated in chapter 4, through the use of elementary statistics. Moreover, at every moment, we have the actual current value and enough history to be able to gauge the approximate meaning of the new measurement, based on past behaviour. This is the best we can do in a non-equilibrium system.

We've now covered enough statistics to understand a central part of the theory of communication by Claude Shannon in his 1948 masterpiece, and how it applies to Computer Immunology. Shannon realized that information was not merely a stream of symbols, but that it had unique content, and that this could be measured. One might transmit a message, for instance, and then repeat it a hundred times, adding no extra information to the first transmission. Repetition is merely redundancy. Shannon therefore defined a notion of intrinsic information, using the statistical distribution function for a message. The intrinsic information was the minimum size to which a message might be compressed without compromising the ability to recreate the full message.

His measure is simple to write down. If one imagines a message being composed of C different kinds of symbols (so $C = 2$ for binary 1 and 0), then Shannon defined the intrinsic information per symbol of any message to be:

$$\text{Intrinsic information per message symbol} = -\sum_{i=1}^{C} p_i \log pi.$$

where p_i is the frequentist probability, or normalized frequency, of finding the symbol i in the message. Because the value is given per symbol, it is an average measure for any specific message, so it cannot tell us what the message is about, only measure its overall complexity. If a message contains only a single symbol, repeated any number of times, then the information is zero, as there must be some variation to encode information. The information takes on a maximum value if every symbol in the alphabet is used in equal amounts, so that there is the greatest mixing of content.

This is called a maximum uncertainty distribution, as mentioned above[148]. Here, uncertainty refers to what the next symbol in a message might be, as in the code-breaker frequency analysis of the Vigenère cipher. Obviously, that is maximal if every symbol is used equally often.

The intrinsic information can be understood quite easily in pictorial form (see the left hand diagram in figure 8.6)[149]. Every message we can create is like a unique path through a lattice of symbols. This is easiest to draw for binary messages with just two symbols 1 and 0.

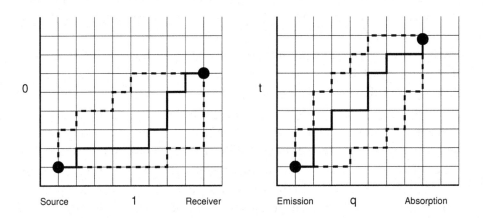

Fig. 8.6. Informational messages and quantum trajectories share the same basic construction. The solid line is the specific message and the dotted lines are alternatives with the same constraints.

The two axes count the frequencies of the symbols 1 and 0. The dots represent the points where source and the receiver emit and absorb the message. The message on the left figure thus represents the message 1011110100101.

The rectangle demarked by the source and receiver dots contains every possible path between these end points, with the same kind and number of symbols, i.e. all the messages of the same length and same probability distribution. A particular message is one out of this total number, and we need to label each one to distinguish one from the other. The intrinsic information is thus defined as the length of a message we would have to send someone to communicate this label, and identify the message uniquely, against the alternatives.

In chapter 4, I pointed out that the Feynman-Schwinger formulation of quantum theory was closely related to information transmission. We can now see this pictorially. The right hand picture in figure 8.6 is the diagram normally used to show Feynman's 'sum over paths' version of quantum mechanics. Each path is a digital message. Instead of alphabetic symbols, it comprises discrete positions and times (coordinates in discrete spacetime). The source and receiver, also represented in Schwinger's formulation, define the limits of the message in space and time, between the quantum transition being measured, and the measuring instrument.

The size of the spacetime message symbols (the graininess of spacetime itself) is so small (the order of the Planck length) that this looks pseudo-continuous to most measurements. Feynman showed that all paths, not just a single unique message, contribute to physical processes in the quantum world. Thus Newton's smooth trajectories are replaced by multiple Markov chains, when we look closely enough. This crowns the deep connection between digital information and physics that I've described in the book up to this point.

It is perhaps strange to think about the movement of physical objects as a kind of message, in which the content is increments of position and time, but that is merest part of the strangeness of the world at the quantum level. This is just formulation.

Shannon's intrinsic information predicts that, if a message contains redundancy, it can be compressed without loss of information by representing the same pattern of variation with a smaller number of symbols. Then one could imagine taking the pictorial representation of the message, like in figure 8.6, and scaling it down to represent the same shape, but using fewer squares. This is how data compression software like 'zip' works. A large message, full of redundancy, can be rescaled as a small one, as long as it has an equivalent symbol distribution. we can say it contains the same amount of variability, and variability is information (recall figure 4.1 where noise increased the amount of information). It might have to be recoded in a completely different alphabet to allow this to happen, but Shannon showed that this was theoretically possible.

In arriving at his definition of intrinsic information, Shannon made an important connection between the general notion of information, and the idea of order and entropy in the statistical mechanics of Boltzmann. Apart from a dimensional scale of the Boltzmann constant, the Shannon intrinsic information is numerically equal to Boltzmann's H function, which he showed was equivalent to the thermodynamic entropy (a measure of energy that becomes unavailable to do work due to its being spread around the system in a state of high uncertainty[150]). Boltzmann effectively showed, 80 years before Shannon's theory, that the information needed to describe the state of a physical system was always maximal at equilibrium. An equilibrium is stable, because it cannot contain any more information, without injecting some from a completely new external source. For that reason, our knowledge of equilibrium states is the most certain knowledge we can obtain.

It seems like a paradox, that we can know more about maximally uncertain equilibrium states than we can about simpler changes. This is a matter of relativity, however. The uncertainty at equilibrium lies in the knowledge of the microscopic processes of detailed balance that maintains it. The knowledge comes from the macro-behaviour, which is constant, and thus requires minimal information to represent it. Once non-equilibrium changes take place, this pendulum swings the other way: now there is less uncertainty in the detailed balance, because the system is more organized and is collectively going somewhere, but our certainty about its total condition is reduced.

Nobel Laureate Ilya Prigogine (1917-2003), whose work on the physics of far-from-equilibrium systems earned him a Nobel prize, wrote[151]:

> "Instability destroys equivalence between the individual and the statistical levels of description. Probabilities then acquire an intrinsic dynamical meaning. We need a 'divine' point of view to retain the idea of determinism. For transient interactions, diffusive terms are negligible. But for *persistent* interactions they become dominant."

Zooming out, from individual parts to the whole, only leads to a radical change of perspective, unless a system is very close to equilibrium. By 'divine' point of view, he implied poetically that one must lift oneself to a higher level, a scale above that is weakly coupled, in order to see the big picture in complex change. The effects of scale can never be underestimated.

Shannon's notion of message compressibility was in my mind when I formalized the notion of convergent operations as part of Computer Immunology[152].

The fixed-point semantics of the CFEngine project's 'zero' operators, discussed in Chapter 5, lead naturally to an equilibrium when applied as a continuous message stream, and also a maximally compressed representation of configuration state.

As long as the symbols in an operator language have a couple of basic properties, then the amount of information required to maintain the state has to incompressible.

1. Change operators must be atomic operations, which can be represented as single symbols, unencumbered by dependencies on one another, else strings of symbols would be needed to express the simplest of things. When symbols are atomic, the order in which they are read and are acted upon does not matter. A message can be read in any order and have the same effect.

2. Change operators should have the 'zero' property, from chapter 5, i.e. they should be convergent (and hence idempotent) when acting on any initial state, so that repetition of a message with respect to intended state has no further effect on the equilibrium.

The CFEngine software's declarative policy language was designed to consist of operators with these properties, to a good approximation, although some practical hindrances prevented a perfect implementation, as we'll see in the next chapter.

In fact, it turns out that these conditions are stronger than necessary. Alva Couch of Tufts University showed that my original idea could be generalized. As long as a system is close to equilibrium, and applies such operations in a cyclic manner, the complete independence of symbols can be relaxed, and some interesting automatic reasoning can take place by coordinating symbols, as we'll also see in the next chapter.

From the viewpoint of relativity, and the distributed systems of today, such a description is optimal because it can be communicated in order to replicate information over a wide area in a highly compressed form. This was CFEngine's modus operandi: the ability to replicate complex system states with a high degree of uniformity in time and space, using a simple and highly compressed declaration of policy. CFEngine's alphabet of convergent operators is thus, to a good approximation, an optimally compressed form of information.

The behaviour of CFEngine's convergent operators has a close analogy to the behaviour of DNA in cells. The DNA code is constant and has no decision-making power. It is used when cells are built, and replicated; but it is also used in daily operation: it is repeatedly examined by cellular maintenance processes. Fortunately, its code is cached in every cell, so no message has to be transmitted from a central organ like the brain. Decisions are made locally, in the context of the local machinery that interprets the DNA. The machinery in each context knows how to extract what information it needs from the total code book. If we replace 'DNA' with 'policy' and 'cell' with 'computer', we have an accurate description of how CFEngine works in computers.

Learning and repairing are thus the two strategies one can build into a system to mitigate uncertainty, and we may add another item to the gallery of fast-and-slow variable divisions, in Chapter 4:

$$\text{Actual state} = \text{convergent application of intended state}$$
$$+ \text{ convergent learning historical state}$$

The relationship a device has with its surroundings makes it an inescapable part of the conditions of the present and also of the history of the recent past, while its policy gives it an eternal sense of right and wrong.

Science has no notion of truth about reality, no absolute knowledge. We sometimes hear phrases like 'scientifically proven' and 'exact science', however these phrases are used for mainly for media grandstanding and have little to do with science itself. What we call science is principally a collection of methods for freely admitting ignorance, managing uncertainty, and building idealized guesses (dignified by the term 'hypotheses') to explain *consistent* views. This stems from a belief that open admissions of uncertainty are the best way to approach a controlled level of certainty. The closest approximation we have is a state of equilibrium between doubt and confirmation.

Science is disloyal by nature (which is why scientists rarely find themselves invited into politics or the boards of different companies), to data, interpretations, and even conclusions. Certainty is fragile to the flow of new information; boundaries that prevent flows play a critical role in whether equilibrium can occur.

As we experiment with technology of all kinds, whether mechanical or digital, we are faced with a stark reality. Determinism has its limits, and those limits are decided by how connected something is to its environment. Measurement is uncertain, and any information system that draws input from outside itself is engaged in a measurement. System must be able to cope with the likelihood of incomplete information and even instability.

The world of computers and information systems offers a fascinating arena in which to experiment on the philosophy of science, because computers exhibit many complex phenomena to rival the natural world. We know that computers are artificial with a core of determinism in mind, but that does not make their behaviour deterministic. So we must explore this problem further. The story about convergence to equilibrium is now complete, and what remains is to look at the least well understood cause of instability: semantics.

9

Clockwork Uncertainty

The arms race between reason and complexity

Kirk: "I'm curious, Doctor, why is it called the M5?"
Daystrom: "Well you see, M1 to M4 were not entirely successful. This one is. M5 is ready to take control of your ship."
Kirk: "Total control?"
Daystrom: "That is what it is designed for."
Kirk: "There are some things that Men have to do to remain Men, your computer takes that away."
Daystrom: "The computer can do your job ... One machine can do all those things that Men do now. Men can go on to do greater things..."

-Star Trek: *The Ultimate Computer*

In the early days of science fiction it was popular to write stories about how computers would go mad and destroy the world[153]. To many who use computers today, this prophesy might have a ring of truth. The fact that computers have taken over the world is clear: they pervade our society from the kitchen to the supermarket; they are in our washing machines, our cars, our supermarket checkouts. They are responsible for monitoring and communicating the movements of a global economy, which, to a large extent, is stylized by the very computer technology it uses. They are in our televisions as well as our PC's, in video games, and in wristwatches. We are now wearing them and soon most likely even implanting them.

Dependence on technology makes society vulnerable to its failures. When a key system fails, the machine stops, it no longer performs its function and the loop of symbiosis is shattered. Not only are humans dependent on technology, but technology is dependent on humans. We live in a human-machine symbiotic society, and increasingly an information rich one run by computers.

The danger of this inter-dependency has to be taken seriously today. Computer warfare is now an everyday occurrence. All one has to do to cripple a society is destroy its information infrastructure. This is the first thing an invasion force does in modern warfare.

Interestingly, some of these issues have been explored before, by people who think up ideas for a living: science fiction writers. During the 1940's, biochemist and science-fiction writer Isaac Asimov (1920-1992) began to consider what kind of problems would result from a society dependent on machines. His machines were robots, i.e. mobile computers with great physical strength, some of whom appeared like humans, and his future society was extremely reliant on these robots. He realized that machines would have the capacity to do great damage, as well as great good, unless they were constrained with a tight leash.

Asimov's answer to this problem was to endow the automata with a set of rules which curbed their behaviour, and prevented them from harming humans. In a sense, a theoretical immune system for humans against machines. Asimov, and his editor John W. Campbell, Jr, together invented the Three Laws of Robotics[154]. The laws went like this:

1. A robot may not injure a human being, or through inaction allow a human being to come to harm.

2. A robot must obey the orders given to it by human beings, except where such orders would conflict with the First Law.

3. A robot must protect its own existence as long as such protection does not conflict with the First or Second Law.

These laws were supposed to protect both humans and complex machinery in unpredictable circumstances. The first law was to protect human safety. The second law placed human decision making at the top of the decision hierarchy, allowing robots to be sacrificed for human needs. The third law was a self-preservation rule: robots would be expensive pieces of hardware, so you would not want to lose them if it were avoidable.

It was clear to Asimov that people could quickly become dependent on machines, and thus there was a need to be able to trust them implicitly. Of course, he also knew that this can never be: no matter what kind of rules one creates, there are always unforeseen circumstances which probe for loopholes in a set of rules, and many of his robot stories were based on the mysteries arising from these loopholes.

In the aftermath of two world wars, science fiction writers almost universally saw machines, robots and computers as being the paragons of certainty. Their 'logical' approach to analyzing the world was hailed as something nobler than human intuition and emotion. Asimov, however, was the first person to really challenge that view in a systematic way. He said, effectively, that if we oversimplify the complexities of the world with simple-minded rules, we will run into semantic ambiguities, or edge-cases where the rules do not apply.

Having formulated the three laws, he then wrote a number of stories exploring the interactions of these idealized rules with the real world, and showed, quite entertainingly, that a set of general rules like this is highly vulnerable to semantic instability. The intended meaning could often be misconstrued in an unexpected context.

As written, Asimov's laws are much too vague to be applied to machines. The rules do not provide clear semantics, or a detailed interpretation of meaning. In order to even define the basic concepts used in the statements, like 'harm', there would have to be a complex model of the world that included a sense of human judgements. Nonetheless, Asimov's thinking was prescient, and his laws do have their analogues in different kinds of machinery today[155].

The robots of today are not much like Asimov's vision. Apart from the mechanical manipulators on factory floors that assemble cars and other machinery, we have automated physical processes all around us in more subtle ways. Planes, trains and automobiles are the most obvious mechanical devices to take on robotic enhancements. They can now drive themselves and soon they will probably refuel automatically too.

A perhaps less obvious robotic system is online shopping. In online shopping, we state a preference or give an order, and a fully automated process begins. Occasionally humans are involved in the production line, say when ordering goods, but consider something like video on demand: you browse for a movie or a television show, and within seconds machines whir somewhere in the cloud of the Internet, and content is delivered directly to your television set, without a single human hand being lifted (except perhaps to point the remote control at the TV). This is not a human form robot, but a distributed automaton.

What would constitute harm to a human being in these cases? In transport systems human lives are at stake. In online entertainment, perhaps moral offence, censorship could be considered the objectives for Asimov's laws. We see the equivalents of the laws in technology around us, in automatic braking systems, and under-age content-filters.

These rules are fixed policies rather than smart adaptations, however. They say 'if X happens, don't do Y'; but, could technology measure harm to a human in a more general sense, so that we could effectively design a machine to know when someone was suffering harm as a result of its actions, and would we want it to? This is a problem fraught with complexity.

One could, for example, begin by attempting to measure something, some indicator of harm. The problem here is that the word 'harm' is too vague: it's an umbrella term for many kinds of injury, so the concept is too broad to make sense out of. One could try an indirect route and attempt to infer harm from some kind of measurable signal. Like Descartes, we might suppose that pain would be that signal, which could be measured by electrical activity in the brain, or from facial recognition. However, now there is another ambiguity: mental or physical pain? If a person feels physical pain, how do we know it is as a result of the television program and not a broken leg? If a person feels mental anguish, how would the technology know that it was a result of the television show and not a completely unrelated case of love sickness?

The relativity of information and observation makes decision-making highly vulnerable to information partitions. The default state of any part of a system is ignorance. That only changes if it is both equipped to received messages about external state, and such information is transmitted to it. Descartes made it clear that we cannot know state with certainty. We can try to *infer* certain conditions from evidence, by measuring presumed causes or indirect consequences of harm, but this requires a sophisticated model that can adapt to individuals or groups. There is inescapable uncertainty.

Automated decision making is clearly not a simple matter. The more we try to out-think a situation, the more potential errors of judgement it is possible to make. When computers 'go mad', when technology behaves unexpectedly, it is often a failure of inference, and that reasoning builds on information measured from somewhere. The uncertainties from measurement cause inevitable instabilities of interpretation. This is why basing predictability on predetermined stability, on policy and fixed rules, is a more likely strategy to succeed than a risky search for the best answers to context-dependent questions.

Can programmed rules increase certainty? Can conditional reasoning based on relative information make technology dependable and safe for humans, or does it merely take us to the brink of instability? There is clearly a trade-off that involves both semantics and dynamics of computer software. We must decide whether the goal is to make technology dependable or merely functional.

The opening quote of this chapter is from an episode of the 1968 show *Star Trek*, one of several occasions in which Captain Kirk talked a computer into self-destructing, by convincing it that its behaviour was illogical. It is a shameless piece of dramatic fiction, but it is also not as far fetched as one might think.

True, computers do not reason with natural language as we do, otherwise we might see office workers chiding their workstations to repent from inexplicable behaviour all over the planet.

The logical error of the M5 computer that caused it to go haywire, was a result of a lack of introspection about its own behaviour: it was only applying its Asimovian rule sets to the incomplete information about a partial and relative view of the external world, instead of also feeding back information about the consequences onto its own behaviour and applying the rules again to converge to a consistent equilibrium. This is actually a common mistake in technology design.

There are many examples of this. Denial-of-Service (DoS) attacks on computer systems are possible because machines follow one part of their smart behaviour with singular resolve, but ignore a broader view of the environment in which they exist. DoS attacks are attempts by malicious parties to bring down computers by giving them too many things to do, thus denying their legitimate users from the services they provide. DoS attacks work by barraging a computer with questions from many sources. Because the computer is programmed to service such requests without question (Asimov's second law), as the questions build up it uses more and more of its resources until it hits a critical limit and collapses from the load. Had all parts of the service chain been programmed to recognize such a critical limit by introspection of their own state (Asimov's third law), with or without some kind of smart recognition of intent, such attacks would be much harder to accomplish, though never impossible.

Once systems start to make decisions based on the subjective world they inhabit, there is intrinsic probability of instability, because the external world will then drive the system uncontrollably. A form of strong coupling is created. Then the effect of a simple and even innocuous change in response to observations might have a profound effect on system dynamics. This is particularly true when information is sparse, and intrinsically noisy (see Chapter 4).

In Chapter 5, I alluded to the way in which chains of dependent messages lead to 'bifurcations' or branching of behaviour. The implication was that system behaviour has branching points, also known as 'possible worlds', that hinge on the details of messages transmitted between parts in a chain. Computer programs are built up in this way, so we should expect every conditional branch 'if X is true then do Y else do Z' to be a hinge that can unleash unstable dynamics.

It's worth relating a few anecdotes to support this idea. These examples illustrate how the relativity of a singular perspective can distort reasoning so that it favours outcomes not always compatible with goals in the bigger picture. The thread that runs through these examples is the presence of a decision, based on semantics, that ends up unleashing a dynamical instability on systems. Decisions are the source of instability, and we witness evidence of the deep coupling between dynamics and semantics.

In the 1990s, network mountable disks were common because storage was expensive and networks were cheap. Accessing disks over the network could be somewhat unreliable, however, so the semantics of reading and writing were to ensure that reads and writes succeeded above all else[156]. If the network went down for some reason, as it often did in the early days of the Ethernet, computers with critical data on network disks would wait for the network to respond before continuing execution. However, the network code was a critical dependency in the kernel of the operating system, and when it became unavailable, the computer would basically come to a complete halt until the network came back. The fragile cabling that was often strung around like a cat's cradle in those days became a critical switch for all other behaviour.

A slightly different problem with disks occurred on at least two different computer operating system designs I have experienced. System log files are archives of messages written by the system about errors and events it wishes to record. The amount of logging performed is usually a configurable choice. If the choice was deleted accidentally, default settings would take over, and try to keep a diligent record of every detail, without any cropping of the archive. Until relatively recently, disks were divided into partitions of fixed size, and the thus, as the log archive grew and grew like a cancer, it filled the hard-limit of the partition, preventing other processes from being able to write information. An accidental deletion effectively reprogrammed the host to kill itself.

This is a classic case of the tragedy of the commons. With the best of intentions many systems have been created over the years that were literally programmed to be unstable, by plunging a system into a conflict of interest out of ignorance of the environment. One could make this argument for fossil fuel consumption and global warming, for example.

One of the strangest conspiracies of instability occurred one Sunday morning a couple of years ago, when I awoke to an email that plunged me into a 10 hour phone call over an ensuing crisis at the site of a CFEngine user in the United States. The user had planned to upgrade the part of the CFEngine software called a hub, which acted as a calibration point in each network region. It's fairly common practice for enterprise customers to make system upgrades at the weekend, so as not to allow them to interfere with normal weekly business. Furthermore, being a major international organization, they chose to upgrade their installations all over the world in a single weekend.

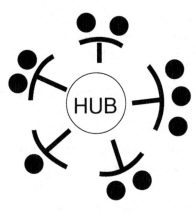

Fig. 9.1. CFEngine's hub is a parallel measuring instrument, a point of calibration for aggregated observations. It divides collection into parallel groups for efficiency and pulls them in to the central store.

A hub is specifically responsible for aggregation of observations made locally on individual computers (see figure 9.1) to a single location, as calibration of the data requires comparison at a single point. It behaves as a massively parallelized measuring instrument, where messages from thousands of computers are received and calibrated on a common scale for further observation. A hub is therefore a bottleneck, but not a single not point of failure as nothing else depends on it.

The customer had three main sites, one in Asia, one in Europe and the largest in the US. The first two site had been upgraded flawlessly that Saturday, to jubilant messages; but the email on Sunday morning saw this elation crumble into panic as the final US upgrade was failing miserably.

The sites had been upgraded in order of size, smallest first. At the time, the Asian site had about 400 computers attached, the European one about 800, and the all-important US hub had 1,600 hosts to gather data from. All three hub servers were near identical machines, with the same hardware specifications, and all of them should have been massively over-capable of handling the task. More importantly, all of them had been managing the task before the upgrade was initiated.

From my conservative estimates, based on simple dynamical scaling laws, I'd calculated that about 5,000 hosts would be a fair number to expect for a hub with average hardware. However, these machines were leviathans, with 16 processing cores and hundreds of gigabytes of memory. They should have laughed at this meager load. Indeed, before the upgrade they had.

However, when the US hub was upgraded, the load on one of the 16 CPUs went into overdrive, and hit 100 percent utilization; the updates seemed to take longer and longer, and the entire machine became painfully slow. To the customer, this all looked very dramatic, as a side effect of this was that one by one the machines turned blue on their console (code blue, meaning dead). This was a major and somewhat misleading surprise, and certainly not the kind of existential experience one hopes for on a Sunday.

In fact, the client machines were not dead, but their heartbeat signals could not be detected by the hub, because the message queue was completely overloaded. At first, my colleagues, working through the night, had hoped this was a temporary artefact of the upgrade and that it might settle down. However, as the problem persisted, they became increasingly nervous about these predictions. A sudden reduction in capacity of the server did not make sense. As I joined them in the morning, my first thought was that there had to be a new scale introduced somewhere that was interacting with the process (such is the burden of a physics education), and a limiting timescale usually meant a mechanical disk drive.

In moments of panic, logic abandons even the most rational of minds, and one begins to doubt everything from one's understanding. Incomplete information feels like a vulnerable position, so one also starts blaming oneself. Obviously, it had to be the upgrade's fault, something that had changed. As it turned out, the relevant scale was not in our own software but in the database it made use of, but pin-pointing the issue was an excruciating exercise in inference from minimal information.

Information relativity became a hurdle to overcome in diagnosing the problem, as the company's own security partitions prevented direct access to the system. In this case, the situation was made almost absurd as security protocols meant that all information we received was filtered through a somewhat disinterested local system administrator by chat, Email. and telephone. We had to hope that his information was accurate, and complete, if it came at all. It didn't help, for instance, when the system administrator decided to go out for lunch without telling us, and then promptly fell asleep in his chair for an hour during our diagnosis.

Nevertheless, with three heads on the job, we found the answer. The CFEngine hub parallelized the collection of data in such a way as to complete all updates within a couple of minutes. Since each message from a computer to the hub was quite small, this would allow updates of thousands of machines to take place very quickly, and at a frequency of up to 5000 machines every five minutes. Given that this was easily achievable by the hardware, I expected the main bottleneck was expected to be the disk write channel, which is the slowest part of any computer and the part we knew the least about. Technologists know that disks require mechanical motion, which takes a long time, so they try to avoid writing to the disk by keeping data in memory, in order to keep updates fast. This very strategy became the reason for the problem: a conflict of interest between wanting to write to the database and wanting to cache the whole thing in memory.

Each update of the 1,600 machines was taking longer to process than the five-minute interval in between updates, so they were piling up on top of one another, like the traffic-jam queueing instability in Figure 4.6. This didn't make sense. Why the sudden change? The statistics showed that the disks were performing well, however. In fact, the database seemed to be keeping data mostly in memory and flushing changes to the disk for permanent storage only occasionally. There did not seem to be much disk activity at all. Then my colleague noticed that, each time an update interval was reached, there would be a massive surge in *paging* and the CPU rate would go through the roof.

Paging, also known as swapping, is something that computers do in order to maintain the illusion of having more memory than they actually have. It is called virtual memory. It is measured differently to normal disk operation, so its interference was not visible from the perspective of normal writing. Paging of memory is another example of 'pulling it apart to keep it together' (see chapter 6). The computer atomizes its memory, dividing it up into slots called pages. If a memory bank becomes full, a single page of RAM can be archived to disk and then the empty space can be re-used.

The situation is something like trying to park your car at an airport or supermarket. Because not everyone can park close to the processing terminal, there is short-stay and long-stay parking. Then, if this becomes full, there are two options: first one could park further away in another block of memory. A second option, however, would be to start moving cars into long term storage, like a valet parking service, but this takes a lot longer to deliver and fetch the cars. This is called paging or swapping, because pages (contiguous blocks) of memory are swapped out to disk to make room for incoming. The strategy is a behavioural decision (a semantic choice), and it can therefore lead to instability. Imagine a sudden flood of cars arriving a a valet parking line.

Because a physical disk access is needed, paging is a very slow operation. It requires the actual physical movement of mechanical parts, which is thousands of times slower than the movement of bits in memory. Thus any time a computer starts paging, there is a large performance degradation. This was what was happening now with the upgraded database. The question was: why had this now begun to happen? There was no shortage of total memory on the machine.

One might have expected that memory was a uniform, homogeneous pool of resources, and that incoming data were being written to disk more or less immediately. Both of these assumptions were wrong, due to unknown limiting scales that were triggered a decision to page. Classically, databases would write data to permanent storage immediately, even in multiple copies, in case of a system error in which data could be lost. This was essentially a case of 'write it down before you forget it'. The upgraded database did not use this approach, however. Instead, it adopted a strategy of keeping data in RAM to enhance performance. It used 'memory mapped files', which piggy-back off the virtual memory system, so that disk writes were performed by paging instead of writing.

The accidental discovery of a system message indicated that the processor architecture of the hardware running the database used something called a Non-Uniform Memory Architecture (NUMA). This is a design for computer hardware with multiple CPUs. It is an attempt to solve the problem of parking memory quickly at the lower level scale of the CPU itself.

CPU processors today are very fast, but the message channels from CPU to memory are comparatively slow, especially when there is a lot of memory, since messages have to travel quite far. Also, if processors have to share the same uniform expanse of memory, it will take longer to find a parking space, and there is more likely to be a conflict of interest, with different processors wanting to 'exploit the commons'. In NUMA, the idea is to make private memory for each CPU (recall the private bathrooms in Chapter 4), so that it can write immediately and quickly without having to share. However, this local memory has a limited size, which therefore introduces a new dynamical scale into the problem: the size of the local processor's private cache.

The question is: what then happens when the local memory becomes full, i.e. when the dimensionless ratio of

$$\frac{\text{private memory used}}{\text{private memory available}}$$

approaches 1 (not to mention all the other combinations of memory limits for the other 15 private and public areas)? After our upgrade, the updated database had adjusted its semantics to fill up its private RAM and then begin paging immediately to disk, instead of looking for memory elsewhere. The result was that everything became throttled by the weakest link in the chain much sooner than necessary.

A sudden change in data rate to three orders of magnitude slower had to result in a transition to a completely different kind of behaviour. The system underwent a semantic instability that forced it to paging contention and coupled the disk strongly to the system. There was a 'phase transition'[157] to a regime of slow data. The system could no longer cope with the data rates we had planned for, and so it choked on the incoming data.

This was a bold proposition, based on fragile evidence, but reasoning left no real alternative. The problem was solved by removing NUMA handling, changing the semantics at the threshold to avoid paging. In an instant, what had taken all 1,600 machines more than 6 minutes to update at 100 percent CPU, updated in 18 seconds without breaking a sweat. Instability solved.

A hidden and unintended semantic change ended up unleashing a scaling instability in a resource queue, which slowed the server to a near standstill, as if it had been dumped into treacle. In fact, ironically, had they been less powerful machines with fewer cores and no NUMA architecture, the problem might not have happened at all.

For technology designers, an important question arises. How does one avoid unexpected interactions like those in this anecdote? How adaptive and responsive should infrastructure be? We might compare the strategies evolved in biology and homeostasis. The science is clear: avoid the appearance of too many scales.

This episode illustrates nicely many of the principles of stability we've discussed so far. In particular, it proves that one cannot ignore dynamical scales when deciding semantics, nor can one ignore semantics when predicting dynamics. In technology, dynamics and semantics must be understood together[158].

I view this episode as a triumph of theory over practice, and strong evidence that information infrastructure is balancing on the brink of instability, with too many unknowns and few models to understand the strange interactions of scale. No amount of testing or poking at the software would have systematically been able to discover the NUMA memory scale. You simply cannot see beyond the scale in which your tools reside. We could not have predicted the existence of a phase transition any more than Newton could have predicted the Einsteinian relativity, or the ancient Greeks could have known about quantum mechanics. Scale is a harsh mistress.

Interestingly, there are indeed several parallels with quantum mechanics here. In a computer, there are only certain intrinsic properties one is able to observe, as in the quantum world there are certain 'eigenstates' you can measure. Thus our entire understanding of what goes on inside the black box is limited by a projection of some deep-rooted behaviour onto this small number of states.

Observations were contaminated by noise, because the act of measurement had violated the 'second assumption' of making no effect on the system: in this case a distortion of our measuring instrument—our thermometer was melting!

The trick of handling scenarios where information is limited lies in being able to use this limited information to reason about the system, without knowing anything about some underlying deterministic mechanism. Statistical inference is one tool, but computer science teaches of another: logic.

Logical reasoning was instrumental in diagnosing this database episode, and decision-logic was the reason for the problem in the first place. Logic clearly plays an essential part of developing an understanding of systematic behaviour, and we need to explore this further.

Logical reasoning is a kind of rational *story-telling*, or narrative that we find plausible or satisfying. It comes in many forms, and it has a reputation for being a kind of pure form of thought, but we should be careful in drawing that conclusion. Stories can, in some cases, be proven true of false, offering the illusion of certainty, but it is important to shatter the myth that logic represents certainty. In a sense, logic lies at the interface between the dynamics of messages and the semantics of messages. It is a centrally important topic, but it is as much the source of our problems as it is a tool for solving them.

Two important kinds of narrative used in reasoning are known as *induction* and *deduction*. The Scottish philosopher David Hume, and English-Austrian philosopher Karl Popper (see Chapter 7) developed these notions in particular[159]. Induction is a kind of bottom-up inference in which one draws general conclusions from specific instances. For example, we believe that there is a law of gravitation, because hammers and other objects fall when released. It happened before and thus we expect that it will happen again. Deduction, conversely, derives specific examples from general rules. We know the law of gravitation, therefore we deduce that a hammer will fall if someone releases it. Hume pointed out that induction implies that we draw uncertain conclusions from limited experience. Popper used this to discuss his ideas on falsification.

These ways of reasoning with natural language and human concepts are part of everyday life for thinking creatures. They reach heights of entertainment in the stories of Sherlock Holmes, Asimov's tales of robots, and in the modern entertainment about crime-scene forensic pathology. However, when we speak of logic today, many have acquired a cultural notion of logic that has been bent by exposure of computers, and there is a tendency to confuse the true and false nature of binary systems with a kind of deterministic certainty.

Logic is not just about stringing together pathways of sequential connections. Formally, logic is about *semantic consistency*, or the compatibility of certain statements. To use language from this book, we could say it is about probing semantic stability, whereas so far, the book has mainly been about the idea of *dynamical consistency*, i.e. the uniformity of properties from time to time and place to place. The sleeve of a book on my shelf contains the following delightful excerpt[160]:

> "If an man supports Arsenal one day and Spurs the next, he is fickle but not necessarily illogical. If a legal system helps the rich but not the poor then it is unjust but not illogical. The type of consistency which concerns logicians is ... compatability of beliefs."

Logical consistency is about whether statements have compatible interpretations, at the same time and place. For example, you might declare the following:

> I am over 18.
> I am 21.

These two statements are logically consistent. They might not be 'true' statements, but they are at least consistent, and might therefore suffice to get us into a drinking establishment. We can tell that they are consistent from the properties of numbers (an impartial scale which calibrates such statements). Since 21 is greater than 18, we conclude that both statements are consistent. Not all inferences are so simple, however. More pursuant of information technology, we might declare the following:

> Mark should have access to the data.
> Mark does not exist.

We recognize that these two declarations are not consistent, but how can we tell? As human beings, we are quite good at reasoning, because we are able to imagine things, i.e. search all kinds of references to things we know about, and fill in gaps in our observations. In this case, we know that the property of existence is required to have the property of access, but that might not be obvious to everyone, certainty not a computer which is trying to solve such constraints automatically. It would have to be expressed as a rule of inference.

In all cases, the modern approach to formal logic would be to arrange for all propositions to be formulated in such a way as to make them either true, false, or undetermined.

The concept of 'truth' is hardly a simple or trivial thing to explain, but somehow we all have an intuitive understanding of what it means (just try to explain truth without going around in circles). To get around this, it can be treated as a semantic primitive: an unquestioned building block for reasoning.

Unlike the knowledge discussed in the previous chapter, the realm of logic pretends that certain facts are simply irrefutable, i.e. they are *assumed* to be true.

We call these axioms. They are 100 percent accurate by assumption. Theorems are logical arguments that prove an alternative form of an initial assumption. A measured quantity could only be considered a fact in the sense that it were true that the measurement yielded a value (either it did or it didn't), not whether the value is correct or accurate.

Declarations made in a logical framework are thus either *facts*, things that we know to be true, or *intentions* that might become true in the future. A fact is defined to be something that is either 'known' or that has been 'proven', but we already 'know' from the previous chapter that knowing is not such a simple matter, so this will bear further scrutiny. Again, the concept of truth is as elusive as it is intuitive.

The kind of logic we employ in technology has to be more mechanical than these linguistic examples. When computers reason, they can typically verify only very simple conditions, and use that as a notion of truth. There is very little room for implication or indirection to fill in gaps. Indeed, this is part of the problem, so we should try to sketch out what it means.

A brief history of logic makes a useful and instructive diversion to complete our working notion of uncertainty. Since the Renaissance and Industrial Revolution, logic has been very much entwined with the philosophy of machines, and its champions lay close to the major thinkers of their times.

The earliest formal body of work about reasoning came from Aristotle, whose studies spanned narrative forms in discourse, from rhetoric to syllogism. His works were collected together under the title *The Organon* (the instrument). It described early forms of induction and deduction, and its influence was broad and deep. Centuries passed, in fact, before any substantial improvement was made to his work.

The history of formalized logic, in a sense, goes back to the highly influential Thomas Hobbes[161], and his fascination with the mechanical, deterministic essence that he saw in the behaviours of things and Men around him. The particular concept of reasoning that logic imputed was heavily influenced by the prevailing view of determinism, prior to the 20th century, which sprang from a world obsessed with ballistics, and the computation of trajectories for projectiles in warfare. Hobbes' studies of society and his insistence on seeing causal mechanisms for the trajectories of society, led him to believe that rational thought was synonymous with computation[162]. He saw the evolution of things to be like a game of billiards, where one ball strikes another, setting in motion the next phase of a trajectory. Hence one should 'add many things in sequence' to form a logical argument. This would also form the basis of the 'difference method' of Newton and Leibniz (see Figure 9.2).

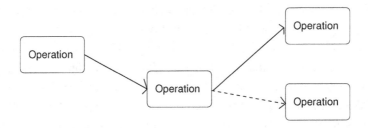

Fig. 9.2. A ballistic view of logic, or a transition system with decisions providing possible branch points (bifurcations).

Hobbes also understood the importance of observation on his machines, however, and protested the metaphysical implications of Descartes in favour of a more pragmatic reality. He wanted a more mechanical, less fanciful view of causation:

> All which qualities called sensible are in the object that causeth them but
> so many several motions of the matter, by which it presseth our organs
> diversely... For if those colours and sounds were in the bodies or objects
> that cause them, they could not be severed from them, as by glasses and in
> echoes by reflection we see they are: where we know the thing we see is in
> one place; the appearance, in another. And though at some certain distance
> the real and very object seem invested with the fancy it begets in us; yet still
> the object is one thing, the image or fancy is another.

Leibniz was impressed by Hobbes writings, and his own mathematical sophistication allowed him to propose a formulation of *symbolic logic*, based on the binary notions of true and false. A symbolic logic attempts to abstract away ambiguities of natural language into semantic primitives, or symbols that have undisputed meaning: atoms of reasoning. Thus, logic too was able to make use of the strategy of pulling something apart in order to glue it together.

To fashion a process for reasoning that was deterministic, inevitable, and as free of human whim as possible, Leibniz proposed a mathematical form of logic, based on symbolic statements: digital messages coded in symbols that not only passed on information, but whose semantics were expressions of logic. Each message added up a succession of logical transitions (deductions, inductions, abduction), resulting in an end point of the trajectory that we may call a conclusion. He was not able to implement it in his lifetime, however.

As noted in Chapter 5, Leibniz's view of truth was also preemptive of modern ideas about 'many worlds' interpretations of causation, and so-called modal logics (see Chapter 10). He bridged the language of reason with the abstraction of context, by pointing out that truth could be made consistent with a sense of outcome if one identified that *necessity* is that which is true in every possible world, and *possibility* is that which is true if it holds in some. Saul Kripke developed this concept of possible worlds in the 1950s and 1960s in the context of modal logic, and Hugh Everett used the idea as an interpretation of quantum mechanics in 1957 in what is now the most famous many worlds interpretation of causation. Leibniz made a mechanical calculator, preempting Babbage's Analytical Engine, and he even imagined a pinball-like computer made of spherical bits in 1679[163].

In spite of all this, his ambitions in logic did not come to fruition, and his programme rested until the mantle could be passed on to a worthy successor. George Boole (1815-1864) became perhaps that successor. An English schoolmaster, who later became first professor or mathematics at Cork, Boole's formulation of what we now call Boolean algebra was a major contribution to symbolic logic.

Boole's essay, *An Investigation of the Laws of Thought, on which are founded the mathematical theories of Logic and Probabilities*[164], written in 1854, realized Hobbes' and Leibniz's vision in the sense of showing how arithmetic and his algebra of true and false could be derived from one another. By assigning the numerical value of 1 for true and 0 for false, he went even further and related these to burgeoning science of probabilities. The words we use for logical narrative: reasoning (reckoning) or ratiocination (from the Latin), from which we have rational, ratio, etc., almost preempt the relationship between thinking and arithmetic, formalized by Boole. The title of his essay placed the joint notions of logic and probability on equal footing.

Although frequently glossed over today, Boole realized that we do not increase certainty merely by trying to shoe-horn outcomes into two categories of true of false. This neither creates nor implies new certainty. He wrote:

> The slightest attention to the processes of the intellectual world reveal to us another state of things. The mathematical laws of reasoning are, properly speaking, the laws of right reasoning only, and their actual transgression is a perpetually recurring phenomenon. Error, which has no place in the material system, occupies a large one here.

In other words, true and false might be the labels on two sides of a tossed coin, but predicting which of them one concludes with is still a matter for chance and error. One can project uncertainty onto true or false outcomes, but the uncertainty does not go away, it merely gets cut across a knife edge. John von Neumann, a formidable mathematician and physicist, and one of the inventors of the modern computer, also recognized that logic did not remove the need for error and uncertainty. A century later, he wrote *Synthesis of reliable organisms from unreliable components*[165] to much the same effect.

The fact that the limitations of discrete mechanisms only project uncertainty into fewer outcomes, without actually increasing the prevailing certainty, might have disappointed Hobbes, as it continues to disappoint users of technology today. The separation of systems into parts is often argued as a strategy for reliability, but, as we've seen, it is the weakness of coupling between the parts, rather than the number of possible outcomes, that allows greater predictability.

Every parameter, every lever, switch, and button to push, Boolean or not, adds communications channels to mechanisms that increase coupling and can amplify errors. The statistical theory of errors and the Schwartz triangle inequality in mathematics makes it clear that the statistical uncertainty can only increase with each button, level or parameter we add to a functional mechanism:

$$\text{Uncertainty} \sim \sqrt{P_1^2 + P_2^2 + \ldots} \geq P_1$$

Uncertainty does not get reduced by greater parameterization. Thus certainty can only be improved by taking these parametric levers and buttons away altogether.

Symbolic logic developed gradually until reaching its crowning achievement, with the publication of a treatise on modern symbolic logic, known as first-order predicate logic, by David Hilbert and Wilhelm Ackermann in 1928[166]. This is the logic on which all modern computers base their operations. First order logic has been embraced for a diverse range of purposes, and it pervades much of our modern culture, just as Newton's laws do. But, in spite of its undeniable successes, what initially seemed like a triumphant conquest for the omnipotence of logical certainty turned out to be a short-lived fancy. The proof that symbolic logic and binary computation were not the end of uncertainty was just around the corner.

At the International Congress of Mathematicians in Paris in 1900, one of the mathematical leaders of the 20th century, David Hilbert (1862-1943), put forth a highly influential list of 23 unsolved problems in mathematics[167]. Apart from showing his deep understanding of the state of mathematics, it laid out a remarkable manifesto for years of research to come. Echoes of Hilbert's challenge still ring throughout cloisters of mathematics, not to mention over the air-waves of contemporary culture. It included major issues like Fermat's famous Last Theorem, and, in particular, one problem that was to have the greatest impact on scientific reasoning: the consistency of the rules of arithmetic: the very laws which Boole had used in linking arithmetic to logic and reason.

Hilbert's second challenge asked a deceptively simple question: is arithmetic consistent and complete? Given the equivalence of arithmetic and Boolean algebra, it effectively asked: if we start with any question, can we always produce either a proof or a refutation of it, within the framework of arithmetic? In other words, can we decide whether the answer to every question can be determined true or false, but never both at the same time?

The second challenge struck at the very foundation of logical consistency. Hilbert himself went on to seek out a complete system for arithmetic logic, leading to the formulation of his first-order logic in 1928. Essentially, it offered an expressive symbolic framework for formulating consistent, conditional statements about sets of 'things'. It would later be extended and specialized in a rich variety of ways for different purposes, but first-order logic remains the backbone of what is represented in information systems and digital technology today[168]. However, it did not answer Hilbert's own challenge.

The implied breadth of Hilbert's question is hard to comprehend, because we assume so much of the foundations of arithmetic and logic in our everyday lives today. It could seem like a crazy one to even ask, because it involves great subtlety. Which ever way one looks at it, answering such a question did not seem like a small feat, Remarkably however, an answer came just three years after Hilbert's own publication of first order logic. from a young mathematician of extraordinary talent named Kurt Gödel (1906-1978), and his answer was a resounding 'no'.

In his doctoral thesis of 1929, Gödel proved first a so-called completeness theorem which said that, in first-order predicate logic, every universally valid formula was provable. This was not at all bad news for Hilbert's programme, seemingly supporting the idea that arithmetic was consistent. However, just two years later, Gödel extended his work, turning that optimism upside down with two devastating *incompleteness* theorems. He was able to show that, not only was arithmetic not consistent and complete, but in fact, no 'finitary' formal system that included arithmetic could be both consistent and complete at the same time. Arithmetic, and hence the reasoning of Boole, contained fundamental uncertainty.

Gödel's theorems were as remarkable as they were paradoxical: their implications were that if arithmetic were consistent, there would have to be undecidable statements, making the idea of proof itself inconsistent. The result is known as

Gödels first incompleteness theorem. In the same paper, Gödel also showed that, if arithmetic were indeed consistent, a proof of its consistency could not be formulated within arithmetic. This denied Hilbert of another hope, of finding a finite proof of consistency. It is known as the Second Incompleteness Theorem. Two Incompleteness Theorems were published in 1931.

Gödel's incompleteness is often likened to the so-called Epimenides paradox, which has a similar self-referential logic. Epimenides was a Cretan who made the statement: "All Cretans are liars." The paradox arises because the sentence implicitly refers to itself in the negative, creating a recursive semantic instability. It can be rephrased as:

"This sentence is false."

If the sentence is true, it must be false; if false, it must be true, and so on, in a never-ending unresolvable loop. This paradox was used as the unresolvable logic that sent countless computers to their deaths in science-fiction movies, with Captain Kirk of *Star Trek* the 'quintessential devil' of those matters.

Gödel's incompleteness theorems dashed hopes of achieving Hilbert's second challenge, and more importantly showed that logic was not equatable with certainty at any level. Regardless of whether a statement could be proven within some framework, there would still be doubt about the framework itself.

The effect of Gödel's theorem was something akin to the shock of quantum theory and the uncertainty it introduced. Gödel cemented the 20th century's position in history as the number one undoer of certainty, and put the final nail in the coffin for determinism. Indeed, quantum mechanics offered actual proof that the world can (and in fact) does exist in states that are neither true nor false, at least within the framework of our own understanding of it. Both states do occur at the same time in physics, proving that nature does not respect Hilbert's second challenge (ironically the way one shows this in quantum mechanics is with a Hilbert space).

Alan Turing went on to use his work on computation to prove his own version of the theorem, using his prototype computer, the Turing machine. He considering the so-called *Entscheidungsproblem* or *halting problem* for a machine to answer a question. The idea here was to know whether every problem fed into a computer could be resolved with a true or a false answer. Are there results that are not computable at all? Turing showed that it was possible to construct problems that could neither be proved true nor false. By assuming the discreteness of time and state, and the sequence of cause and effect as in logic, he showed that there were problems that were undecidable. Far from being a disaster, however, this realization opened the door to entire new fields of mathematical understanding, like algorithmic complexity theory, which I return to at the end of this chapter.

Logic alone is clearly not a panacea for bringing certainty to information systems (or to prevent them from going mad). To synthesize a compelling model of information systems, we need to insert the stable aspects of logic into the picture too. The dynamics described in the first part of the book already display limited reasoning capabilites, in the sense that a computer immune system can decide when a system is not in its desired state, and effect repairs. To complete the picture, it makes sense to explore the pros and cons of additional reasoning capabilities, and see where they belong in the model. By the time the details of Computer Immunology were being implemented, this work was already underway.

One of the fortuitous encounters I had at the 1997 LISA infrastructure conference, where Computer Immunology first occurred to me, was kindred spirit and Tufts University researcher Alva Couch. Alva surprised me by being both friendly and enthusiastic about my work. Academics do not usually compliment each other (let alone complement each other), so I surmised that there had to be something deeply wrong with him. Naturally, we became good friends, and occasional collaborators.

In the year following my Computer Immunology paper, Alva and his student Michael Gilfix embraced its concepts and showed that CFEngine's approach to convergence state could be likened to another kind of desired outcome: logical verification. He began to apply some ideas from semantics to my physics inspired dynamical ideas. It was not quite Captain Kirk talking down the M5 computer, rather it used a more well known language of logic programming, associated with artificial intelligence and computational linguistics, known as Prolog[169].

Within this framework of programmatic logic, Couch and Gilfix compared CFEngine with Prolog, and opened the door to a discussion about the relationship between the purely dynamical approach of convergence, and the deeper traditions of logic and programming.

In Prolog one declares what one intends to be true (or one might choose to say what *should* be true) as 'facts'. One then proceeds to evaluate the consistency of these different facts by applying rules. They showed that CFEngine's behaviour was essentially the same as that of a simple Prolog model they could construct about the state of a computer. In Prolog, a user executes a query to determine whether a fact is true, and if not make it so. Once a fact is true, the semantics of logic and the constancy of facts mean that it will remain true. In CFEngine, the computer itself continually executes convergent 'zero' operators that quickly converge into a definition of truth known as a fixed point.

Couch and Gilfix showed that CFEngine's primary achievement was effectively to transmute intentions into facts, these were the building blocks for certainty in atomized systems. Decisions and separated regions ('possible worlds') are represented in Prolog as preconditions, which play the role of

> if *pre-condition*, then X will be fact, else Y will be fact

in a more subtle way. This does not seem very different, in substance, from ordinary reasoning. However, the framework of logic programming does not view reasoning in the same ballistic, blow-by-blow stepwise manner, normally used in programming or flow control. It represents only a descriptive level of the problem, where the underlying manipulations are abstracted into higher level definitions. This mapped well onto the 'smart operator' approach to evaluation of state used by CFEngine.

In spite of the dumb machine-like nature of the convergent operators, this work implied that even something as mundane as common or garden maintenance operations were capable of a form of reasoning, though not in the usual sense of a story based on deductions. CFEngine was able to reason in the same way that the growth of plants follows from arranging to water them or not, or in the way our immune systems seem to recognize invading organisms and viruses and make decisions about whether or not to fight them. In other words, convergent policies could implicitly recognize and fend off faults in computer system configurations.

We can frame this in the way of the earlier chapters by returning to the operator evolution language I've used throughout the book. Logical facts are to logical reasoning as state is to a change operation, or as inputs are to a computer. Equivalently, we could say that facts behave like the boundary conditions on the process of reasoning, just as boundary conditions ground the beginning of a solution to an equation of motion in the mathematics of Newton and Leibniz (recall Chapter 3). Rules thus become the equivalent of the 'equations of motion', in the laws of machine behaviour, that determine how to infer new facts about those inputs.

(Operate on) state	$\rightarrow$	outcome	(General propagation)
(Reason about) boundary values	$\rightarrow$	outcome	(Logic)
(Rules applied to) facts	$\rightarrow$	outcome	(Prolog)
(Convergent operator) initial state	$\rightarrow$	outcome	(CFEngine)

Evolution of the state of a system, in the real world, is defined to be causal, i.e. it obeys the laws of cause and effect, just as logical arguments take one step at a time. There is thus a representation of time that underlies these steps. The changing information, altered through the process of symbolic reasoning, actually makes an interpretation of time happen, by the very act of measuring the states. To call the change mechanism clockwork is literally true, since the symbolic messages form a symbolic measuring scale against which the change can be measured. Logic thus becomes a digitization of change, and thus of time.

This raises a question that has been pressing ever since we discussed equilibrium: what happens when more than a single desired state converges, and in what order should convergence happen? We understand that time passes when one state is transformed into another, by the action of a operator. One tick of the clock is:

(Operator) state $\to$ new state　　$\leftrightarrow$　　(Tick) time$\to$ new time

This ticking of the clock will continue until a fixed-point equilibrium is reached, at which point time stops because there is no longer anything observable to measure it by. Then the system has reached stability.

(Operator) end state $\to$ end state　　(clock stopped)

But what happens when more than one kind of operator exists to change different parts of a system? Then there are two different kinds of clock ticks, two kinds of time. If those different parts depend on each other somehow, for example because they have been tied together in cooperation, then they are related ticks of the same clock, and the order of the changes must matter to the final outcome. If they are independent, then that ordering is irrelevant. Moreover, what if the operations cannot converge? Does the system continue to change?

There are several ways in which this could happen. Suppose $\overline{A}$ means 'undo A', then this does not converge:

$$A\overline{A}\ A\overline{A}\ A\overline{A}\ A\overline{A}\ldots$$

Recall from chapter 2 that a system need not necessarily converge to a single state, but might end up in a constant orbit:

$$ABABABAB\ldots$$

If so, is this different from

$$BABABABA\ldots$$

but the two clocks tick at the same rates. Consider the two operations:

A = Fill in name and address

B = Move house

It is easy to see that these compositions are not the same, that the order matters to the outcome of these operations:

$$AB \neq BA$$

On the other hand, some operations clearly don't affect one another:

C = Eat sandwich

D = Drive car

The outcome of these is the same in either order:

$$CD = DC$$

and

$$CDCDCD \ldots = DCDCDC \ldots$$

So we could just as well run them in different threads:

$$\frac{C}{D} \frac{C}{D} \frac{C}{D} \frac{C}{D} \frac{C}{D} \frac{C}{D} \ldots$$

or in different simultaneous 'possible worlds'. This is called parallelism, and it's quite unlike the simple linear narrative of first order logic. Two processes that do not interact—i.e., which exchange no messages, no information (not even implicitly, like the address above)—are truly 'irrelative'. Relativity is irrelevant because they have no causal contact[170], indeed their ticking clocks can run at completely different rates of change. That doesn't matter unless the threads come back together and interact again later, in which case there is an analogue of Einstein's twins paradox, where one thread might experience information from the other as being older or even outdated, relative to the larger environment.

In most real systems, certain parts of a process might happen in parallel like this, and then the threads would have to join together to continue in a serial fashion. For instance: $\frac{C}{D}B$, meaning eat a sandwich in the car as you drive to your new house.

The ordering of operations is an extremely subtle and important matter in technology. It affects everything from the smallest quantum processes in the universe to eating your sandwiches before taking off the wrapping. In the quantum world, our best understanding of the mechanics of the information transitions, similar effects occur. Measurements are represented as observational operators because there must be an active mutual interaction to measure at the quantum level. Such operations can have inequivalent interpretations when computed in different orders. We say that the operations do not commute, or are non-commutative if $AB \neq BA$.

This can only happen because the observed properties share a common information structure somehow, a common point of reference. The possible worlds bifurcate into the alternatives. Once you have moved house, you address is determined. Once the state has been encoded, it is committed, and is irreversible, so the total state resulting from the two orderings is inconsistent because the actual state of the encoded state information was dependent on the outcome of the operation. This is the many-worlds interpretation of quantum mechanics, and it is the effect of any logical precondition in a machine.

Each transition that drives and measures the time evolution of the machine leads potentially to every possible outcome. No one knows what this means for quantum mechanics in terms of physical reality (because no one really understands the relationship between the quantum theory and physical reality), but the logic of it is clear and present in computer software and any other information system. The future hinges on decisions of causal ordering.

From the view point of the quantum theory's mathematical formulation, it appears that the act of measurement (which is represented by the action of a measurement operator) breaks the symmetry between the different possible outcomes, and thus select one, making an irreversible choice of world. This is the way the theory of quantum mechanics is constructed. It is sometimes discussed as a 'collapse of the wavefunction' (like seeing which way a spinning coin lands) and sometimes as a many-worlds branching. Either way, it is an interactive alteration of state information, and we have no better understanding of it than that. In machines, these symmetry breakings happen through interactions with environment around them, which includes users.

Of course, one should not draw analogies too far: the quantum semantic world might not be directly analogous to the human semantic world. Filling in your address does not automatically cause you to move house, and vice versa, there has to be a separate correlation between the information. However there is a bifurcation point, a *precondition* on which these different outcomes hinges, which is like Prolog's logical representation of reasoning.

If we want to make a usable technology from this basic mathematics of conditional narrative change, these matters play a role in ensuring correct behaviour. Typically we do not want our technological infrastructure to be a clock, changing from moment to moment, but we do want separate atomic facts and prerequisites to coalesce into a consistent equilibrium end-state, no matter how temporary. To help move away from a view of time-based reasoning, to desired state, it helps to restate transitions as intentions. Consider these intended facts:

- Mark has an account.

- Mark has access to the data.

We want this clock to stop as soon as possible so that user 'mark' can reach equilibrium with this state of the world. Logically, we don't have to state these in any particular order, as any convergent process of reasoning that makes use of them will be able to try and see how to determine the order with which they fit together. A rule that would make these statements consistent would be something like

> Access to data requires there to be a valid account.

The kind of problem description used here is thus called *declarative* because it is all based on saying what should be considered true, not on how one might go about making that happen, or the order in which they should happen. Again, we may speak of a desired end-state. One could also imply from these statements that the 'facts' are intended to be true, even if they initially are not, and thus there is an implied initiative to make them so.

Many of us are not used to thinking in this way, however. The alternative and more usual form of machine programming (the kind one learns in school) is called *imperative* programming. It is based on the step-by-step, sequential flow of instructions, as in the ballistic methods of symbolic logic described above (see Figure 9.3). In an imperative approach, the problem might be expressed as follows:

1. Open an account for mark. (tick)

2. Add mark to the access list for data. (tick)

Unlike the declarative form, the repetition of these actions is not 'idempotent' however, meaning that, if we repeated them, we'd end up with mark having multiple, possibly conflicting accounts and being added several times to access lists. This can be fixed by the addition of preconditions:

1. If mark does not have an account, open an account for mark. (tick?)

2. If mark has an account AND mark is not in the access list for data, add mark to the access list for data. (tick??)

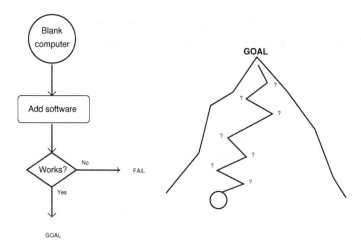

Fig. 9.3. A flow chart is a sequence of transitions that build on top of one another, with bifurcation points at each decision to make a new transition. Each ? represents a precondition. The predetermined chain starts from a known initial state and proceeds towards a goal, if it passes all the decision tests. If the environment changes in an unpredictable way, the predetermined chain will not arrive at the expected goal.

Declarative logic programming is different: it tries to search through known facts in order to reason whether new facts are true. One describes the end-state and looks for a valid path to justify it. In imperative programming one starts with the initial state and adds pieces step by step.

I call the flow chart method a hill-climbing approach to a desired end-state. It's like building a Tower of Babel. You start from the baseline and climb the mountain, step by step, according to a predetermined map with instructions (see Figure 9.3). As long as the instructions match the environment you meet at each step, and nothing fails, you will reach the top in a one-off singular train of thought. The map is more of a recipe, because it only tells you how to get to the treasure if you start in the right place. You can't start in the middle, or even from the end, without computing a new set of 'rescue' instructions.

The alternative to hill climbing is the convergent fixed point approach that I presented in chapter 5 (see Figure 9.4). No matter where you start from, you can just follow the intrinsic property of the artificial environment and roll to the desired state in an inevitable way. As long as there are no obstructions, like preconditions or dependencies, nothing can prevent this.

The way operations converge towards an outcome in CFEngine can be a lot simpler than Prolog, because CFEngine's main goal is to retain dynamical sim-

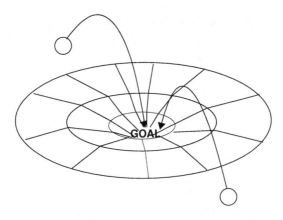

Fig. 9.4.   A convergent operation is single transition with no questions or bifurcation points. It starts from any unknown initial state and proceeds towards a goal, insensitive to changes between the initial and final states.

plicity, by making all declarations atomic. Alva Couch pointed out that this gave the CFEngine of 1999 'incredible speed', but not much expressibility, moreover system managers could verify but not validate the correctness of configurations[171]. Later in 2007, my graduate student Kyrre Begnum showed a way in which this might be done, using a language analyzer called Maude[172].

Which formulation is best to guide operations into the correct end-state? Imperative linear logic steps or a convergent potential well to roll into? Might listing imperative steps improve certainty, or just increase complexity?

This is an interesting question indeed. In 2001, a controversy began to stir around whether CFEngine's convergent approach could lead to a correct system or whether a hill-climbing approach was needed. My friend, Steve Traugott, then a consultant for NASA, had experimented with CFEngine and another project called IsConf. He had been early in promoting the concept of a stable information infrastructure, and spoke about the use of virtualization ahead of industry, in 1998 when I was talking about Computer Immunology. By 2001, he was not convinced by the notion of fixing the end-state, rather than fixing the starting point of a construction process. He became the first of several to parry the notion of convergence with the idea of *congruence*, meaning to follow an equivalent path exactly each time from the same initial state (a blank 'out of the box' computer)[173].

Steve argued that the only way to build the most general possible infrastructure, i.e. a completely arbitrary pattern of resources, was to compute the result with the full power of a computer. In computational terms, one needed a Turing machine (see Chapter 5). CFEngine's convergent operators could not represent a Turing machine, as they were built around absolute 'zero' operations, whereas a Turing machine could also perform operations relative to the current state, like addition and subtraction (arithmetic).

However, the boundary condition for this type of computation was an initial state, not a final state, but that made it fragile to the sequential instability discussed above. It meant that one had to wipe out a computer completely, taking it out of service, to repair the smallest problem. Today, at the time of writing, there is a return to this kind of thinking in the world of the 'cloud', or virtual datacentres, where it has become very easy, and relatively quick to simply wipe out a computer and make a new one in a congruent fashion. Because of virtualization, Steve's vision is currently winning the race for mindshare, but it cannot get around being a destructive approach, so it cannot perform non-intrusive repairs like an immune system.

The thrust of the argument against convergence is that, because it deals with purely atomic operations, it is not able to generate every possible pattern one might dream up. Indeed, it is known, from Chomsky's classification of patterns (see chapter 5) that certain patterns require a certain level of computational complexity to support them, including the ability to perform relative computations. A convergent approach seems, at least superficially, to be incapable of relative computation, and thus handle operations where the order of building matters. However, this is not really true, and a deeper question is whether there is any value in reach such arbitrary states.

To get an idea of the challenge, imagine a simple example of a machine that edits a document on a computer (CFEngine does this on a daily basis). One can easily change simple attributes of a file, like its owner, its name, or its access rights without a sense of order. These are simple because these attributes are independent; they require only a change of value. One can change the name without affecting the owner, and so on. However, a much harder problem lies in determining more complex structures convergently. Editing the content of the file, for instance, is difficult because files really do have internal structures that are order dependent. Words and sections occur in a particular order, and words occur within sections, so there are containers to think about.

Suppose you wanted to make sure that the second chapter of a book contained a reference to a document after the name of an author. You would first have to locate the second chapter, understand what the semantics of a chapter are, then find the name and insert the reference at the right location, if it were not already there. Repeating the operation should have no further effect. This is harder than it sounds, and there is no guarantee that it is always possible.

Chomsky's proved that there is a hierarchy of structures (called formal grammars) for ordering symbolic information, and that one can not place symbols into arbitrarily complex patterns without the full computational power of a Turing machine. This had been part of the argument made by Steve Traugott against convergence.

There are ways of solving this problem in a wide range of cases, however. Indeed, CFEngine has several models for performing this kind of file editing, with generic file formats, to adjust the settings on computers. Essentially, the model of processing logic gets encapsulated within the definition of the convergent operator. It becomes a black box, or a 'closure'. It is unlikely whether arbitrary repairs can be made in this way, but we can cover the most important cases easily. One may then discuss whether the stability of convergence is more important to system safety than the ability to make completely arbitrary changes. Some sacrifices could be worth making.

With this, the answer to operational ordering is essentially to exploit the use pre-conditions outside of the black box logic, also know as guards in programming[174].

An interesting counter-argument to the suggestion that only imperative programming could solve the ordering issues of the Chomsky hierarchy was also provided by Alva Couch and his student Noah Daniels, as a generalization of CFEngine's operator convergence which they called the Maelstrom property[175].

One of the concerns that Alva Couch had expressed about programmatic change on computers was that, with incomplete information, one could not know whether a system might enter unsafe states, for an exploitable period of time, while finding their way to a desired end-state. Naturally, the meaning of 'unsafe' requires an interpretation, just like 'harm' in Asimov's laws, but an aspect of system design lies in preventing malicious parties from exploiting windows of opportunity. Security is one of the semantic conflicts of interest experienced by designers of information technology[176]. Alva later proposed the use of domains of semantic predictability called *closures* to address this for operators, exploiting limits on information visibility.

Couch and Daniels demonstrated what they called the Maelstrom property, which both described CFEngine's behaviour in 2001, and showed how it could be trivially extended to solve a key issue about the cyclic maintenence model[177]. They generalized the property of order independence, showing that one could fashion sets of operators that would fall into the right order by themselves using preconditions, even if the system was feeding back on itself. Thus, it was possible to satisfy the constraints of strict ordering without sacrificing the self-healing properties. Thus they turned self-organizing atoms into self-organizing molecules. In doing this, they showed that an alphabet of atomic convergent operators, each of which could be closures, could satisfy the ordering problem well enough, dispelling the notion that the ballistic approach to logic was necessary.

Couch and Daniels said, suppose you are working in a cyclic maintenance regime, like CFEngine, repeatedly verifying convergent properties over and over again. Then it needn't matter what order these operations are applied, because it is possible for them to generate the correct order simply by saying what preconditions have to be true before the operator's latent function will become switched on. The result is a little like gene activation in cells. Suppose we insist on having the order ABC for three operators. As long as the semantics of the operations are such that B is only active if A has already been done, and C is only active if A and B have already been done, already done, then even if the symbols occur in exactly the wrong order CBA, as long as the application is cyclic, the correct ordered sequence will appear automatically:

$$CBA^* \rightarrow CBA\mathbf{C}\mathbf{B}AC\mathbf{B}A \rightarrow ABC$$

The bold letters show when they are activated. This is a very primitive form of reasoning, using preconditions, much as Prolog reasons: C is only a possible fact if B and A are already facts, but what is important is that this is sufficient to solve many problems. Indeed, if a higher level of reasoning is required, it would only introduce further instability. For even this to work, observation of the state of the world has to be performed continuously.

The Maelstrom property, (named after a whirlpool at the confluence of two rivers in Northern Norway), was implicit in the way that CFEngine worked, but added the idea of using additional pre-conditions to a convergent operator. This meant that a given operator would have to wait for a certain observation to become a 'fact', before proceeding to converge to a fixed point. If the condition were not already true, it would do nothing. It is the standard approach to orchestrating convergent operations in CFEngine today, but it remains controversial amongst traditionalist imperative programmers. The process has intrinsic stability, but it fails the programmer comprehension test for those who need to see an explicit step-by-step flowchart.

Uncertainty seems to reside not only in the incompleteness of information, but also in the instabilities of reasoning. The question remains how one could measure or at least gauge the potential risks of logical (and illogical) behaviour.

The example of the NUMA-database instability showed that logic can be hidden in a multitude of interacting parts, each of which is sensitive to different physical scales. Boolean logic's insistence on projecting such complexities into just true/false or on/off choices, amplifies these effects into distinct modes of operation, forcing actual semantic bifurcations onto behaviour.

The problem of instability in software thus seems to be inflated by an eagerness to reason arbitrarily about data that are not constant. It comes from treating something environmentally measured as though it can be simply true or false within a model. Attempts to outsmart the environment, like a frantic King Canute, will lead to bifurcations and instabilities.

Computer Immunology was a reaction against that mode of thought. The convergent operator maelstrom was an effort to desensitise the system to and, where possible, eliminate unstable decision thresholds altogether, by engineering it towards an inevitable state. All decisions made automatically had to be intrinsically stable, and any other changes were forced into a human-supervised process of policy-making. The unsupervised learning (see chapter 8) used to measure actual state, deliberately used statistical averaging to desensitise thresholds to sudden anomalies, and all responses would be stable by definition, provided one did not explicitly abuse the use of pre-conditions. Computer Immunology could not prevent instability, but it could minimize its likelihood significantly.

Companies like IBM and Hewlett Packard began to take on a similar approach in their 'Autonomic Computing Initiative' after 2001, imitating the methods of electrical engineering's control theory feedback to regulate web services. Each of these cases grew out of an understanding that reliance on binary decision logic was like walking a tightrope between the frying pan or the fire.

The final piece of the puzzle to identify decision thresholds as a culprit of complex instability came, quite surprisingly, from the notion of Turing machines themselves. It was surprisingly, because Turing machines were used above as an argument against the notion of convergence in the strong ordering problem.

In 2003, a formal proof of CFEngine's algebra of convergence had finally appeared in print[178], and, across the Atlantic in Boston, Alva Couch was in the process of engaging a bright young PhD student by the name of Yizhan Sun, whose talents lay in formal mathematical methods. Armed with a new sense of optimism for using mathematical approaches to modelling infrastructure maintenance, the timing seemed perfect to begin to develop some better models for understanding the questions surrounding stability, and the relationship between dynamic and semantic behaviour.

Alva and Yizhan began to look into the algorithmic complexity of infrastructure maintenance, using methods of mathematical computer science, to see if one could place some kind of a value on the difficulty of reasoning forth solutions to semantic instabilities, or at least estimate the difficulty level[179]. The methods for approaching this kind of problem grew out of the aftermath of Turing's work on computability.

When Turing proved the halting theorem, echoing Gödel's incompleteness result, it opened the way towards a systematic study about the computability of certain problems, potentially allowing one to ask: what makes a logic problem hard? Why should we or shouldn't we try to control, micro-manage, or pursue the detailed balance of technology systems based on reasoning? Naturally, Turing's work did not consider the implications of the dynamics of information; it was a theoretical abstraction focused on only one issue. Nevertheless, it gave a solid foundation on which to build.

The complexity of a piece of logic has two apparent dimensions, which turn out to be related. These are what might be termed 'easy' and 'simple'[180]. We say something is simple if it consists of only a few parts, and requires only a little information to describe it. Simplicity can be associated with Shannon's intrinsic information. If a description of something requires little intrinsic information to describe it completely, then it is simple. Simplicity is therefore a measure of the structural complexity. We say something is easy, on the other hand, if it is accessible or close at hand. Solving a problem might be considered easy if the solution could be obtained with little work, in a short time or from a near location[181].

Building on Turing's work, a field of *algorithmic complexity* thus came about, characterizing the ease by which one might logically answer questions. Could it be possible to put a measure on how easy or difficult a problem is to solve by a systematic, stepwise process of reasoning? The idea was simple enough: most problems can be ultimately be phrased in a form that leads to an answer being either true or false, provided they are simple enough in structure. If the question can be written in this form, one may then construct a chain of reasoning (a computer program), using a sequential Turing machine, to search for the answer to that question.

One could then measure either the amount of time, or the number of steps it took for the Turing machine to complete a search for the answer (to see how easy it was to reach the answer). The value would be measured relative to the size of data fed in at the input, so that the measure takes on the characteristic of an intrinsic efficiency, or dimensionless ratio. This gave it a more plausible interpretation, without specific reference to the amount of data fed in. Algorithmic complexity is thus a measure of how far we need to go, riding on a Turing machine, to reach the conclusion.

This method has developed into a field of research in computer science, that attempts to decide how difficult certain computational problems are to solve. The difficulty of a piece of logic is called it algorithmic complexity. Research has shown that different kinds of problem fall into just a few different levels of difficulty. For example, if a program takes an amount of time that is directly proportional to the number of symbols fed in, it is said to be linear, or of order N. If the time taken is proportional to the square of the number N^2, its cube, or some other finite power of the input, it is said to execute in *polynomial time*. All of these answers makes up a large class of problems, answerable in polynomial time, and are said to belong to the complexity class **P**.

It turns out that all of the questions considered computationally feasible belong to **P**, but that there are also very hard problems that do not belong to it. By definition, this class **P** represents the problems it might take a computer a 'reasonable amount of time' to compute. The remaining problems that are not considered tractable, using a sequential Turing machine, belong typically to classes **NP** or **PSPACE**.

A problem that lies in the class **NP** might still be solved in polynomial time, only if supplied with some lucky guesses, i.e. with inputs obtained non-deterministically, such as by flipping a coin. They represent conditional branching points in the algorithms, of the form:

if (coin toss $\rightarrow$ HEADS) go left, else go right.

Perhaps this sounds an unlikely approach to solving a logical problem, but imagine searching the surface of the Earth systematically to find some buried treasure. That could take years. If, on the other hand, you stick a pin in the map and start from a random place, you have an even chance of finding the treasure more quickly, because you might end up a lot closer to the treasure.

Without such a hint, it could take a systematic method exponentially longer to complete an exhaustive search. Using a random, non-deterministic algorithm is perhaps a strange idea, but statistically it turns out that one can get lucky by using randomness, and chance upon a decision that brings you much closer to the answer. Such methods are called Monte Carlo methods for computation, because of the gambling connotations.

The exact boundaries of the complexity classes are not fully understood, but it is believed that **P** is a subset of, **NP** that represents the most tractable problems, and that **PSPACE** encapsulates even more complex algorithms. In other words, **PSPACE** is just about the worst case scenario in terms of complexity. The problems that belong to **NP** and **PSPACE** are amongst the hardest problems known, such as those used to protect encryption keys from being cracked.

The major questions about difficulty are answered by placing it in one of these classes. The argument is basically this: if we know that X is very far away and Y is close to X, then we also know that X is also very far away. Thus a problem is 'easy' if it is close to P in terms of computational reasoning, and hard otherwise[182].

In her doctoral thesis Yizhan Sun showed that finding an imperative chain of reasoning to locate a solution to a general infrastructure maintenance problem was an NP hard problem. In other words, it is not computationally tractable. This did not mean that performing infrastructure maintenance would take a computer millions of years (luckily, as that would not be very good for business), only that, if we tried to compute the knowledge that we currently put into maintenence, using automated reasoning, it would take that long in a systematic search to get the answer right. In short, you can't take human knowledge completely out of the loop if you want to maintain your infrastructure, as it would take too long to work it all out independently.

Think about the complexity in biology, for example. It contains the result of billions of years of random evolutionary searching for ways to make successful organisms. DNA, together with the environment of chemicals around it, has encoded those results in a hard-wired technology that has already flipped all those coins to get to where it is. That means that computing a new cell does not take a long time, because it does not have to search for the right answer every time. However, trying to solve the entire problem of life from the beginning, without the DNA would be an intractable problem. You would need more than a cup of coffee when the computer said: 'Please wait...'. The same principle applies to devising mechanical solutions to problems. The reason CFEngine's convergent operators worked so well was because the convergent operators encapsulate (hardwire) the relevant knowledge about how to interact with a model of their environment, in their 'DNA'.

Couch and Sun's work on intractability was not really as gloomy a prediction, as it seemed. What was interesting to know, however, was whether dumb convergent operators might actually be easier to find than imperative solutions. That is not an unreasonable question to ask, since not every problem can necessarily be made convergent, so there are perhaps fewer things to find.

Following Alva and Yizhan's lead, my colleague Lars Kristiansen and I considered a different approach to study the complexity[183], looking at just the operator approach to maintenance, described in this book. We found that, even when restricting to maintenance to convergent operators, this did not reduce the level of difficult in answering the questions. In fact, the problem was PSPACE hard.

These studies helped to give a small level of credibility to the problem of understanding the challenges of information-rich infrastructure, at a time when keeping it alive was considered low level labour, by essentially putting the problems of its maintenance on more of an academic footing. We built a tenuous bridge between the physics and a tradition of mathematical computation. Yet none of these results actually helps technologists to find answers that help manage smart infrastructure.

DYNAMICS	OBSERVATION	SEMANTICS
QUEUES		TRUE/FALSE
SIZES / DURATIONS		IMPLICATION
RATES / SPEEDS		INFERENCE
CRITICAL POINT		CONSEQUENCE
INSTABILITY		DECISION
CYCLES, LIMITS	MEASUREMENT	PATTERN
FIXED POINTS		RANDOM
EQUILIBRIA		CONSTANT
COMPLEXITY		FACT
INFORMATION		COMBINATION
MESSAGES		COMPLEXITY

Fig. 9.5.   Summary so far of the interface between dynamics and semantics.

Understanding how complexity arises, through the influx of conditional points, where non-determinism flexes its muscles, helps us to see ways we might avoid it in the first place. Could we actually hold complexity at bay, and make machines that are more semantically stable?[184].

The lesson that I see in these studies is that every decision, every point at which a computer program stops to decide something, based on information from an outside source, leads to a branching or bifurcation in the space of possible states the program might go on to visit. It is a ticket to deterministic chaos. Each decision increases its fundamental complexity, from the point of view of 'bugs' and unexpected behaviour. For those of us who come to rely on these systems, this is not good news.

This perspective inevitably brings us back to a speculation made in chapters 5 and 6 that reasoning itself is a source of instability. A recent NASA report about software stability certainly supports this viewpoint[185]. The more an environment

interacts with systems, the more programmable we make them, the more we
generate complexity, and the less stable they will be to unexpectedly running
off the rails. Dynamics and semantics have to be understood together. Figure
9.5 contrasts some of the points we've covered up to this point, and which side
of the line between semantics and dynamics they lie. The bridge between these
worlds is good old Shannon communication.

Designing systems to reason about their environments is hard. There are many
things that might go wrong, many misunderstandings to be made. As long as
there is input, from a noisy channel, there is no way to separate semantics from
the dynamics underlying it. Every decision will be affected by the way we
interpret a measured scale or symbolic alphabet.

At the time of writing, programmability of infrastructure is actually encouraged at a level that would be frightening if the systems were mission critical[186].
My prediction is that this trend will have to change for us to build systems that
are truly safe for human survival. Several high profile outages have been attributed to software instabilities to date[187].

The paradox of certainty is that the very controls we add to steer by, the levers,
the buttons, and the functions, work mainly in instability's favour to undermine
that control. In a sense we can say that the greatest certainty in a smart environment, is a state of blind ignorance (see Figure 9.6).

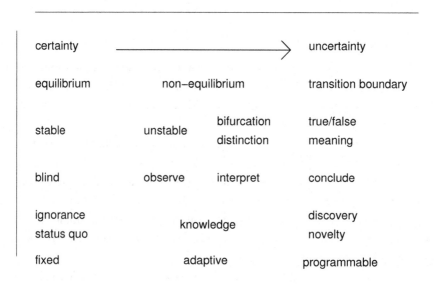

Fig. 9.6.   The spectrum of certainty.

Science fiction writers saw machines of logic as the paragons of certainty. Logic was hailed as something nobler than human intuition, but Asimov was really the first person to question that view, by systematically investigating the flaws in the assumptions of simple reasoning. If we oversimplify a complex situation, with easy rules, we can miss a lot of edge cases.

The future quite probably lies in embracing a tradition that has long held sway in natural science and engineering, but which is still an uncomfortable subject in information science: *approximation*.

Part III
Promises

The chemistry of autonomous cooperation

10

The Concept Of Promises

Or why behaviour comes from within

"A new scientific truth does not triumph by convincing its opponents and
making them see the light, but rather because its opponents eventually die,
and a new generation grows up that is familiar with it."
–Max Planck

In the foregoing sections, we've seen how science has tried to come to grips
with the three main challenges facing our mastery over the world: scale, complexity, and reason, and how the resilience of anything we care to build—not
least infrastructure—depends on how well we maintain its state. We've seen
how the expense of brute force methods, along with the uncertainties of reasoning about the state of things, causes fundamental problems for reliability in
information systems. All this ushers the critical mind to pursue a different approach altogether to the brute force methods of the past: an approach based
more on what is knowable rather than what is desired, based on approximate
reasoning, less sensitive to errors of input and intent. We want to base system
outcomes, as far as possible, on intrinsic stability, because we surrender to the
inevitable: scale, complexity, and reasoning are all subject to uncertainties, and
the inconsistencies of multiple observational 'worlds'.

In this final part of the book, I want to suggest how to adopt a different way
of thinking about human-computer infrastructure, more ambitious in scope and
more practical in nature, that has the potential to go beyond today's art, to make
infrastructure smarter and more resilient, balancing intelligence with inevitability. This final section is about how to make the relativity of information work to
our benefit, at multiple scales and locations, in order to express intent fit for human purpose. Without this capability, information infrastructure has no chance
of succeeding for the good of the world. Let's begin with intent.

The story of logic told in the previous chapter would not be complete without a brief appendix, on the subject of *modal logic*. Indeed, appendix might be the right word, in the sense of a vestigial organ that occasionally becomes inflamed. Modal logic was, in a sense, imagined in the work of Leibniz and his experiential 'possible worlds', but it could not be properly formalized until after the publication of the first-order logic.

Modal logic is a family of logical languages that attempts to construct a calculus of intentionality, i.e. to qualify certainty about the state of the world[188]. This would seem to be what we want to design and discuss an information infrastructure, allowing for uncertainty. It garnered a small wave of attention during the latter half of the 20th century in an attempt to design a perfect language for legal documents. It was later used to describe the limits of what was and was not allowed in information systems, not so much in the sense of how logical agents can be made to reason, as in what they should and shouldn't do. Modal logic is a curiously baroque ornament, a peacock on the runway of formal design. Nevertheless, its intent to explicate the very intent we seek deserves a passing mention, if only to point the way towards a more practical instrument.

Rather than using the tools of statistics and probability to represent uncertainty, modal logic seeks a description in terms of modifiers of natural language, which it could formalize within a purely symbolic framework. A modality, in language, is something that qualifies or quantifies a statement. It takes us from the unapologetic stature of true and false, to express a *degree* of certainty. How true is true? Can something be more true than something else? Can a thing be partially red, i.e. reddish? Can someone be partly competent, or sufficiently competent? These modifying, qualifying terms express degrees of the digital properties that simple first-order logic could only express bullishly within a framework of true or false.

The kind of statements modal logics consider include the following:

> X is usually true
> It is necessary that X be true
> It is believed that X is true
> It is possible that X is true
> It is obligatory that X be true
> It is forbidden that X be true
> X will become true in the future

By formalizing terms like 'it is required', or 'it is forbidden' as symbols, first order logic was extended to discuss modalities.

Alas, this is not as straightforward as it sounds. From the primitives of modalities, one can say things like: if it is not *necessarily* true, then it *might* be true, i.e.

it is *possibly* true. The concept of *truish*, for instance, does not beam with the nobility of formal mathematics, and yet its intent is completely obvious to any child. The goal of modal logics was thus to make it possible to say something vague with precision![189]

The programme of modal logic is somewhat artificial, and fraught with difficulty. It attempts to capture the flexibility of words like 'possible', but only by formalizing the meanings of the words to such an extent that they no longer have that flexibility. For example, one of the axioms of modal logic is that, if something is 'not necessarily untrue', then it is 'possible'. But in English the term necessary does not have the right connotations to be able to say:

> It is possible that it might rain tomorrow.
> It is not necessary that it will not rain tomorrow.

In the stiff, formal meanings attributed to symbolic logic, these sentences are the same, however the commonplace meaning of 'necessary' does not quite convey the right sense. Similarly, to keep algebra simple, modal logic assumes that if something is necessary, then it is necessarily necessary. Again, the assumption of inevitability of necessity is artificial and easy to argue against. Further objections find evidence in behavioural psychology.

If we want to reason about humans and machines in concert, because we want to make smart public systems, then we should also be aware of an asymmetry between the perception of what is possible and what is necessary. Whenever loaded, or threatening words like 'necessary' are used, a sense of foreboding kicks in and our 'risk aversion' instinct tends to prejudice us against it[190]. Consider the following cases of modal equivalence. Some of them work as intended, but most of them don't. The reason is obvious: when humans read language, we don't merely process the formal semantics of the words, we engage all kinds of associative inferences about likely context and meaning that prejudice our understanding.

> It is necessary to not walk under the ladder.
> It is not possible to walk under the ladder

> It is necessary to have sufficient vacation.
> It is not possible to not have sufficient vacation.

> It is necessary to have an account in order to be able to log onto the system.
> It is not possible to not have an account in order to be able to log onto the system.

> It is necessary for you to be at the meeting.
> It is not possible for you not to be at the meeting.

> It is possible the system could be in error.
> It is not necessary that the system is not in error.
> The system is not necessarily not in error.

Clearly the subtleties of linguistic semantics sabotage the intention of modal logic to have a simple language of clear, unambiguous statements.

One of the modal logics that has been studied the most is known as deontic logic, from the ancient Greek deon ($\delta\epsilon o\nu$), 'what is right'. It is the logic of obligations, or statements about what is allowed and forbidden. It originated in the philosophy of law, in a kind of Hobbesian approach to proving right from wrong with a language precise enough to avoid ambiguity. For example, one might say:

> It is obligatory that X be true
> It is forbidden that Y be true

e.g., where, say, X means 'Mark Twain pays his taxes', and Y means 'Mark Burgess walks on the grass'.

In the 1990s, deontic logic rose to minor prominence as a way of defining how information systems *should be*, i.e. a formal language of specification[191]. These were declarative statements about what was allowed in an information-rich system, such as how network security 'should be' (see chapter 6). Superficially, this was like the idea of the CFEngine project's fixed points, except that merely stating something is not the same as knowing that there can be an automatic fixed point associated with the statement. Deontic logic could formulate statements like:

> File X should be available to person Y.
> It is permitted for person A to speak to person B.
> Process P is forbidden after 6 p.m.

As I finished work on my book *Analytical Network and System Administration: Managing Human-Computer Systems* in 2003, I explored the idea of using modal logic to fill in a missing link in the puzzle of how to formalize a model for Computer Immunology. The language of dynamics, explored in the book, did not offer a complete framework to model intentional semantics like 'allowed' and 'forbidden'. One could say how fast, how slow, how efficient, even how likely something would be to happen, but the closest the book came to formalizing the semantics of policy decisions was a discussion of strategic game theory. There was a pressing need to synthesize a more complete, over-arching theory of distributed information, specifically for modelling something like CFEngine, but also going beyond it. That framework would have to be able to answer dynamical as well as semantic questions about systems: who, what, when, where, how, and why.

In computer science, two poles of writing prevail: totally abstract mathematical work with proofs that seem far removed from practice, and more heuristic discussions of specific system designs. There is relatively little work of a more discursive nature that lies in between. It seemed important to be able to analyze Computer Immunology independently of its implementation if there were to be any chance of exceeding the current state of the art. What I craved was a physics of computer system behaviour, with kinematics and dynamics, extended by the semantics of a technological setting.

From the outset, I wanted to preserve important principles that had been learnt in the CFEngine implementation, as these were well tested in the field. The character of CFEngine's approach to Computer Immunology was that its agents operated independently of a central controller. Each agent was a sovereign entity that could ultimately decide its own behaviour—a singularly frightening idea to most technologists, trapped in the ideology of determinism. It was not possible, by design, to force instructions upon a CFEngine agent from outside. The agents could choose to follow one another, but they could not be forced into it. This was both part of its security model, its ability to scale to very large numbers of computers by complete independence, and also a principle that agents should able to repair computers even when unable to communicate with one another. Put concisely, CFEngine was relativity friendly.

CFEngine's behaviour could be called *autonomous*. Autonomous systems have the right to decide for themselves. However, the meaning of autonomy has become quite confused in the literature of computing. Even now, the closest kinship to this idea in the literature lies in the school of *multi-agent systems*, which spawned off from Artificial Intelligence and robotics. Autonomous multi-agent systems were supposed to be robots that worked alone, but followed a central design plan that instructed them from outside. The research community had a notion of 'commitments' and the 'beliefs, desires and intentions' software model (often called just BDI) that seemed initially interesting[192]. However, inexplicably, these models both based themselves on modal logics of obligation, obliging agents to behave in certain ways from an external controller, without any reason to suppose that they might be able to comply. They were not autonomous agents in the sense that CFEngine was and there was no way to calculate the likelihood of something succeeding, because it was simply assumed that the agents would succeed. There was still no pre-existing theory that I could use.

My view, which was then still deemed unorthodox in the world of infrastructure management, was that one should model a human-computer system as being composed of human and machine entities on an equal footing, i.e. human and machine agents both played important parts in a collaborative effort, rather than software being like a kind of loud-hailer for a human voice to reign. This is tantamount to saying that one ought to hold out for a model that would apply to both.

Modal logic initially seemed to offer a reasonable fit, but that hope faded quickly. Quite apart from the moral dimension to deontics, the reactionary discomfort of agents (human or machine) being told what to do and how to behave by remote control, this mode of description was (and is) simply impractical and fraught with inconsistency. The very property of consistency that logic was supposed to eradicate was not upheld[193].

After a just few weeks of studying it, I had serious doubts as to the viability of obligation as the paradigm for talking about distributed systems. The concept of an obligation for a system to behave in a specified way seemed to suffer from the following basic flaws:

1. Obligation is a *non-local* concept. Each agent is obliged by an external agent to behave in a particular way, but what ultimately happens is only up to the agent being obliged. Obligation comes from without, but behaviour comes from within.

2. Obligation is not relativity friendly. It quickly becomes inconsistent without global knowledge. There is nothing to stop Alice and Bob from both imposing contradictory obligations onto Charlie, leading to an inconsistent set of requirements that Charlie might not even know anything about (see Figure 10.1). This was the problem Kripke's many world semantics were supposed to solve, but they still didn't address the fundamental issue of non-locality.

3. Obligation (in the sense of law) is often used as if it were a kind of irresistible force, but there is nothing to guarantee that an obligation will be met. Obligations in law are social contracts, built up over generations around social norms that people are basically willing to accept. Obligation only works in society because of individual self-determination, but technology has no such notion. In technology, or otherwise, there are many reasons why agents might not comply with obligations. They might not want to or be programmed to, they might not be able to, they might not even know about them.

4. Obligation has the familiar illusion of control: that which is obliged is not inevitable, and may even be impossible; it takes us back to the King Canute syndrome from chapter 1.

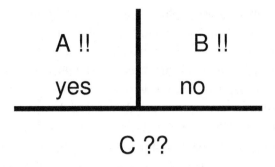

Fig. 10.1. Obligations are not relativity friendly, because they are *non-local*. If there are information flow partitions, inconsistencies flourish. Suppose Alice, Bob and Charlie do not know of each others' existence. Alice makes a rule obliging Charlie to only say yes, Bob makes a rule that Charlie only say no. Charlie does not even know that he is in the middle of a conflict of interest.

Kripke had tried to solve some of these problems by using a many worlds approach to limit the scope of obligations so that one could model who was affected by them, but this alone does not solve the fundamental issue of non-locality and self-determination. Modal logics, fraught with difficulties due to the incompleteness of information, seemed to beset the idea of obligation with fundamental limitations. It didn't matter whether they were used to describe people, natural or technological systems.

One of the reasons for my dissatisfaction with modal logic was that Kripke's semantics do not naturally capture the essence of a network. Networks are extremely important for understanding information systems, because they are everywhere. I wanted to place the behaviour of computers on the same basis as any other description of natural systems of incomplete information, like physics, and there is no theory of obligation theory in chemistry or physics[194]. The idea of networks seemed natural and obligations seemed artificial.

To describe public infrastructure, something simple and intuitive was needed, and it seemed clear that networks had to be part of it. By 2003, I had spent several years looking at another theory of distributed parts, called graph theory (see chapter 2), with Geoffrey Canright and Knut Engø Monsen of Telenor Research. Graph theory is the branch of mathematics that studies networks in a general way. We had already looked at the most basic scaling properties of networks, and we'd gone on to look at simple ideas of partitioning networks into logical regions.

The thrust of networks-as-graphs research was being done by physicists, and it was purely dynamical in nature, but Geoff and I also showed that basic security semantics (i.e. intent and behaviour) could also be derived from the dynamical properties of networks themselves. The phenomenon of *percolation*, for instance, is what happens when water is passes through a sponge, or a porous rock. This can be described using graph theory, and the same theory may be applied to computer security, where people penetrate a system. The semantics of traversing a boundary can be modelled and understood without human intent entering the picture at all. This showed, once again, that semantics cannot escape the dynamical confines of the environments in which they reside: dynamics trump semantics. However, it also showed how to incorporate networks into a system description.

In a conceptual project called Archipelago, with undergraduates Tuva Stang and Fahimeh Pourbayat, we had shown a way of visualizing network connectivity by turning it into a number of loosely connected islands, centred around peaks of denser linkage. This made a simpler representation of infrastructure, in terms of its effective components, capturing *scales*, and it allowed one to look not only at computer networks, but also integrate social networks, and human interactions, bringing any kind of interaction between players into a unified view.

We could see the possible security implications of information flows[195]. In computer security the problem of unintended, or covert channels (hidden channels by which information can be transferred unwittingly), is one of the main design errors in security systems. The idea of networks of *intent* was becoming a common theme, crying out for a general analysis.

Archipelago was unveiled at a seminar for the Norway's forensic computer crime squad in 2003, as a way of helping to discover these channels of social engineering[196], and Tuva presented the work at the 2003 LISA infrastructure conference in San Diego.

With all the drawbacks of obligations, and the immediate range of techniques available for network analysis, graph theory was an easy choice to pursue a new kind of theory for network behaviour that was both local and causal. Using some of its results as guidance, I began to write down some of the algebra of different intended infrastructures, as graphs, based on some practical examples worked out together with doctoral student Kyrre Begnum and visitor John Sechrest[197].

After a few months, having struggled with prototype mathematical formulations of intent, trying modal logic and even the pi-calculus, two things surfaced. The first was that the kind of theory one needed had to be an atomic theory (the directed graph formalism was a good representation for that). The second was that it should provide a 'calculus' for working out the effects of interactions, which could handle arbitrary constraints.

The graphs started to look surprisingly like a bunch of Feynman diagrams, in which the nodes of the graphs were either known states or interaction vertices, and the lines links between them were informational messages about their properties. Even more interestingly, the 'many worlds' experienced by observers due to the fact each observer projected outcomes into their own scheme of interpretation had a direct analogue here. We were looking at a kind of dynamical similarity between the Feynman-Schwinger formulation of quantum electrodynamics and coordination mechanisms of autonomous agents.

The idea gelled in April of 2004 that autonomously specified declarations of intent were simply *promises*—something conceptually opposite to obligations, or any other kind of declarative or imperative logic. Promises could be defined as a network that was not necessarily the physical network between computers, more like a network of self-imposed constraints that we call intentions. This was the beginning of a theory that could work.

Emerging was a theoretical model for a kind of smart, intentional infrastructure based on graphs of autonomously made promises. This graph theoretical approach was an altogether more plausible and scalable approach to locality than deontic logic. Indeed, graphically, it was easy to see how the problem of incomplete information was made worse by the idea of obligation (see figure 10.2). In a theory of promises, one could expect a kind of voluntarily maintained determinism; in obligation theory one could never have that level of certainty. Voluntary promises are immune to relativity's bad effects, since all their information is localized by the promiser.

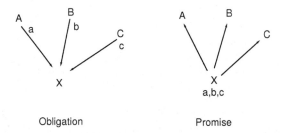

Obligation   Promise

Fig. 10.2. If three agents try to impose three different kinds of behaviour on agent X, the information a, b, c is distributed elsewhere than X, and X does not automatically have access to the information required of it. If agent X promises its behaviour autonomously, all the information is localized at X.

My attention to graphs held me fixated on the apparent connectivity of promise interactions, until Jan Bergstra came to visit me at the University College in Oslo, in the spring of 2004. He brought with him a different perspective from formal computer science.

Although we had totally different backgrounds, Jan and I shared the same attitudes and philosophies about science and research, and we quickly became friends as well as collaborators. Coming from formal computer science, Jan was both intrigued and sceptical that promises were a new way of thinking about systems; but, once the thought processes began ticking, he threw himself into the problem with his unique depth of careful reasoning. This was the beginning of a highly enjoyable collaboration that continues when ever we have time, and has resulted in important progress in formalizing a clear notion of promises[198].

Jan encouraged me to set aside the formalism I had been coveting, and begin by stating the motivation for promises as clearly as possible. This turned out to be excellent advice, and resulted in a paper that I presented at the *Distributed Systems Operations and Management* conference (DSOM 2005) in Barcelona[199]. The paper sparked an immediate interest. It seemed like a way out of the sense of 'same old', though this did not last for long before the audience wanted cold hard tools to use the theory. I held out for three more years, refining my understanding of promises before succumbing to pressure from the academic community to prove the model by writing version 3 of the CFEngine tool, based as closely on the strict theoretical model as I could.

Let's review some of the basic properties of promises and the reasoning networks they form, and try to get a feel for how they might help to explain and design an information infrastructure. It helps to start with quite mundane things. Consider this definition:

> A promise is an autonomous declaration about some intended behaviour that is yet to be verified.

We say a promise is autonomously made, because making a promise is a voluntary act; it comes from within an individual or a device, not by external coercion. This immediately makes it compatible with relativity, as every agent has its own private viewpoint, and knows what it knows. A promise is a declaration of an intention, so it forms a message that has to be transmitted from the originator of the intention. If the originator keeps an intention internal, then no one knows about it and nothing has been promised. It is by making networks of promises that collaboration between individual parts leads to collaborative systemic behaviour.

Intended behaviour need not be about the future; you might promise to have already fed your neighbour's cat, or that you took out the trash, but promises make no sense if we know the outcome, so a promise has not yet been verified by the promisee. They are about incomplete information. Similarly, you might promise that it wasn't you who let the cat out, knowing that the cat was indeed let out, but the thing to be verified is whether or not it was you who did it.

The following points help to summarize the essentials of a promise, and distinguish promises from obligations.

1. Every promise is made autonomously by an agent, to one or more other agents. The agent may be human, machine or a part of something else, i.e. any distinguishable object. The autonomy of agents implies that promises are made 'voluntarily' (the opposite of obligation).

2. An agent can only make promises about its own behaviour. It describes local behaviour. Any behaviour an agent wants to encourage in other agents must be arranged through other promises made by the other agents.

3. A promise is made by a promiser[200] to one or more promisees (to whom the promise is made), and a scope (the set of agents who receive the information in the promise message). The promiser has special status as the agent principally *affected* by the promise, due to locality.

4. A unique promise is a unit of information. It can be compressed into a single symbol, and transmitted to the agents within scope.

5. Incompatible promises are promises that an agent cannot make at the same time. Some promises might be lies or deceptions.

6. Promises might or might not be kept[201]. This judgement requires an assessment, which connects promises with the idea of observation. Different agents might make different assessments about whether a promise is kept. This makes promises compatible with relativity.

7. A promise made does not have to be accepted by the promisee. The acceptance of a promise given (usually denoted with a $+$) also requires a promise to accept, called a use-promise (usually denoted with a $-$). The transfer of something promised requires both $\pm$, like a charge neutral equilibrium.

This final point is the key to understanding relativity and 'many worlds' perception. A key idea in promise theory is that each observer experiences obervations of the world according to what it individually promises to accept. Like quantum mechanics, it is the observer who is the only accessible measuring instrument, projecting whatever hidden goings-on that take place into their own framework of understanding or set of of traffic-light states. This is compatible with relativity.

It might seem surprising that these points are all that is required to govern a distributed human-computer system, to within approximate but quantifiable limits, but indeed they are.

Promises are entirely localized in a single agent, at the smallest scale, so all the information required to discover inconsistencies, arising from conflicting promises, is automatically located in only one place. That means each agent is, by design, capable of resolving its own inconsistencies without any external help. This is a huge step forward for individual certainty. An agent might promise that it will feed the cat, and that it will not feed the cat, but, if so, has only itself to blame for being inconsistent[202]. Thus, one can never directly have a situation like that in Figure 10.2, where an agent is not aware of a conflict. The only subtlety comes when an agent makes a promise that is explicitly based on information from another agent. We'll see how this complicates the issue of locality in Chapter 12, but also how the concept of promises helps to clarify such matters of relativity.

Does the idea of promises really make sense? It is too human an idea? Some of the benefits of a promise viewpoint are not immediately obvious until you start to think in a promise manner. Culturally, we have been conditioned to think in terms of laws, rules and obligations, which are also human notions. However, the world makes a lot more sense if you switch to thinking in terms of promises. Promises allow us to pull systems apart and put them back together again, without losing sight of their intended behaviour.

The challenge that first-time readers often have to swallowing the kind of loose, anthropomorphic language of promises, lies in divorcing oneself from the idea that promises are a purely human thing. What does it mean for a computer or some other machine to blame itself for being inconsistent? In fact this is easy to answer: intentions all get traced back to the humans originally responsible for making, deploying, and programming the machine. We don't have to think of these humans directly, we can think of their remnant merely as the ghost in the machine, the *deus ex machina*.

Inanimate things can make promises by transference, or because a human observer interprets their behaviour to be consistent with the existence of an underlying promise. We even use this in daily life, e.g. 'the weather looks promising', 'it promises to be a fine day'. Intentionality originates from humans, but it need not flow from a human, as such. For example, here is how to make furniture promise you a sandwich.

> John promised you a sandwich.
> John, who works at the reception desk, promised you a sandwich.
> The reception desk promised you a sandwich.
> I promise you, the desk promised me a sandwich.
> The sandwich doesn't look that promising.

The advantage of abstracting the intentionality is that, even when John is off duty, you know you can ring the reception desk of your hotel and ask them why they didn't keep their promise. It depersonalizes the concept of what has to keep the promise, and allows us to associate abstract roles to groups of agents (people and machines), like 'service desk'. This is exactly what we want for describing infrastructure services[203].

So what does promise theory do for us? It creates a uniform framework for thinking about systems of all kinds, no matter whether the agents are human, biological, mechanical, or inert. To appreciate promise theory as a tool, especially for technology, we need to make it more formal. What this then promises (pun intended), is to encourage a mode of thinking, in which the behaviours of independent parts of a system are coordinated through information, i.e. the possibly non-deterministic arrival of messages, passed in the form of promises and assessments. Such messages set expectations about the behaviour of the parts for a certain amount of time.

As an information theory, promises allow us to examine a system from any perspective, and set expectations about their certainty. We might invent an imaginary 'godlike' observer who can see all promises from a high level, or we can change from the viewpoint of one agent to another in order to see what they might know or believe about one another. We must concede that we cannot guarantee when or if promises will be kept, but we *can* attach probabilities to the outcomes based on past frequentist behaviour or Bayesian belief. Hence we see a way to fuse logical reasoning with numerical probabilities and beliefs in a way that respects relativity and indeterminism. Promises are an honest approach for grappling with incomplete information, rather than attempting to deny it, as obligations do. They can also be used as a basis for constructing mathematical games[204].

Let's explore the relationship between promises and natural behaviour a little more and try to unify a number of different points of view about how the world works. As we know from Feynman and Schwinger, the forces of nature behave very much like transfers of information. In their view (or my version of their view), a quantum source promises a receiver information about all the different possible messages (visualized as paths) that transform from one state to another. The receiver promises to listen to all of these alternatives, add them up, and compute its final state based on all of them together. There is a dynamical similarity to thinking in promises.

We can practice further thinking in terms of promises by reformulating 'laws of nature' in a promise language. Here are Newton's three laws[205]:

1. Every agent promises to remain in the same state unless unless it accepts a message from another agent.

2. Agents promise to accept messages (impulses) from other agents and adjust their steady state behaviour according to the importance (momentum) of the message.

3. To transfer an influence, each + promise must be met with an equal and opposite − promise. Moreover, each agent must promise to respect the integrity of message accounting. If an agent promises to receive a message, then it acquires the value of the message, and the sender loses the same value.

Physicists recognize these laws as expressions of conservation of physical accounting measures: energy and momentum, and would doubtless be horrified by the gross anthropomorphization of physical law; however, the point is that the description works and the language of 'promise' is really no worse than that of 'law'. Notice how energy and money look very alike in this formulation (see Chapter 1 and Chapter 3). There is no reason why all promise-oriented systems should follow these laws, but these are the promises made by our physical universe.

Promises are not ballistic messages sent from source to receiver. Ballistics are a classical, *force*-oriented way of thinking. In a digital information world, we have to think about autonomy of the objects and how their promises might lead them to change their state or behavioural orbits, based on what they learn.

Thus a promise does not crash into an agent and change it. Rather, the agent promises to accept messages that transfer information, promised by other agents and possibly act upon them. There are two kinds of message:

- Messages associated with signalling the existence of new promises.

- Messages that are exchanged as part of the keeping of promises.

The initial signalling of a promise, when it is created or expires, has some similarity to a particle creation or annihilation event in physics; though, once a quantum object exists, its promises are determined (we call those promises the laws of physics), and they are constant. In the technological world, promises come and go much more often. We begin to see why we should not underestimate the uncertainties that can arise in a complex infrastructure. It is a harder problem than dependable physics.

A few basic message patterns come immediately to mind. These help as eye-openers to the way we might express models using promises. The first of these is the basic transfer mechanism for intent, on which everything else rests. It is the analogue of Newton's third law (see Figure 10.3).

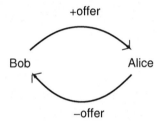

Fig. 10.3. To exchange something, it has to be both offered and accepted. Bob makes a promise with some offer (+ means give), and Alice signals her willingness to accept (− means use).

The figure shows a one way process of offering a service of some kind from Bob to Alice. The fact that Bob is offering something to Alice does not make her accept. She might ignore Bob's promise entirely. If he sends her letters, she does not have to receive them. For symmetry, in promise theory, we required Alice to promise to 'use' or accept Bob's promise, to bind them in an agreement of transference[206].

The need for mutually matching 'give-receive' promises is new in the semantic world. One is able to take force transfer for granted in physics, because the laws of physics have constant semantics: when something is offered, it is received, no questions asked. Indeed, all our descriptions of physics assume this and take it for granted. The same is not given in a world of agents with autonomous intent, however. There, one is at the mercy of voluntary cooperation alone: that which is offered is not necessarily accepted.

A second and more interesting promise graph takes us right to the heart of the concept of economics, stability, and equilibrium. Consider the exchange of promises in Figure 10.4. This makes use of a new idea: that of a *conditional promise*. A conditional promise is actually not (yet) a promise at all, but it might

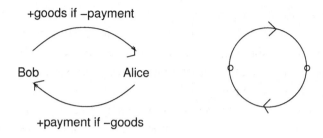

+goods if –payment

Bob   Alice

+payment if –goods

Fig. 10.4.   The basic promise graph of trade (with use-promises suppressed) shows a two person Nash equilibrium, or 'loop diagram' which generates a long term relationship. This currently represents a deadlock situation, or reversible process, or unbroken symmetry. The deadlock needs to be broken for it to generate an arrow of time.

become a promise in the future. A + conditional promise might say: 'I promise to give you the goods if you promise to pay me'. The counterpart (promisee of the goods promise) retorts: 'I promise to pay you if you promise to give me the goods' (see Figure 10.4).

When faced with a pre-condition of this kind, we need the condition to be satisfied before the promise becomes valid, like in Prolog. Thus, what we end up with in this pattern could simply be a deadlock, in which neither of the potential promises can be realized, let alone kept, until the other has been given. But this depends on the behavioural semantics of the agents. We need to clarify this.

We may look at this and reason that these two conditions are self-consistent. Thus, in a world of agents that trust one another, agents could be satisfied with such promises and begin trading. The loop might result in a long term exchange of money and services. If we do not insist on deterministic semantics, we can imagine that goods and money flow in both directions at random times, but how much and when are not determined.

Now suppose, we change the semantics so that the precondition requires the pre-condition promise to actually be kept before the giving promise activates, not merely that such a promise exists. Now there is a true deadlock: 'You'll get your goods when I get my money', and 'You'll get your money when I see my goods'.

Jan Bergstra and I first discussed this example, sitting on the train between Amsterdam to Utrecht, having struggled to buy a ticket for me from a vending machine. Jan pointed out that the symmetry between these two promises had to be broken in order for anything to happen[207]. Symmetry breaking is a well-known process in physics, with deep significance—yet another connection between physics and information. This was a very exciting observation, displaying how the connection between symmetries and dynamics emerge from the otherwise static promise graphs.

Compare the right hand side of Figure 10.4 with the Figure 4.9. As we mentioned in Chapter 4, this dynamical equilibrium structure is a generator for all basic behaviours, including those that deviate from equilibrium. All we have to do to start a process is to break the symmetry with an appropriate boundary condition. In this case, we ask: does someone pay up front, or does someone deliver the goods first?

In Schwinger's quantum source language, the symmetry is broken by the presence of a source, which injects either goods or money (creation of particle or antiparticle) at a certain place. This is easy to see. Suppose some agent (the 'external source') sets an initial condition of payment to Bob, thus breaking the symmetry, then now Bob promises Alice the goods, and Alice's precondition is met, hence she promises payment, which in turn primes for another round (see Figure 10.5). We have actually generated the motor of economic trade by breaking the symmetry on a simple pair of promises.

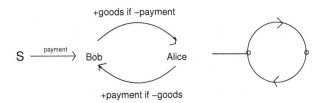

Fig. 10.5. The deadlock symmetry is broken by the presence of an external source, to start the loop. If the promises are not restricted in time this becomes a motor for exchanging goods and payment.

With hindsight, although simplistic, this simple promise configuration might be the most fundamental and important graph of all. Why? Because it represents a state of equilibrium, and as we know equilibrium can be the generator of all possible processes. Not only that, it does not care whether the equilibrium is static or dynamic, deterministic or non-deterministic. It is a completely structural representation of the semantics of trade for money, free of the dynamical details. Each bubble represents not just a single moment in time, but potentially an ongoing relationship, like a clock, that can be set in motion by breaking the symmetry. Time is actually generated by this diagram, as it realizes transactions between the agents.

It is not hard to see how this simple 'one loop' diagram is the basis of all trade, and therefore an awful lot of economic issues. It is the basic pattern for a contract: one agent offers something for another agent in exchange for something in return.

Doctoral student Siri Fagernes and I showed that we could map this promise diagram onto different kinds of two-person games, as studied by von Neumann and Nash[208]. Then one sees that the equilibrium represents the minimax or Nash equilibrium described in Chapter 4.

Economists and philosophers struggle over the definitions of contracts, because they have rooted their notion of promises in the philosophy of obligations[209], but promises also help to explain an argument about whether or not a contract is an exchange of promises in philosophy. Jan and I showed that a contract may be considered a document of bilateral promise proposals, i.e. promises that were not yet agreed to. What was missing was the agreement itself. Obviously the signing of the agreement represents a use-promise for the promise of the whole document, from each of the parties. Only on this signal is the agreement full of proposed promises activated. With the simple idea of a promise proposal, no one has to 'go first' and be weakened in a negotiation. A signature is a promise to use the collection of bilateral promises as a unit. It is a voluntary act. We pretend that it is binding, but of course compliance is entirely voluntary.

The name Promise Theory was coined at the meeting in Barcelona in 2005, and it stuck. It was an absurdly simple idea, but one that had great analytic power. As a theory, promise theory has its limits, but it is enormously helpful as a way of looking at problems of complex but intended behaviour. Of course, its main purpose here is to approach a trouble-free description of information infrastructure.

What promises offer is a language of small intentions to describe and discuss cooperative behaviour. They have the capability to unify many of the topics we've already touched upon in this book. If you start with a highly expressive language that allows to you describe any scenario, with necessary detail, then you can answer difficult questions. For technology, we can place things in a common framework and decide between them. "How sure can we be that this will work"? And "at what rate"?

As an atomic theory, promises give us a table of elements (basic promises) from which any behavioural substance can be put together, like a chemistry of intentions. Once an intention about self is made public, it becomes a promise. Its founding principles exist to maintain generality, and to ensure that as few assumptions as possible are made, such as recognizing that every agent's world-view is incomplete in relation to the whole.

What is unusual about promises, compared to other scientific models is that it models human intentions, and it does it in a way that is completely impersonal. By allowing contact with game theory models, we can also see how cooperative models ultimately have an economic explanation (often referred to as bounded rationality). Why should I keep my promises? What will I get out of it?

To apply promise theory to a new problem, one starts like this:

1. *Identify the key agents of intent.*

   An agent is any part of a system that can change independently. To get this part of the modelling right, we need to be careful not to confuse intentions with actions or messages. We are not talking about the moving parts of a clock, or even an Internet search request, but the motivations that play a role in making everything happen. Actions may or may not be necessary to fulfil intentions. Maybe inaction is necessary!

   To be independent, an agent only needs to think differently or have a different perspective, access to different information, etc. This is about the separation of concerns. If we want agents that reason differently to work together, they need to promise to behave in a mutually beneficial way. These agents can be humans (as in the business-IT bridge) or computers (as in multi-tier server queues).

2. *Deal with the Uncertainty.*

   There is no absolute certainty. Promises might or might not be kept, so plan for that. Even a machine can break down and fail to keep a promise, so we need to model this. Each promise will have a probability associated with it, based on our trust or belief in its future behaviour.

3. *Turn 'requirements' into autonomous promises.*

   The goal in cooperation is to ensure that agents make all the promises necessary so that some imaginary on-looker, with access to all the information, would be able to say that an entire cooperative operation could be seen as if it were a single entity making a single service-promise.

   How we coax the agents to make promises depends on what kinds of agents they are. If they are human, economic incentives are usually the answer. If the agents are programmable, then they need to be programmed to try to keep the promises. We call this voluntary cooperation.

   Is this crazy? Why not just force everyone to comply, like clockwork? Because that makes no sense. A computer follows instructions because it was constructed voluntarily to do so. If we change that promise by pulling out its input wire, it no longer does. Cooperation is voluntary in the sense that it cannot be forced by an external agent, without perhaps actually attacking the system to compromise its independence.

4. *Eliminate conflicts of intent.*

   If all agents share the same intentions, there would be no need for promises. Everyone would get along and sing in perfect harmony, working towards a common purpose. The fact that the initial state of a system has unknown intentions means we have to set up things like 'agreements', where agents promise to behave in a certain way. This is what we call orchestration with relativity.

The capacity for individual agents to change independently is what characterizes locality. Local actions and interactions are what one has the best chance of controlling: short distances, short times, small changes. The accumulation of many such small, controlled changes could then be examined to discover what long-range properties might exist.

The challenge for technologists seeking certainty is thus to harness individual parts as a collection of individual agents, arranged like a network, and then try to constrain them to lower the number freedoms they can exhibit so that they can be predictably close to equilibrium. To do this, we have to decide at what level of composition in the discrete hierarchy of scales we wish to model.

Just as in physics, what we treat as atomic is not necessarily actually the smallest thing in a system. What is important is how we identify the things that are independent. If we model atoms that are too big, it becomes impossible to resolve sufficient information to describe the behaviour. If we resolve atoms that are too in time or space, we end up with too much redundant information (see Figure 10.6)[210].

For example, if our aim were to study traffic, we might choose individual vehicles as the atomic parts. We would not choose the components, like doors and wheels, that make up the car as being atomic, else we might have to promise that they all moved at the same speed at all times, and were stuck together! This is just the same as physics. If we want to describe a material, we don't talk about the protons and electrons of every atom inside the material, we treat a piece of material as an agent.

A model in terms of atomic promises places the responsibility for correctness inside the affected object, and helps us to see the impact, relative to the other parts. In designing the formal language for promises, the identification of the correct scale becomes a part of the definition of the promiser.

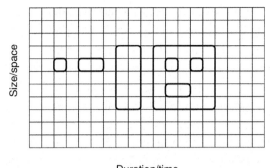

Duration/time

Fig. 10.6.   How we choose the artefacts that we consider to be atomic at the appropriate level of description. Some might contain other artefacts we don't care about.

Consider these promises, to keep restrooms clean in a restaurant. First we could make a promise at a high level of granularity:

Promiser: Restroom
Promisees: Customers, health inspectors
Body: Ensure clean and supplied every hour.

Or, realizing that restrooms have internal structure, i.e. different parts that can change independently, it could be broken down into different promises, with different schedules:

Context: Every day between 10:00 and 23:00

Promiser: Floor
Promisees: Customers, health inspectors
Body: Be clean and without litter, every two hours

Promiser: Toilets
Promisees: Customers, health inspectors
Body: Be clean, with freshener, plenty of paper, every hour

Promiser: Towels
Promisees: Customers, health inspectors
Body: Plenty of towels, check every hour.

This collection of agents (floor, toilets, towels) could be given the status of a single high-level meta-agent, just as an atom contains multiple sub-atomic particles.

In each case, the promiser identifies what the affected object is, and what is formally making the promise. The body of the promise explains the details of what is promised. The context of a promise explains where and when it applies, e.g. all restaurants, every day between 10:00 and 23:00. Then there is the explanation of why the promise was made. This complete declaration becomes essential documentation with a simple semantic interpretation.

You might have noticed, in the example, that the toilet itself formally promises to stay clean, but it does not say how this is achieved. It might not have the technology to maintain itself, in which case it might have to rely conditionally on promises made by human or robotic cleaners.

Promiser: Floor
Body: Be clean and without litter, if robot promises to help

Promiser: Robot
Body: Clean restroom floor every two hours

These are details that we might or might not want to know. The value of having the affected object make its own promise is that assessing whether or not the promise is kept, can be done independently of keeping the promise, and the work-item still needs to be measured according to what is promised, not according to what was done.

In the management of information systems, the same situations occur, for different resources. One of the issues faced by engineers is how to repair systems that drift out of a healthy state. Changes occur, some intended, some unintended, and these need to be countered by some kind of immune system. This was the central thesis of Computer Immunology.

When a computer drifts out of its desired state, it might be a result of human error, or a clumsy upgrade, sent perhaps by a vendor, that changes a small part of a file. It could also be a dynamical instability caused by crossing a scaling threshold. One then has a dilemma. What level of atomicity should be respected during the repair? Do we try to edit just the offending part of the file? Do we replace the entire file with a new one? Do we reinstall the entire computer to make sure that everything is correct? This takes us back to the convergence versus congruence discussion in Chapter 9.

Choosing the right level at which to make promises is a tricky design choice, with potentially many conflicts of interest. For modelling, we may do what we like. For the the actual real-world implementation, there are several criteria to consider in choosing the atoms to manipulate in order to keep a promise, i.e. *at what level or scale* must a promise be kept? The criteria include: what is easy to think about or manipulate, what is safest or causes least impact, what is fastest, what is cheapest?

It might sound like a strange discussion to have, but we make such choices based on the available tools and the economics of the change. If the branches of a tree intrude onto your house, you might trim the branches or cut down the whole tree. Computer engineers sometimes try to fix errors at the level of a broken part, but if that takes too long, they often reinstall the entire computer, even though this means killing it or taking it out of service. This is fine as long as nothing is lost by throwing away the part. In biology, the atomicity of cells is what allows the immune system to replace parts without killing an organism, as long as there is sufficient redundancy. Killing a skin cell is no problem, but killing off neurons or anti-body memory cells would impair the organism. In a computer, the equivalent of DNA is information held in system promises.

In a mission-critical situation, one does not have the option of killing a computer just to fix a bad file, unless there is massive redundancy and no one would notice. Certain kinds of services can be replicated to allow this kind of redundancy, but many cannot. Today, in so-called cloud-computing datacentres, it is relatively quick and easy to kill and rebuild a computer. Thus, in the absence of other tools, many companies use this approach. It is a biological strategy: if you lose a few cells, it doesn't matter much, but only if the machines themselves don't matter much. These dynamics are constantly changing as a result of technological progress.

CFEngine 3's approach followed promise theory, actually vice versa. Promise theory says: look for the smallest part that can change independently and maintain it as a separate promise. It advocates a bottom-up approach to constructing systems, because if you maintain the basic parts, then the whole is more likely to hang together. If we think top-down, changes to repair low level issues often involve *ad hoc*, unplanned actions, because one doesn't have a model of the system at a low level. This results in cables strewn around rooms, *ad hoc* piles of equipment, extra power splitters, improvised shelves, duct tape holding things together, and so on. In this case, there is little alternative but to destroy and rebuild, because one has wandered into a situation of not just incomplete information, but inadequate modelling[211].

By applying the abstract idea of promises to model the behaviour of automation, I realized that one important thing about a promise is that is it *not* an instruction, or a step in a flow control diagram (see Chapter 9). It is information about intended outcomes that would be maximally useful if it could answer the basic questions: about *what*, *when*, *where*, *how*, and *why* promises were being made. It was a meta-level description, in the same kind of way that quantum mechanics could well be a meta-description of something that we cannot fully see the details of. But it provides enough to be predictive. Another important thing was that every promise could be associated with a convergent operator whose semantics captured precisely those hidden details to keep the promises. That did not make systems deterministic, but it maximized the chances of predictability through promises being kept.

It was on New Year's Day 2007 that I woke up in the quiet of the morning, after an evening of celebration with friends, and decided that the time had come to apply promise theory to the muse that had inspired it. I wrote the essay 'Promise you a rose garden'[212], to explain how to think of computer networks using voluntary cooperation, and thus began the effort to apply promises to the actual world of information infrastructure explicitly.

Promises emerged out of the failures of deterministic logic to describe distributed systems. In this chapter, we migrated from a logic fraught with formal difficulties to a theory built on networks with dynamics and semantics unified, and the notion of *intent* finally came to the forefront, as a crucial part of the puzzle of technology.

Before seeing how to apply promise theory to understand information infrastructure, in all of its complexity, we have to discuss the other side of promises' dual personalities, and explore intentionality itself. In particular, there are deeply human issues at stake: the informational aspect of promises ties one to the need for learning over slowly varying time, not only about the environment in which a system functions, but also about the reliability of the system itself, our expectations of it, and the economics of it.

A promise-based theory of infrastructure not only pulls a system apart into atoms that see their own world view, in order to put it back together in a comprehensible and maintainable way, it also documents intent and context about the world in a way that humans can and must relate to. It is not about instructions for change, it is about expressing the desired end-state to achieve human goals and aspirations, at the level of the fundamental mutable parts.

Perhaps just as importantly, individual human issues and desires have finally entered the description of science and technology, and society's serviceable information infrastructure, in a natural and integral way.

11

The Human Condition

How humans make friends to solve problems

"While any new technical device may increase the range of human freedom, it does so only if the human beneficiaries are at liberty to accept it, to modify it, or reject it: to use it where and when and how it suits their own purposes, in quantities that conform to those purposes."
–Lewis Mumford, The Myth Of The Machine

The SOS Morse code signal 'Save our souls' is one of the most recognized hails on our planet. Although it is based on a phrase in the English language, its significance transcends the language of its origin. The simple pattern of dots and dashes (. . . – – – . . .) is so clearly recognizable that anyone could discern it and learn its meaning. Morse code follows a tradition of nautical signalling using simple coloured flags. A good signalling code is easily discernable under difficult, noisy and foggy conditions.

Today, a whole generation of mobile phones, with custom ring-tones has weakened the association of this signal with the *m'aidez* cry for help, and the SOS signal is instead associated with certain brands of phone. This reveals that the challenges of communication are not just in the content of a message, but also in its interpretation. Where humans are involved, how we promise *meaning* is at least as important as information.

Morse code is a set of audio symbols formed from two atoms: dots and dashes (or dits and dahs). It was designed as part of the single wire telegraph by Samuel Morse and Alfred Vail between 1837 and 1844. Its advantage lies in turning the alphabet of Latin characters and numbers into a representation of sequences of these atoms, easily distinguishable sounds on a background of noise under difficult conditions. Its drawback lies in having to be learnt.

In the early days of communication, voice transmission was not a realistic option, and a high fidelity encoding of text was highly valuable. The ability

263

to record sounds with the phonograph was not invented until 1877, thus simple digital codes were the best approach to telegraphic messaging. Each Morse sequence, always promised the same alphanumeric symbol. The stability of a simple set of promises allowed robust delivery in spite of environmental noise. The trade-off asks humans to work harder to make the job easier for the technology, but, at the time, it was the best compromise.

What Morse's code enabled was the rise of a global network communications technology. The Victorians were demonstratively daring, as is witnessed by the feats of engineering completed during the 19th century.

In 1853, a handful of enterprising men laid the first telegraph cable across the North Atlantic Ocean, principally to carry messages between the trading centres of London and New York. It yielded the first working communications link between Britain and the United States[213]. The economic incentives of global trade made it important to build a closer relationship between the two countries, meaning more regular interactions. Morse code made that possible, with the technology of the day. Digital communication thus emerged during the industrial revolution, from the promise of responsive and closer relationships.

Sir Francis Ronalds (1788-1873) pioneered telegraphic communication. In the first publication on the subject in 1823, he proposed a method for locating faults on a telegraph line, realizing that it was not enough to promise a service unless one knew how to maintain it over time. Samuel Morse, on the other hand, had the idea for electrical communication in 1832 but did not produce a working telegraph in the United States until 1836. Morse carried out experiments in London which showed that signals could be promised through 2,000 miles of cable. Politics and rivalry intervened however as the more well-connected surgeon Edward Whitehouse, who had an aristocratic interest in telegraphy, proclaimed falsehoods about transmission lines, suggesting that very high power was needed to transmit over long distances[214]. It was left to Lord Kelvin (William Thomson) to show that low power signals would be transmitted best. Using his invention for detecting small signals, the mirror galvanometer, he was able to signal effectively over huge distances.

From there, it required simple bravery. The first attempt to lay an underwater cable began on 28th August 1850, when the steam tug Goliath drew a single copper wire insulated by a half centimetre of gutta percha[215] from Dover out across the ocean to Cap Gris-Nez. Unfortunately, after only a day, the cable broke around the French coast[216]. In treacherous seas, at the very limits of possibility, many failures were endured before, finally, on the 27th of July 1866, the steamboat Great Eastern delivered a cable from England's Valentia Bay to Heart's Content in North America[217]. It is a marvellous testament to the Victorian engineers that one section of Atlantic cable, placed there in 1873, was still in use in the 1950s.

This brief narrative captures the essence of the human condition. It illustrates the drive for human involvement, as well as the value we derive from it, how we attribute meaning, why we seek out communication, and why we pursue certain avenues of technology over others, and, not least, our desire to make a difference.

The superficial appearance of technology in the story could distract from what is really going on: the gadgets stand out as novelty more than age-old human platitudes. Nevertheless, most important of all is the impact of the technology. A telegraph could pretend to be cables and electricity, but it really embodies communication, relationships, monitoring, and awareness and comprehension of the world. These are the things of human value that drive us to build in the first place.

The telegraph is an example of an enduring digital technology that enabled humanity to amplify it endeavours, through the coordination of activity. That was its grand purpose; but, that coordination would not have lasted long unless it could keep its promise to deliver information repeatedly and comprehensibly. For that to occur, trusting *human relationships* had to prosper, and be replaced by *proxy relationships* via technology. Relationships are the basic ingredient of socio-economic activity, thus the relationships we build to our basic infrastructure becomes a critical aspect of its success.

Promises lead to relationships, and relationships sustain promises over time. As they grow, we learn, and we build infrastructure to satisfy the human desire to know and comprehend it, like a friend. To understand these dynamics of relationships better, we need to explore this evolving symbiosis more fully, by delving into its science, beginning with the economic theory of dilemmas.

A dilemma is a decision process, known as a 'game' in mathematics, in which players compete against one another, with no particular incentive to cooperate in the short term, but where they can win out in the long term by building a cooperative relationship with one another (see Figure 11.1). Recall the two-person promise interaction described in the previous chapter, and its relationship to the economic motor, and you will see the connection. You might be familiar with the original 'prisoner's dilemma' game, as this has been widely popularized to discuss problems in economics, evolutionary biology, and also as a general model of non-cooperative behaviour.

Keep$_1$ Break$_1$

	Keep$_1$	Break$_1$
Keep$_2$	*(R,R)*	*(S,T)*
Break$_2$	*(T,S)*	*(P,P)*

Fig. 11.1. A 2 person dilemma game. The values in the matrix show what payoff each agent gets if it keeps (or does not keep) its promise, given what the other player decides. The game can be played in many rounds. For the game model to qualify as a dilemma game, the symmetrical payoffs for each player should satisfy $T > R > P > S$, and $R > \frac{(T+S)}{2}$.

In a dilemma game, both players, i.e. both 'agents', meet one another in multiple rounds. This represents a model for how people seek each other out in real life, if they find the relationship valuable. The agents are completely autonomous, so they may choose either to keep their promises to the other, or not. They can make this choice on any round of the game, and they can even give up the game if they want to. They are motivated to meet and play only by what they expect to win. However, if we assume that they are guided by the incentive of profit, (making them rational players, in the eyes of most economic theory), then they would seem to be compelled to make a rational choice to maximize their winnings.

The business of rational choice in economics is a peculiar one. Psychologist, economist and Nobel laureate Daniel Kahneman and collaborators have shown that humans do not really make rational choices: our brains are too easily fooled by simple illusions (for example, see Figure 8.5.). There is an asymmetry in the way we think about reward incentives that makes the classical arguments about rational pursuit of reward over-simplistic. The threat of loss casts a larger shadow than the attraction of a win, for instance[218]. Nevertheless, this only helps the argument that both humans, and their purely rational machines, would favour the formation of long-term relationships.

In the dilemma game, the players each have two possible choices: whether to keep their promises to one another, or not. They decide based on what they see as the economic outcome, possibly combining multiple reward currencies in what is known as bounded rationality. Agents meet a certain number of times (rounds of the game), and they play on each round by being challenged to keep their word.

If you are inclined to reason through the details, the numbers in the matrix of Figure 11.1 are the 'payoffs' to the agents, i.e. what they expect to gain from the interaction, written in the form:

(agent 1, agent 2)

The rows represents the choice made by agent 1 and the columns represent the counter choices made by agent 2. The values in the boxes of Figure 11.1 represent the payoffs if they play their respective strategies labelled in the rows and columns. R is the reward for cooperating, T is the temptation to not keep their promise (which is greater than the reward), and S is the sucker's payoff when the other agent keeps its promise only to be tricked by the other. Finally P is the punishment if both players fail to keep their promises[219]. Both players choose at the same time on each round, but both can also remember what happened on previous rounds. The cumulative payoff accrued by each player by the end of the rounds decides who came out best.

The crucial detail in the setup, which encourages agents to defect from keeping a contract relationship of mutual promises, is that there is a temptation T to not keep the promise, which offers a quick short-term benefit over keeping the promise (T is greater than the normal reward R). In other words, if either agent looks at its immediate options (labelling the rows and columns in figure 11.1), it sees that it can make a quick win by reneging on its promise.

Suppose, for example, you promise a bank each month that you will laboriously verify the security of its information systems, and for this you are promised a modest subscription reward. Each month, there is a temptation to slack off and not do the job properly (defect on your promise), as that will give you more time to work for more money from other customers. You might succeed, and temporarily profit from that, but this betrayal will inevitably be discovered by the bank, and so the next month, one of three things might happen:

1. The bank ignores the betrayal and pays the usual fee as promised. (Possible in the interest of fostering amity, but unlikely.)

2. The bank retaliates, and breaks the promise to pay any commission.

3. The bank ends the relationship, and perhaps seeks retribution.

At any time, either you or the bank can terminate the relationship, but if either loses out by being tricked, there is a chance of winning back losses by continuing with the long-term relationship. Relationships are valuable; stability is profit.

What encourages cooperation in a long-term relationship is the fact that the punishment for not cooperating is harsh. It might seem clever for an agent to trick its counterpart once, but that will likely meet retribution the next time they encounter one another. If players know that they have to meet each other again, they will likely try to punish the other for betrayal.

So, in order for there to be multiple encounters, and long term profit on both sides, there has to be a reinforced trust about the keeping of promises. This is what makes the world of business go around. It is the economic motor, I discussed in the previous chapter.

This dilemma model was designed to represent a situation between human players, but there is no need to assume any particular intelligence in the actions of the agents. The responses are entirely automatable. Information systems, mechanical devices, or even the forces of nature could be taken as the agents, pitting their behaviours (rational or not) against one another.

The specific values in the boxes of Figure 11.1 also don't matter as much as their relative sizes. One agent might be operating on a scale 10 times that of the other, and it wouldn't matter: each agent lives in its own partitioned world. We imagine that 'rational' agents are trying to maximize their payoff and do as well as they can, given whatever circumstances they have to deal with.

What the dilemma game does is to say: if we add up the payoffs from these autonomously made, unstable choices over time, can we still reach some kind of an equilibrium or profit, without some external agency forcing the agents to cooperate? In other words, is there a strategy for choosing, even simplistically, to get the best possible long-term outcome for both players.

A model that projects choice down to yes or no, true or false, is like the binary logic of Boole. We know that this leads to critical bifurcations and semantic instabilities, so the conclusions are potentially simplistic. What makes them reasonable is that one seeks the stable equilibrium, as Nash predicted one stays away from trouble.

Political scientist Robert Axelrod, of the University of Michigan explored the idea of games as drivers of cooperation in the 1970s. He asked: under what conditions will cooperative behaviour emerge, without the existence of a central authority? This was very much like the question asked by Thomas Hobbes, centuries before. However, whereas Hobbes concluded erroneously from his own logic, that a central authority was necessary (because he wanted to curry favour with the King), Axelrod showed that Nash's simple model of the bargaining problem in economics game theory allowed cooperation to take place quite autonomously. The payments could be quite asymmetric as long as they showed consistency in keeping promises. Each agent has its own subjective view on the scale of payment, after all: value is in the eye of the beholder. There is no need for a central authority or currency.

Axelrod's simple yet profound contribution was to apply the dilemma game to study numerous practical real-world problems. He also looked in a very general way for optimal solutions to the problem, by setting up a competition to pit different strategies against one another. Of the many submissions to play against one another in tournaments, Anatol Rapoport's submission, from Toronto University, was highly successful and nearly always won. It was the simple strategy of 'tit for tat', i.e. whatever you do to me, I will do to you.

It is well worth reading Axelrod's own account of these games, as there are several subtleties[220]. The basic lesson, from the tournaments, was that winning strategies were those that were 'nice', in the sense of not being the first to break their promises. Giving the benefit of the doubt would lead to longer term value in a relationship.

The central point, for me, is that cooperation cannot begin unless parties meet regularly. In a sense, they rehearse their cooperation by reminding themselves of the value of it on a regular basis. This fits our everyday experience of getting the most out of a relationship when we practice, rehearse, revise, repeat, on a regular schedule. Scattered individuals who meet on an ad hoc basis will not form cooperative behaviour at all. Thus, the on-going relationship may be essentially equated with the concept of lasting value.

Agents' recall of the past also plays a role in how they judge trust. Agents will inevitably forget what happened between them in the past, as time goes by. This is not only normal, it is desirable for adaptation. Forgetting gives a clear advantage in a dynamical environment, as conditions are changing all the time. Stubbornness doesn't pay.

Axelrod arranged for the value of older games to be discounted in a predictable way, somewhat like the gradual forgetting of data in machine-learning of Chapter 8. He found that having a long-term relationship (low discounting of past behaviour) meant that there was a possibility of a finding stable equilibrium of cooperation, with long-term mutual gain. If agents had only a short memory, they would not stabilize so easily, but would tend to be tempted to break promises. This is really all we need to know to observe the importance of relationships between agents that act in their own selfish interest. The shadow of the future, or the fear of damaging a relationship, turns out to be a major factor in consistent behaviour.

This final part is significant, because it implies that we may invoke the argument of relationships promoting stability in the presence of any agent that has incomplete information about its external environment. Any agent with access to only local information, and a certain amount of memory, will see value in any relationship of positive payoff.

The theory of economic games offers an interesting perspective on what we attribute to value: it shows implicitly that communication is central to value through the regular interactions that groom intended and promised behaviour. Regular communication underlies the keeping of promises, and builds trust over some time horizon, as we gradually forget the past.

Particularly significant here is that the agents in these dilemma games are completely autonomous, and have not only incomplete information about one another, but no information at all other than what they win. In spite of this, they stabilize their relationships. The conclusions are highly reminiscent of Boltzmann's methods of statistical mechanics, used in finding stable equilibrium distributions by looking for 'maximum uncertainty' configurations.

The 'tit for tat' strategy, with long memory, low discounting, is a Nash equilibrium, a kind of settled behaviour which brings long-term value. Promise-breaking, on the other hand, is a non-equilibrium strategy. We should be careful about imbuing too many ethical arguments about the breaking of promises, however, despite the human flavour in these discussions. There might be good reasons to break old promises as new scenarios and circumstances come along. Remember that a system in equilibrium is essentially 'dead', frozen in time.

In Chapter 8, I preemptively suggested that a relationship with observation was needed to achieve certainty, i.e. that we need to revisit observations to really 'know' them. I even used the expression 'to know things like a friend' to emphasize this relationship. The suggestion is that the value of knowledge is about grooming it and reiterating it, so that it can be sustained[221].

What we get out of a long-term relationship, i.e. what learning confers on us, is the amalgamation of two things: observational experience and *context*. These two things together give a perspective that is more valuable than any individual episode, because the whole relationship is robust to environmental noise. Long-term memory, or knowledge retention is perhaps an economically motivated adaptation to the benefits of learning.

The real driver, however, is likely the economic value of the robust relationship itself: it has survival value in a noisy environment. Learning is not merely a stream of facts or data we observe, but a contextualized history of information, sifted for relevance. If each repetition of an act, in a new context, confers a positive value, then repeating it clearly causes the total value to add up.

It is surely no accident that the most successful technologies in human history have been related to forms of communication that allow us to maximize our possible input of experience, build and maintain relationships. Indeed, I have gone to some lengths, in the earlier chapters, to show that communication is that most fundamental of mechanisms that enables change to take place at all scales. The human predilection for communicating is deeply significant from an economic survival perspective, and no understanding of technology could be complete without at least considering its impact.

So, if communication leads to value, why not just babble continuously and be done with it? In a sense, this is exactly what humans do, in between survival acts, using whatever technology we have at our disposal. In the 21st century, we have begun to do this in electronic social media at a greater rate than ever before. There are limits to this, however, and we have to understand what they are, as well as to consider what subjects one should be talking about.

A clue about why frequency of communication is important to relationship-building came from a quite different investigation about the human brain itself.

During the 1990s, Professor of Psychology Robin Dunbar of Liverpool University, proposed the idea that relationships and language are intimately related. He proposed that the evolution of language in humans grew as a substitute for the kind of grooming that other animal species perform as part of their cooperative behaviour. Animal grooming, like picking the fleas out of one-another's fur, is a social activity, and is associated with group relationships (see Figure 11.2).

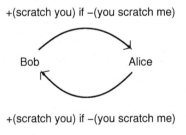

Fig. 11.2. Another promise trade relationship. Grooming: if you scratch my back, I'll scratch yours.

Dunbar looked at the size of a part of the brain called the neo-cortex, or grey matter, and asked what its role was in these evolved collaborative rituals. The neo-cortex refers to the newest evolutionary part of primate brains. It is responsible for thinking, analyzing, and for language, in particular. He was specifically interested in the question of why human brains had evolved to such a great size. As he plotted the size of the living-groups formed by different primates, he noticed an interesting correlation between group size and the size of the neo-cortex of the animals. It suggested that our brains actually evolved to handle the complexities of social relationships. This was contrary to the oft-held speculation that brain size was associated with body mass.

By extrapolating the trend, Dunbar was able predict an expected group size for human beings of 100—150 acquaintances, which he then found to be essentially a universal order of magnitude in humans. Do not be misled: certainly, humans can remember more individuals than this number, and we can also be in reasonable chance of contact with more by writing down lists, like telephone directories or using social media sites, but these do not really help us to maintain a relationship with them. We do not exceed the limit of 150 with technology, because maintaining a relationship requires the work of grooming, and writing a list does not help us to process the list. Social media and telephone lists merely ask someone else to help us remember basic facts, like layers of a fossil record in a museum. There is no relationship.

The number 150 became known as the Dunbar number[222], but, in fact, Dunbar's work continued and he revealed a hierarchy of numbers associated with a human brain size, that is very interesting. By studying different kinds of human groups, he found that the same human brain can only maintain relationships of increasing closeness in inverse proportion. The more intimate the relationship, the more work it costs us, and the fewer we can manage. He found that we manage around 5 intimate relationships, around 15 in a family-like group, about 30-40 in a tribal or departmental working relationship, and 100-150 general acquaintances. Whatever semantics we associate with a group, i.e. whether we consider someone close a lover or a bitter enemy, family, or team, it is the level of cognitive processing, or intimacy, that limits the number we can cope with. Once again, dynamics trump semantics: the brain seems to have a scale which has a limiting processing threshold.

The more intimate a relationship, the more brain power it consumes. The fact that these limits exist, means that there must be limitations on other kinds of relationships too, such as what we learn and plan: knowledge of systems and strategic issues. Exactly what the number of such relationships is doesn't matter precisely. How many theories of special relativity can we know like an intimate friend? How many pieces of specialist software can we know? How many aircraft can we fly?

Dunbar's work indicates that we have to make economic trade-offs. Maintaining a relationship with your boss might be a much more intimate relationship, needing a bigger investment, than maintaining a relationship to a customer, or vice versa. There are some economic choices to be made here, which we see even in social circles. Some choose to become 'a friend of the people', while others choose to become 'a friend of the King'.

What I find particularly interesting about Dunbar's findings is that they point to what it costs us to know something. His work suggests that knowledge itself is a relationship that has to be rehearsed and practised so that we eventually 'cache' or retain it in our more primitive brain areas—what psychologists call 'system 1', colloquially known as 'muscle memory', i.e. that it is through rehearsal and mutual interaction, with something or someone, that we transfer thoughts from hard work to learnt by rote.

When we study for an exam, we artificially revisit old material with the aim of memorizing it for a short while. This usually has only a short-term effect, like an acquaintance. It is the experiences we encounter, shape, and wrestle with on a regular basis, as part of daily life, that we become experts at: they are things we know intimately. This is why experience always wins over paper credentials when are looking for expertise.

The fact is that we also have relationships with the tools we work with. In the modern world, where work consumes a large part of our re-purposed cortices, we spend probably more time learning how to use certain tools (in my case, the text editor I am writing with) as interacting with close loved ones (though hopefully we know more significant buttons to push in the latter). Musicians think of their instruments as an extension of themselves, so close are they to a single instrument.

Further evidence of our finite mental capacity comes from thought processing in language. In the 1960s, MIT researcher Noam Chomsky analyzed language patterns and argued for the innateness of certain linguistic processing mechanisms. Indeed, he demonstrated the existence of a close link between pattern recognition and language processing, through the Chomsky hierarchy (see chapters 5 and 9). Amongst other things, he showed that the parsing of parenthetic remarks required a higher level of computational complexity than mere pattern repetition. In the view of Turing and Chomsky, computation was language.

All of us have probably experienced getting lost in parenthetic remarks at one time or another. It is called clausal indirection in linguistics, and it further evidence that our mental capacity is limited. Studies seem to show that there is a limit to the number of nested linguistic remarks we can make until we lose track of which was being said[223]. The average human seems able to manage about

4—5 levels if indirection without losing track of where we were. For example, consider the following sentence:

> I was about to say to Janet when I was walking to the shop, you know the one where that dog always stands on the corner, God I can't stand dogs, especially when they look all mangy, I think there is actually some kind of disease, if you can call scruffy looking a disease.

These sentences are not only hard to read, but hard to write! You might notice that the original train of thought in the sentence never got completed, because the speaker proceeded to open up level after level of clausal indirection. We never get to find out what was the speaker was about to tell Janet, and he don't much care by the end of it. In formal languages, like those used to program computers, one often uses parentheses to mark out such levels of nesting explicitly:

```
(
I was about to say to Janet
... (
... when I was walking to the shop,
...... (
...... you know the one where that dog always stands on the corner,
......... (
......... God I can't stand dogs,
............ (
............ especially when they look all mangy,
............... (
............... I think there is actually some kind of disease,
.................. (
.................. if you can call scruffy looking a disease
.................. )
............... )
............ )
......... )
..... )
??
```

To parse a structure like this, a finite state automaton needs a memory structure called a stack, which is like just keeping a pile of post-it notes to remember your place in the sentence for each parenthesis. Each time you open a new parenthesis, you put a new post-it on top, recording what you were thinking before it started, and each time you close one, you take the reminder from the top of the pile. In this case, we didn't take all the notes off the pile and complete the original sentence.

This finite stack size problem for parsing sentences is a limitation to our thinking, like the relationship number. To my knowledge, it has not been shown that these are related in any way, but I would be surprised if they weren't. Game theorists also have a version of this which they call the Cognitive Hierarchy Hypothesis, which suggests a maximum number of moves that we can think ahead, when playing games like chess.

I believe that the significance of Dunbar's result goes far beyond friendships and grooming. Measurements are a kind of relationship with data, in which we repeatedly revisit estimates of a numerical quantity in order to increase our certainty, or knowledge of it. Thus, monitoring of information systems must also be considered a relationship that we maintain at some level of intimacy. If we care a lot about the behaviour of a piece of technology, we need a rather close relationship to it, to 'know it like a friend'.

The science of relationships has a lot to tell us about technology, how we design it for a purpose, and how we use it. I believe that we cannot really progress towards an honest theory of the science of technology unless we attempt to, at the very least, pay lip service to human concerns.

A conspicuous element of relationships that I've not mentioned so far is the sense of dignity they bring us. A relationship gives the feeling that we make a difference, and covets a sense of purpose. It is a key human motivator, and this is something we should take pains to preserve when introducing technological infrastructure.

This is not a fully rational feeling either. Studies made by psychologists indicate that humans generally over-estimate their own importance in ensuring a successful outcome of events. In a surprising number of cases, simple systems of rules have been shown to be more effective at coping with tasks, where we often feel human judgement is important[224]. Automatic transmission (gears) in cars is a good example. For all but the most demanding cases, modern automatic gearing is, on average, more than adequate. It might make different optimizations than a human might make (e.g., fuel economy rather than acceleration performance), but it is highly effective. Of course, anyone who has driven a car with automatic gears knows that there are good and bad implementations of this technology. The point is that, if the implementation is good, human skill is quite redundant, even if we don't want to hear it.

Self-driving cars are perhaps the latest demonstration of this. Soon, smart cars will be able to drive as well as, or better than most humans. Autopilots have existed in aircraft for years, but we don't mind the idea of an autopilot as much, because it does not replace the large majority who cannot pilot a plane.

Cars, on the other hand, are our guilty pleasure. They are as much entertainment as transport.

Passionate discussions about the ethics of automation and technology replacing humans recur each time a new technology comes along to take a job, no matter how inhumane the working conditions. The sense of dignity that comes from contributing to a group overrides almost every other consideration. When ever it happens that a machine takes over a function that was previously performed by a human, we feel threatened. From the punkah wallahs who were employed to fan air in Asian residences, to the universal air-conditioning systems of the United States, or from the factory production line labourers to the shop floor robots, eventually the ignominy passes, and we move on to the next battle. Ethics is not a topic one normally associates with bringing certainty to infrastructure, but when it comes to the tools of society, one cannot ignore the issue of human involvement[225].

Let's come back to technology for a moment. The evolution of human involvement in systems follows a pattern. Although I am not aware of any proper studies that were made on this, my causal observations suggest that Dunbar's hierarchy explains human involvement in information systems quite well. Leading up to the point at which the scale of computer installations approached the Dunbar number, system engineers actually did treat computers like friends or pets. They tended computers by hand, logging onto them manually to tend to their needs, like groundsmen tending a garden, nurse-maiding their ailments, even changing their electronic diapers. Engineers gave computers names, like friends or pets and thought of them as having personalities, just as captains personify ships. As computer installations grew further in size, this did not scale well, and a militarization of systems came into play, breaking them up into tiers.

Military organization has been hierarchical for much of human history, if one discounts guerilla groups, and historically, all but a few humans societies have grown in a hierarchical manner[226]. This seems to be a dominant pattern that forms around centralized power structures. In engineering terms, hierarchies are usually represented as tree-like structures (see Figure 2.6), which can be fragile and inadvisable; however, economically, they make perfect sense as a growth pattern, and military hierarchies are emulated in technology as a form of command and control perhaps because they form simple growing *spanning trees* of human networks. A result in graph theory tells us that, given any network of collaboration, we can always make a tree (a graph without loops) that provides a unique path to every node; this is called a spanning tree. It's a very useful concept in networks. In military hierarchies, tree structures are de-personalized: names are replaced with serial numbers, and command hierarchies are constructed like spanning trees to make organization the chain of command unique through every branch.

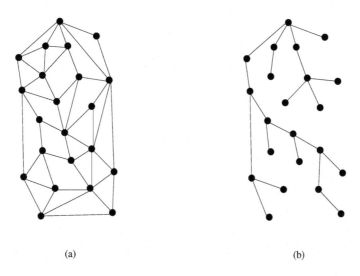

(a)   (b)

Fig. 11.3.   A spanning tree is an acyclic graph that covers all the points in a network by only one route. They are often used to plan network traversal, to avoid having traffic go in circles. Hierarchies are usually formed from spanning trees.

Knowing that our cognitive capacity is limited, it makes sense that this would affect our ability to cope with scale. We start maintaining computers intimately like family or pets, naming them; then the level of intimacy falls off as the numbers pass the various Dunbar limits. As the scale of computer installations grew larger still, hierarchies indeed fail to keep the promise of economic scaling. They become unwieldy, due to what we may call the 'depth versus breadth' problem. This is the cognitive limitation of comprehending such a large structure, analogous to the Dunbar and clausal indirection limits described above. A tree has breadth and depth (see Figure 11.4), which places a burden on us to understand it. If we have trouble relating to large numbers (breadth) or great indirection (recursion depth), this will limit the comprehensibility of the structure.

Plausibly, the breadth of a group in a hierarchy will be bounded by some kind of Dunbar limit, and the depth of the tree by clausal indirection, thus we have limited the kind of tree we can meaningfully comprehend to shallow fat trees of limited dimension. On economic grounds, one can then see how a network of promises would grow into a hierarchical structure and then collapse: it would start with the allegiance of a few helpers to a central command authority, form-

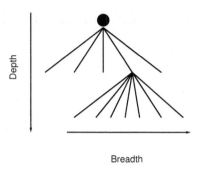

Fig. 11.4.   Breadth and depth in a tree.

ing a first level star network (see Figure 2.6). As the number of members or satellites in the star exceeds a Dunbar limit, it will break up into sub-groups, each with an appointed leader and a membership smaller than the limit. This will continue as the sub-groups also grow, until several levels of depth have grown. Now we have preliminary scaling, but at the cost of bottlenecks and single points of failure in a fragile structure (see Figure 2.4).

At some point, there must be a tipping point in which the conflict of interest between the fragility of all the single points of failure, combined with the difficulty of maintaining tree depth, outweighs the benefit of breaking the structure into hierarchical levels. Then the command and control paradigm breaks down. At this point, one has little option but to return to agent autonomy, under general constraints, as a model of governance. Exactly when that happens, depends on the amount of brute force the tree can exert to keep itself together.

Admiral Grace Murray Hopper is quoted as saying: 'Life was simple before World War II. After that we had systems.' Systems are a symptom of scale, a point at which we de-personalize activity and mechanize, but if this is not done in a way that respects human comprehension, the system eventually fails to perform.

What does it look like when a system returns to an autonomous model? The symphony orchestra is often used as a model for autonomous governance under constraints. The players in an orchestra work quite independently of their neighbours, playing music in front of them, and watching for guidance from the conductor. The conductor does not command every instrument, channelling messages to the players from his podium. This would be unworkable. Instead, he distributes the music for everyone to read (this is delicately known as stigmergic cooperation), and instead promises to provide a few coordinating signals so that everyone knows when to start and stop, and feedback about how the whole thing sounds. For this reason, autonomous coordination is sometimes called orchestration.

Autonomy also is recognized as an organizational principle that gives a preferred sense of human dignity in workplaces[227], while hierarchy is often considered dehumanizing. If you are at the centre of your own universe, it's hard not to feel special. Moving from individual, uncoordinated work, to a command and control structure, back to autonomy with governance is a path to stable scaling as well as human sense of worth. The conclusion is more or less implicit in the first part of this book, and the framework of promises helps us to see that there is actually nothing personal in the conclusion. Regardless of who makes and keeps the promises, the conclusions are the same.

American writer and futurist Alvin Toffler described the ascension from manual labour in three waves of society, from manual labour, through industrial amplification of effort in which we try to limit variations to prevent breadth, then finally comes the Third Wave, in which variation is held up as being the goal itself, and technology finally serves humanity rather than limiting it (see chapter 6). He points out that the second wave of industrialization is a deeply de-humanizing phase of growth in which humans give up their humanity essentially to lift themselves out of poverty.

Toffler's Third Wave is very much about making the best possible use of information to give humans what they want. However, it should not be taken to mean that the whole of society switches to Third Wave practices at the same time. On the contrary, examples of first, second and third wave enterprises are all around us. They co-exist and evolve at their own rates.

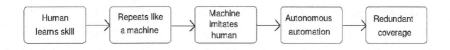

Fig. 11.5. The stages of human involvement in automation.

Leading up to a Third Wave organization, it is easy to see the pattern of evolution, from human involvement to automated scaling, shown in figure 11.5. The stages describe a shift from the belief that human involvement is necessary in order to control a process by rational then irrational judgement, to a fully throwaway commoditized mass-market approach:

1. A human agent figures out the skill 'the hard way', i.e. through raw analysis, or a trial-and-error relationship, often flying by the seat of his or her

pants. The human re-solves the job each time, calculating and reasoning forth a solution, learning on each round. This is a human 'system 2' cognitive control approach. It is the cognitively expensive relationship building of Dunbar, that Kahneman showed is somewhat precarious, so we progress quickly to the next stage having learnt an equilibrium from the relationship.

2. A human memorizes the equilibrium task and begins to imitate a machine, repeating common parts of the job mechanically, forging intuitions; practice makes perfect. The human transfers to 'system 1' muscle memory, or goes on autopilot.

3. A machine is constructed that imitates a human doing the job. This is a scripted automaton, or a mechanical Turk. It does not try to optimize because it assumes the machine is only a dumb replacement for a human.

4. The results of the scripted automaton are optimized and de-personalized as an information system. Commonalities are cached or commoditized to be 'off the shelf'. Results can be kept in a database or a warehouse for instant recall rather than reworking from scratch each time. Some rule-based computation could be involved. Now we shed the shackles of imitation and scale for the mass market.

5. Parallel replication and redundancy of the delivery service are now needed to exceed the limitations of a centralized approach in 1—4. De-centralization is achieved by atomization of parts for delivery at scale[228].

This is a reasonable description of scaling in commodity systems. It does not address the need for bespoke engineering (which always remains an exploratory enterprise), but it is a common path to industrialization. To reach a Third Wave, there has to be yet another step: a level of enlightenment beyond reliable mass production.

For information infrastructure, this is very much where we are today. It leaves us with the question: how do we progress beyond simple commodity industrialization to an information society, based on customized variations that suit the wants and desires of an exploratory audience? Second Wave industrialization is about optimizing the dynamics of systems, so the natural answer to the Third Wave must lie in the semantics.

Interest in the question of infrastructure semantics grew around 2005, when Hewlett Packard researcher Claudio Bartolini challenged the industry to pay attention to the problem of how to align information systems with the needs of businesses to deliver human-centric services. What caught my attention was the obvious connection to promises, given that promises build trust and the trusted relationship is a central part of what makes a business work[229].

The 2000s were the adolescence of information technology, because it was only then that online commerce truly began to take hold. Organizations could no longer afford to maintain computer installations for their own sake, as they had done up to that point; they needed to actually achieve the larger goals of the organizations that owned them. The 'land owners' were finally insisting on having their land farmed, and used for productive purpose, rather than merely letting it grow wild and plucking a few berries along the way.

All this seemed like a good test for promise theory to be able to predict something about business purpose from low-level purposes. I was particularly interested to know what a high-level purpose would look like as a model.

Through a series of workshops, Claudio Bartolini and Jacques Sauvé of Universidade Federal de Campina Grande, pursued the idea of alignment with business purpose, and by 2007 had inspired me to apply promise theory to this idea of business relevance. For the keynote of the Business Driven IT Management (BDIM) workshop in Brasil 2008, I had worked out a simple model which displayed some crucial features[230]. It was enough to make sense from a business perspective, not merely a technology perspective.

It posed a simple question: what relationships should people and technology have in order to collectively keep a promise to customers, given that both no one can keep all the promises by themselves, and that no one can make promises on behalf of anyone except themselves. Ultimately it was about how to understand the likelihood of cooperation through a more objective lens of expectation. Carolyn Rowland of the National Institute of Standards (NIST) and I developed this idea into a template for business alignment, from a human perspective, in the period between 2008 and 2010[231].

Promises always form networks, thus they describe structure without even trying. This is interesting, because much of the writing about business on the structural side was about the necessity of building command hierarchies[232]. Whether promise structure is physical, inter-personal, conceptual, or relational is unimportant. To a scientist or engineer, the only goal is to understand the parts of the system, irrespective of whether a function is performed by human or by machine. Often promises can be made in the form of templates and reusable patterns. The traditional visible boundaries of buildings, departments, and walled enclosures were made irrelevant by the mixture of humans and technology, as well as the virtual channels for communication enabled by the Internet, and with so much of business being done via information networks, across borders of every kind.

Siri Fagernes and I spent some time trying to understand how organizational boundaries could be made sense of in terms of promises, without referring to physical apparatus like buildings and departments. Quite simply, a collective group may be considered an organization if every member of the organization promises to be a member, and this promise is accepted by everyone in the group. Essentially, if they give you a uniform and you wear it, then you're in. This was a simple and liberating definition that didn't involve politics or agenda, but it did not lead to any particular notions of business-technology alignment.

To get closer to the idea of business alignment, I went back to basics and looked instead at a simple model, somewhat like that developed by W.E. Deming and his descriptions of factory workflows (see Chapters 6 and 9). Deming's idea that parts of a workflow cooperate to optimize locally and globally can easily be understood through the relationships the links in the chain have to one another. One ends up with a workflow or value chain[233]. Processes could be simplified by keeping the promises themselves simple and putting intelligence inside parts rather than in the combinatorics that worked between them.

Optimizing the flow of work between even the simplest two-part collaborative chains is still widely discussed today: Development and Operations, or Production and Delivery, Computers and Network. Each link is a dilemma relationship between the agents in the chain. From this, it is a small leap to see that a business process is a sequence of dilemma games, or promise trades between links in a value chain (see Figure 11.6).

Fig. 11.6. A cooperative chain should be something a collection of back to back promise trades, here unlabelled.

A promise diagram like Figure 11.6, even without labels, can offer a misleading impression of the workflow, however, suggesting something being passed from agent to agent. In promise theory, that would only be a secondary effect of sorting out the logic of the promises. Rather, the diagram shows intent to keep a promise.

In a business setting, the question we really want to answer is: how can we organize the different agents to keep a specific promise to a customer, using the mixture of human and technological workforce at our disposal? What promises would they each have to make for us to trust in the outcome? This is a structural composition of intent—call it *promise engineering*. Different agents will have different skills and will be able to keep different kinds of promise.

Suppose there are two stages called 'produce' and 'deliver'. The agent with the hammer can produce, and the agent with the truck can deliver. We might think of the producing agent as a factory, a kitchen, or a person; we might think of the delivery agent as a truck, a waiter, or as the post office. The names do not matter as much as knowing what promises are required to keep the final promise to the customer. In fact, this will prove to be important.

We start by writing down the most important promise: the business promise from some customer-facing agent to its customers. It could be a shop, a provider, or a dealer, e.g. I promise to deliver the car that you have ordered. As soon as we write this down, we begin to realize the magnitude of what this promise represents. Even assuming that there is a simple template for making the car itself, so that the agent does not have to promise the wheels, the doors, the lights, etc, as separate components, there is still a significant challenge to coordinate the different agents behind the scenes in the total system from production to delivery. The dealer cannot make this promise unconditionally, because it relies on the factory to make it, and the transport company to deliver it. It can make a conditional promise: I will promise to deliver the car you ordered, if the factory makes it and the transport company delivers it to me first.

This example is specific, but the problem is generic. We could construct a dynamically similar problem from purely information technology: e.g. I promise to deliver a web page when you click on this link, if the database returns some valid data and the network in between us doesn't fail. The dynamics are similar, and the semantics are similar, but they are not precisely identical.

Now the promise theory viewpoint unravels interesting assumptions as we deconstruct what these promises represent. The rule in promise theory is that an agent may not make a promise on behalf of another agent, only on behalf of itself. Moreover, a conditional promise is not a promise at all, as one is left wanting to know if the factory has actually promised to deliver the car, or the restaurant's kitchen is going to make your dinner. So we need a promise from the agent on which the customer-facing agent depends too, in order to have a complete promise, or an expression of intent on which to set expectations.

Trust plays a clear role here, but trust does not spring from nowhere. We begin with a default level of trust based on naivete or experience of general cases, then our relationship with a specific agent modifies that trust based on whether the agent keeps its promises. Trust comes from the long-term relationships, as studied by Axelrod, sometimes passed on through reputation or the experiences of others[234].

The simple view of a chain gets rapidly complicated, as we add in all the promises that have to be made and kept to fulfil the complexities of assumptions about agent behaviour (see Figure 11.7). It actually gets hard to draw them. When a promiser relies on subsidiary agents to deliver promises like *make* and

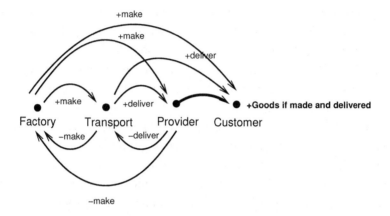

Fig. 11.7.   A cooperative chain actually looks more like this.

deliver, there is an explosion of complexity.

The provider promises a car if the factory makes one and delivers it. The delivery company promises to deliver one if the factory makes one. The factory only promises to make one if the provider promises to accept it. The factory has to promise the delivery company, the provider, and the customer that it will make the car: after all, none of these agents can accept responsibility for something they cannot promise. In fact, the number of promise relationships must grow like the square of the number of intermediaries in a value chain. We know that there always has to be uncertainty about whether promises can be kept, regardless of whether the agents are human or machines. This affects the certainty that the promise to the customer can be kept.

Now, if the sale of a car to a customer is a one-off transaction, then the promises of the factory and delivery company are of little value because there will be no long-term relationship, however the relationship between factory and provider, and delivery company and provider and factory are all repeated inter-actions for different customers, so there are dilemma games going on between them all the time, pumping value through the chain.

Even this simple example shows just how much trust and intent lies behind simple cooperation in a delivery chain. The promise methodology gives us a more or less mechanical way of breaking down a promise into necessary and sufficient promises by intermediaries when there is a workflow of agents cooperating to keep the final promise. This results in job descriptions for each agent. The value of the promises themselves becomes even more apparent when we add the *mean time to keep promise* into the story. Once there is a timescale involved, we no longer have to think only of the semantics of the promise design, the dynamics of keeping the promises also enters, as it must. Now we are back in the world of instabilities and bifurcating thresholds. In the world of business, there are so-called Service Level Agreements (SLA) between customer and provider. My colleague Tore Jonassen from Oslo University College, Siri Fagernes, Kyrre Begnum and I showed how this instability of cooperation could grow in a promise network in 2005 on entirely general grounds[235].

This ecological growth seems much too complicated to sustain. Each promise dilemma uses up an agent's Dunbar slot to keep track of the relationship, and the longer the chain becomes the worse it gets. That is certainly one argument for automating the relationships, where possible. Another way to simplify it would be for the customer-facing provider to simply lie to the customer about needing to have a promise from the factory and delivery agent, or even gamble on whether one of its subsidiaries could deliver on its promises, without a specific agreement in place. This would be risky, but it happens.

On the other hand, one could try to make the likelihood an agent gets what it needs to keep a promise so high that there is no longer any practical doubt as to whether the promise will be kept, in spite of it being conditional. A strategy of having multiple subsidiaries addresses this; then, if one of them fails, there will also be another to choose from. This is a very expensive over-capacity, leading to a duplication of cost, but often it is the only answer. The pursuit of certainty can be extended to more than two providers, just in case two failures were possible. Neither approach is attractive unless the cost is very low. Automation reduces cost, so (again) automation is often a preferred approach to bring predictability in a cost sensitive world.

What happens, then, if we try to introduce redundancy into the picture of a value chain? To begin with the network of agents will no longer be just a simple chain; it will start to resemble the right hand side of figure 2.4. But, if we choose our scale focus judiciously, and the promises that make the chain work are suitable for scaling, we can avoid seeing the details of redundancy and hide it entirely within the agents, making *pools* of agents to keep the promises.

Instead of single-celled agents, we can make agent organisms that can tolerate the loss of one or two single cells. This is called a fault-tolerant strategy. I'll return to this topic, to show how this can work, in the next chapter.

Again, the value of the promise abstraction is that it places all kinds of reasons for faults on the same level: actual physical loss of hardware or forgetful loss of intent are made equivalent. The reason for the failure to keep a promise matters little to the keeping of a final promise. If we add probabilities for promises being kept to the diagrams, it is even possible to compute the likelihood of the final promise being kept.

Before looking in more detail about the dynamics of collaborative promise keeping, we need to elaborate further on the dual aspect: the semantics of purpose. Because all technology is for human purpose, irrespective of whether that intent is channelled through mechanical devices or not, we are ultimately concerned with the semantics of processes. The end state matters more than the details of how we get there (even if ethics are brought into the argument, we can formulate the problem in this way without sacrificing decency). Having clear promises between the collaborating pieces is a way to build confidence in the outcome. In information systems, one often calls these promises 'interfaces'.

As it turns out, this is a partly misguided obsession. The challenge of the value chain is that of *inter-operability* between agents that occupy their own world, with their own relativistic view. Once a basic algebra of cooperation has been achieved between these worlds, the chance of eliminating bifurcating instabilities lies in reducing the importance of those semantics to a minimum level, so that specific choices no longer matter to the final stable outcome.

The dynamical issues with infrastructure had been quite well understood by 2005, so my own attention began to switch from the dynamics of processes to their semantics. Having worked as a teacher in a variety of contexts for many years, the role of knowledge relationships between humans and technology grew in my mind as a necessity for keeping a network of humans and machines self-sustaining. Once knowledge of a system decayed, the system could go unstable in a number of ways: either because a human or machine was unable to respond to known patterns of behaviour, or perhaps because the channels of causation and the key dimensional scales of the problem were not appreciated. Either way, a human would ultimately be responsible and concerned with the outcomes.

Thanks to discussions with Jan Bergstra and Siri Fagernes, a formal model of promises was beginning to take shape, and could be applied to human-technology scenarios in equal measure. The experiences with using CFEngine in datacentres around the world had effectively revealed promises not only as a way of maintaining predictability in information infrastructure, but as a form of documentation about intent. Moreover, since promises encouraged repeated interaction to effect maintenance over time, they offered a basis for relationships to form, which could lead to knowledge about themselves. Promises provide a basis for knowledge to emerge as a subsidiary effect of merely writing them down. Such knowledge would have two aspects:

1. The fuller understanding of the intent behind the promises, obtained from repeated study of the promise declarations, in relation to prior expectation. (Semantics)

2. Knowledge of actual state of compliance with that intent, which comes from observing the state of a system repeatedly over time. This could include a revision of expectations and emergent effects that were not planned for or understood. (Dynamics)

Monitoring the actual state of a machine, by any and every available method, had not only been routinely achieved before 2005, but had indeed been unstoppably pursued ever since machines were first created. However, being able to define an extensive 'knowledge equilibrium' (see Chapter 8) between intended state and actual outcome, relative to a changing environment, and with only a single model implemented on a massive scale, was indeed a step forward from the state of the art for information technology. The technique eventually became a trivial side effect of CFEngine 3's normal operation, thanks to its reformulation in terms of promise theory.

Siri Fagernes and I went further and showed that we could understand so-called *emergent behaviour*, or unexpected side-effects, from the viewpoint of a system observer quite easily in promise theory[236]. An emergent behaviour is a semantic illusion that arises from a dynamical process, like the swarming of birds, or how insects build apparently intelligently designed structures, complex pattern formation in physics: any case where something unexpected arises from the cooperation of apparently dumb entities. If a dynamical system can be interpreted by an observer as appearing to keep a particular promise, then the observer cannot distinguish this from a situation in which the system actually promised the behaviour. We would then say the behaviour was emergent if we happened to believe that the behaviour was not explicitly promised, but the collective behaviour appeared intentional. This is a purely semantic mirage, experienced by our brains' projective model of the world.

The connection with knowledge is a vital part of the human experience, as our desire to know is strong, but that experience is fragile where information rich infrastructure is concerned. The inner workings of the infrastructure we rely on are, almost by definition, not something that we typically have a very close relationship to. We expect to take them for granted, until something goes wrong. At such a time, we wish we'd paid more attention to the training, the manuals, or we look for the contact details of that former employee who built the system originally. But imagine if the very design of information rich infrastructure could help us to get to know it better, in a shorter time, by telling us about itself in a way we could understand. Imagine if we could amplify our capacity to quickly form a working relationship to essential infrastructure by using some form of knowledge engineering, going beyond a directory of parts to a kind of social-media experience, a forum of 'friends' both human and machine. It would have both didactic benefits and immediate actionable benefits.

A model based on promises could theoretically have that property: it describes a stable outcome, it has clear semantics, and each atomic relationship can be learnt and documented over time. There are three essential reasons for wanting to develop not only self-healing, self-learning infrastructure, but also self-teaching infrastructure; they are, quite simply: our past, our present and our future.

1. Past: to see the *impact* history of past interactions, both intended and unintended, to appreciate the channels of cause and effect.

2. Present: to offer situational *awareness* and *comprehension* right now, i.e. knowing the current state of health, what is going on?

3. Future: to plan for change in *capacity* and ensure *disaster* readiness.

This kind of knowledge would assist cognitively limited humans in their ability to form an understanding of systems through their many message channels, including covert channels, which are often exploited catastrophically by the environment and by attackers.

In the commercial world, the term for this kind of information is 'analytics', but simply providing the information does not make it actionable. Turning analytics into working knowledge within a human participant is the real challenge. Of course, it is the challenge that every teacher faces in coaxing students to learn. The only difference here is that we are looking for a way to short-cut the lengthy process of learning for quick actionable results, because there is a situation that exceeds current working knowledge.

Put simply, if we subscribe to the viewpoint that analytical information is not truly knowledge until someone relevant has a relationship to it, then promises are not knowledge in and of themselves: we need to encourage a relationship with them to grow.

One thing in their favour here is that promises do map directly to useful knowledge, gathered automatically, from the record of the outcomes they represent. This knowledge could arise in two kinds of relationships: between the system and the engineers that maintain it, and between the system and the users that profit from it.

In my work with computer immunology, the repeated, cyclic heartbeat verification of promises by CFEngine, provided exactly the regular relationship between intent and verification required to be able to speak of certain knowledge about information infrastructure. In a sense, using CFEngine successfully transplanted part of a human relationship between man and machine into an immune-system-style machine-machine interaction. This freed up a Dunbar 'slot' that human engineers could use for something more profitable.

The next question was: could one extend this simple concept of knowledge relationships to the point where human participants could deposit anything they considered important into a knowledge bank, with sufficient documentation of experiences, in such a way as to accelerate the acquisition of that knowledge by someone else who needs it in a hurry?

This question was not immediately answerable. Reducing information was easy: patterns or rules are the way we reduce the amount of information, to bring message compression (see chapter 5). This could be a way of factoring out the repetition inherent in a relationships. It is the trick used in market branding[237]. Yet, the business alignment agenda had identified a way to explain the purpose of infrastructure in terms of a pattern of networked promises, that documented the collaboration of parts. Comprehending this inter-operable network of man-machine promises has since become a major issue in managing today's online infrastructure, due to its huge growth. So it all points to the need to design new technology for the maintainers, whose burden is to improve their limited ability to cope with three uncertainties (scale, complexity and reason) of that seldom-visited underworld: massive scale, intricate complexity, and a lack of knowledge.

A possible way to approach the building of a smarter relationship with information infrastructure was suggested to me in 2006, when I was invited to become part of an international collaboration of the European Union, called EMANICS, bringing together researchers in network management as part of the European Union's research initiative[238]. In this so-called Network of Excellence the research focus was on network management rather than the information server infrastructure. John Strassner, a researcher at Motorola, collaborating Joan Serrat of the Polytechnic University in Barcelona, was advocating *knowledge engineering* as a way of surpassing what traditional database models of information could accomplish.

The traditional approach of using databases to model infrastructure, as with SNMP/MIB and its successor in the Common Information Model (CIM), had simply bloated out of control, with tens of thousands of tabular forms to represent the states of different kinds of manufactured devices (see chapter 6). Strassner believed that a more dynamic model for discovering capabilities was needed to model environments where even the hardware was changing too fast for the model to keep up.

The approach he was advocating was based on an outgrowth of the World Wide Web, called a *semantic web*. The idea of a semantic web is to try to enrich the meaning of information on a web page with hidden meta-information that describes what it is supposed to mean (i.e. its semantics), so that a smart browser would be able to better understand the content within a web page. Text information is just text: we don't know if a paragraph is biographical, or technical, whether it is fact or fiction, what language it is written in, and so on. Ordinary hypertext links have the simple interpretation 'click here for more information'. This is nice and simple, but also very unspecific, and you don't know where you will end up. A human being can draw their own conclusions about information, based on their existing knowledge, experience and reasoning, but information technology is dumb and cannot infer without explicit assistance.

In a semantic web, information may be tagged with interpretations so that smart browsing technology could also divine its presumed meaning. If a text paragraph were marked as a fictional quotation, a browser would not try to recommend this as biographical data, for example. The main idea of the semantic web and its tools was to bring certainty to the semantics by standardizing or normalizing the way terms were used to describe things. A prescribed set of standard meanings called an *ontology* was used for this, based on a form of descriptive first order logic. The idea was that, if one had a logical basis for labelling content, this would enable machine-assisted reasoning.

John Strassner's interest in semantic richness lay initially in its application to an experimental technology called 'cognitive radio'[239], a smart wireless transceiver for phones and computers, which could discover what communications channels were available to it and adapt to the best the environment had to offer.

Trying to discover the inter-operability channels between devices using the old form-based approach of databases was not likely to succeed, as one would have to know the precise question to ask whatever device encountered, and there were as many forms as there were device models. The database schema approach was essentially a continuation of ideas from paper bureaucracy: databases are essentially rigid tabular structures that can only represent pre-defined relationships. Each new device would bring a new kind of data, so no rigid structural data models were going to cope with the problem of discovering a device's unpredictable surroundings. If the forms between infrastructure and device did not match, there would be no relationship established between them.

Data rigidity is easily explained using an analogy. As a hi-fi buff, I experience its limitations every day. To get the best quality digital music, I have to convert my CD collection to digital format. When this happens, the information about the tracks recorded in CDs is read and inserted into a database of music. However, the track information on CDs turns out to be supplied in a form that is quite chaotic, yet the conversion software attempts to feed the information it finds into a rigid database, with categories of artist, composer, title, and so on. For popular music, the model works reasonably in many cases, but for classical music it is quite broken. CD producers cannot decide whether the composer or the conductor or the orchestra or the soloist are the 'artist'. They cannot decide how to spell transcribed names.

For example, if I look for Shostakovich, I cannot find all the music I already know that I have by Shostakovich because sometimes the word Shostakovich appears in the album artist, sometimes only in the track title, sometimes in the title of the album. To make matters worse, it is sometimes spelled in the German transliteration Schostakovich. In some cases the artist is replaced by the conductor, or the orchestra, and there is no encoded data about the composer at all. That information probably appeared on the album sleeve in print, but that is of little use to the digital representation in my music library. It means I have to browse through the music from start to finish hoping to recognize something related to the composer, even the small picture of the album sleeve. Thus, I need to use a lot of human effort, based on indirection or associative matching, to find my music.

A semantic database would have solved this problem more flexibly, allowing for a greater inter-operability between CD standards. If information were annotated with meta-information, each CD manufacturer would simply be able explain what each of the bits of information was supposed to represent, and how they had filled in the CD with information. If they were allowed to define the model as well as the content, there would have been no confusion. There is no reason to suppose that two arbitrary communicating pieces of technology would share the same set of standards for labelling music. There is relativity, not of data, but of semantics.

Strassner and his collaborators had proposed to handle the corresponding problem of device interoperability with the idea of a machine *ontology* language, borrowed from the semantic web. They designed a standard 'knowledge representation', for a machine-machine communication. It was an advanced handshaking mechanism for use between electronic devices, so that applications sitting on top of an information infrastructure could advertise capabilities and services to one another.

Ontology, in philosophy, means a world-view. A world-view is related to a 'possible world' as discussed earlier and used by Leibniz and Kripke, amongst others. However, in information technology, ontology has a specific technological meaning, relating to how a particular agent understands names and reasons about concepts. An information system ontology describes a set of agreed names for categories of things, and the possible logical relationships between them. Descriptive modal logics are typically used for this. The World Wide Web consortium has sanctioned a particular implementation of this idea based on standardized tools. The Web Ontology Language (known as OWL, through an A.A. Milne spelling transformation) is such a standard, though it would be an exaggeration to say that it was widely used. The OWL framework was originally designed for 'knowledge representation' in artificial intelligence research from the 1990s. The meaning of 'knowledge representation' in this case is usually just some kind of archival form of how to interpret the world.

The information technology concept of an ontology is based on an extension of the more familiar idea of *taxonomy*. Taxonomies have a much longer history, and all of us have seen one at some time in school. A family tree is a kind of taxonomy of familial relationships. A taxonomy is a tree of things in which we use branches to separate parts we want to distinguish, and in which we place everything into its correct branch of a tree. Given a network of things that are related, we know that this is always possible: the answer is just a particular spanning tree, but there are two flaws with spanning trees: they are not unique, and they do not preserve the closeness of things to one another from the original network. One can make different trees from different points of view, and each one can make very artificial distinctions, depending on how you choose to divide up categories.

For example, imagine a taxonomy of life: the so-called tree of life. You might begin by dividing living things into animals and plants. This seems like an obvious distinction, at least until you go under water and look at anemones and jelly fish. Mammals and egg laying creatures seem a safe bet, until you meet a duck-billed platypus that is warm blooded but lays eggs. Birds and lizards seem to be a clear distinction until we learn about dinosaurs, and so it goes on.

Our conceptualization of the world was not really intended to form non-overlapping, mutually exclusive categories. Indeed, the father of binary logic George Boole did not even propose such an artificial separation of things. This is a modern affectation that has been exaggerated by the true-false myth of computers.

Forcing things into categories is precisely the problem of projecting complexity onto a finite set of choices that leads to semantic instability during reasoning (see chapter 9). After all, a taxonomy is merely a decision tree, mapping out a process of reasoning, known as a branching process in mathematics. If we make the wrong decision, the tree is not a record of truth, merely a genaeology of the thought process we used to arrive at the erroneous answer. It has no significance. The blunder lies in mistaking a branching process for an authoritative hierarchy.

Taxonomies have fallen in and out of favour throughout history, but there was a particular fascination with them during the Victorian era. The Swedish botanist Carl Linnaeus (1707-1778) ushered in a renaissance of taxonomy, which led to the The Tree of Life, the phylogenetic tree, and other classifications of living things, usually bent to satisfy the thinking of the church so as to place Man above all other creatures.

The problem with spanning trees, taxonomies and ontologies is: how do you decide on the criteria for dividing things up? You could choose to divide up things alphabetically. Instead, one chooses more abstract ideas. This tendency was repeated during the heyday of Object Oriented programming, where class hierarchies flourished. Once you have made a mistake, or if you change your mind, with a tree decomposition, you usually have to unpick the whole edifice and start again. This can be very expensive if you have built something from the structure. The very structure of ontological spanning trees embodies a prejudicial reasoning. Following a path through such a tree, you cannot avoid inheriting a whole ream of associations: a duck-billed platypus is a mammal and an animal. This seems harmless in this case, but it becomes more sinister when your ontology is based on good and evil, and evil people includes the sub-category of people with tattoos and moustaches, and people who double-park?

The idea of using ontology to avoid inflexible database models goes like this: a smart device does not have to know the precise details of its environment to be able to find out how to talk to it: it only needs to understand some basic categories of information. As long as both parties promise to use the same ontology, they will be able to adapt to one another in a generic way. Trying to standardize an ontology to make a universal language of categories is no easy task, however. The formation of a standard can be more restrictive than helpful. The so called Dublin Core forms a standard for meta-data and a forum for efforts to standardize, a kind of United Nations of ontology design. The power of language, however, lies in its creative flexibility, and on individuals' abilities to abuse strict rules.

The hierarchical nature of OWL ontology, and its use of formal logic, made me sceptical that it was a useful way to represent knowledge that was not artificially constrained. That approach would be fine for a machine-to-machine handshake, but it was unlikely to be flexible for any kind of learning. However, because of promises and their potential for representing knowledge, I wanted to learn more about ontological approaches to information technology.

As a test, graduate student Margaret Adaa and I tried to use OWL for representing knowledge about some familiar problems in infrastructure management[240]. Maggie Adaa tried to build an ontology for infrastructure management and anomaly detection by starting from first principles. By attaching names and relationships to the parts that make up infrastructure, and the states they could be in, one should be able to reason about how they are related: perhaps even use those relationships for fault diagnosis.

Maggie was interested to see if the machine-learning capabilities of CFEngine could be incorporated into the reasoning. After all, machine-learnt data form a strong argument for acquiring knowledge, as they are based on continuous monitoring. She wanted to to see if one could reason about anomalous changes in a computer installation, and thus enhance ideas about anomaly detection and fault diagnosis using ontology. The states of a system were categorized into values that were increasing and decreasing, above threshold, below threshold, and so on. These were then entered into a hierarchical model using OWL. Network services, people, devices could all be represented and reasoned about.

We found that consistency checking of the model was a useful property to the designer of an ontology, but the need to design an ontology in the first place required the work of an expert in knowledge representation (not in infrastructure engineering), so this was adding more burden to humans not relieving any. Moreover, if one used a model based on promises, the need to verify consistency became unnecessary, because the locality properties of promises make it impossible to make an inconsistent promise model. Each agent lives in its own Kripke world[241].

Hierarchy and spanning tree design also became a problem. Unless the user of the OWL ontology knew about the details of how the systems parts were categorized, it became almost impossible to ask questions about the system. There are two approaches to finding information in any knowledge representation: browsing and searching. The first problem we encountered was in knowing how to search the network without knowing the entire ontology. In order to search categorized information, you needed to know which category the thing you were searching for belonged to in order to get the right answer. If you didn't know the model, you'd get stuck and find nothing at all. If you did know the model, you would have to type so much to specify a search that you could only ever find what you'd already entered!

The problems with this kind of linguistic categorization are the same as those we encountered in Chapter 10 with modal logics. The significance of such terms is easy to understand in human language: they are approximate categorizations that trigger more complex sensations in a human brain. However, logic needs strictly defined symbols that trigger nothing more than instant recognition. Describing shades and degrees of state is what numbers were invented for.

We thus ended up with the same problem as in modal logic. Describing relative terms like 'necessary', 'greater than', 'safer than' is hopeless with language, it requires numbers. Maggie was more enthusiastic about the likely success of OWL than I was, but eventually we concluded that promises could manage without this form of knowledge representation.

Each time we tried to search for a non-obvious association, the search returned nothing at all. The reason was straightforward: humans think of knowledge as something to explore and brain-storm around, but logic is not designed for brain-storming, it is designed for whittling. Instead of a whittling mechanisms, what a human operator needed was a mind-expanding tool.

Ontological systems fail to provide useful assistance because they are designed to solve the wrong problem. They refine a set of possible things into stronger and stronger constraint groups: like exploring a labyrinth, when there is only one correct path amongst many, more often than not, you hit a dead end. An obsession with hierarchal structure works against you: like Zeno's paradox, splitting up categories into ever smaller pieces and forcing them into a single spanning tree leads to a proliferation of over-constrained pathways.

By chance, in 2008, I stumbled across a possible solution to this problem that offered a way to develop human learning, and fit more closely with the concept of promises. Ironically, the bridge came from the very intersection between Shostakovich and semantic networks, through my friend, Steve Pepper.

Steve, with whom I share a passion for classical music (Shostakovich being a favourite of both of us), was one of the main advocates for a different kind of semantic technology called *topic maps*, a knowledge representation that grew out of a model for a electronic book indices in the 1990s. Topic maps could represent much of the same information as OWL, but in a less constrained model that was designed for human interaction, not for machine reasoning. One could end up with all the same problems as with OWL, but it was also possible to steer clear of them. The specific atomic properties of the topic map model were notably compatible with promise theory, in a way that OWL was not.

One reason ontology failed to make headway in human knowledge gathering was a basic limitation on human willingness to get involved in highly technical reasoning: we are ultimately lazy, except in unusual circumstances. Modelling knowledge with logic is very hard, and requires a level of rigid discipline that is an unnatural state for humans. Our knowledge acquisition is based on human faculties, which are seldom fully rational and are never uniquely structured. Logics are not a good model of this. To force human users to discipline themselves further in order to even get started with knowledge mapping, would cost them more Dunbar slots, when the aim is to free up such slots for better use. For humans, complex ontology is counter-productive.

A topic map starts somewhat more simply, with fewer constraints. It maps information using an index model, which Steve called the TAO:

- Topics, or subject fragments (knowledge atoms).

- Associations, that show relevant related topics.

- Occurrences of independent information about topics.

Every knowledge item we want to talk about is a topic which has a name and a type-category. Relationships to related issues are made by association, analogous to the 'see also' in a printed index. Finally, occurrences are pointers to specific documents or other representations of knowledge that are relevant to the named topic.

A focus on human interaction was already a step forward from OWL. What we needed was a way to include humans more in the process of interacting with information, not exclude them only to push an eventual answer in front of them. In order to trust the answer, a technology would have to help them to think about the material regularly enough to build a relationship to it. Facts are useless if they are merely thrust upon us, with no context of trust.

The problem in human-technology systems is often that there is too little of the right kind of human involvement. The purpose of automation is to take away pointless relationships so that humans may be brought into the loop on only relevant concerns. The problem of a lack of relationship to technology is that it results in incomprehension: not understanding the monster you've created. CFEngine's core immunological approach was a way to take pointless and bothersome relationships away from humans, freeing them to think about issues more worthy of human dignity, but what would be left? How do they get connected to the relevant observables and make friends with them?

In a complex information infrastructure, fraught with issues of partial visibility, and the inconsistencies of relativity, living between these many worlds is a confusing vantage point. If we search blindly for some data, we could end up with information from some other world, bereft of context. Some kind of semantic map was certainly going to be necessary to transform and relate different perspectives about dynamic and semantic information around the system, but exactly what that would be proved to be elusive prey. It was time to take a step back.

In the history of human thought, there have been many ideas about how humans actually think, and what that might imply about understanding. George Boole wrote his treatise on logic or the 'calculus of deductive reasoning', believing it would help us to build a model of how we think. He based his model of Boolean logic on the tradition of narrative reasoning, or argumentation about cause and effect that went back to Aristotle, but he also considered the new tools of probability in equal regard. Several cultures have grown up around these more or less artificial ways on thinking. Human thought is clearly not logical in nature, yet we tell ourselves logical stories through induction, deduction, abduction, and so on. Numerical arguments are also told as narratives, but based on processes that either characterize distributions of average behaviour or specific chains of process. There is a definite and practical need to understand this better.

A more modern version of the speculation, from the 20th century this time, came from thesis advisor to Claude Shannon, Vannevar Bush (1890-1974). Bush published an essay in 1945, entitled "As we may think"[242], in which he foresaw our modern ideas about associative networks. Bush was an electrical engineer at MIT and was instrumental in developing analogue computers. Some consider Bush to be the grandfather of the World Wide Web: in his article, he described plans for a hypothetical machine he called the 'memex', which he envisaged as allowing the user to store and retrieve documents linked by associations. This linking was very similar to what is known today as hypertext, and fits nicely with the model of topic maps. Indeed, Ted Nelson who later did pioneering work with hypertext, prior to Tim Berners-Lee's World Wide Web, credited Bush as his main influence. Bush hoped that the memex would transform an information explosion into a knowledge explosion. Topic maps are perhaps closer to this vision than the Web as we know it today, and they also claimed to represent a process of reasoning somewhat analogous to humans thought.

At a Topic Map Conference in Oslo in 2008, Steve Pepper related some of this history of associative documentation, but most of all I was struck by a remark he made about the basic properties of the topic map design. By design, it was possible to merge any two topic maps, because each occupied essentially a local world view of its own. Unlike the constrained logics of semantic web, this meant that topics were free and atomic properties of the worlds they belonged to. This was exactly the property of promises, within a many worlds interpretation. It meant that topic maps and promises were compatible with one another, and they could both be relativity friendly.

The possibility of constructing a semantic network was intriguing to me. From the work Geoff Canright and I had done on percolation of semantic links, we had used idea of tracking the traversal of influence across a network, whether it be intentional, as in the network traffic routing[243], or entirely unintentional, as in the case of security breaches. Percolation (see Chapter 10) is what happens when influence can squeeze through the cracks in a network in an unexpected way, by solving the maze of links and connections to find a route from one place to another. Although the project had been a simple and preliminary idea, the Archipelago project had sparked the beginning of this interest in mining the possible semantic information of a network of diverse connections to see how different kinds of connection arise.

Today, when a crime is committed, forensic investigators can gather evidence like films and photographs and label them within a semantic network. What people are in the picture? What they doing? When was the picture taken? What global coordinates? All of this information can be analyzed for 'covert' or un-intended semantic pathways that might link cause and effect. If a criminal left a trail, this technique allows the whiff of cause and effect to percolate through the network of connections.

The same approach could easily be applied to information infrastructure, how it works, or how the effect of faults propagates. We have to be able to model business too, and the flow of parts that contribute to commerce. This too involves semantics. What does it mean for us to understand whether technology keeps its promises, and keeps to its intended purpose?

The way we find meaning in system behaviour is a complex issue, involving observation and interpretation. Currently, one relies entirely on human expertise for the interpretation of data, but this is only possible if we are lucky enough to have the right person available who has a strong enough relationship to the kind of data to be able to interpret them. Looking at observational data is wholly insufficient for understanding observations, if you don't know what you are looking at.

The paradox is that, while numbers communicate the state of a system best, we cannot read numbers easily. We need pictures and stories to explain them. At college, students are told to explain results in words for this very reason: mere data are meaningless. This is where topic maps could come in, to form a kind of semantic substrate from which to extract an explanation.

A graph or a table is not useful without an explanation to accompany it, a story about what we believe it means. Once we have sufficient experience, telling these stories from tables and graphs can be ad libbed, but that requires the experience of a long-standing relationship with the skill.

Semantic networks have an important role to play in mapping out a local world of thought, around an agent's basic concepts, because understanding requires us to think associatively in breadth and depth. Semantics are the basis of how we build a model of understanding.

Imagine a more mundane example: when we say cake, we don't just think of a description of physical attributes, we think of many different kinds of cake, the cake granny made on Saturdays when we were small. We think that it was like the one in the cafe the other day. We think, not of one cake but all cakes of different colours, shapes, and sizes—and of all our experiences eating cakes at parties. Perhaps we think of a cookery program on the television or of a famous chef. From one starting place, our thinking diffuses into every niche of possible meaning, and this is what brings new ideas. Those who are good at diagnostics, are often those who are good at this random walk of association.

In other words, concepts are not isolated things in our minds. The robustness of meaning has only to do with the competitive strengths of different interpretations. There is no unique search-key, like a simple look-up that tells us how to think. There is no unique way of attaching meaning to memory, rather we tie memories into many different models of meaning, which compete for attention.

This feature of human cognition is what we exploit in blending systematic thinking with the apparently random walk of imagination. It is how we solve problems and diagnoze causal change. It is not at all like how databases work: we don't simply find information on a shelf at a particular place, alone and independent, with nothing else related, no free relationships forged.

Imagine then that we were in possession of a network of semantically labelled connections, between every kind of object, person, place we can imagine. If the links could be comprehended simply, the possibilities for divining relationships would be limited only by the imagination. For instance:

- Looking for intended and unintended behaviour (semantic pathways).

- Looking for possibly transitive relations.

- Looking for percolation of cause and effect.

- Identifying faults and possible causes.

- Identifying impact of changes.

- Identifying covert channels

- Locally understanding the significance of an item

I spent a year studying topic maps and making models relating to promises, with some coaching from Steve Pepper, and eventually wrote about the connection between topics and promises between 2009 and 2012. I was able to show that a topic map could be seen as a collection of promises, i.e. promises about how different topics were associated with one another, without the need for a formal pre-determined hierarchy[244]. The promisers or agents in a topic map were the topics themselves. This had a useful symmetry, because a topic map could also represent a meta-description of a promise, and thus the models were intertwinable in a mutually beneficial way. From this, I was able to implement an approximate topic map language based on promises in CFEngine 3, and used this to explore ways of representing brain-storming connections between system resources, their promises, and the impact they had on one another.

The barrier to contributing knowledge to a topic map, and learning from it was related to the need to understand an official, authoritative ontology of things. However, it was straightforward to simplify the topic map model to make it less hierarchical, using context instead of type. This removed the analogous problem with OWL, and other type-based classifications, i.e. the need for a pre-existing model to pigeon-hole ideas.

There was a simple design error in the formal definition of topics that prevented this from being realized[245]. The design had fallen into the classic trap of trying to control the growing structure, to achieve tidy structural uniqueness, by imposing mutually exclusive categories so as to form a spanning tree of taxonomic types. However, this simply led to conflicts of classification that pushed the burden onto the user trying to deposit knowledge. Once that was removed, the barriers to contributing knowledge were also removed, and no one would have to be aware of the model to contribute to the topic map. This was more true to the atomic, merge-able property which had attracted me in the first place.

The solution was straightforward. Instead of thinking of 'cat' as something belonging to the category of animals with fixed semantics by virtue of its location in a hierarchy, one can think if it simply as a linguistic atom (just a word), used in the *context* of another linguistic atom 'animals'. The word 'cat' can also be used in the context of industrial manufacturers (a company making cranes and digging equipment), or as a command abbreviation for 'concatenation' in computing, and so on. These different meanings should not be tied to rigid places in the network. Meaning can emerge from its usage, as with promises.

There is a world of difference between these two interpretations. Topic categorization is about putting things into the right box (meaning you have to work hard to find the right box before you can learn anything), topic context is about flexibly allowing multiple interpretations in a local region of knowledge (make as many boxes as you like). One is restrictive, the other expansive.

The formal model of topic maps had proposed the former, but for modelling collaborative knowledge sharing, I chose the latter, as it allowed free and uninhibited growth without requiring any previous knowledge to bootstrap from.

It took several years of failed experimentation with topic maps to discover the importance of context over category, and it has not yet been fully tested in a significant real setting yet, but the initial signs are promising, and it now offers the most likely approach to mapping out semantics to date.

Getting someone's expertise into a map representation is one thing, however. There was still the question of how to use it once it was there. Accelerating new knowledge acquisition in someone who needed it was the motivation for semantics, so that analytics could become domain knowledge quickly and predictably. The answer now seemed to lie in the simple idea of *approximation*. To understand why, we must go back to the basics of communication and the difference between symbolic message and natural language.

Morse code might have been the first form of electronic digital communication, but it is not the earliest man-made form of digital communication. That would be *writing* itself.

Writing is a form of symbolic (digital) data, written approximately as a sequence, which allows us to express very complex ideas, and indulge in even more complex relationships. It is not the only form of expressive communication. Painting, for instance, is a non-digital, non-sequential form of communication. It is not entirely sequential either, rather it follows a pattern called a grammar, which on a detailed level might have complex word orderings, parenthetic remarks, and other digressions, and on a larger scale conventionally follows an approximately causal time-ordering, which we call a story or narrative.

The history of writing itself is only a few thousands years old. Maryanne Wolf, of Tufts University, calls reading and writing the greatest invention in the world, and points out that writing is much too new in the history of the world to be something we have evolved specifically to do. The invention of writing seems to hijack a part of our brains designed for something else, perhaps navigating terrain along sequential paths. Wolf also notes the close association between reading, writing, and human innovation[246]. Creating symbolic patterns on stone tablets, on papyrus rolls, or on paper, has allowed humans to codify memories and experiences, to record history and pass on learning with high digital fidelity. In other words, writing allows us to build relationships to things that happened at other times and places.

We place an extremely high value on written communication, whether it is with ourselves in diaries and notebooks, or with others through letters and telegrams, or their modern equivalents Email, instant messages, and social media channels. The sequential nature of language is both clarifying and limiting. It binds us to think about systems in an unnecessarily linear way, and we often confuse that convention with necessity.

Our oldest notion of logic, syllogistic reasoning, is based on narrative. It is remarkable that few authors have remarked upon the obvious connection between logical reasoning and simple story narrative. It is way of thinking that we only use when we tell stories in natural language, yet it is not the only way we think, in other cases.

Most of our thought processing happens completely unconsciously and transparently, without us even being aware of it. Although we sometimes talk to ourselves in our minds, thinking about our thinking, this is a kind of rehearsal, or role playing that we use to reinforce learning. If Maryanne Wolfe is right, it is when we engage language that we turn this thinking into practice.

Freed of the need to verbalize my thoughts, I very often have flashes of insight that make bold connections between diverse imagery, which I later struggle to write down in some plausible form. This kind of thinking is far from linear and sequential. It comes in a flash, and the imagery is gone just as quickly, leaving only a feeling like an after-image of the answer. Suddenly, we somehow know the answer to something, but we cannot easily retrace a sequence of steps that made us arrive there.

Human writing is immensely sophisticated. Compared to simple digital signalling, text narrative exploits not only precision for expressivity, it includes many other dimensions, such as order, emotional and metaphorical levels as well as purely descriptive. This makes it a poor medium for transmitting certainty, because the meanings of our words are context dependent. Yet, I propose that it is exactly what we need to help humans gather knowledge quickly.

Formal ontologies were one approach to providing precision, based on artificial types, but an unsuccessful one, in my view, due to their rigidity. Something more robust, at the symbolic level is needed. Could there be a Morse code for semantics?

A simple digital message, in Shannon's model of communication is a Markov process: every symbol has a meaning independent of what came before it. In human language, however, what we just said can change what we now mean:

> Let's go to the vet. Bring the crane.
> Let's go to the building site. Bring the crane .

We understand from the context of the sentence whether we mean crane as animal or as industrial machinery. The more descriptive of details we are, the more text we add, the more fragile the story is to misinterpretation. This is why dumb, insensitive signal messages (digital messages, flags, dots and dashes) are more robust. The closer we get to natural language, the more ambiguous discussions become and the harder it becomes to reason reliably, as we enter the realm of semantic instability. Long descriptions require us to reinforce coupling strength between parts of sentence structures distributed over a wider scale. This ties together scale, semantics, and dynamics together. Narrative thinking is fragile, but emotionally stimulating.

Human language even goes as far as to flirt with misunderstanding[247]. The dominant use of metaphor in human language, the complex grammars and their chains of dependent words and phrases, i.e. the non-atomic nature of communication, make it highly susceptible to error. Yet, so strong is our conviction that we'll be able to communicate, that we even flirt with ambiguity for emotional effect: sarcasm, hyperbole, exaggeration, understatement. Metaphor is the basis of creative writing. Cockney rhyming slang is a great example of how we use indirection for amusement and play. It consists of a simple substitution codebook of phrases that rhyme with the actually intended words. Why would we deliberately cloak intentions in ambiguity? One answer is that this self-imposed riddle acts as a kind of code, which forces the initiated to build a closer cultural relationship in order to understand it. It is a culture club.

> "The old Trouble and Strife's out with the Bin Lids."

This combines Britain's wicked sense of humour with a rhyming indirection:

> Trouble and strife → wife
> Bin lids→ kids

A simple token (a noun) gets inflated into a semantically laden phrase. Unwitting machines (including several people I have met) are unable to understand a lot of indirection, without forewarning. The counterpoint of indirection is the so-called domain specific language. A domain specific language uses conventional words in more precise ways. Instead of relying on metaphor, it used words with special coded meanings. For example, the word 'catastrophe', in mathematics refers not to a cataclysm, or a failed calculation, but a particular kind of sudden change in the shape of a curve. Every specialist terminology services the basic purpose of increasing certainty, or reducing semantic instability. Yet, even with special meanings, we look for narrative.

Rousing stories of human ingenuity, the heroic narratives or sagas, are something we all aspire to be part of, at some level, even in our daily lives. We assemble information into stories rather than merely blurting out fact strings. Our daily stories need not be the epic poems like the Iliad, Odyssey, and the Aeneid, but they serve to wire information into our sequential memories. Sequential narrative seems to be an important part of our minds' situational modelling, related perhaps to our more long-standing adaptation to tracking causation, and path navigation through an environment.

Something about stories caught my attention at the start of 2009, having worked with topic maps for about a year. I could see stories in topic maps, by traversing them along different alternative paths, and these seemed to be able to say important things about the worlds modelled in these networks. If one built a semantic network to document things and relationships, real and abstract, it was possible to probe into a system in a way that was not possible by simply dumping numbers into a table or a graph.

Inevitably the stories could be rather specialized, but it seemed worth trying to elucidate the principle. Imagine a network with nodes: 'apples', 'fruit', 'healthy', 'Mark', 'vitamins', etc, or equivalent things in information infrastructure (computer, payment system, database, etc). Then suppose there are labelled associations between them (in italics). By traversing them we might get a sequence of connections forming a story:

Person		Computer
Mark *likes* apples		Payment system *requires* smart tables
Apples *are a kind of* fruit	or	Smart tables *are a kind of* a database
Fruit *contains* vitamins		A database *contains* data
Vitamins *make us* healthy		Data *make us* updated

The first chain of associations might lead us to the conclusion 'Mark might be healthy', or the 'Payment system is up to date'. These are potentially valuable insights, just out of reach of the raw data. The idea is that, by stringing together a story based on associations we know to be true, we may attach meaning to the entire path that goes beyond what can be seen in the collection itself.

The conclusions we derive may or may not be true, but the story itself shows us connections that might be used to draw such a conclusion. Interpreting such a story is easier for a human than for a machine, but finding the connections is easier for a machine than a human. There is a possibility for both to play a meaningful role.

The challenge in turning this idea into a technology is to find a set of rules for interpreting associations that lead to stories, and would allow us to replace the entire path with this short cut conclusion. In a different traversal, we might pick out a different set of associations that have been left to discover:

> Vitamins *are found in* apples
> Apples *are eaten by* Mark
> Mark *denies being* healthy

This seems to lead to the opposite conclusion, suggesting that multiple viewpoints might lead to contradictions. This is always a risk in a complex system, if we ask for donations from independent agents. Thus we cannot expect a semantic network to be a treasure chest of truth, merely a mine of assorted semantics. However, its potential is broad. If we try non-sequential reasoning, funny things can happen:

> Vitamins *are found in* apples
> Vitamins *are found in* Mark.

From this, we might conclude that Mark is like an apple. If you think this sounds silly, then think again. In fact it is a quite reasonable interpretation if we extrapolate: both apples and Mark can be places in which we might find vitamins. Both apples and Mark can act as containers, or both apples and Mark are chemical in nature. Some parallel inferences, like this, tells us about generalizations of concepts. The rules of semantic inference are clearly very complex, and reference potentially multiple pathways through a network.

The stories and metaphors we construct, in order to relate and discover meaning about the world around us, shape our thinking; they inspire and inform us at the same time. They seem to be a far cry from Morse code, yet we know from the structure of the Chomsky grammars that (at least, at a practical level) this is just a matter of encoding. The fact that they inspire us taps into our human nature.

Occasionally science and technology try to eliminate human aspects from discussions of technology, but as I've mentioned throughout this book, we cannot eliminate humans from a discussion about society. It would be an empty discussion. In semantic networks, I believe that there is a possibility to give renewed meaning to the connection between Man and Machine, at a practical level, by encouraging relationships between the two that strengthen the bond rather than make artificial distinctions.

In the spring of 2009, Alva Couch came to work with me at the University College in Oslo, and I told him about my idea for stories derived from topic maps. He immediately caught on to the significance for fault finding in computer installations, and began to develop the notion further.

The problem we studied was this: how might we provide non-expert infrastructure engineers with a illustrated camp-fire stories about the complex workings of a human-computer system (words and pictures), so that they can become experts for a hour, for a day, or for kickstarting a long-term relationship so that they know it like a friend?

In technical terms: suppose one is given a network of different topics, all related to the state and behaviours of some information infrastructure, and linked by a mesh of semantic associations; then, suppose one explores this network, starting from some particular topic (perhaps because it is something we are worried about, or something we would like to achieve). How could this help us to obtain a quick situational awareness and history of the issue, and gather together all of the ideas and concepts we need to think about to build up that picture?

There are three sources of input for such a story: the promises that describe *intended* behaviour for the system (its supposed purpose), the machine-learnt patterns of *actual* behaviour gathered by automated observation, and the *expertise* and experiences of humans who have shepherded the whole thing over time. The hypothesis then is that, by constructing some kind of semantic network (possibly a kind of topic map, but certainly something associative), it should be possible to generate interesting and relevant stories in a human-comprehensible form about the state and history of the total system.

As always, there are two ways of looking: *browsing*, for when we don't exactly know what we are looking for, and *searching* for when we have a specific question to ask.

Since we are looking for a path to integrate a number of incremental contributions, a story also needs boundary conditions for searching, much like solving a difference equation, with fixed end-points. Boundary (start and end) points place limits on where we start and where we can end up. For example, one possible approach would be to choose a starting topic and the end topic and look for a reasonable story connecting them. Another approach would be to specify only the starting point, or end-point and look for all possible stories about a particular topic. Specifying both the start and end-points for a stories, Alva was able to use Dijkstra's notion of a shortest path through a network to find simple relationships between pairs of topics[248].

We found very early on that the main problem with semantic networks was that, without engineering the topics and associations very particularly, searches were usually over-constrained, or under-populated, resulting in no stories at all. The kinds of associations that could be chained into meaningful stories could also limited by the order in which they occurred in a fairly 'sophisticated' way. This story is not very interesting:

> Computer X *signals alert* disk fault
> Disk fault *can be caused by* loss of power
> Loss of power *can be caused by* diesel generator
> Diesel generator *is manufactured by* Acme Generator Company
> Acme Generator Company *is a special case of* companies
> Companies *employ* people
> People *have* legs.

It begins as a wild goose chase, and ends in absurdity. A very stupid inference, from these connections, would be that computers have access to legs, which is certainty true in a far-fetched sense, but is hardly useful. Again, this shows that meaning is in the eye of the beholder. The search for connections cannot be faulted for going awry, for how can a machine know what the associations mean?

However, this was a luxury problem. In practice, even specifying a random start topic, and looking to see how association 'percolates' from it through the network, led to few non-trivial stories, in our experiments, or simply nonsense. This was related to the percolation problem itself, well known from the physics of materials. If there were few paths for interpretations going from topic to topic, then percolation tended to stop or end up in strange contortions out of desperation. Percolation theory tells us that connected pathways only emerge in random networks when the density of the associative connections reaches a certain critical level. It means one needs a minimum level of input before there will be any valuable output. The practical use of such a network was more of an issue than the construction of one, and it was limited by simple density. Dynamics always trump semantics.

What was new here was the fact that every link in the chain was a different *kind* of connection, with a different interpretation. Moreover, the fact that every kind of association also had an inverse was also a cause of trouble. Consider this exercise in nonsense generalization:

> Computer X *signals alert* disk fault
> Disk fault *is a special case of* fault
> Fault *has a special case* bad data

> Bad data *is a special case of* fault
> Fault *has a special case* disk fault
> Disk fault *is a special case of* fault ...

Pathways through networks may contain loops, and steps can be retraced form-ing a kind of semantic labyrinth. Fortunately, techniques for avoiding some of these issues are well known from network traffic routing (spanning trees are one way). This made the problem technically challenging as well as semantically challenging.

As we presented some of our preliminary thoughts to colleagues at conferences and meetings, the response was frequently one of surprise that we should bother trying to make infrastructure talk to engineers in a kind of automated human language. Why not just show them a picture of some monitoring data and be done with? That was the state of the art at the time. My problem with this was that it assumed too many things: that the human operator was looking at the right picture at the right time, and that they were able to understand what they were looking at. One could not assume that they would have sufficient experience to know what the possible causes and impacts were just by looking at raw data from instruments.

What might happen if the situation were much more complex, and one was looking at multiply correlated conditions across diverse regions of a system, where relativity distorted or even prevented a single individual from having the necessary relationships to have a chance of understanding?

If an analogy helps, then imagine a mission critical situation like a plane in flight. We've all seen the movie where the human expert, i.e., the pilot, is sud-denly unavailable and a novice is expected to fly the plane. They have to wait for someone on the ground to talk them down. If the technology was semantically aware, it could help the novice automatically.

There is no doubt that asking a machine to assist in skills where human ex-perts excel is a tough problem, but it seems eminently solvable. More impor-tantly, Steve Pepper's notion of a semantic network proved to be of general utility. Even if associations themselves don't link up into long stories, one could still search for isolated 'molecules' that had particular relationships or proper-ties, more like a regular database, but without the need for a rigid schema[249]. Semantic networks have properties in a similar way: small molecular bonds can play just as important as role as extended narratives.

The same is true for any semantic association. For example, we might search an information infrastructure for computers that provide or use a service, by looking for anything that has this kind of relationship to something else. We might find people, computers, software, or even components in an information system. Or, one could look for all objects that might be affected by a particular resource (a broken disk) to know its impact. In a classic tabular database, this kind of reversal would be an expensive brute force search that would have to be pre-arranged; in a network, it is straightforward to find from randomly collected hints. The advantage of the network is that it allows us to freely explore indirection, and even embed metaphor. However, the richness of natural language for expressing relationships makes searching harder.

Alva realized that one could use the idea of ontology, during this narrative reasoning, in a much simpler form than for semantic web, in order to classify associations by their usefulness. Never mind their conceptual categorization, classify them rather according to what they could do for us! This would bring us a step closer to the dots and dashes of a kind of Morse code. The key observation was that associations that combine into stories are relatively rare, but that approximate inference could reveal more connections than we might expect in a rigid interpretation. To find long range connections, logic normally requires *transitive* relations. Transitivity means that, if we chain together two relationships, then the end-points of the chain behave as if there is just a single relationship with no intermediary. So if something is true between A and B and separately between B and C, it must also be true between A and C by implication. For example:

(A is important to B) and (B is important to C) → (A is important to C)
(A is inside B) and (B is inside C) → (A is inside C)

Inference allows a connection to teleport over an intermediate agent. We can make triangles from such relationships (see Figure 11.8). Moreover, once you can hop over a single agent, you can do it for any number in a chain.

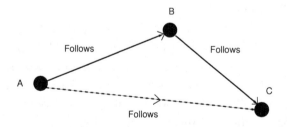

Fig. 11.8. The transitivity of inference leads to triangles where we can effectively short-cut past an intermediate agent. This is the prototype for interpreting a semantic 'mean value'.

Then there are subtleties due to causation. Suppose, A collects everything from B and B collects everything from C, then A also collects everything from C, but we might disagree depending on the order an frequency with which we interpret the actions. If A collects everything from B before B collects everything from C then A will miss out on some of the things it could have collected from C. That discrepancy could be quite important, if this were a data backup strategy we were talking about.

This was where promise theory helped considerably. This would not work for just any model, but it could work for certain promises. If the relations were not one-off actions, but promises to be kept over time, then an equilibrium could form. The order would eventually become irrelevant due to repeated promise-keeping, just as in the maelstrom effect. However, if one tried to think in terms of imperative actions instead of self-healing promises, there would be ordering problems. Understanding such subtleties was something else a tool based on a semantic network could help an inexperienced human to unravel, in the thick of daily work.

Alva realized that the reason transitivity worked boiled down to a few simple truths about causation. Consider these:

> A provides a service for B
> A has information for B
> A is a master for B
> B depends on data from A
> B takes input from A

All these really said 'A can influence B'. For all the different ways we had of expression relationships, there was really only a small number that mattered to transitivity. We boiled it down to three kinds of relation: causation, structure, and willingness to acceptance messages (i.e. to cooperate). This was exactly what promise theory predicted.

He also realized that one could greatly increase the density of useful associations by reducing their logical certainty (see Figure 11.9). For example, if A affects B somehow, and B affects C somehow, it is not necessarily true that A has affected C, but it is possible. If we say it *might* happen, then we can add an association that will allow percolation of influence, without saying anything incorrect or artificial. Ironically this is a return to the modalities we rejected from logic, but the key difference is that one adopts a pragmatic rule of maximum uncertainty instead of looking for provable correctness.

In promises, there are very few transitive intentions one can make. Since each agent is responsible only for its own promises, $+$ promises are immune to transitivity, and $-$ promises can transmit mainly the three causative associations mentioned above. However, by using approximate inference, we could add commentary about possible repercussions of promises. We were merely putting words on probability estimates in order to tell a story about their interpretation in context, not adding any creativity to the inference.

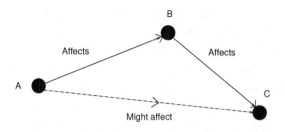

Fig. 11.9. The transitivity of inference leads to a principle of least certainty, for semantic averaging.

Allowing greater uncertainty in our characterization of local relationships actually increased the certainty of finding a possible percolated link between separate parts, because one is always more likely to find a vague connection than something specific. Also, it made it easier to automate the generation of topic map associations about the commentary as a direct result of the promise theory model. It was quickly clear that we could not expect human engineers to type in all of their experiences as knowledge promises. Rather, the process of extraction would have to come from automated inference, from comments added to the promises themselves, and data about how frequently promises were kept.

A kind of 'Morse code' of semantics was beginning to emerge. It did not have to compromise on expressivity, but it had to give up the idea of high resolution certainty. This is what I would have expected, as science is not about certainty, it is about uncertainty and how to keep it under control. To a physicist it does not seem paradoxical that, by averaging out specificity at a low-level, one can obtain greater certainty at a large scale: a kind of semantic mean, based perhaps on multiple viewpoints, votes, or simply blunting meaning. This was even reminiscent of studies made by Nobel laureate Elinor Ostrom, in studying human institutional rule-based behaviour[250]. This is the essence of scaling. Now, there was also a way to apply this both to statistics and semantics.

Technology cannot be understood without taking into account its purpose; this much is clear. Intentions come exclusively from humans, as does technology's role in a larger ecosystem of human-technology activity. Models of technology therefore make sense only if we involve humans both in motivating behaviour and in executing the actual work.

The question is how to scale that. The most extreme datacentres today have hundreds of thousands of computers run by only a handful of humans. In the past, this ratio would have been more like one person to every 30 computers (like a Dunbar tribe). Those days will not return, but we cannot escape our cognitive limitations either. We can borrow the illusion of a close working relationship with a massive infrastructure, by providing quick awareness of a situation at a particular scale, displaying numbers, graphs, and indicators, equipped with useful semantic signals, but the knowledge can only be superficial. A pilot can see status from dumb instruments, but cannot know how the aircraft will fly from these dials. That would require a deeper relationship.

Today's instrumentation of infrastructure is still dumb. It provides raw data, and burdens humans with the interpretation of it. We cannot ask the instrumentation for the worst-case scenario, but in the future we could, and indeed will have to.

Having worked on a semantic foundation for CFEngine for a number of years, and observed its failures and minor successes, I've seen that the biggest challenge of semantics lies in over-constraining intent: trying to fall back to command and control thinking. This was the mistake of security consultants over the years too: locking down systems to the point where they were unusable. Classical thinking was authoritative: this led to constraint, spanning tree thinking, and the fragility of a branching tree structure. If you don't get rigidity exactly right, you just kill information.

- Users cannot be expected to work too hard to interact with knowledge.

- Knowledge is not a logical framework.

- Users will categorize things as they like, we cannot impose an ontology on them.

Descriptive logics failed, like modal logics, because they are artificial and over constrained. To connect past, present, and future into a seamless relationship, we need a kind of periscope onto the system that can see into experiences of past, present and possible futures, and can measure these against the goals and aspirations that were intended. The economic value of semantics lies in how humans contribute to problem solving: through heuristics that break the barriers of algorithmic complexity.

The language of promises, as an atomic theory of intent, helps us in three ways, by allowing us to unify coordination, economics, and documentation into a single framework. Unlike the convergence (zero operator) property, the tool of a semantic network is not a targeted solution to any single problem in information systems, rather it is a foundation on which to build a battery of customized solutions in different contexts. It lies in the nature of semantics to be non-universal. Semantics are context specific, subjective, relativistic, and rightly so, as this is the nature of the human condition. Promises, on the other hand, form the skeleton for this flesh.

If stability and predictability increase as we eliminate reasoning about the environment, then putting humans in front of a remote control is bad, but asking a machine to guess is worse. The goal cannot be to build infrastructure washed and rinsed of semantics, but to strike a balance of predictability, while still allowing playgrounds of creativity on top. What we seek, in pursuing human-computer relations is a balance between the dynamical stability and semantic creativity. It must allow the business of society to prosper in a predictable and trustworthy way. These techniques are only the beginning of a better relationship between Man and Machine. The next step is to weave this unified web of dynamics and semantics into fabrics that we can use.

12

Molecular and Material Infrastructure

Elastic, plastic and brittle design

> The history of attempts to prevent cracks from spreading or evade their
> consequences is almost the history of engineering.
> – J.E. Gordon

In the first part of this book, I explained how our apparently predictable and
continuous world is really discrete and non-deterministic at its heart, and how
one of the major achievements of the 20th century was to come to terms with this
insight. Along the way, we've seen how ideas that are dynamically similar to that
insight appear in descriptions of information technology too, providing clues
about how to develop a more sophisticated view of our electronic information
infrastructure.

One place where the discrete nature of information infrastructure is especially
apparent is in the giant datacentres that feed our Internet services. In this chapter, I want to describe how the concept of promises can help us to understand
and recover a notion of *scaled continuity* in those places that keep services running, unifying performance and intent without sacrificing the benefits of the autonomous point of view. This is how to equip systems with the ability to evolve
to the next level of pervasive infrastructure, in which datacentres break apart
and grow to cover the entire surface of the planet, embedded ever more locally
into smart environments. To get there, we need to picture semantic and dynamic
aspects of human-computer systems as a single resilient *material*.

In true automation, an enclosed mechanism (say a clock) makes something
meaningful happen by mechanism alone, without humans intervening or pushing buttons. In software systems, such processes are often emulated or virtual-
ized entirely in software. In hybrid human-computer systems, even today, many
of the systemic connections are made implicitly through human intermediaries,

working on behalf of machines. The division of labour is often motivated by mistrust of machines rather than by a need for human input. Promises allow us to understand both parties' roles in a single framework.

Cooperation between Man and Machine is about delegating processes at different scales properly. The human's timescale is long and strategic, the machine's timescale is short and tactical. Technologists generally concern themselves more with machine inter-operability than with human inter-operability. Yet favouring the former, they risk making people feel uninvolved or detached from processes. After all, humans should not be asked to act like machines, else they may actually do so, shutting off self-correcting common sense, or even riling against the system rather than enhancing it with their essential qualities. Similarly, putting decision-making into the hands of automation would elevate the machine above the human.

The good news is that overcoming the problems needn't be difficult, or even steeped in lengthy psychology, if we just have a unifying approach to modelling semantics and dynamics in the combined system. Promises offer that. Nature then shows us two kinds of solution: dumb replication of structures that form uniform 'promise crystals' at one end of the scale, and smarter biologically adapted 'promise organisms' with significant functional semantics at the other. The concept of smart human-computer materials then becomes a useful way to think about these issues across diverse environments[251].

An interesting example, which effectively fuses these two extremes, is the story of how the video streaming service Netflix redesigned its operations to both work faster and become more resilient to failure[252]. Netflix scaled up the delivery of home video to a fairly reliable world-wide service in a short number of years by designing a human-computer network of promises for resilient infrastructure. Their streaming service requires not only the delivery of video data, but also the on-going development of a number of web services, for searching and subscribing to content, not to mention the service promises to maintain global cooperation of a highly distributed set of third party infrastructure resources.

Rather than building a model of machine redundancy for service continuity at the datacentre level (which would address dynamical continuity but not the need for greater rate of semantic improvement), software developers who designed the services built a model of individual human responsibility, which they called *micro-services*. This coupled service designers directly to their own creations' outcomes in a strong feedback loop, and in small group failure domains. Humans and services bonded in a strong-coupling relationship for rigid feedback, but the services themselves coupled weakly to allow scaling and resilience.

By coupling humans strongly to the outcomes of the technologies they built, they were motivated to keep promises out of an autonomous sense of pure shame. The approach was referred to as micro-services due to the large number of small domains. The development organization became like a gas of strongly-bonded but weakly interacting human-computer molecules, all individually fragile and important, but with small impact in case of failure. Each developer promised to accept responsibility for all failures and repair them quickly. Continuity was not specifically due to parallel redundancy now, but also incorporated rapid serial repair, just as in Computer Immunology.

On the operational side, it was the opposite: replication of the delivery channel in the datacentre was achieved by a so-called 'immutable server' model, in which no repairs were ever performed on server infrastructure. If a server atom broke, it was allowed to fail over to another redundant server, to eventually be replaced with a new one on a longer timescale.

The Netflix approach made the service timescale robust by (parallel) material replication of *dynamical* behaviour, and the functional timescale robust by repairing (serial) human-computer *semantic* behaviour. Many companies had designed systems for dynamical robustness before, but making *semantics* (represented by the human team) robust was the real innovation. The key was making small creative units *more* actively responsible for the customer experience (semantics), by forcing a closer relationship between Man and Machine, while severing the relationship to make humans less responsible for the dynamic scaling[253]. This plays to the opposing roles of dynamics and semantics, described at the end of Chapter 6.

In any system, human-machine promises can be built up incrementally to accumulate a sense of purpose, starting from the bottom up. If we think of each agent like an atom (or a micro-service, using Netflix terminology), then the promises between agents are like chemical bonds, binding agents into promise pattern that is a kind of 'molecule' of intent. From there, we can begin to think about the general chemistry of intention (see Figure 12.1). In the physical world, we design molecular substances and devices to have different properties at different scales. For example, a knife is hard and sharp at a small scale, but easy to hold at a large scale. This is the lesson engineering must absorb for information infrastructure too.

Promises give us a language of design for human-computer systems by which to architect outcomes, and reason about uncertainties. Some promises are structural (see Figure 12.1), and others are actionable. Promise theory tells us that we need both promises to *give* and promises to *accept* in order for information,

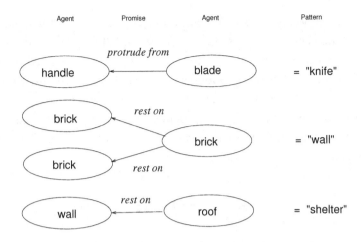

Fig. 12.1. Modelling relationships as 'molecular' promise graphs.

comprehension, and value to be exchanged. It allows us to think in terms of basic commoditized materials, like 'load balanced service dispatch'.

It is thus plausible how a network of promises might be used to design a collaboration between agents at multiple scales, one which is continuous, self-repairing, and self-informing at the top level. Continuity does not have to be represented by some kind of flow or a chain of events, though there is something in our human psychology that predisposes us to want to see things in a timeline. Down below, the world is not a simple flow, networks are involved, and acausal effect abound, but the flow is an illusion of storytelling that we desire and construct after the fact. So how do we tell such a story and restore this kind of comforting determinism to a world that doesn't really work that way?

Let's return to dynamics amoment, to understand resilience and how to keep the engine running. Recall how Shannon's digital messages enabled errors to be corrected with a minimum of effort, because the symbols in a message were atomic and immutable. Every 'A', for example, is indistinguishable and exchangeable with every other 'A'. A symbol could be replaced, or mistaken for another symbol, but the alphabet was stable, and therefore correctable. This basic strategy may be repeated for promises too, if we build a continuous message of indistinguishable, healable components. Immutable Shannon alphabets are thus *replicatable*, interchangeable units. They imply systems that can be repaired quickly and cheaply. Nature too has evolved into this strategy, through the emergence of DNA replication and cellular replication.

From this basic lesson, engineers have learnt to atomize processes into exchangeable commodity parts. This allows error correction, either by replacement or redundancy, as well as the ability to pull things apart or pack them together for transportation, and compressibility by seeing repeated patterns. If we find a fault in one of the symbols or replica units, we can either repair and work around it, or discard and replace it. Continuity restored.

Let's see how that works. Process chains, like in Figure 12.2, can be reinforced so the points and links themselves are not allowed to fail. The key to this lies in Figures 2.4 and 11.7.

Fig. 12.2.   A simple link in a chain is fragile, unless the singular points and links are merely schematic for something more robust.

Redundancy means that, for every agent, you have at least one other agent that could do the same job. It is a multiplicity for no other purpose than to allow failover. Failover means that, if one agent fails to keep a promise, one of its equivalents will take over and make sure the promise is kept.

This can be extended into the simple chain of promises, if we imagine that each 'super agent' is indestructible because it is made up of many smaller agents that can take over in case of trouble (see figure 12.3). In order to make this work, the agents inside this 'super agent' have to have a cooperative relationship with one another, so that they know who is going to do the job and when. If we take this idea to its logical conclusion, then we can do the same all the way along the chain (see Figure 12.4) for multi-stage processes. We'll see below what these formal super agents of promise theory look like in a physical system: they are not necessarily cellular in physical form. In fact, we know these super agents well from daily experience.

In this redundant form, there have to be promises from each of the internal agents in each 'super agent' to each of the individual agents in the next 'super agent', and so on. This adds superficial complexity, but it also brings resilience. The complexity added through redundancy is not 'real' complexity, in the sense that it is a completely predictable pattern, so we can factor it out of the big picture. Indeed, that is the advantage of looking at the promises at different scales. We can zoom in if we want to see the details, and zoom out if we don't. The less we zoom in, the more continuous everything seems.

The example in Figure 12.4 is based on a basic pattern for increasing channel

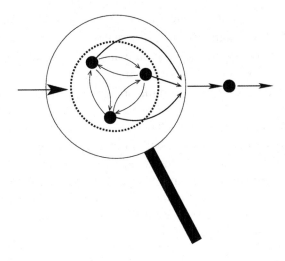

Fig. 12.3. Magnifying a resilient agent, we find pools of collaborating agents all in the same role, at the microscopic scale.

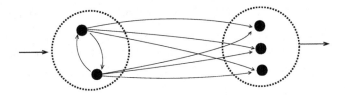

Fig. 12.4. Resiliency of the promises between the agents follows automatically from having pools of multiple agents through the chain. The agents within a pool can work together so ensure that only one of them keeps the promise.

capacity for service delivery, such as web services. The initial agent in the chain would be called a 'load balancer'. Its function is to divide up the incoming requests from users and route them to a server that will dispatch the request. I base this on web services, but the pattern is equally valid for a warehouse shipment. The load balancer has to be redundant, in case one of them is sick or offline, so both have to promise to listen for requests from the same incoming stream and dispatch to the same group of servers. Similarly each of the servers has to promise to fulfill the incoming request before taking on another. This pattern of promises, whether fulfilled by humans or machines, is simple and repeatable. The redundancy brings fault tolerance and increased capacity. In this way, we see that the details of redundancy and failover are not really separate from scaling.

At the start of this book, I indicated that we have reason to think about technology as we think about matter itself. It is now not such a leap of the imagination to see why. Massive parallel replication combined with smudging of detailed promises into coarser promises is just what happens in material science.

At the microscopic level, every atomic or molecular substance is a network of atoms bound together by promises of attraction, and chemical affinities. Then, as we pull back to the macroscopic level, we abandon the focus on atoms and think about compound objects with bulk properties. In mechanical or chemical engineering, one does not even bother to refer to physical materials as continuous; we simply take for granted that the physical world continues to exist and that it does not fall apart except under duress from the environment. We speak rather of these bulk materials (super agents), and we describe their resilience to continuous loads. For example:

> Stress   A load or force applied to a material in tension or compression
> Strain   The amount of stretching per unit length due to stress

Stress is a perturbation of a material by a bulk external force across its cross section (see Figure 12.5). It is usually applied at the edges of an object, and results in a state (called strain) that is distributed throughout the material. Stress applies to solids; in fluids we talk about pressure. Stress may be caused by a sudden impact, but as we shift attention to continuous systems, it is more normal to think of sustained loads.

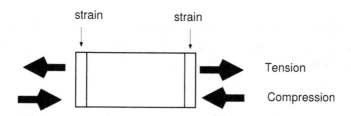

Fig. 12.5.   Stress applied to a bulk solid.

There is a straightforward analogy between physical load and transactional load placed on information systems by demand for services, in terms of transmitted force messages. Strain is the response of the system to a stress. For small stresses, it is usually an elastic response in materials: the material stretches and usually recovers once the stress is removed.

> Strong   Resistance to total failure under tension or compression
> Stiff   Resistance to deformation, bending, flexing

We say that a material is strong if it is difficult to break apart, either when compressed or stretched. A strong information system would be one that could not easily be made to fail under stress. Here are some definitions:

Elastic	Able to absorb temporary stress and recover afterwards
Plastic	Able to adapt to load by changing shape
Ductile	Linear plastic deformation
Hard	Resistant to changing shape under load

A system is elastic if it recovers its shape when stress is removed[254]. Elasticity usually only applies for small perturbations; after that, a system breaks or deforms. A plastic material is one that can change its shape easily as force is applied. The parts can move and flow over one another. The term malleable is also used. Ductility is a similar property that allows materials to be drawn out into threads or wires, by plastic flow. Plasticity is associated with weak couplings.

Plastic materials can deform or adapt without losing their essential properties. In a plastic material, you allow parts of the system to re-organize themselves to cope with the stress. They can do this because they are weakly coupled in the first place. As they re-organize, the system will take up the load differently, and survive, but with a permanent deformation of some scale (see figure 12.6).

Fig. 12.6. A plastic material will deform to cope with stress.

The final terms I want to mention have to do with material defects. Most solids have some kind of network (crystalline) structure, which is imperfectly formed. The surfaces of solids materials are marred by cracks that have an important impact on their strength. If cracks open up and spread easily (the technical term is propagation), then we say the material is brittle. Brittleness is associated with strong couplings which transmit force directly, toughness with plasticity. More definitions:

Brittle	Susceptible to crack propagation
Tough	Resistant to crack propagation

We fear the concept of brittleness perhaps the most, because it is often associated with sudden and dramatic failures, relating to bones or glass. However, brittleness is not a special condition of weakness, it is the normal state of all simple non-metallic solids[255]. Indeed, jelly is brittle: try nicking a crack in jelly and it will shear straight through and break. In modern times, we have learnt to overcome it in clever ways, by introducing impurities like fibres or alloyed interstitial atoms into materials which 'catch' or stifle the propagation of cracks.

Cracks propagate when materials are under tension because the load becomes unbalanced across the section transverse to the direction of the force. In a material lattice (see Figure 12.7), the load is normally spread evenly, giving the maximum resistance to stress, i.e. maximum strength. However, a crack removes essential bonds, leading to a *stress concentration* at the tip. If a material is strongly coupled, the force gets transmitted to the next nearest atom, at the tip, diverting extra load onto a smaller number of bonds. This tends to make the stressed bonds break and the crack opens further. Once this starts, it is usually a cascade failure which causes a material to break easily along the crack. (As mentioned earlier, I always think of this mechanism when nicking a banana skin with a knife to open it.)

If the material is stiff enough (jelly is brittle, but not stiff), the sound waves generated by a sudden force can open several cracks at the same time, and the material shatters as glass does. Before glass manufacturing methods improved, glass was very weak because it was damaged by the manufacturing process, riddled with cracks.

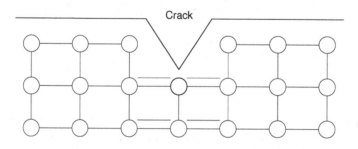

Fig. 12.7. A crack begins at the surface of a material and leads to a concentration of stress around the missing linkage. The stretched binds are more fragile and weaker which tends to open the crack further causing it to spread or propagate.

Strength is a property of the networks of atomic bonds, so it is not surprising that information networks have similar properties. The only difference is that, when characterizing human tools, we need now two measures of resilience: as always, based on both *dynamical* properties and *semantic* properties.

There are few lattice structures that exactly resemble Figure 12.7 in information science, today; but cracks can form nevertheless. Recall, however, the queue at the supermarket from Chapter 2. A number of queues apply pressure to a battery of service checkouts. The structure of promises in these queues is essentially like the lattice in Figure 12.8. Each agent, played by a customer in line. The horizontal promises are to stay behind the agent in front, and to leave the queue once processed by the checkouts. The agents can also change lines, if they promise to allow this (vertical bonds).

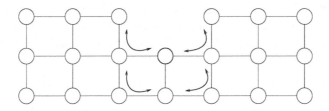

Fig. 12.8.   A lattice is a redundant structure that can reroute load around a failure, but it is still vulnerable to stress.

If one of the lines becomes blocked or there is no checkout, then there is a constriction in the flow and the stress on the remaining cross section increases. This increases the likelihood of failure in the queueing. From a high level, this is a reasonable picture of a supermarket queue, or even a queue to a number of web servers. We zoom in, however, to look more realistically at the promise molecules around a web server.

Now let's compare these pictures with the world of information technology. Figure 12.9 is schematic diagram of a classical multi-tier service architecture, e.g. as used in delivering web site information. Dispatchers promise to receive incoming service requests and queue them to a battery of servers; servers promise to pick up from the queue and dispatch with the assistance of helpers (typically a database). The stress of service demand is caused by users requesting web pages.

The dispatchers promise to collaborate, in balancing the load across a number of equivalent servers, just as the stress in a solid is balanced across its cross section. However, unlike the lattice, the servers don't actually bond: they don't

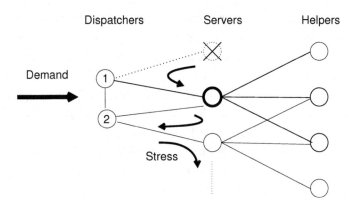

Fig. 12.9.   When a server under dispatcher 1 becomes inoperative, a stress concentration forms at the bold ringed site. If this also fails, stress will be shifted to the neighbouring channels around input 2, shifting load and causing the failure to propagate.

make any promises to one another. Their cooperation is handled by the dispatchers, so effectively:

$$\text{dispatcher} + \text{server} = \text{bonded queue lattice}.$$

If one of the servers fails, this acts like a crack, because the dispatcher has to then re-route the load transversely through the remaining servers, which increases the parallel strain on them. This might cause other servers to fail under load, propagating the crack further, or it might cause the dispatcher itself to fail, pushing the load onto the redundant dispatcher, causing the crack to propagate diagonally. We have much to learn from solid materials in designing better systems.

What design steps can we take to make information infrastructure less weak and brittle? Things that make promises dynamically strong are typically sufficient resource capacity to keep the promises, failover and response speed brought about through automation. Toughness, or crack resistance, is all about weak coupling or averting cracks before they can propagate. The latter can be achieved in two ways: by buttressing with redundancy, or by repairing with fast error correction and countermeasures, and statistical memory (hysteresis). The former adds non-productive overhead; the latter was the concept of Computer Immunology, which might be too slow, so we need to balance strategy intelligently.

The things that make promises semantically strong include the avoidance of branching uncertainty in decisions and conditionals, where we project environmental complexity across a true/false edge. Semantic toughness comes from avoiding decision making altogether (dumb devices, with the zero property), or at least have multiple voices voting to eliminate uncertainty, multiple viewpoints like dual security keys, multiple pilots (semantic averaging).

In metallurgy, the technique of heating up a metal to introduce random imperfections that favour plastic flow over brittle crack propagation is used to toughen metals. This is called *annealing*. Simulated annealing is used in software as a method of introducing random noise into information systems to avoid getting locked into states that are sub-optimal. Basic randomization of pathways leads to the same effect in information infrastructure. The converse, i.e. hammering the metal to squeeze out those imperfections, is called *work hardening*. Its aim is to restore brittleness. The success of steel is largely due to its ability to be tough on the inside, and hard on the outside, which was traditionally good quality for sword-making. The analogy of 'hardening' of information systems is sometimes used as a concept related to security, favouring inflexibility at risk of complete failure over uncertainty of a possible intermediate state[256].

Going beyond single systems, we can rise above individual services and look at the larger scale of the physical fabrics that host them. Thanks to the separation of scales, software developers of the past have mostly been able to ignore how programs actually work at a physical level. However, at heavy load, the increased risk of dynamical failure places the burden of handling those semantics back onto the programmer's shoulders[257]. All of the software complexity has to be carried by the communication infrastructure, or network[258].

To bear the load, and maintain reliability at the same time, it has been necessary to move away from the simplistic, top-down hierarchical structures of local area networks (see Figure 12.9), to a more sustainable model. The past 10 years has seen a number of large datacentre engineers rediscover an architecture from the era of analogue telephony, allowing engineers to build networks that work like telephone operator patch boards, with built in spanning tree properties. Charles Clos[259], an employee at Bell labs wrote a paper in 1952 exploring the graph theory of so-called non-blocking networks[Clo53], i.e. networks which continue to connect points together despite the loss of key components. These networks remain attractive to network engineers, as they still follow the pattern of a simple tiered hierarchy, which is most familiar and which seems to avoid the problems of loops in network routes.

Figure 12.10 shows a 2x2 non-blocking Clos network (also called a fat tree, as it is shallow but broad). This is a special case of Figure 12.4. Examining the links, one sees that every major link from top to bottom is doubled up redundantly, so that a simple failover would take place in case of failure. Naturally, this assumes that the total capacity of the failed network remains sufficient to bear the total load, as in the case of a load bearing beam. If not, cascade failure or crack propagation will ensue as before. What is important about the Clos design is that is attempts to keep failure domains as localized as possible prior to cascade failure.

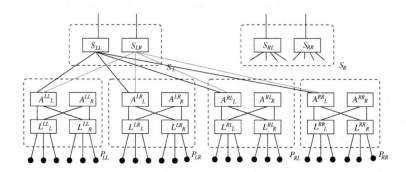

Fig. 12.10.   A simple 2x2 redundant Clos non-blocking network or fat tree network. Half the top links to the right hand nodes of the second level are missing for clarity.

External traffic load enters from the top, via one of the two backbone switches, and is passed down the ranks along the duplicated pathways to the leaf servers at the bottom. The pattern is also called a leaf-spine architecture.

The regular patterns of nodes have the regularity of a crystal, but not the simplicity. Indeed, this looks more like a cat's cradle of tangled wool than a smooth diamond. The reason for this will become clear in a moment, and is caused by a conflict of interest between the spatial symmetries of the human space and the technological space.

If we look at the arrangement of computers in racks in datacentres, there is a superficial likeness to sites of a simple cubic crystal lattice, as the black dots in Figure 12.11. We stack most kinds of warehouse in this way. However, what spoils the analogy is the way the sites are connected together. Try to imagine a datacentre design actually like Figure 12.11, including the connections between the nodes. It would be very simple to change a connection or a broken node, and every component would be simply addressable using well-known Cartesian coordinates. It would be simple mathematics of the kind we learn in schools. Instead, however, we have irregular container addresses using network container prefixes and then arbitrary numberings that are unrelated to the symmetries of the physical hardware. This makes managing datacentres unnecessarily complex.

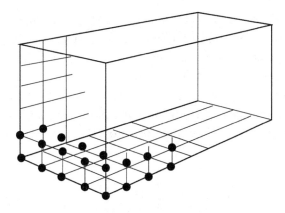

Fig. 12.11. A cubic lattice has the symmetries of racks of computers.

The simplicity of form in space is offset by an increased complexity in find one's way around this latticework structure, without getting into loops. There is now more than one way to get from A to B. In principle that is a good thing, but it complicates algorithms. How does one choose? Thus it seems that there is also a possible conflict of interest between the ease of finding a route and the robustness of having many different routes. In fact, the natural world has found ways of solving the corresponding problem using potential gradients to lead the way, e.g. in the chemotaxis between cells and in foetal morphology. But, perhaps there is a compromise to be made?

Consider a network similar to the Clos architecture, shown in Figure 12.12 that has somewhat similar properties. When drawn in two dimensions, like the Clos case, it has a somewhat similar tree-like structure. It does not have quite as good coverage in case of failure, but the risk level is somewhat similar. Drawn

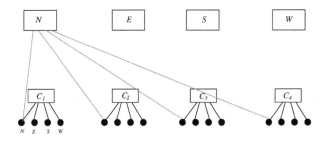

Fig. 12.12. A Body Centred Cubic (BCC) lattice.

in this way, it does not seem to confer a particular advantage over the Clos network. However, if we re-draw it in three dimensions, it turns out to be a very well known structure in material science: a body-centred cubic lattice, similar (but not quite identical) to that of Iron (see Figure 12.13). A cubic lattice is quite close to that shown in Figure 12.11, and thus we see that there is a possibility to have both the advantages of redundancy and the easy of connectivity if we just draw the picture to exploit its symmetries properly.

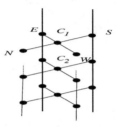

Fig. 12.13.   The BCC lattice in three dimensions.

Indeed, our inability to think well in three dimensions leads to the complexity of real and current datacentre designs. Racks and servers are mounted in a three dimensional cubic lattice structure, because this is how we humans design our spaces, but the network devices are connected in a two-dimensional tree-like form (Figure 12.10), with a radial symmtry. The amount of criss-crossed and folded cabling required to perform this unholy union leads to mind-boggling cabling complexity inside datacentres with thousands of nodes.

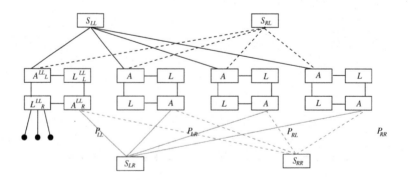

Fig. 12.14.   Re-drawing the 2x2 Clos network, still in two dimensions.

Could this be avoided? The simpler cubic lattice suggests that we might have our cake and eat it. In fact, the more robust Clos network can also be redrawn in a simpler geometry. If one looks at Figure 12.10, any mathematician would immediately notice a regular radial symmetry. Indeed, if we begin to unravel the topology by re-drawing and un-twisting the connections, in three dimensions, a surprising thing happens.

The first step is shown in Figure 12.14. Instead of thinking about the network as a muddled hierarchy from top to bottom, we can use natural the symmetry of the structure to avoid crossing cables. The remaining cables at top and bottom, which seem to cross, do so because we are projecting a three dimensional structure into two dimensions. If we bend the middle layers into a torus (doughnut) by rotating them 90 degrees and arrange the outgoing connections as in Figure 12.15, then we can unfold the entire structure as a toroidal geometry as shown in Figure 12.16.

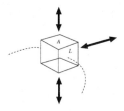

Fig. 12.15.   Three dimensional thinking allows us to optimize connections.

The advantage of a radial design is that all nodes can reach on another by line-of-sight connections, or perhaps with a simple mirror to reflect back inside the inner annulus, thus avoiding the need for expensive fibre-optic waveguides (which need replacing as they grow brittle). Lasers could connect separate units directly. Perhaps such datacentres will be built in the future, allowing for rigidity issues in earthquake zones. Similar transformations can be made for larger Clos networks too.

Another incidental advantage of this simple case, as a three dimensional tower, is that cooling air could be drawn up from underground from top to bottom. This is a well known design, inspired by termite hills. In spite of being baked in the desert sun, termite mounds remain quite cool inside, because they are ventilated by air channels that draw in air that is cooled by feeding it underground. The heating of the tower leads to a natural convection which drives a cooling engine. The power savings alone might justify this kind of design.

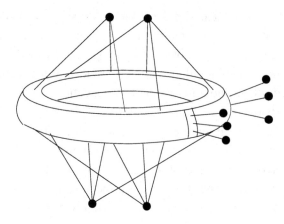

Fig. 12.16.   The Clos network can now be unfolded into a radial geometry with line-of-sight connections that could be maintained by direct fibre-free laser optics.

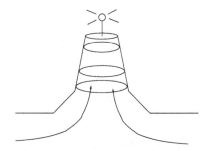

Fig. 12.17.   In the future one might imagine datacentres looking more like these towers, with cooling air drawn in from underground instead of air conditioning. This has a more biological material structure than solid crystal form.

An infrastructure that society can rely on craves a level of certainty that is not merely based on a throw of the dice. We have to know how to combine parts to make what we need, and immunize systems against uncertainty by using what we know of structure. Much of the semantic complexity of systems lies in combinatorics of parts and purpose. Figure 12.18 shows a hypothetical parallelization of workflows, essentially independent, that are then combined at a single point, like when a factory combines independently made parts into a single entity, or when software relies on data from multiple sources. The joint becomes a point of possible failure, and a stress concentration, because it is strongly coupled. This is a simple model of a manufacturing system in which multiple parts are assembled independently then combined.

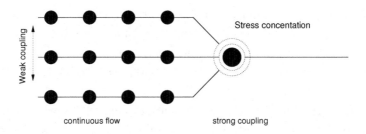

Fig. 12.18. Mixing stability with regions of creativity by componentizing can create a stress concentration at the joint.

Robustness comes from what game-theorists call a mixed strategy: a diverse broad base to support you. The more specific a role structural arrangements play in the properties of a design, the more brittle the information infrastructure is likely to be.

Structural physics of lattices opens the door to many phenomena that we need to understand. Lattices not only propagate cracks, they can also propagate information, but with a cumuluative delay. Recall that one of the problems of distributed systems was the matter of consistency of knowledge in a network, as a result of relativity. The finite speed of communication caused information from one location to be either unavailable to another locations, or to exist in multiple inconsistent versions.

To copy information by transmitting it through a chain or lattice of machines, we have to take into account the dynamical scales that arise from the periodicity of the lattice itself. Threshold behaviour related to the period (as in chapter 2) is inevitable. The matter of CAP inconsistency of data, discussed in chapter 7, now raises its head. We may also view that effect as a dynamical material property[260]. Suppose, then, we want to make this discrete process look like a continuous flow, as approximately deterministic as possible: what would that take?

The answer has to depend on how often the information changes at source, compared to how often the information is distributed around the network, and how fast that transfer is. One could achieve this with simple promises to copy the information from neighbours at regular intervals. Eventually, keeping these promises would lead to equilibrium. The equilibration of the network cannot be instantaneous, however, as there is a finite speed of information. Constructing the dimensionless ratios of times, we would expect there to be a resonance between the time to copy between a host and the size of the total chain, somewhat like in Planck's quantum hypothesis, where one has integer multiples of discrete times in each dimension. Then, if the lattice were broken somewhere, perhaps because a computer is non-functional, the information would have to flow around the crack by a different route, adding path lengths that would complicate the resonances.

In 2007, graduate student Matt Disney and I wanted to know how effectively this kind of relay-race of information equilibration could be made based entirely on autonomous agents with a minimum of cooperation, to determine their bulk properties. It felt almost like revisiting the early days of statistical mechanics, experimenting with laws of expansion and contraction of gases to make steam engines. Matt studied the way a consistent state was transmitted through a chain of agents, in a promise-based periodic updating scheme, inspired by data aggregation work of Rolf Stadler from the Royal Institute of Technology in Stockholm[261].

A few tens of agents, arranged in a chain, promised to update themselves independently, at the same regular interval, and Matt measured how long the process took, varying other scales in the system to look for threshold behaviour. We compared the results to a simple model based on a even probabilistic unidirectional flow of promise-keeping to see how well the concept of a regular flow modelled the results.

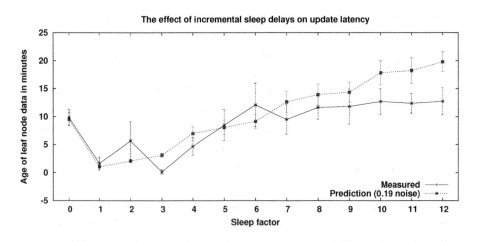

Fig. 12.19. Measured and predicted timings of message transfer in a chain (reproduced courtesy of Matt Disney [Dis07]).

Figure 12.19 shows some of the results from actual tests in the lab. A change would be made in an agent at one end of a chain, and Matt measured how quickly the change propagated to the other agents. the graph shows the total trip time to reach the other end. The simple flow model captured the results only approximately, to within the bounds of observational uncertainty. In the real system, which was constructed using CFEngine agents, there were unseen couplings through the underlying infrastructure that sustained the agents, that we were were not able to model. It was also expected that we would see resonances between the length of the whole versus the update interval, where standing waves could play a role due to the quantized intervals. These produced some qualitatively surprising effects, by causing the agents' behaviour to be correlated in invisible ways. Had the information been allowed to flow in either direction along the chain, the results would have been significantly more complex.

As we increased the periodic interval at which the agents woke up and synchronized with their neighbours, the time to synchronize actually went down before rising again. That was because, in a periodic time framework, a delay from an earlier round can actually look like an early arrival: the maelstrom effect can be counter-intuitive.

The effect of this kind of scaling instability on transport times in, a real world organization such as a bank trying to synchronize financial information, could be potentially problematic. This is why buffers and limits on financial transactions are used to limit risk in the fact of incomplete information.

Even a small amount of noise in the distribution of starting times could lead to unexpected effects in the equilibration time, sometimes annealing the material, sometimes disrupting it. This made the illusion of determinism difficult to promise. The lesson was that there is more to scaling than a simple model can predict, when one deals with small numbers. The continuity we experience in bulk materials comes from many more orders of magnitude of averaging that a few tens of agents. Most of our information infrastructure today is more akin to nano-engineering.

If promises express the properties of agents as real chemical atoms express their properties by virtue of their electronic structure, then one would expect that, as the number of agents in a human-computer material increases, promise structures must begin to behave more like bulk materials. Randomness from environmental noise could then bring so much dynamic and semantic averaging as to make semantics relatively unimportant to the outcome of the material. Dynamics always trump semantics. This is good in the sense that it would eliminate a source of instability, but it also means that materials could lose the ability to be very 'smart' at massive scale.

In material science, there are smart materials of different kinds, and at different scales. Studies are going in the opposite direction, however. Nanotechnology is scaling down atomic systems, emphasizing the importance of semantics and potential instability[262]. In the meanwhile, smart infrastructure for our day-to-day society is caught somewhere in the middle of these scenarios. The model of promise networks puts us into a position of being able to perform analysis for general dynamical and semantic networks, and to understand their cooperative, bulk behaviours.

While datacentres are increasingly looking like molecular crystalline materials, composed of large arrays of interchangeable parts, with very simple semantics, biological structures in nature show much more functional differentiation. Biological organisms forms organs and cooperative entities, as well as uniform tissues, at different scales. They are more sophisticated information systems, of the kind we need to pay attention to.

Today promise graphs of what goes on inside a simple piece of infrastructure currently resides at the level of medium complexity molecules (see figure 12.20). Some organizations build structures that look like crystals: media providers have extremely uniform systems that can be scaled without semantics. Others (like banks) have complex interactions between different services that follow more of a biological paradigm. The graph of promises in an organism is riddled with strong coupling dependency, making it formally brittle, so instead of redundancy the strategy should be rapid repair. The purpose of Computer Immunology was to close such cracks in systems, even in systems that could not play the numbers game of pure redundancy.

What impediments might we face to resilient infrastructure? Semantic uniqueness works against dynamical redundancy. For example, redundant agents have to promise to share the same identity, and therefore contend for resource. They also have to agree to coordinate which of them should respond to a service request, so that there is no duplication of effort leading to contention. Contention for competing interests could also lead to corrosion of material properties, as different concerns vie for control. We may summarize the situation neatly in the following table:

CONFLICT	SINGLE		MULTIPLE
DYNAMIC	POINT OF FAILURE	$\rightarrow$	REDUNDANCY
SEMANTIC	UNIQUENESS	$\leftarrow$	CONTENTION

The arrows point in favour of increasing certainty. Semantic and dynamic stability end up being at odds. This makes the Netflix cultural model especially interesting.

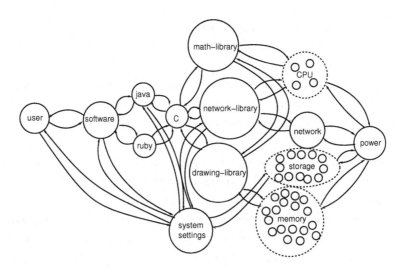

Fig. 12.20. Promise diagram for software systems, composed of many separate agents, making complicated promises to one another, with little redundancy. This is not a crystalline material. There are single points of failure allowing cracks to cut into the system, breaking it in some aspect of its behaviour.

If we are going to make smart robust infrastructure on the material scale, we are going to have to understand more than we do today about the scaling of semantics. Putting 10,000 units redundant that fail at the same rate does not necessarily make you more resilient, if you have no repair, it just buys you a little time. A fatal crack can still undo the whole thing. Plasticizers that give systems room to adapt to load will be an important development.

The ability to test this level of scale and complexity is currently a hindrance. What one needs is something analogous to a *wind tunnel*, as used in the transport industry to test aerodynamic designs. Wind tunnels are a development of the idea of dynamical similarity[263]. One builds a scale model, based on a system having the same dimensionless ratios for its dynamical properties. Today, we do not have tools capable of determining such models. As we saw in the NUMA-database anecdote of chapter 9, this would be very difficult to achieve for computers. The sheer number of interacting scales is very high, and we know little about them all. The only way to achieve it would be to assume incomplete information, and try to ensure a weakly coupled system, with comprehensible dynamics. This would offer the hope of understanding the dominant effects.

Testing a combination of semantics and dynamics has, to my knowledge, rarely if ever been achieved. How would you test 'town planning', for example? This is a pretty good analogy for a complex information system. User testing of a prototype is almost never good enough, because it is too hard to reproduce how it behaves under duress. Fitness for purpose comes from the combinatorics of many bulk and environmental effects. Software engineers tend to test for limited semantics, but as we've seen, it is dynamics that provoke the instabilities. We are still at the nano-engineering level in information systems.

As infrastructure becomes more diffuse, the diaspora of embedded and mobile devices looks less and less like the regular crystalline world of a datacentre. Why would we expect such a crystalline regularity at all?

In material science, the natural state of diffuse atoms is a gas. Mobile users form a gas of devices, weakly coupled to one another by a variety of radio technologies. Gases condense into closely packed solids only when the need to bind exceeds the need to move around. Atoms have physical attractive forces to bring them together. So why would mobile devices form stable structures and coalesce into a different phase? The attractive force for humans with mobile devices is the economic value of working together and trading. This is easier to understand from a promise theory perspective than for simple communication.

In 2005, doctoral student Siri Fagernes and I were sketching out models of promises for human-computer systems, looking for examples of individuals coming together to form spontaneous but stable 'molecular' cooperation. This is analogous to condensation of a gas. At the time, there was much discussion of so-called pervasive computing, smart homes, intelligent spaces, where the molecular viewpoint is particularly relevant. *Embedded devices* is the name given to computers built into the world around us, in refrigerators, televisions, security systems, temperature regulators, and so on. Embedded devices are designed to work in close contact with an external environment, and bond typically more tightly to the human world than to other computers. Siri and I were adamant, even though writing for an audience of computer scientists, that we should not imply that the promise model was just another kind of network communication between inter-operating devices. There was also an important human cooperative and economic aspect behind it.

To emphasize this, we wanted to show promises in an indisputably pedestrian human-computer environment, where infrastructure had a clear meaning as something that would support society at large. Siri came up with the idea of a shopping mall, based on smart infrastructure. We called this (reaching new heights of imagination) the Smart Mall[264].

The smart mall consisted of agents of different kinds. Some were super agents representing the management of the mall, some were shop owners, some were

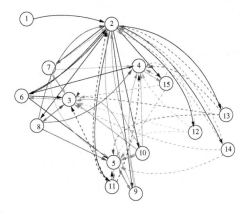

Fig. 12.21.   The smart mall consisted of many agents in different patterns forming a thick mesh of promises.

customers. We looked for the kinds of promises that would sustain an economic relationship between each of these, based entirely on different forms of voluntary cooperation. Paying for goods became a last resort for us: it was just a little too obvious[265]. We wanted to look at other forms of cooperation. Figure 12.21 shows the network of all the promises. One idea was that customers could

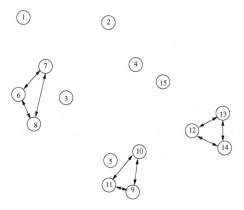

Fig. 12.22.   Customers form a treaty with one another to avoid junk advertising.

win credit for passing on recommendations and advertising to other friends and customers. This was handled by a subset of promises, and resulted in a particular molecular pattern (see Figure 12.22), within the whole. Several such patterns could be identified, according to the different interacting relationships or chemistries.

We were a number of years too early to see how Netflix's micro-service human-computer molecules exploited exactly this mechanism for cooperative binding in a very different environment. Truth often exceeds fiction.

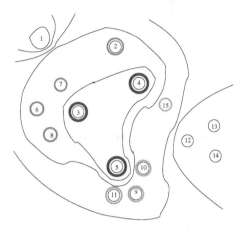

Fig. 12.23.   The smart mall consisted of many agents in different patterns forming a thick mesh of promises.

A further advantage of seeing the promise network in its entirety was that one could then apply the techniques of network analysis to the promise graph. The work I'd done with Geoff Canright and Knut Engø Monsen on ranking the importance of the different agents could be applied to the whole. In Figure 12.23, for example, we ranked the nodes according to how much pressure the agents were under to fulfill different promises, or how encumbered they were with promises. This could represent a fragility in the system, since Axelrod showed that agents expect reciprocity to sustain their own interest in keeping promises. Humans don't want to be exploited, and machines typically need to receive something to produce something.

The most straightforward kind of network analysis is to look for regular patterns that might be used to compress the description of a network into a small amount of information. This was the goal of CFEngine in information infrastructure, and promises clearly play the same role in a generic way. Any agent that keeps the same set of promises must be expected to behave in the same kind of way (all else being equal) thus one identifies *roles* from patterns of promises.

The numbers of promises each agent held could be plotted and were also significant. The results were drawn as a contour plot, showing a landscape of connectedness. To a physicist, this drawing is rather telling. It has the definite appearance of a potential, pressure or stress-energy concentration map. Moreover, for certain classes of promise, which would be held continuous by message flows, the graph views could be traced like control flow diagrams in control theory—a more established method of seeking control by force. We were thus able to represent the illusions of continuity and control from a framework based entirely on voluntary cooperation[266].

This model had almost no solid characteristics, making it very resilient to failure on a large scale. The failure domains were tiny. In terms of materials it was a gas. The Netflix example showed how such a gas, imbued with more complex semantics, can even become a society. It seems then that the concept of continuous materials from atomic parts is only one way forward to scaling up systems. Elasticity and plasticity apply to fairly rigid couplings, but gaseous models can also be applied to cases with more freedoms.

This intriguing idea, that networks of promises form spacelike structures, is more than mere fancy. It actually tells us how a network needs to be designed to address the issues of both solid resilience and fluid mobility. Today, the addressing of devices connected to the Internet is not designed with a regular coordinate system in mind. In spite of the apparent solidity of cables and datacentres, the Internet is still (logically) a gas, not a predictable lattice. This leads to considerable complexity when arranging to find things. Promise theory, and the notion of smart 'semantic spaces', can help to resolve that deficiency. There are also intriguing parallels between semantic spaces and brain research, concerning the representation of our spatial memories[267]. Work to develop these ideas as operational technologies is already underway[268].

Humans and machines working together, as a single smart material, with purpose but without ego. Imagine that. Would they be equal partners? Very few people would agree to that position. Nearly everyone has some kind of an agenda, or position on the question.

Systemic human-computer cooperation has been studied by several authors. In particular, the concept of Joint Cognitive Systems, in which humans and machines cooperate in performing critical processes, discusses this matter more from the human sensory perspective[269]. David Woods and Erik Hollnagel write:

> "Consistently we observe oversimplifications that claim ... that consistent computer capabilities substitute for erratic human performance."

In other words, the aim should not be to replace a human on principle, but rather to find a meaningful understanding of the mutual cooperation. Writers in this field focus on what humans bring to the table in terms of semantics, and tend to downplay the importance of automation, but this seems to be a defensive posture. They are not concerned with continuity (automated responses of constant semantics), as much as active creativity (basing decisions on awareness), and dignity. In my view, neither one should outweigh the other.

Sometimes we need simple continuity, in which case it is best to take human concerns out of the loop: dynamics can wash out semantics completely and bring predictability. At other times, we need to override such continuity in order to evolve, and push the boundaries. Then we need to force a process out of equilibrium by providing an overwhelming signal against the noisy background, like a monument or tower ripe with symbolism to draw attention, and human intentions have to play a role in that, as I will argue in the final chapter.

Meaning and purpose are human phenomena. From a promise theory view, meaning arises in the observer through the lens of a use-promise. There is no intrinsic meaning given by the things we observe, it is for each of us to decide whether we find meaning in what we see. But let's be pragmatic. The goal must be to help humans improve themselves through technology, without getting stuck in a dead-end job, aping cogs in the machine. We have not made peace with this division of labour yet, perhaps we never will, but the tools for building a more meaningful total system concept lie in the concept of promises.

We are developing the technology to bring both dynamic and semantic linkage, coupled with the kind of stories described in chapter 11. By revealing semantic context and experience along side the equivalent of statistical learning, we can learn to master the technology of scale from all sides, building up from nano-technology to macro-technology, to support and smarten our environments at every level.

13

Orchestration And Creative Instability

Or why the conductor does not promise to blow every trumpet

"The composer should picture to himself the exact harmonic formation of the piece he intends to orchestrate."

–Nikolay Rimsky-Korsakov, *Principles of Orchestration*

"It is true, that certain living creatures, as Bees, and Ants, live sociably one with another, (which are therefore by Aristotle numbred amongst Politicall creatures;) and yet have no other direction, than their particular judgements and appetites; nor speech, whereby one of them can signifie to another, what he thinks expedient for the common benefit: and therefore some man may perhaps desire to know, why Man-kind cannot do the same. To which I answer,
"First, that men are continually in competition for Honour and Dignity, which these creatures are not ... these creatures, having not (as man) the use of reason, do not see, nor think they see any fault, in the administration of their common businesse: whereas amongst men, there are very many, that thinke themselves wiser, and abler to govern the Publique, better than the rest; and these strive to reforme and innovate, one this way, another that way; and thereby bring it into Distraction and Civill warre."

–Thomas Hobbes, *Leviathan*

Amongst the many forms of intentional human expression, we have traditionally only music and dance that capture multiple, simultaneous, overlapping voices, unifying them into a single collective experience. As artistic languages, these embrace the interactions between parallel parts and players, and use the combined effect to tell a story. Perhaps this is why the terms *orchestration* and *choreography* are frequently co-opted when speaking of complicated processes

341

in the world of information technology[270].

The successful 'orchestration' of human-computer systems has come to be regarded as an ultimate test of control in information technology. It is about composing and arranging the behaviour of all parts of a system so that it performs according to a preconceived plan.

The kind of smart infrastructure we have come to expect involves designing and implementing quite complex interacting parts, as well as updating, maintaining, and renovating these arrangements over time. Consider the following scenario:

> You are walking through the city with your smart phone or smart wrist bracelet. You consult the map on its display about your current location and find: you are standing on a street corner which is connected to streets X and Y. It shows information about these streets under several categories: important tourist attractions, restaurants, shops, and friends who live nearby. Advertisements now leap out of the pages, nearby billboards and other smart surfaces that have identified your location on the street around you. You can go to the list of shops, and then choose and find about its wares, even statistics about its stock inventory. Based on your previous activity the map provider can guess how interesting you will find the tourist attraction, and how busy it is expected it to be at this time of day.

The smart infrastructure that enables this experience captures the semantics of your situation and presents you with a number of possible futures to choose between. Lateral and vertical assisted reasoning is all done in the blink of an eye to show a selection of possible worlds, possible bifurcations of your timeline.

To create the illusion, you need a working connection and working information services that can cross reference one another. Those services have to scale to potentially hundreds of users passing by each second, on a normal day, just in your immediate surroundings. If there is a flash crowd, the capacity needs to be increased to maintain service. If there is a bug, or a failure in one part of this information ecosystem, it needs to be detected and repaired quickly. Ultimately, this involves coordinating both people and automation from multiple providers, over multiple locations and times. A skilled orchestrator makes this possible, balancing dynamics and semantics of the applications, as well as business needs and technical challenges against planned upgrades and renovations, delivering what we want from our smart environments without relying on continuous human intervention. Orchestration must plan for everything going on at the same time.

Aspects of orchestration include designing, building, repairing, upgrading and decomissioning constellations of computer hardware and software, all of which are distributed over a potentially wide area. Once assembled, services must be integrated and composed to interact successfully, like the molecular patterns of the previous chapter. It is also about keeping the output of services flowing, in spite of a changing environment and changing needs. Even the process of creating new software can be woven into the picture. Orchestration is a cauldron of intent and process.

The dimension of *time* is what this adds to the purely material view of continuous infrastructure, described in the previous chapter. We dare to tackle the design of out-of-equilibrium processes, bringing about significant intended change, so we must involve intentional instability, and tolerate external interventions. Some change can be absorbed into steady state equilibria, by rescaling, as we have seen in previous chapters; some will not fit into this pattern, but might be viewed as boundary conditions or impacts on continuity. Orchestration is the most non-trivial issue we face, and it is widely believed that human supervision must play a dominant role in guiding its details. From a scientific viewpoint, that still remains to be justified.

The information technology industry uses the term orchestration in a less grandiose way, more often as a metaphor for phased deployments of change, or interventions: 'first do step 1 on these 120 computers', then 'do step 2 in 37 other computers', and so on. To many engineers, orchestration is completing 'to do' checklists through sequences of interventions. Repairs and renovations are often treated as if not part of the system design, but rather part of the ambient backdrop of unregulated external state. This can leave systems, after an intervention, in an unmodelled state. Overcoming ad hoc interventionist thinking is currently the biggest hindrance to progress in this field.

From a research point of view, remarkably little is understood about the science underpinning total orchestration of systems, in spite of some honest attempts to think about the problem. The challenge one faces in technology is always how to separate general science from a particular implementation of the technology itself. The foregoing chapters contain my own attempt to synthesize a plausible set of ingredients, but a general theory is still in its infancy. In this chapter, I shall sketch out the issues and challenges that I see for the future of information infrastructure, and explain why I believe current practice needs to make way for a new and more ambitious approach.

There are three parts to orchestration: specification, collaboration and coordination. We have discussed specification at length. Think 'coordination' and you probably imagine someone directing individuals to perform different tasks. Think of 'collaboration' and the main pictures we have are of individuals working together to carry something, or of a group sitting around in a meeting waiting for their turn to speak. These represent *parallel* and *serial* processes, respectively.

Team activities come easily to mind, when we think of collaboration, because (as we know from Dunbar) we care more for intimate interactions than for background activity; but, what about the less glamorous jobs in a system— the ones that allow organizations to scale up? These also crave the attention of the orchestrator. Consider cleaners, garbage collection, mail sorting, or a phone answering pool. These roles also work in parallel under the umbrella of a common organization. A method for orchestration has to account for them too.

Avoiding complexity, and maintaining comprehensibility in the design process is essential to success. If an organization is only weakly coupled together, it might be possible to view it as a number of *components*, working side by side, thus using patterns to factor out similar roles. The voices of the orchestra are a good example: strings, woodwind, brass. The same can be said about the abstract processes performed by these components: themes, accompaniments, counter-points. Weakly coupled components can be rearranged, taken apart and made into something else, assembled into a meaningful composition. They can be understood separately or as a whole.

The electronics industry has been effective at working in this way. Think about the components you see inside electronic devices: there are resistors, transistors and capacitors, and more. These commodity roles make specific promises about what they will do to an electric current. These may also be viewed in patterns to think of clusters that form oscillators, timers, adders, amplifiers, etc. These, in turn, can be combined in many ways to make radios, televisions, clocks, and so on. Designing a set of reusable components is one of the parts to orchestration. Another is deciding how tightly parts should be coupled together. We know, from Chapter 12, that strong coupling leads to precision but fragility.

Promise theory provides principles to understand this decomposition, as if a form of material science (see in chapter 12). But, like electronics, promise theory captures the steady state more naturally than it does long-term temporal and structural change (see Figure 4.2) or interventionism. On the other hand, a promise viewpoint can easily integrate a collaborative team and a cleaning service, without undue distinction: both these are natural parts of a total operational plan. If the promises are described fully, in context, they will fit together into a unified picture of the whole.

Call it a human limitation that we tend to overlook those promises that do not play a visible role in the main narratives about purpose and success. We prefer to emphasize episodes of creativity and achievement, and de-emphasize the supporting 'keep the lights on' promises, like cleaning, garbage collection, directory services, message routing, and the like. Background tasks fade from view and become part of the environment, but that does not make them unimportant. When agents collaborate implicitly through what they change and leave behind, rather than what they actually say to each other, it is called *stigmergic* collaboration. This is how Thomas Hobbes' ants and bees coordinate (see the quote at the start of the chapter), leaving trails of accomplishment behind them, and building wondrous structures without a centrally guided purpose.

Because we favour interventions, orchestration is often considered to be a kind of singular performance, like a rocket launch, some say a 'fire and forget' event. In business, one speaks of 'managed projects', bringing together expert skills, to design and build some kind of metaphorical or physical rocket, and which then runs the mission control centre for the duration of the episode. There is a countdown and a roar, and the episode ends with a splashdown, often unrehearsed at high risk[271]. These focus on acts of building, or re-working. Now, contrast this with something more like our invisible infrastructure: the successful delivery of electricity to our homes, across international boundaries, and all over the continent. Symphonies may open dramatically and end with a crash, but there is also background music that continues almost unheard while some other performance is going on. Both forms of music require orchestration.

In a sense, orchestration is like managing the air traffic around an airport. The total air-space activity is a combination of many flight 'interventions', which pass through several stages of preparation: boarding, pre-flight tests, a runway, and which then end up in a complex inter-dependent soup of promises, some related to goals, and others related to inter-operability and co-existence. Without air traffic control serving as the total orchestrator, it would be every plane for itself—an inefficient way of using resources.

Quietly organizing the delivery of resources for consumption involves many independent activities and coordination of supply and delivery that go beyond building. Does such a steady-state change require orchestration, or is it only creative change that has to be described? Engineers are inclined towards interventionist thinking, but sustained processes are what keeps the lights on. The real challenge is therefore to integrate both into a single design process.

The canvas of 'the human-computer infrastructure' is broad, and its processes are diverse. In this final chapter, we need to tackle the matter of how we deal with the design of promises, involving adaptive and creative change, in a framework where promises are kept, altered, improved on the fly.

Orchestration is a useful analogy for discussing this topic, but it is only a partial analogy. As with music and dance, what we need to complete our mastery of dynamical infrastructure is an understanding of how to make full use of both space and time, at multiple scales. The goal of any process might not be to reach a particular frozen end state (there might not even be one). Rather, the goal could be the continuity and consistency of change itself, just as the great evolutionary search of biology renovates the components within a living ecosystem.

We've seen that stability comes from the separation of scales through a weak coupling of parts, but now we have to confront the proverbial elephant in the infrastructure, namely how to use *instability* creatively to bring about intended change, to adapt to surrounding circumstances. How do we redefine purpose, or rescale intent, alongside a basically stable ecosystem? At what scale should promises be made and kept? To what extent will the voices of the infrastructure orchestra continue to express parts of a single composition?

Change can be intended, unintended, inevitable, preventable. It can be interpreted with many worlds, equilibria and relativity. It is something we perceive up front, and something that goes on behind our backs. The question is, how should change take place? How is it scheduled, and organized? These are not trivial questions.

To get the final handle on this subject, we must return, full circle, to the start of the book. We have to know how to separate scales from one another, to bring a measurable predictability to infrastructure: fast versus slow, long versus short, discrete versus continuous, meaningful versus meaningless, creative versus eternal, semantic versus dynamic. The split between semantics and dynamics implies that this has two parts:

- Changes to *intended* state (semantics).

  We must be able to alter a collection of promises kept by infrastructure, analogous to altering the score of a musical performance.

- Changes to the *actual* state (dynamics).

  We must be able to alter the actual infrastructure, analogous to the playing of the music itself.

Being able to maintain a persistent distinction between the two implies a separation of timescales. This sounds like a straightforward matter, but it is not. Infrastructure is not only persistent, it is distributed, which means that change has to be made in several locations in parallel, and humans are stuck reasoning only one thing at a time. Relativity (the finite speed of information) creates horizons and scales that have dynamical significance, bringing potential instabilities.

Just a few years after the millennium shift, when Computer Immunology was bringing stability to many companies around the world, through an effective if somewhat immature CFEngine 2, online commerce exploded into the world, like a new beginning. The sudden need for scale, based on commodity services, refocused attention away from stability onto change itself, and the idea of disposable systems arose. This allowed companies to focus on the value they built on top of a commodity infrastructure, rather than the infrastructure itself. New minds, unaware of past successes, began to look for ways to grow the larger and more monolithic systems craved by Internet services. Progress towards smart infrastructure slid backwards a little during those years.

Some years later in 2009, the idea of using 'smart' computational reasoning to control information infrastructure took on a new dimension. Phrases like 'Software-Defined Datacentre' and 'Infrastructure as Code' were coined, to express the idea of programmed changes to infrastructure[272]. Network connections could be re-routed on-the-fly, and new virtual servers could be brought online following demand to handle changing business needs[273]. The use of Application Programmer Interfaces (APIs), as the analogue of the push-button remote control, began to take hold, enticing software engineers with a promise of control (or at least change).

The frameworks for controlling the infrastructure thus became, once again, like remote controls, usually scripted in the traditional linear narrative logic of flowcharts. Unaware of the limitations of linear narrative, engineers tried to scale processes by imitating human reasoning (phase 2—3 of Figure 11.5). During the 19th century, scalable operations were orchestrated with the help of fixed punch-card patterns used in industrial looms, turning out reams of continuous fabric without distracting semantics, but in the new economy individual human power has been amplified through information technology to the point where change is viewed more like a shooting range, trying to knock coconuts off a pedestal to win a prize.

When I proposed Computer Immunology, the idea was to get beyond episodic surgery on computers, to a point where systems self-healed automatically 'from within'. You merely had to 'pop a pill' (of desired end-state policy) to reprogram their immune systems and they would morph into a new kind of organism without manual intervention. The pill was a fully edited orchestral score for the total system. Orchestration was described as a kind of complete architectural plan, written as a collection of promises to keep for every contingency. The distributed autonomous agents used this score to perform their changes and repairs without the need for a conductor[274].

The norm for instigating change in information infrastructure in 2013 is still to make libraries of 'scripts' or 'recipes'[275] or 'runbooks' available to engineers to quickly cobble together modifications to infrastructure, through as series of human-guided surgical interventions. Systems would be anaesthetized, halted, operated on, by a skilled team with a waiting list. Hopefully they would not perish on the table. Runbooks are essentially computer programs that are followed like recipes to take the raw materials of computers and networks and turn them into functioning services: 'do this, do that', provided one starts from the correct initial state (see chapter 5). They guide one through a single episode, but do not maintain the state of those creations persistently in the face of an environment that is eating away at them.

Engineers often argue that they can get by with this kind of interventionist thinking. Many hold to the belief that once technology has been erected, nothing significant changes until its human masters intentionally change it. Information technology typically sets aside the notion of 'corrosion' in dynamical or semantic structures, although corrosion must be taken seriously in any chemistry.

Studies of the use of CFEngine in the field show that corrosion is not only present but rife: with no intended changes, the agents repair *millions* of minor drifts from promised intent every week, across larger organizations[276]. Engineers do not see these drifts because they are not aware that they need to measure them.

Risk management researchers, who look at common factors across many different industries, have learnt to pay more attention to system drift, however. They dedicate much attention to discussing how both human and environmental change can cause human-technology systems to 'drift into failure'. The route to catastrophic events is often through a series of small, apparently innocuous changes that eventually build up to major corrosion of system integrity[277]. In the language of chapter 12, this is classic crack propagation, by stress concentration.

A deeper problem with recipes, scripts, or runbooks is that they are strong-coupling regimes, and hence do not naturally support the separation of fast and slow timescales (see figure 4.2), because there is only one level of description: modules that bundle scripts. They cannot offer a high level overview to comprehend the large-scale plan for making them in the first place[278]. This makes it harder for human interests to co-exist with automation, as there is no record of the larger narrative behind the interventions. They support the idea of long-term purpose poorly, which makes alignment of services with business intent hard.

Orchestrating certainty of outcome in a public information infrastructure, at the level of scripted contraption-building, leads to strong-coupling, and instability, because the ballistic reasoning forces one into chains of dependent actions, usually with decisions to bifurcate pathways into instability. Society has been witness to several high profile outages that have already resulted from these practices, from *software defined networking* (SDN)[279]. But getting around the limitations of engineering is both a technical and a cultural challenge in the information infrastructure world. For the reasons mentioned above, decades of teaching programmers to think in flowcharts has stymied the discussion of a sustainable, scalable approach that avoids the semantic instabilities of imperative thinking[280].

Judging from the quote at the start of this chapter, Thomas Hobbes did not believe that human decision making necessarily helped in the execution of coordinated activity. Dumb machines, he proposed, might be simpler to manage, averting unnecessary conflict of interest. This is one of the thorny issues of human-computer interaction. Many still view change orchestration basically as a matter for human command and control, a flow of work, punctuated by human decisions.

Promises might be of help here, acting as a bridge between these views. Promises operate in a fundamentally more stable manner than scripts, because they already decouple intent from action. In place of 'do this, do that', promises rely on the notion of *constraining* the freedom a system has to change, while maintaining state continuously.

Recall from Chapter 6 that the word 'management' comes from the old Italian for horsemanship. Engineers often begin by thinking about system control as holding the reins of a metaphorical horse (strong coupling), but that model does not scale up to handle a herd of horses. To steer a herd, you need to abandon the idea of direct control and adopt a very different way of thinking: shepherding (weak coupling). The discussion of algorithmic complexity, and **NP** complete methods in chapter 9, showed how one may relax determinism in order to obtain results quickly in reasoning. Letting go, with weaker constraints might actually increase certainty.

Herding systems, instead of riding them, i.e. governing through constraints, can take us a long way, if we are willing to believe in the creative power of indeterminism. Evolution works by randomly exploring all reachable possibilities, constrained by environmental fitness; why not information systems? Business and financial plans also fall into the category of loosely specified plans that allow unspecified activities to take place underneath. Science speaks against trying to control systems, without adapting in response to scale.

Serial programming and ballistic problem solving clearly dominate computing, and bring with them significant baggage. Our world has to progress beyond this view in order to understand information systems fully. Let us consider how to let go of the Newtonian, and embrace statistical, parallel thinking, just as

Boltzmann, Planck, and Einstein had to do to move forward in physics. Historically, parallelism and constraints have evolved hand in hand.

The science of coordinated instability starts with making room for parallelism. A workforce is scaled up by putting multiple agents to work at the same time. In information technology, this means putting sequential computational processes next to each other and letting them each work on a different part of a problem in parallel[281].

A modern computer is a lot like a city, with different activities held together by a web of utilities, transportation and services. Maintenance and utility services can (even should) be run as background tasks, so they don't draw focus from more important uses of the computer, i.e. providing core services for human users. Parallelism not only speeds up execution, it allows different processes to interleave and communicate with one another, like the many cells in a living organism. This is called multi-processing or multi-threading. Different threads of logic represent different tasks, executed on different logical processors.

In computer science, parallel process networks were first discussed by German mathematician and computer scientist Carl Adam Petri in 1939, and are called Petri nets. Today, one might consider them to be a form of *control theory*. They are networks that extend the idea of finite state machines of Chapter 3.

Petri nets were an early attempt to cope with parallelism, by extending the ballistic view of reasoning to allow multiple trajectories to interact (see Figure 13.1). One imagines tokens passing from place to place in a Petri net, representing the arrival of messages. The arrival of a token could trigger a new message to be passed on. For example, one could define what happened when a particular part of a program needed a response from two sources before proceeding. Understanding the flows of messages was a level of description above the logic of automated arithmetic, and a step towards a model for breaking up a logical machine into components.

To be realistic, Petri nets need to work non-deterministically, as one cannot say exactly when one result will be finished for the next stage. Given this property, they are able handle some aspects of real-world issues; however, they are also limited. The functioning need not be deterministic, but their conception *is* deterministic, as they model directed linear computation. As static networks, they can not easily model the lack of predictability that comes from the relativity and mobility of computers and smartphones. That is a different kind of problem in which the structure of a network itself changes on an *ad hoc* basis, such as when you connect a wireless headset to a computer. The topic of ad

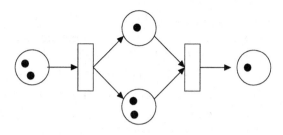

Fig. 13.1. A simple Petri net follows the flow of job tokens that move between processing centres and decision boxes. Parallel assembly lines could be represented in this way.

hoc networks became important during the 2000s, and was worked on by many authors[282]. More sophisticated process models, building on the traditions of symbolic logic, are known as *process calculus* or *process algebras*[283].

Petri nets were threads of linear reasoning chained together into a web, fashioned on first-order logic. They retained a one-dimensional flavour, reminiscent of factory production lines, but they could split into multiple threads. However, they did not represent a paradigm shift in embracing parallelism, and more interesting ways of escaping from a one-dimensional view were not far away.

Cellular automata, imagined by John von Neumann in the 1940s, are one such an interesting example of parallel computation. A cellular automaton is a generalization of a Turing machine, or if you like, a Turing machine is a linear cellular automaton[284]. Generally, cellular automata look like lattice-works of cells, closely packed like the solid crystalline materials in Chapter 12 (see figure 13.2). They compute in multiple dimensions simultaneously by looking at the states of multiple nearest-neighbour cells to determine the new state of any given cell, subject to constraints. This constraint-based computing is often combined with random or 'Monte Carlo' updating to model biological systems. Bacterial computers, based on DNA replication have been used to perform massively parallel computations too.

The power of multi-dimensional computation is that one can keep open several possibilities at the same time and perform both dynamic and semantic averaging on these to distill answers. The noise-cancelling cabling, in chapter 7, is an example of how just two parallel messages can be allowed to develop independently and then be recombined into an average total result. Imagine being presented with a fault and having a computer trace multiple possible semantic diagnoses (e.g. using the methods described in chapter 11) simultaneously, presenting a spectrum of possibilities for human interaction.

Cellular computation is an entirely local computation, fully compatible with promise theory, and made famous by British mathematician John Horton Conway's Game of Life, in 1970[285]. It can simulate complex emergent pattern generation, and display a rich set of behaviours including fixed points and limit cycles. Automata are used as models for cellular life, robotics and even studying material properties: for example, there is a simple sense in which the propagation of a crack through a solid could be viewed as a straightforward computation in a cellular automation. Hårek Haugerud, Are Strandlie, and I used them to show vortex phase transitions in magnetic crystals[286]. The limit is one's imagination.

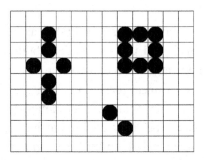

Fig. 13.2.   A cellular automaton, the Game of Life. Each cell changes state in response to its neighbour's states in a cyclic process.

Cellular automata do not have be put into regular lattices. Computation on generalized networks is a natural generalization, more suitable for information infrastructure. Nonetheless, combined with the notion of autonomous promises, cellular computation offers a powerful perspective on reasoning and stability, semantics and dynamics, and they could potentially bring a scalable approach to analyzing the material properties of infrastructure.

A third model for parallelism comes from quantum mechanics. The mainstream view on computers is based on Turing's model of computation, which, in turn, was based on a classical Newtonian view of information, but we know that the world is not fundamentally like that. In the early 1980s, physicist Richard Feynman (see Chapter 3) dared to ask the obvious next question of whether the lower level reality of quantum mechanics, with all of its strange unpredictability might be used as a computer[287]. After all, computers are just analogue devices used in some way as a representation of digital information. There are potentially more ways of doing that.

If you recall, what seems like a linear trajectory in a Feynman diagram is really a whole sea of interfering possible trajectories that compute end states by mutual interference (somewhat like the noise-cancelling cables). This picture of the physical world embeds parallelism on a fundamental level. There is no question of forcing it into a convenient linear narrative for human digestion. This is one of the reasons why quantum mechanics is hard for us to understand, and also one of the reasons why it could be efficient at computation. To extract results from a quantum computer, we have to constrain it with certain boundary conditions. The details are quite beyond this book, but principle is plausible.

We know, from the foregoing chapters, that multiple messages, both coding both dynamics and semantics form pathways of cause and effect, analogous to Feynman path integrals. The tools of the future have to unravel this picture in a comprehensible narrative for engineers.

Parallelism and constraint based computation is not only possible, it is a fundamental part of modern computer systems, and the world around us. The challenge we have in harnessing it lies entirely in translating a fundamentally difficult viewpoint, for humans, into a comprehensible method for technology.

The prolific composer and orchestrator Nikolay Rimsky-Korsakov (1844-1908) wrote, in his treatise on orchestration, three principles[288]:

1. In the orchestra, there is no such thing as an ugly quality of tone.

2. Orchestral writing should be easy to play. A composer's work stands the best chance when the parts are well written.

3. A work should be written for the size of orchestra that is to perform it.

These principles translate well to human-computer performances too. The first says that we should be open minded in realizing a system's intent; it is up to the designer or composer to exceed the limitations of convention to achieve the desired business purpose. The second says that we should keep changes simple and inevitable if we want the best chance of success. The third says that we may need to adapt our implementation technique depending on the scale of the change. This last point tells us to beware of trying to make techniques that are successful on a small scale work on a large scale. We cannot expect to build infrastructure with the same tools and methods of the past[289].

Rimsky-Korsakov wrote that orchestration was a responsibility of foreseeing an entire parallel process that could be played out from start to finish, in the simplest and most convincing manner. I believe the same is true of any change process. The fact that we are able to comprehend polyphonic music ought to tell us that we are capable of comprehending parallel processes in general, at some level, so we should not fear them.

The word orchestration is helpful if it encourages a composition that is intentional, parallel and comprehensive; however, we should not become too quick to control every aspect of a system. As Hobbes pointed out, emergent behaviour reminds us that pattern generating behaviour can also be harnessed reliably, based on purely dynamical effects. Some things can be allowed to run wild and still be predictable. For instance, a farmer does not control the production of every sheaf of corn by micro-managing processes, he allows independent growth, then harvests the result, perhaps selecting good from bad after the fact. In other words, he constrains the relatively free dynamics of growth, and constrains more tightly the semantics of harvesting maize from wild oats.

It could be time to reconsider our views on intentionality. We could learn to satisfy ourselves with building on what is sustainable, i.e. what can reliably be created, rather than what we ideally would prefer to have. Semantics can be bent more flexibly than dynamics, so it serves us to consider adjusting creative desire to that which is dynamically sound, rather than attempting the reverse. Darwin's lesson to us was simple: that which can be sustained will outlive the things that cannot, regardless of their beauty or meaning. Dynamics trump semantics.

Insects teach us the following: where humans might think of getting to a preconceived end goal, and brushing talk of obstacles aside, insects merely pursue an ongoing process, relentlessly battling their environments as an equilibrium, and caring nothing for conclusive goals. When we look at an ant-hill or a beehive, the structures seem intentional to us, because we perceive a finished product, and project onto it those semantics. To the insects, these are merely ongoing processes to maintain continuously.

To software engineers, holding the reins of their ideas, with remote controls and imperative runbooks and scripts, probably feels like controlling the system, but, as we know, programmed logic invites instability. This linear approach to control results in a single scale viewpoint, analogous to flying a fighter jet with continuous microadjustments. Stability, won through separation of scales, emphasizes that the information about where to go, and how to survive the journey, are best kept separately. We can see that by attending to processes at three timescales, from the short fluctuations of random noise, through short intentional change, up to long-term experience. Summarizing the earlier chapters, we have:

TIME SCALE	NAME	PROPERTIES
SHORT	MICROSCOPIC	FLUCTUATION REPAIR, DETAILED BALANCE, EQUILIBRIUM
MEDIUM	MEZOSCOPIC	CONTINUOUS IMPROVEMENT, LEARNING, CREATIVITY
LONG	MACROSCOPIC	TRENDS, SEARCHING FOR GOALS

Fluctuation repair could apply equally to maintaining operational state or application software, i.e. bug fixing. Consider how to use this split to base a scaled approach on sustainable promises. These are the things we know:

- It is possible maintain stable intended state, by designing fixed points using zero operators to build a periodic maintenance relationship on a short timescale.

- A set of promises can be evolved over a medium term timescale to evolve the purpose of the infrastructure.

- It is possible to model the semantics of purpose and meaning without a rigid pre-defined ontology.

- One may observe and learn and forget about the actual state of infrastructure predictably via a periodic observational relationship.

- One can arrange for continuous chains of information to 'flow', merely using conditional promises.

A future-proof approach to infrastructure would thus synthesize these properties into a new practice for governing the multi-scaled human-computer activity: one that copes with the three major uncertainties: scale, complexity and purpose. Let's see what that parallelism looks like, in action.

If you have not played in an orchestra, you might wonder what it is that keeps an orchestra playing together so perfectly—and, if you've ever heard a bad performance, you will know that this is not inevitable. It is an impressive achievement indeed to combine so many agents in a single performance. When I pose this question, a common answer is that it is 'the conductor' who drives the performance. This is not correct, but it illustrates our cultural predilection for thinking in terms of command and control.

The conductor does not convey or command all the necessary information to play the symphony to the players. He certainly does not play every violin or blow every trumpet. The thing that keeps the orchestra playing together is, first and foremost, the musical score. Then, there is the communication between players through the sound they make (stigmergic cooperation). These are constraints on the otherwise complete freedom of the players to do whatever they like. We can separate out and identify the scales of the orchestration process too:

SCALE	AGENT	PROMISES
MICROSCOPIC	PLAYER	PLAY SCORE
MEZOSCOPIC	CONDUCTOR	REHEARSE COLLABORATION
MACROSCOPIC	COMPOSER	ARRANGE THE TOTAL EXPERIENCE

The main role of the conductor is to bring a continous feedback relationship, from a scale above the microscopic to the lower levels. He has an overview. It yields a weak coupling between the adjustable microscopic changes and the larger trend. A symphony orchestra usually plays an intentional composition, but smaller groups (especially in Jazz) often improvise music, with no conductor, based only on the feedback from the music itself, and learned musical experiences of which overlapping patterns bring a satisfying result. The difference between unstable improvisation of a small jazz ensemble, and the stable scored performance of an orchestra, is like the difference between a marching band and a group of acrobats. Agility through quick communication allows adaptation on a small scale over short times, but does not necessarily scale automatically to a large scale ensemble.

The role of the conductor is thus one of shepherding with helpful advisory constraints, as one scales up. Each player in the orchestra is an independent agent, with only their own music in front of them; they do not know, a priori, what the other instruments are going to play. Players have, in other words, incomplete information. Each lives in a separate 'world', partially connected through observation of outcome. The conductor has complete information, and also the best overview of the sound, so he can provide a service to the players, giving signals to help the players follow the score, and advice about timing and volume. He also promises to align this guidance with his interpretation of the intention of the music, just as agents were asked to align their local promises with larger business goals in the previous chapter. The conductor manages the relativity of the orchestra.

The agents receive information about their task and coordination from the coding of sequences on the score, from the feedback of the musical outcome itself, and from a few signals from the conductor. Players also gain knowledge of the music from *rehearsal*. They develop a relationship to the music that allows them to predict what is coming, avoid errors, and to perform well, both dynamically (pacing their breathing and correct use of strength) and semantically (interpretation and phrasing). Rehearsal is a problem for infrastructure change.

Thinking of orchestration as an exercise in voluntary cooperation (keeping promises) has proven to be an important technique for scaling up organizations too. A number of users of CFEngine that I have had occasion to consult for have found this viewpoint essential in surviving mergers and acquisitions. When distinct cultural groups are thrust together in a company merger, the best possible way to preserve efficiency and dignity is to allow the groups to maintain their cultural expertise and knowledge. At least two major companies I have worked with have used the approach of shepherding autonomous players to integrate their information technologies, having failed with the use of brute force 'obligation'.

The feedback model above was essentially the same model I used in CFEngine and Computer Immunology for maintaining information infrastructure. Each computer has its own copy of system policy (meant to encode a symphony of health and happiness, or at least working services), and the separate software agents would pick out the parts that were relevant to them, and ignore the rest. A policy composer would be able to see and design the whole picture. Coordination signals could be passed between the agents to keep them working together. Each agent is able to learn, and a conductor part is embedded into the technology in a decentralized way.

SCALE	AGENT	PROMISES
MICROSCOPIC	AUTOMATION/CFENGINE	MAINTAIN AUTONOMOUS OPERATION
MEZOSCOPIC	OPERATIONS ENGINEER	MAINTAIN COLLECTIVE OPERATION
MACROSCOPIC	SYSTEM ENGINEER	ARRANGE THE TOTAL EXPERIENCE

The same basic separation is present in biology: each kind of cell has its own 'score' coded in DNA, and chemical signals keep them orchestrated to behave as tissue, say a heart. The organism's morphology or large-scale structure is a single composition enacted from conception through birth to death. The life-cycle of a cell (player) is quite different from the life-cycle of the whole organism.

One thing we should note about the orchestra, however, is that it has a single point of failure in the way biology usually doesn't: by using a single conductor as the agent of coordination, the orchestra is doomed to be a local information technology: it will not scale to very large size. Dynamical limitations, like the finite speed of information and relativity of information ultimately kill off the orchestra model. This is easy to see. The speed of sound is about 340 metres per second. That means that in 0.1 seconds (a perceivable amount of time), sound will travel only 34 metres (about the width of a parking lot). Thus, if the conductor and players are using sound to coordinate, and the audience is to hear music played by all the players at approximately the same time, then the orchestra cannot grow much larger than this size else people will start to hear the time lag between the timpani and the violins.

One could scale up performances by parallelizing the orchestra and playing in multiple cities around the world with separate centralized groups, but they could not coordinate as a unit. This would be a weakly coupled hierarchy. Sometimes coordination doesn't matter, sometimes it does. To within the limits of uncertainty, multiple performances by different unrelated orchestras might be an entirely good enough way to disseminate the information, like multiple queues at a supermarket checkout. There is no guarantee that the interpretation or experience would be completely uniform. But who cares? Semantics are in the eye (or ear) of the beholder anyway.

Computer science has virtually no body of work on how to approach the orchestration problem at the level we are describing here. The science of dynamical scaling is relatively well understood, if not always well applied, but how do purpose and meaning scale from the small to the large? Is everything we do on the small scale pointless, when viewed on the large scale? This will surely depend on how weak or strong coupling is across the scales. But we have no laws of scaling for semantics. The science is seriously lacking here.

Similarly, how do people, perhaps in the role of conductors, maintain a 'knowing relationship' with a massive, complex system, in order to feel a sense of certainty? From earlier discussion, this has to depend on the frequency and closeness of the interaction one has with it. In an orchestra, the players get to rehearse the score before putting it in front of an audience. In information infrastructure, however, this can be harder to achieve. Infrastructure is in continuous use. One cannot close down society for rehearsals. Finding a suitable time or place for such a test is no simple matter. Moreover, information systems need to be tested both dynamically and semantically.

In aviation and vehicle design, simulations are carried out in wind tunnels and testing grounds are used to develop high risk projects that are expected to perform flawlessly at high initial investment (see chapters 5 and 12). Dynamical testing often has to be woven into the general fabric of everyday change. What about semantics?

One technique is A/B testing, in which one injects a small amount of modified version B of a software component into 'live production' of version A to see how it performs. If it goes badly, unlucky users might experience inconvenience, but the damage can be contained. A more conservative approach is to maintain limited 'staging environments' in which new design versions progress through a number of checkpointed testing grounds for moving from 'wild idea' to 'seems to be stable' to 'approved for public consumption'[290]. In practice, all this too must be part of the orchestration process, in translating design into a performance.

These are some of the issues we have to consider when designing processes to allow humans and machines to reach a dynamic and semantic equilibrium through rehearsal of repeatable promises.

There is considerable disagreement about what planning human-computer behaviour means. Is it just about making interventions? Is it only about installing new kit? What happens in between these times? Shouldn't normal operations also be orchestrated for the best possible experience? How are promises kept in the long run? The lack of a plan for continuity of infrastructure is undoubtedly why there is considerable variability in the quality of the information services we rely on.

A partial answer to some of these questions can be found from the world of manufacturing, and is implicit in the world of W. Edwards Deming. To explain the point, I shall have to distort Deming's language and reinterpret it somewhat in the context of computing. The essence of it is to eliminate discontinuity altogether by manipulating the timescales and processes to bring material continuity. For dynamics, this is relatively straightforward; for semantics, it is harder. The trick lies in turning one into the other through the use of constraints.

Transforming semantics completely into stable constrained dynamics is an approach that was tried empirically by Deming and his disciples. It is also an approach used by modern 'constraint solver' software to try to allow design requirements to act as obligations across a distributed system[291]. If one can program the entire symphony of an organization's output as a self-correcting, parallel process that simply goes on and on, without significant decision-making, then all of the problems of rehearsal and change become simply different aspects of a purely dynamical problem. The worst thing to deal with then is the dimensionless thresholds. The main thing holding us back from this it the matter of design, of creative human involvement.

Research indicates that, if we were able to properly orchestrate processes in this way, a smooth, stable, self-healing system could be assured; alas, we know of no generic method for deriving such an orchestration. Indeed, the work on algorithmic complexity suggests that this is **PSPACE** hard. Fortunately, there is hope that promise theory might offer a framework for tackling the issue robustly, if not uniquely.

However, also known, is that fact that heuristic solutions to such problems are always possible. Thus, it is always difficult for us to foresee how this can be achieved, but that doesn't mean it is impossible. Just as infrastructure engineering struggles to escape from the idea of the episodic performances, from the single rocket science approach to change, battling from campaign to campaign, so it is hard to see how any semantically unique event can be seen as part of a continuous process. And yet, that is exactly what engineers are able to do, time and time again, in technology.

In the years following my involvement with Claudio Bartolini and Jacques Sauvé's business alignment project, I saw an example of this in a simple picture. I chanced upon a photograph of a Boeing 747 airliner, parked next to an Ariane space rocket. This struck me a nice illustration of what it means to embrace constrained parallelism, with a complete redesign of process.

The rocket is a perfect illustration of an early stage technology, where one brings together dedicated experts to build a prototype: a one-shot, episodic intervention to solve a problem (the term 'fire and forget' is sometime used). The rocket is built for one purpose, it will have a pre-programmed destination and this will not change. The flight will have a start and an end, and nothing else will be planned. There is no rehearsal, because this is an expensive, high risk venture. This is runbook automation. Hence, one tries to manage the huge uncertainty through an abundance of caution. The project drags out over months and years to avoid making any mistakes. On launch day, you can only guess what is going to happen. Either it works or it doesn't.

You would not try to make a commercial aviation business using this kind of rocket science, because you could not scale this process to cope with many flights per day. If you are going to have simple, predictable business continuity, you need something much simpler, something that can be rehearsed and repeated over and over, without the experts who designed the system on call.

The 747 is an icon for repeatable, well-rehearsed flight, with built in automation and monitoring that allows trained operators to fly again and again, building up confidence through a continual relationship between technology and purpose. The planes can be mass produced, and you don't need Cape Canaveral to launch one. Essentially, you are saying; replace design experts with trained operators, and helpful automation. The expertise needed to build a service, and run a service are not the same. Putting the right knowledge in the right role will lead to scalable parallelism, and operational polyphony.

The orchestration of the 747's process is about the entire process of manufacturing the planes, training the pilots, to welcoming passengers into the airport, bringing food on board the planes, planning the flight schedules, and so on. A vibrant, mainstream business cannot be based around such a singular process as a rocket launch, but discrete launches can be rescaled into a continuous process.

From a scientific perspective, it seems to be perfectly possible to bring continuous adaptation and operation to processes, but that does not mean there is still a clear model for how to do this. The problem is quite similar to the one studied by Deming.

The answer might begin by factoring out the semantics of a process completely into a different level of description, leaving behind a purely dynamical one, without risk of semantic instability. The role of the 'composer' is then to design a performance that is stable and repeatable, with a continuous viewpoint. Essentially, the composer's job is to decide what high level promises need to be kept, leaving everything else to be an inevitable, self-healing, dynamical processes at the lower levels. This is a kind of software design, but it is structural like Prolog rather than procedural like a script.

The delivery chain example discussed in chapter 11 illustrated how promise theory could predict the relationships needed to establish a state of cooperation in a production line. However, long before promise theory was imagined, Deming had already figured this out by statistical modelling of empirical cases, summarizing his thoughts around the transformation of the Japanese car industry. Deming wrote[292]:

> Each stage works with the next stage and with the preceding stage toward optimum accommodation... 'Here is what I can do for you, Here is what you can do for me' ... I could do a much better job if I knew what the program is to be used for ... [my punctuation]

Deming's work was based on empirical studies and simple dynamical models. In its own language, it emphasized the need for deep knowledge relationships, and Shannon-like error correction of the production chains, to assure promise quality. He too considered the operation of an organization to be a stability problem. He did not speak explicitly of semantics, but his writings were quite informal and are easily couched in a promise-compatible language.

Deming's famous 14 points, addressed to human managers of manufacturing process, can be summarized by the following: leadership needs deep understanding (knowledge) and commitment, deep cultural relationships are more important than specific tools, and a holistic orchestration of the system is needed to bring value to the promise to the end user or customer. All of these things should, by now, be obvious from the preceding discussions, but they are not easily implemented as part of a larger human-computer fabric.

On the topic of reactive interventions, versus pre-planned continuity, Deming used a simple experiment dropping ball bearings through a funnel to parody. Formulating a sequence of responses, based on monitoring of the current state of a system (like improvising jazz) rather than on an absolute orchestrated plan, leads to a random walk and highly unpredictable results, he claimed.

Jazz is an expression of exploratory creativity, and can be part of a research programme for gestating new ideas, but if you want to produce something for sale, Deming proposed, it had better be consistent in form and quality: forget one-off rockets, give us repeatable 747s. For all its value to creativity, improvisation meant destabilization of the dynamics.

A key point made by Deming, which flies in the face of much current industry practice, was that mass inspection, or testing and monitoring of results *after the fact*, was a useless strategy for delivering quality. If you only examine the result when it is too late, you have wasted time and resources. This paints the current state of the art for information technology in a rather poor light: independent *ex post facto* monitoring is the norm. Quality has to begin with intent, Deming said, i.e. with the promises one makes.

A key benefit of the promise model, which became clear as I was implementing CFEngine version 3, was that it gives you an automatic way of monitoring every promise directly, in a continuous closed circuit relationship. Instead of requiring two different models for keeping promises and monitoring them, the zero operator method gave you both in one. Thus every promise written in CFEngine would automatically have built-in compliance monitoring for no extra work. It removed the need for arbitrary mass inspection, by disconnected systems.

A cycle of improvement, which he called the Shewart cycle, now often called the Deming cycle, described a process of continuous improvement, which I will describe in terms of promises below. It is essentially an equilibrium compromise between divergence and convergence. To use my own terminology, each link in the chain would be a self-healing promise equilibrium, with promises aligned with business goals. Indeed, reading between the lines, and the different language, what Deming encouraged was the notion of building long-term continuity from short-term discrete actions[293].

These ideas began to reach software engineering at the end of the 1990s, as pressure to deliver rapid improvements was driven by the rise of online services. The notion of bringing continuity to the processes of service improvement and delivery, i.e. abandoning the rocket science approach to change, became a credible idea[294], thanks to the new delivery mechanism of the Internet, and it became imperative from a business viewpoint, from pressure of competition in online commerce..

Computer software is where the value chain begins in the information technology industry, and it evolves quickly, tracking new ideas and taking on board improvements of design; it also requires little in the way of initial development investment, so it can adapt to changing demand and new ideas faster than almost anything else. A decade ago, it could take many months to get a new piece of software into the hands of users, and most of that delay was caused by human process. Likewise, at conservative institutions I have worked with, internal procedural bureaucracy has meant that ordering a new machine could take up to six months from order placement to working machine. These delays limit the performance of the value chain.

If one takes orchestration seriously, then getting the delivery processes right, with all the players contributing at the right levels, from the software that makes the systems work, to the last mile availability, must all be taken into account. Two human roles are instrumental in orchestrating system behaviour: *software developers*, who design systems and are specialists of semantics, and system *operations engineers*, who are specialists of the dynamics of continuity and performance. The way in which these parts play together is thus a key concern to scaling and reducing complexity.

In the software engineering part of the industry, delivery of new versions of software, bug fixes, and improvements had traditionally taken months to achieve. This was partly because the delivery part of the software production line involved copying the software onto tape or CD/DVD and distributing physically at great expense. As the Internet itself came to be used to distribute software, there was no reason to wait for months; new versions could be shipped at basically zero cost. Rapidly crafted improvements could thus be transmitted to end users in smaller, more frequent increments. This was a competitive advantage.

The terms 'continuous deployment' and DevOps (signifying a cooperative relationship between software developers and service operations engineers) were coined in 2009 by a number of individuals, who pioneered a move away from the limitations of the rocket science approach[295]. Arguably, most attention has been given to the practices of large, high-profile web service companies, whose development processes are somewhat easier to put right into production on a self-made web-site; however, several authors pointed out how the ideas were equally applicable to more diverse organizations. The strength of this increasingly active movement has been to show how, once again, small discrete semantic changes can be viewed as contributions to a higher level of purely dynamical continuity. Software improvements could flow continuously from programmer to end-user, through multiple links in a chain, just by forging the right promise relationships.

A key point to Deming's legacy is to point out the role played by stability, in bringing about reliable continuity. Orchestration is not about episodic surgery, and isolated interventions, it is about the entire composition. The explanation goes right to heart of the separation of scales: continuity derives from the slow variation at higher levels, even as the lower levels seethe with rapid activity. A model of unifying, achievable goals is needed to prevent mezoscopic change from simply becoming like the random walk of Deming's funnel.

A couple of years ago, I made the simplest possible experiment around this, using a semantic association network (a modified topic map) to describe a number of business goals (see the story in chapter 12). Promise architects could make these goals 'stakeholders' or promisees for the low-level promises, so that the technology could track which promises contributed to which goals, and display the results as a simple measure of goal alignment. The result was a very simple bridge between the language of business and the language of low level infrastructure. When I presented this, informally, at conferences, I was amazed by the ooohs and ahhhs, as if a new world of meaning had been opened up to engineers. Such a simple thing was able to inspire a human level of cooperation.

DevOps, as a philosophy, focuses mostly on the human aspects of CAMS (culture, automation, monitoring and sharing)[296], while Continuous Delivery focuses on getting goods and services quickly to market, with a detailed methodology. Deming's work unifies these views so that one may see them as facets of the same thing. A promise formulation has an advantageous role to play here, which follows from the basic structure of a promise:

affected object (promiser) $\rightarrow$ *interested parties and goals* (promisees)

body or details of the promise

Each promise is not only a statement about a dynamical equilibrium about the state of the affected object, it represents documentation of intent transformable into a purely dynamical process, but with context that may be separately coded into a semantic network, applying equally well to human and machine. It is thus a tool for bringing about knowledge. Knowledge about system state comes from watching the promiser in context, knowledge of cooperation and relevance comes from seeing the promisees or stakeholders, which can be either persons or abstract ideas like goals. Finally the operational semantics become knowledge from the predictable zero operator behaviour described by the body. Thus, by encoding intent as promises, we end up with a multi-faceted, orchestrated score that can be played out, studied, and improved.

In 2006, I stumbled across another connection to the idea of continuous delivery from the field of logistics, while looking at business alignment modelling, making a link between continuous improvement and the refilling of supply inventory[297]. The models of inventory management confirmed that there is an optimal average time interval for maintaining business value in a pseudo-continuous model, based on the timescales of supply and demand, giving a precisely definable meaning to continuous delivery.

Supply chain thinking makes the dynamics of inter-agent orchestration particularly clear, but the cultural aspect of the human role in the system is even more important in organizations with more complex semantics. The maintenance theorem showed that consistency and long term stability force us to think about small changes to maintain local stability, superimposed onto a longer term variation. Rapid correction is thus the way of maintaining stability in the face of intended change. Put simply, speed is of the essence.

Establishing the beginnings of a science to understand the orchestration of an infrastructure value chain is one thing, convincing engineers to develop methods for handling the necessary parallelism will be another. DevOps and continuous delivery sprang up in engineering to draw attention to the issue of efficient process design in a human-computer system, but they have not yet attracted universal acceptance, nor have they brought an unambiguous message. Their main contribution has been to spark a debate, and even a rethink of old practices.

Few subjects decline into religiosity faster than those claiming 'the only possible approach' to determining the outcome of a process, and many engineers do not believe that one can compose a process that will come together from many independent parts into an orchestrated whole, without serializing it for manual inspection. As Arthur Schopenhauer (1788-1860) wrote: "Every man takes the limits of his own field of vision for the limits of the world." However, in spite of the almost mystical attachment to the honorary role of humans in pushing the button, there is precedent for a model that does not cling so desperately to determinism.

A fully programmed view of processes that balances local stability with long term change could be built today, in a promise compatible way. Currently what is available, e.g. through CFEngine is incomplete, addressed at the local level, and is heavily optimized for machine rather than human, but basic processes are supported. The biggest challenge to be addressed is how to make this culturally counter-intuitive way of thinking about change easier for humans to digest and interact with.

The major problem today is that engineers are dazzled by too many freedoms in the way engineering may be executed. This is true even with a fully described promise model. The biggest challenge to consistency thus lies in overcoming the limitations of individual ad hoc step-by-step narratives.

During the late 1990s, when I promoted the idea of convergent zero operators in Computer Immunology, differences of opinion were already rife about whether the serial ordering of actions was necessary to orchestrate services. Two companies I worked with chose opposite strategies for different reasons. Recall the example of a web server and helper database as described in Figure 12.9. It describes a situation in which a web service depends on a database or other helper service in order for its service to work. The program logic therefore suggests that the database has to be working before the web server. This leads to the common 'orchestration practice' of requiring that the database be set up and started before the web-server:

1. Set up the database, start the database

2. Set up the web server, start the web-server

3. Create content for the web server

First, we may remark that the orchestration required to build this service infrastructure is only half the job. The score should also include the possibility of repairing it when it fails. The second thing to note is that, in this ordering, one confuses the notion of pre-requisite to final function with the necessity of making intermediate steps in a certain order. This is a semantic error. It is like saying a supermarket cannot fill its shelves before the warehouse can make deliveries, therefore the supermarket should not be built until after the warehouse is built. If the two are built in parallel, much time can be saved, and the process will converge to a desired state in the end. If you are worried about the end-user experience, you can still keep the doors of the supermarket shut until deliveries have been made, but there is no reason to impose artificial waiting on the construction of the supermarket.

By the same token, if you start a web server before the database, neither of these agents suffers any ill from this, but the web application will not work correctly until both are running. If you want the user to have a consistent experience, then you need to make a strong dependence, and arrange for the application logic to protect the user anyway. Either way, you can wrap the entire experience into a molecule so that it becomes a packaged box[298].

There is a good reason for not ordering these operations forcibly. If one of the parts of the system should fail or crash, what do we do? In a Computer

Immunology view, you would simply heal the relevant part based on the policy score and continue. If you insist on strict ordering, you need to start from the beginning, which requires you first to deconstruct and then rebuild. In a periodic maintenance framework, there is always another chance to bring things back together. Alva Couch's maelstrom effect is more robust than destructive rebuilding, and avoids the workaround of building special Heath-Robinson contraptions to force mechanisms to trigger change in a particular order.

The first of the companies (a financial institution) was not willing to tolerate any plasticity on the part of the user experience. They wanted a hard front, or no front at all. As a result, everything was locked into a very specific and brittle process that was prone to failure. They required an illusion of hard determinism, and paid for it with all or nothing. Thus they sacrificed stability for inflexibility.

The second company (an Internet service provider) used a probabilistic approach, trying to minimize the probability of failure and maximize the rate of repairs. This meant that users might occasionally experience glitches, but that they would likely go away in a very short amount of time. They did not care about the order of operations. In addition, load balancing provided a semantic averaging: if a user failed to reach something once, trying a second time would most likely take them away from a faulty server to a working one, so the chance of inconsistency fell to an unnoticeable level.

The weak coupling process was very robust also but too plastic for hard-nosed environments. The strong process was more tightly controlled, but fragile to error. We know that fragility and weakness with strong coupling have to be fixed with redundancy, which costs additional infrastructure. So the answer for the small Internet provider was to remain as plastic as possible.

The advantage of the fully convergent score is that no matter what state the system starts from, it can converge towards a properly designed final state without human intervention. So if something breaks at any point in the delivery chain, the process (not just the components) will self-heal. This is what rehearsal-free orchestration is for.

Today, this example seems almost trivial, yet a majority of organizations is still held back by uncertainty about issues like this one. The largest companies that distribute content globally have to deal with parallelism on an entirely different level. So-called content delivery networks (CDN)[299] are like distributed amplification services (a kind of network public address system) that replicate web content, on behalf of other organizations, over specially optimized networks. The idea is to move the point of delivery for services closer to the end user, in order to avoid the worst problems of information relativity: if one can make the distance between content provider and content consumer as short as possible, then. delays and inconsistencies might be kept to a minimum. In order to pull this off, organizations arrange for their online domains to be redirected to replicas rented on a content delivery network. This, in turn, points traffic to the closest possible copy to minimize network times. More recently 'Cloud' providers provide more general rentable computing power that can be distributed at multiple locations[300]. Some orchestration can be conducted as a service, whilst some is hardwired into the score.

For static content, like the streaming of video or pictures, this is a highly effective way of delivering content without wasting expensive trunk network capacity. The more quickly content changes on servers, the less effective replication is. The locations of replicas are, by necessity, highly distributed, and their numbers are large, so scaling up the 'order of change' example above to a global level, across thousands of servers, is simply not possible in an approximately predictable way, without long verification delays. Waiting between verified stages of dependent change could lead to significant interruptions of service.

From the discussion in this book, one sees that promises, maintained by a process like Computer Immunology, offer a robust and plastic approach to describing complete process orchestration in space and time, even on a distributed level, provided pre-conditions can be communicated between promises for the maelstrom effect to work. This does not mean that other approaches cannot be made to work, perhaps by brute force—many enterprise computer software products claim to solve all of these problems at a high level. However, I believe that the promise approach is superior not only for its clear dynamics and simple low level semantics, but also because it satisfies all three of the challenges: scale, complexity and comprehension.

For the remainder of this chapter, I want to describe how working with promises might open the way to further benefits, particularly in the area of meaningful human participation, towards a complete and long-term approach to information-rich infrastructure.

All the concepts we need to plan out inevitable performances of information-rich services are basically now in place, so let's try to construct a new picture of orchestration, fully parallelizable, and based on promises, to address some of the weaknesses of a scripted approach. To summarize, three main kinds of process patterns affect our ability to coordinate activity in time and space. They occur at the three main scales we now know and love.

- MICROSCOPIC IN TIME (EQUILIBRIUM):

  Convergent maintenance processes are the basis of a system that is stable by *detailed balance*. These were described dynamically in the first part of the book. In promise theory, they are described by promise equilibria, like those in Figure 13.3 and Figure 9.4. They happen mostly under the radar of human interest.

An agent can keep a promise to restore a desired state using a zero operation as discussed in Chapter 5. This is the basic process of maintaining equilibrium of state.

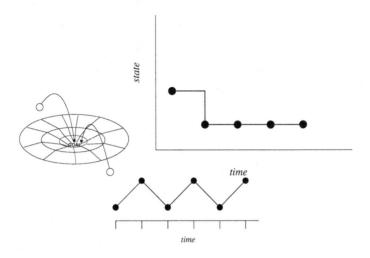

Fig. 13.3. A maintenance process is a convergent sink, attracting any state to a fixed point. This is also called absorption.

- MEZOSCOPIC IN TIME (PATHWAYS):

  Divergent branching processes are used to search for answers, by trial and error (see Figure 13.4). Human interest begins here. Branching is generated by decision options. In promise theory, branching is generated by conditional promises and is pruned by trial and error selection (conditional acceptance).

  This is a bifurcation of possible worlds. It uses instability creatively to seek out possibilities which must then be pruned or selected by some other criterion. Stability is one such criterion.

  Software developers follow this branching pattern when designing behavioural changes. At some point the branching is frozen by selection and the state may be encoded with convergent fixed point operators.

Because human decision making is involved in branching out, engineers often feel that this means they have to push the button on the changes themselves. In a proper orchestration, the composer changes only the score and delegates the execution to the instruments agents of the system.

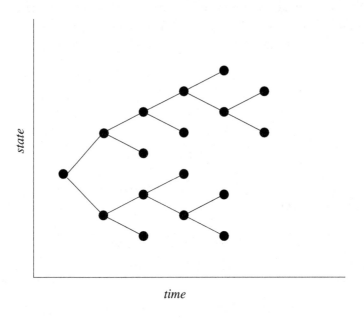

time

Fig. 13.4. A branching process, generalizes the idea of bifurcation process. At each juncture, the system can choose to take one or other of the branches.

- MACROSCOPIC IN TIME (INTENT):

    Goal selection processes are about classifying and annotating promises to climb the knowledge ladder (see Figure 13.5) for business development. This is continuous improvement, on a long-term basis, based on intended goals and experiential knowledge. To be sustainable, the goal has to lie in the dynamical equilibrium between between divergent branching and convergent maintenance, and it should result in an infrastructure design that connects low-level changes with high-level 'why'.

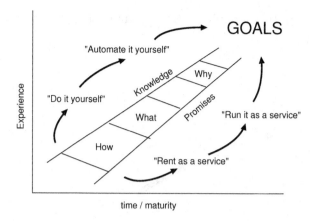

Fig. 13.5. The knowledge ladder, learning about promised improvement.

These three scales each play a role in the evolution of a stable and meaningful system. A similar breakdown of scales exist in space or locations:

- MICROSCOPIC IN SPACE:

  Microscopic in space refers to the ability to make promises about the configuration of resources on individual computers.

- MEZOSCOPIC IN SPACE:

  This refers to the ability to coordinate several computers and persons in a local area network.

- MACROSCOPIC IN SPACE:

  This refers to the ability to promise the state of global patterns of infrastructure, where information relativity is a serious concern to coordination.

Change in space is much easier to deal with than changes in time, though these two are sometimes related by the finite speed of communication. So, how do we reconcile these very different looking processes with one another?

A simple place to start to think about this is to take the shifting of a microscopic policy, depicted in Figure 13.6. This is the basic, lowest level change, moving from one bag of fixed points to another. It is the analogue of reprogramming an organism's DNA. Instead of manually performing surgery on an organism, you alter its genetic instructions so that its own self-maintaining processes make the alterations themselves. That way, you know the changes are documented, and any disease to that state will be counteracted without having to call the doctor. If you don't think this is agile enough, wait until you have 10,000 patients.

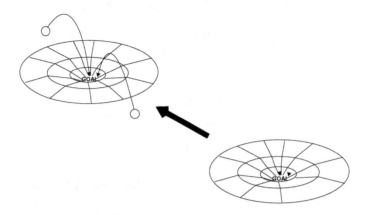

Fig. 13.6.   A policy shift is an adjustment of the convergent desired state. This could mean the addition of constraints, or the alteration of existing ones.

Each bag of fixed points represents a possible world, living at the end of a spanning tree of bifurcation choices, from some initial state. Each parameter may be varied, one at a time, to generate the tree of possible branching worlds. The combinatoric complexity of the possible states grows exponentially.

The process of deciding on a change of policy is a creative one. For example, suppose you made a number of models of a house in different colours, and you chose to paint the house green, of all the possible alternatives. You would have made a selection from a divergent process of variation, and collapsed all those possibilities onto a convergent process of single choice. Of course, it is not enough to paint the house once, the new colour must be maintained until the house is either no longer needed, or there is a new change in policy. In an information system, the analogous properties are computer resources, but the principle is the same.

Each target of desired state in the figures represents a complete set of promises for a single autonomous agent, perhaps a person or a computer. Figure 13.6 does not show us how to string together chains of promises, or the way to encode dependencies between promises. That's because, once you have abandoned one fixed point in favour of another, everything about the first one is, in principle, lost. I deliberately drew the shifted state in Figure 13.6 counter to the normal timeline to emphasize this.

Once we have decided on the states for this bag of fixed points, we leave it to be maintained absolutely by immunological zero operators checking that promises are kept on a periodic schedule. But this does not stop the search for a better collection of promises. Thus, while the system rests in one fixed point, human teams are comparing the performance of the system in relation to business goals to see what needs to be changed. The branching process represents the decisions of everyone involved with improving the 'score'. In practice, the system never sees the forking and branching, because only one of the alternatives is chosen. What the system sees is thus more like a ladder or staircase (figure 13.7).

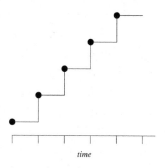

time

Fig. 13.7.   Branching of possible worlds turns into a climb up the staircase of continuous improvement.

The main point is that altering the desired end state is no excuse to not require convergence. Short term fluctuations can still spoil this state, even though you know it is going to change again in the medium term.

At the final scale, of business goals, you would ask the questions, how does the colour of the house affect my ability to attract visitors and bring in business. For this, you need to build a relationship to the information about visitors, track their behaviour as an integral part of the system. A smart infrastructure house can collect that information and feed it back. You are no longer worrying about whether the house is no longer white, you can assume this with confidence, but you can quickly decide to make a change. Or you can see when a visitor left in disgust because there was a wall in a state of discoloration. A part of the policy might be to mow the lawn and turn the lights of the house on after dark. If a light gets switched off by accident, or the weeds start to grow, you want to know that these things will be fixed.

Now, these kinds of processes are somewhat harder to visualize when they apply to many different issues that span tens of thousands of distributed computers.

Part of the difficult engineers have in comprehending orchestration surely comes from the sheer number of issues and locations they have to deal with. This is a further reason to not couple together issues, if possible. Promises that depend on other promises are both uncertain and difficult to understand. The writing of a complete promise 'score', orchestrating infrastructure fully, must contain promises for all of the agents in a system: people, computers, network devices, phones, and wearables.

Where should you start in trying to write an orchestration of an on-going continuous process, written entirely in the language of promises? We know the answer to this too. The goal of convergent orchestration indicates that policy should be build up from a low level to a high level, using knowledge acquired over the proper timescales. This in turn demands that we have a relationship with the parts of the system at the right timescale, at the right level.

If you start building from the top down, you start with an overview and you undertake a branching process to break it down into manageable issues. This can quickly lead to an explosion of multiplicity, and thus complexity. Programmers are taught to start with generalities and push details in underlying layers, out of sight, out of mind. If and when you reach the bottom, you can easily be left with something that is rotten at its core, insufficiently based on the reality at the raw end of the system, because you are focused mainly on the surface layers.

If you start from the bottom up, with simple promises that you know you can keep, then you may begin to expose layers of simplicity by aggregation. This is a converging process, where each layer is a visible simplification of promisable things and their interactions. Statistically, an aggregation of things is likely to lead to fewer moving parts then a divide and conquer approach, because division leads to multiplicity. Convergence from the bottom allows you to see general rules and patterns of structural composition: a kind of molecular engineering, a chemistry of atomic parts.

In Hume's viewpoint, top down is a model that does not represent reality. You can design it, prove things about it, but it will not necessarily result in something related to reality. Bottom up is real, but you have to take what you get. Top down also easily leads to a duplication of effort, as it is a branching process rather than a unification process. If we recall the many-worlds interpretation of knowledge, then ontology forces concepts into different semantic worlds by design. If different branches end up with similar concerns (aspects), they will end up developing private meanings which then have to be eliminated later for consistency and efficiency. In a world of voluntary cooperation, where promise theory prospers, one begins from the assumption that promises have to be made to bring separate worlds together, through cooperation.

Creativity in nature is always a bottom up process, as nature has no imagination to foresee what might be. It can only build on what it has, thus it always leads to stable systems through natural selection. That is a very practical point of view. The lowest levels of any tower should be the most reliable, and where most of the effort should be invested. If a foundation is shoddy, nothing we build on top of it can make it better. Thus, in a top down approach, the deeper you go, the more responsibility is placed on correctness, and the more burden is placed on a human being.

Promise theory is useful here, because it shows how different perspectives, in different worlds, can co-exist unproblematically, and even harmonize their mutual interpretations. One should assume that every agent speaks a different language until they receive the orchestration. It is only through voluntary co-operation to hold to certain standards relating to the major goals that the policy becomes valuable.

In Figure 13.8, I have tried to depict different issues in a system orchestration as different instruments in an orchestral score. A musical score basically looks like a number of swimming lanes. Each 'target' symbol in the figure represents a new desired state signifying a change in behaviour promised by a particular 'promiser'. The planning of such changes might actually happen on the fly, and the timeline implicit in the figure would then be a record of intended change, like a seismograph of shifting of the policy foundations.

In spite of superficial appearances, this view is different to simply scripting one-shot changes, firing and forgetting like a rocket launch. Because each target is an equilibrium, it is the model, not the repairs, that is adapting over time (see Figure 13.8). The development of the system proceeds basically as a series of punctuated equilibria[301]. Some have claimed that this limits the possibilities achievable with promises, however that is not the case.

Graduate student Wei Gao at Oslo University College compared some practical cases of promise modelling against the more flowchart-based Business Process Modelling Language for orchestration in 2009[302], with the preliminary conclusion that promises had at least as much expressivity at imperative flowchart approaches, and with self-healing added for free.

One cannot always guarantee to keep an arbitrary promise without a complex computation. However, practical experience shows that the kinds of states that cannot be represented simply as promises are inadvisable and easily avoided. This is the advice of both Deming and Rimsky Korsakov!

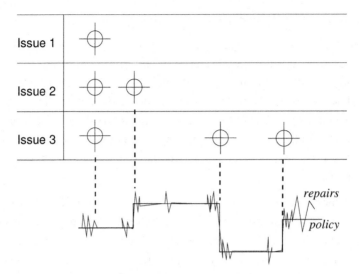

fixed−point policy transitions in time

Fig. 13.8.   Separating the scales in parallel 'swimming lanes', makes policy look like a musical score. Each score change is a change of desired end-state, but repairs to the actual state are still required.

Orchestration is about designing behaviour. It is about getting the right agents to make the right contributions, at the right spacetime coordinates of a human-computer system. These agents have incomplete information, and operate on a voluntary basis. Unlike a piece of music, the score of an interacting human-computer infrastructure is not a fixed performance, under controlled conditions. It is not a 'deployment' or a military campaign. It has to adapt, like jazz, to changing circumstances, but in a continuous way. Coordinating adaptive behaviour on a massive scale need not be problematic as long as one builds robust materials.

How then does one get the various agents, responsible for keeping promises in society's information infrastructure together, to respond correctly in all contexts? What information do the agents need to play their parts? Remarkably little is still understood (at least publicly) about the science of large scale orchestration. If one searches for a scientific literature on this subject, what one finds is a collection of tools and opinions about how to do it. The large installations are in the commercial world, often steeped in secrecy, and highly specific to their particular purpose. There is much work to be done here.

From the title of this book, you will surely appreciate that my own view on this topic is related to managing the uncertainties, dynamic and semantic. Many of the challenges are related to the challenges of incomplete information; others are about having a strategic relationship with the key parts of the system. Finally, there is stability.

A good place to start is therefore to try to maximize the information available to agents, given their locations and observational horizons. This would given them a better chance of being able to make autonomous decisions, which in turn would allow the number of agents to grow to a maximum possible size without increasing the burden of the three uncertainties: scale, complexity and comprehension[303].

I've discussed the low level basis for maximizing certainty at length in the foregoing chapters. Now, let's look at the higher levels and see how the patterns and similarities in the lower levels can be abstracted for human consumption. The basic instability of strong coupling suggests that we need to move away from single-scale mezoscopic change (the API, or push button control), to a properly separated process at multiple scales. We can summarize this in the following table:

SCALE	ENGINEERING FOCUS
MICROSCOPIC	DESIGN OF PROMISE EQUILIBRIA
MEZOSCOPIC	METHOD SEMANTICS, STATISTICS AND ANALYTICS
MACROSCOPIC	GOAL ALIGNMENT AND DIDACTICS

Suppose one separates intent from implementation. The evolution of intent itself is still quite challenging in a typical organization, because of parallel individuals contributing ideas. It is not a simple linear chain, but rather a 'bow-tie' structure (see Figure 13.9), where promise proposals are made by multiple contributors, in different worlds, to describe a unified policy for the human-computer system. Each contributor undergoes a branching process search for ideas, then concludes an intention; these must then be integrated into a single world view. Different intentions, or promise-proposals, are merged into a complete proposal through some kind of checkpoint at the knot of the bow-tie, before being released to all the parallel agents that will try to keep the promises.

Computer programmers have software tools to support this branching process called version control software. The idea is that successive changes lead to new versions of policy, each formally residing in a new Leibniz-Kripke world. The software allows a particular version of a set of documents to 'fork' or bifurcate away from the original, creating a parallel copy and leaving the original intact. The two different versions then co-exist. Thus two different interested parties

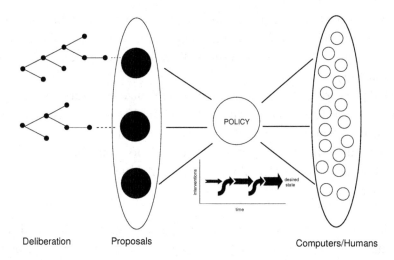

Fig. 13.9.   The bow-tie progress of diverging search for a design in different worlds, converged to a unified view, then dissemination to all agents. All changes, whether short term interventions, or steady state should be integrated into this process,

can evolve their own intentions for infrastructure in different ways, without interference, effectively in different branches of reality. Later, when implementing these intentions, someone must choose which of these versions of reality to implement and where, or whether to merge them somehow into a single re-unified viewpoint. This is where the human role has maximum importance, because merging is a political decision, about goals and purpose.

If one applies this methodology to policy, it represents a many worlds view of planning. Once we commit to a certain branch of intent, then the real-world branching begins to takes place, like cause followed by effect. Modelling thus becomes about finding an equilibrium between these various conflicts of interest and competing ideas that uses divergent branching for trial and error, and convergent merging of these various realities into an equilibrium branch[304].

Working in this way, the desired end-state model of promises becomes increasingly important. As long as engineers try to match the *current state* of infrastructure to the *start* of a chain of events (i.e. the script approach), the result will be fundamentally fragile. It will be sensitive to where and when changes are applied, like in Deming's funnel experiment, in which he showed that by making relative changes to improve over time, one basically undergoes a random walk. The lesson learnt is that focusing on the *end state*, up to mezoscopic scales, immunizes against that fragility[305] (see Figure 13.10).

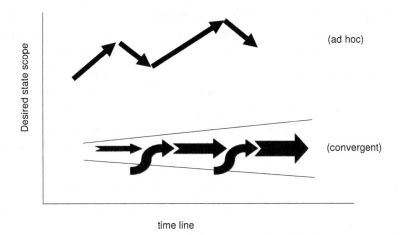

Fig. 13.10.   How we handle interventions is critical to the desired outcome. An ad hoc approach leads to random walk, like Deming's funnel. In a convergent model, an intervention should be a *learning* change, a revision or expansion of the desired state specification, always moving towards the same goal, without discontinuous reset.

Automation should never be so fragile that a ship will sink if you forget to set your alarm, or a building will collapse if you miss the bus. Humans need a safety buffer in which to plan things out. This is why we have architects and engineers in the first place. Civil engineering has total architectural modelling, aviation has autopilot flight navigation, now the information technology world needs mature tools also.

Molecular and material computing, as described in the previous chapter, leads to patterns that can be used as libraries of reusable components. One may draw parallels between this and modern material design for manufacturing. Computer aided design has a long history of taking this approach, in electronics, and very large scale integration in microchip design. This has some similarities to the kinds of circuits we are now trying to make in information systems, at a larger scale. Civil architecture and aircraft design are other examples of complex problems where models and total conceptual planning are essential.

However, information infrastructure architects have nothing like these sophisticated tools, and yet their problem is even more complex, because information infrastructure changes faster and has to be redesigned while it is in operation. For the future, we must develop the necessary tools with a sense of urgency.

Orchestration by promises is essentially about crafting a Shannon message describing the promises necessary to continuously evolve a total system, basing it on the language convergent zero operator symbols (see Chapter 5), across parallel worlds, something like a Feynman path integral: a parallel exploration of the journey from one state to another.

If this all seems daunting and unfamiliar, especially applied to something as prosaic as a few computers, you might be forgiven for your view, but one must now agree that such a manifesto is possible. A chain of zero operators: driving causation through absolutism, not relative change, sounds alien to software engineers, The primary advantage of this formulation of infrastructure management is *certainty*.

Is this idea hard to understand? Perhaps, but shouldn't we worry about understanding up front, rather than waiting until the result doesn't work when it is too late? There is a moral imperative here. Planck spent his remaining life resisting his own conclusions before finally realizing that resistance was futile. Some ideas are hard, but ethically one is bound to seek out the best possible solution. Human lives will depend on the engineering of universal infrastructure. There is only one question to ask:

How shall we make orchestration comprehensible to infrastructure engineers?

As with other statistical theories of incomplete information, the challenge for observers, trapped in their own limited worlds, is to visualize and comprehend the extent of this inconvenient truth. There is clearly room for making great strides in this area. Visualization of scale and complexity, in space and time, in a way that serves human comprehension, is going to be a massive challenge of biological dimensions for the future.

Let me draw together some of the essential points from the earlier chapters. To observe and comprehend infrastructure, we want to answer certain questions:

- What are the dimensionless ratios? Which should one pay attention to? Can their thresholds be mapped out? (Dynamics)

- What continuous relationships do we need to build, and at what timescales? How do we manage the Dunbar slots? (Semantics)

- How do we choose when to immunize against human choice and environmental adaptation? (Zeroing out semantic instability)

- Is there a way to compensate for insufficient learning experience in interactions with technology? (Human assisted reasoning)

- How can we represent the relativity of information to infrastructure engineers, and help them to recognize the limitations this places on engineering and end usage? (Incomplete information)

Helping humans to comprehend scale and complexity, without needing to understand too much physics, and finding the balance between intuition and training is, ultimately, an ongoing social problem, only shadowed by technological innovation. Knowledge and the continuous delivery relationship become the centrepoints of orchestration of total system behaviour.

The tension between experts and trainees is likely to be a hindrance to progress, unless tools can be standardized at an average skill level. In order to scale aviation, or driving, or computer use, to a general public, advances were needed in automation and in dedicated training. This is all part of the evolution of tooling. It was no different when bringing the Internet into peoples' homes, and it will be no different as information infrastructure continues to evolve into smart environments.

Given the importance of comprehension to relationship-building and thence knowledge, I foresee a return for the role of teachers and students of the humanities to technology. The future of infrastructure will not be the sole domain of engineers much longer, simply because there is such a conceptual gap to be filled. One could try to train an army of super-experts, deft in the skills of data analysis and information relativity, but how realistic is that? Society changes when ordinary people are able to contribute to it: it cannot be held together by a few brilliant minds.

Monitoring systems today expect each observer to look at graphs and tables of numbers and simply know what they mean, or figure this out for themselves. That means they need to use up intimate Dunbar slots on learning different systems over time. No one can understand data at a glance, any more than the average passenger would be able to understand the flight deck of an aircraft. It doesn't matter how nicely the information is presented, it remains incomprehensible because it has no meaning without reference knowledge. A better approach would be to place the user into a narrative timeline, explaining the semantics, without having to follow every detail. The path to enlightenment can be shortened and simplified by offering users automatically generated story-lines about system behaviour.

At CFEngine, in recent years, I have experimented with ways to put a user in context quickly to see exactly what is happening now, versus what has happened before, and what might happen soon. By overlaying semantic networks along side promise networks (which is easy because of the promise model), one can capture long term experience, add narrative explanation, and use machine learning to lessen the burden of maintaining low value relationships between humans and machines. There is a comprehensive problem yet to solve, but I remain optimistic that it can be solved, as long as attitudes change.

The semantic networks described in chapter 11 will be a foundation for answering many straightforward questions in a more humane way. Imagine simple answers to the following questions.

> Show me the services running across this city.
> What does service X depend on to work?
> Who is affected by service X?
> If I make a change, who are the responsible stakeholders I should talk to?
> What business goals will be affected?
> What is the average time it takes to make an update between A and B?
> What if I change X, how will that affect the update rate?
> How will the ability to process the queue of customers be affected if I change Y?
> Where are the dynamic and semantic bottlenecks in this business process?

These interactions remind me of the way the crew interact with computers in *Star Trek*. It is natural, simple and does not try to replace human intelligence with a machine. It is machine-assisted reasoning. Answering questions like these could be faked, in a limited way, using fixed-schema databases, but it would be necessary to know all those questions up front and cater to them in a fixed data model. A more plausible approach to answering them is to use extensible associative networks described in Chapter 11.

Alerts and error messages are an excellent example of the interface between humans and machines, promises and information, where we need help because of the basic relativity of promises. When some part of a system fails to keep a promise, it generally informs the promisees (either human operators, or software agents) using some kind of message format. In all my years working with information systems, I don't think I ever experienced more than a handful of unambiguous error messages. Expert engineers eventually build relationships with systems and learn to interpret messages from experience, but this takes years. Thus error messages do not constitute knowledge directly.

Fig. 13.11.   The promised intent of an error message is not necessarily perceived correctly by the recipient, as they might not share a common frame of reference.

The problem with error messages can be seen from the basic structure of promises they make (see Figure 13.11). Error messages often fail to give relevant clues as to what part of the orchestration resulted in the symptom, because behavioural semantics are interpreted by the observer, not the giver. No matter what a message promises, the user must promises to *use* or accept the result correctly. The problem is that the user occupies a different Kripke world, and cannot know the original intent, *a priori*. This was how we explained emergent behaviour. An observer is free to interpret an outcome however they like. Indeed, given incomplete information and only observational uncertainty, it is inevitable.

The example of error messages is a symptom of a much larger issue. Whenever there is a use-promise, there is a potential semantic misinterpretation. This is where semantic association networks can compensate for that improper interpretation, by showing possible alternatives. Our perception of a system is thus limited by our ability and willingness to interpret it.

SCALE	CHANGE PERCEPTION
MICROSCOPIC	EVENTS AND OCCURRENCES
MEZOSCOPIC	CONTEXTUAL MEANING, IMPACT
MACROSCOPIC	BEHAVIOUR

We can envisage many tools to assist humans in their perception and comprehension of large-scale, complex information. A 'renormalizoscope' could help us to transform an understanding of low level material patterns into a high-level bulk properties. Compressed digital coding of anomalies from the machine learning could provide a notion of network interferometry[306]. Principal component analysis could offer a kind of X-ray diffraction imaging of bulk properties of networks. The research community is not short on ideas.

There is one crushing issue that will be the hardest to swallow for engineers: that is the many worlds problem. The most worrying uncertainty is the one that tells us we *cannot* know more. Ultimately, engineers simply have to give up the notion of low-level determinism. We can draw inspiration from the physics of path integrals to help here. Finding an average meaning through a path-specific network of digital transitions, is almost like computing quantum mechanical path integrals. Instead of trying to lock down unique deterministic trajectories, we can do the opposite: allow them to go anywhere and say anything, mean anything, and then present the optimum paths that satisfy the constraints.

In a sense, quantum computers will exploit this kind of parallelism in the path integral explicitly for this purpose. It is a question of interference, like Huygen's pathways of least action. As we combine inferences, we obtain no a principle of least action, but of least certainty. So far, the closest thing to a solution would be the work I did with Alva Couch on semantic network path selection.

The challenge of maintaining the appearance of continuity, for business and society, is the icing on the cake. Before we find continuity, we have eliminate discontinuity. As always, we must ask what scales we are looking at? The illusion of continuity requires us to respond an order of magnitude below the surface, as I showed in the maintenance theorem.

SCALE	LOCAL CONTINUITY
MICROSCOPIC	CONTINUITY OF PROMISED INTENT
MEZOSCOPIC	CONTINUITY OF AWARENESS AND KNOWLEDGE
MACROSCOPIC	CONTINUITY OF GOALS AND PURPOSE

Continuity is a local phenomenon. On a global scale, we must contend with relativity, consistency and simple ignorance. Dynamics and semantics play side by side. The reason there is confusion about information orchestration today is that we entwine explanations of process with their execution, through linear thinking. We cling onto the psychology of the linear narrative, and seem willing to go to any length to avoid confronting parallelism, and multiplicity of viewpoints.

To a physicist, the deepest questions about time and change all boil down to the single question 'what symmetries are broken and why'? The symmetry of equilibrium is often the closest thing we have to a starting point to explain change. The boundary conditions we impose, absolutely, break equilibriums basic symmetry, and interrupt continuity to determine the major transitions of human-computer behaviour.

How shall we live with change when the very foundations of what we build on are altering so quickly that we are uncertain even about what is right? It is all relative to your location and viewpoint. Unless our intentions and condition are slowly varying compared to the fluctuations (quasi-static as physicists would say), how can we even form expectations? The use of promises offers some simple answers. If predictability is the goal, one should abandon the idea of reactive change on a mezoscopic timescale and replace it by absolute zeros of intent. Knowledge is always relative, and intent is absolute.

14

Epilogue

"How we have advanced, thanks to the Machine."
– E.M. Forster, *The Machine Stops*

How do we want society's information technology to behave? Do we expect to control it, or merely live along side it? Should it be centralized (making it easy to locate and brand with identity), or decentralized (making it fast and resilient)? The answers surely depend on how we, the human masters of intent, want to interact with it.

When I began working with computer installations in the 1990s, neither computer science nor engineering had a clear answer on the subject of how to prevent computer systems from going off the rails. Indeed, in spite of minor advances, little seems to have happened to change this[307]. These formative decades of the new millennium have not yet adapted to the underlying challenges, and the concepts of stability and knowledge-oriented cooperation still appear to be too difficult for mainstream consumption; but progress comes in fits and starts.

We now know that we project some of our own human habits onto technoloy: automated decision-making itself is the main reason for instability in software systems, yet still flowchart programmability remains an irresistable temptation in the information technology industry. This is a minefield we shall have to come to terms with, when disseminating smart infrastructure for public consumption.

The enduring challenge of technology is to make the dialogue between humans and their tools complementary. For that to be realized, we have to include humans in the technology equation from the start. The challenge for humans is to not stand in the way of progress. We need to face up to our limitations, a lesson that physicists had been forced to confront many times over its history.

Imagine the following:

> You enter a hotel room, and the video display in the wall pulls your profile
> from your implanted identity chip. You touch the panel to authorize, and
> gradually the applications and services you subscribe to put in their requests
> to shift their hosting platform from the plane you just landed on to the room
> that will be your base for the next 48 hours.
>
> As you check in with social channels, and access some documents, the data
> shift to your local frame of reference, via the content-cloud relativity cache.
> There will be no possibility of inconsistency, no lagging money transac-
> tions, now that you've moved to your new service provider. As you do this,
> the room's entertainment is synchronizing to your current preferences, and
> the music picks up where it left off from the flight. The bathroom toiletries
> are the ones from your permanent travel profile.
>
> As you check in to work, your company's infrastructure rents some service
> capacity on the content-cloud's substation in the hotel. You can run all your
> services here at low cost during your stay, in a private sandbox. The syn-
> chronization cost will be lower than running directly over the trans-Atlantic
> link.
>
> You have a message from your company's energy saving software. The
> server process has crashed four times in the past week. The developers
> have been informed, as have you. This failure could be associated with
> five known causes, all less than 30 percent likely and has two side effects.
> You run through the possible explanations, adding notes of your own for fu-
> ture reference. Something will probably need upgrading, but there are four
> probable side effects. For now, the self-repairing systems will just keep
> resuscitating the faulty server.

Semantic experience rides atop dynamical services—a kind of spacetime with
semantics. Scenarios like the one above are likely to be commonplace quite
soon. To make them happen, technological principles, like the ones described
here, need to mature and become universal. We cannot reach this level of inter-
operability with the state of the art today.

If the continuous adaptation of a smart environment is the future of information technology, if our lives and future are to be entrusted to decisions encoded
in embedded technology, then we have to recall basic laws of scale and stability to make them safe for a general public. One cannot sail a ship through an
electronic storm anymore than one wrought by wind and rain. We shall have
to stop thinking of technology as something invulnerable that is merely used
by humans, and view it as part of a greater cybernetic ecology all around us.
The key distinction in an environment is not between 'natural' and 'artificial',
but between semantic and dynamic: intention and behaviour. Biology has al-

ready drawn these lines, and through us, it will integrate the inanimate with the animate in information systems, until we no longer see a pertinent difference between the two.

Science must be our guide, but even science gets stuck from time to time. Very possibly, the problem with science is that we model our perceptions and concepts of things, rather than what is actually there. Nevertheless, in my mind, the greatest and most pragmatic achievement of science has been to quantify the art of approximation.

We can apply information technology itself to the problem of understanding information technology. We predict the weather, pollen counts, pollution, etc, why not network traffic, behavioural trends, service demand, and resource jams?

System semantics can be scanned for automatically and converted into an interrogable resource of meaning in order to bring more minds into the loop when building a consensus of understanding. Some problems in human-computer cooperation might never be understood or solved exactly; that is unimportant. Human ingenuity lies in intuitive heuristics for solving problems approximately when they are too difficult to compute directly. Often semantics change as we seek compromises in the face of dilemmas and conflicts of interest. When all this is said and done, we may systematize information to build a relationship between Man and Machine. Can we turn it into a familiar knowledge relationship, to place knowledge at our fingertips, where it can be useful? This is a challenge to keep us busy for decades to come. Semantic networks, combined with observational machine learning, and traceable provenance, combine to suggest a powerful underlying technology on which to build systems for the next generation.

Much of the research work I've described in this area could easily be called physics. Well, why not? Physics is the study of how stuff and things work in the world. The traditions of physics are to break systems apart into their atomic pieces, and explain how to reconstruct them from those parts, explaining the scales and phenomena that occur at each new level. This is exactly what we need. But there is also a need for semantics, a more theoretical understanding of intended structures. This is where promise theory's compatibility with physics becomes useful.

We can expect the structure of such a unified theory to resemble the physics of materials: how they are assembled from atoms, how the atoms fit together, what strengths and weaknesses we can find in them, and what phenomena they exhibit at different scales. There is no reason to draw artificial lines between subject areas like physics and information science. Science is science, classification is merely an arbitrary point of view.

Datacentres and data repositories have become the primordial soup of information *evolution*, in which companies spring up and branch out in incremental mutations, and then either die out or survive if they are successful in replicating their messages. This is where the questions of society, of human growth and survival are currently playing out. The future can still take many directions, but the theme of the journey is set: its backbone is information. What will it take to trust it with our lives?

I've covered many of the ideas that might bring that trust in my attempt to describe the state of things. Here is a reminder of just a few:

1. Stability comes from equilibria.

2. Statistics help us to form knowledge equilibria from observations and measurements.

3. Messages carry influence, and are vulnerable to relativity.

4. Semantics are vulnerable to scales.

5. Semantic stability may come from Nash equilibria or simple voting.

6. The notion of promises is instrumental in putting us in the right frame of mind to understand parallel, distributed systems.

Still there are many more topics I could have discussed. The challenge that remains to be solved—the one the best minds today are working on—is how to translate perceived requirements (what we envision) into distributed promises (what can realistically be expected), in spite of distributed, relative, and incomplete information. The three uncertainties: scale, complexity, and comprehensibility taunt researchers to dare new approaches. We do not have to oversimplify beyond recognition and stay stuck in Toffler's Second Wave. We can have variation, as long as we try to minimize unnecessary *semantic* inconsistency, while realizing that we can never limit dynamical variation.

Inconsistency without reason makes learning, and hence trusted relationships, expensive. Complexity can be hidden, however, provided its outcome is prerehearsed and designed to be inevitable. We should not have to worry about it. These challenges are solvable, if the world of engineering can tear itself out of a time warp, and move ahead.

Science was never a eureka moment of discovery, but a long, slow climb through philosophy and reason, not to mention trial and error. There are elements of belief in science, just as in religion and other 'non-rational' systems of thought, but science's strength lies in its ability to be self-correcting, or self-healing. Science is society's immune system against the onslaught or random information and of foolhardy approaches, keeping us close to a healthy state of understanding. Computer science itself is at a juncture where traditional theory has fallen short of practice. These are exciting and challenging times.

The quest for certainty is an enticing sport, both in technology and elsewhere. It feels like a fool's gold that lures in the unsuspecting, and even the suspecting onto the rocks of hubris. We would all like certainty, we all seek to increase certainty, but we can never have it absolutely. Our experiences are limited, our senses and even our brains are trapped by scales; and then, at the very bottom of it, there is an indeterminism in the world that we are currently not able to fathom at all. Ours is a world of imperfect information.

Occasionally, we fashion constructs (devices, models and stories) that offer fictional certainty: we make machines that are highly reliable and exhibit predictable behaviour, but these are Faustian bargains with a world that is basically fickle. Instead of trying to cheat uncertainty, like death itself, science tries to make the best of an imperfect lot by gauging it, living with it, and even embracing it to make the best of it—all with superb creativity.

Perhaps best of all, we humans have shown that, against the onslaught of inevitable confusion, we are worthy and creative adversaries.

Summary and storyline from the chapters

Part 1: Stability

Or how we base technology on science

1. King Canute and the Butterfly

How we create the illusion of being in control

- We believe we are in control of a process when we choose to ignore all the factors that seem inconvenient or unlikely to make a difference to its outcome.
- We always live with incomplete information about our environments.
- Limiting information actually helps with the illusion of control, but what is really controlling outcomes if not us?
- All phenomena are associated with particular scales in space and time (e.g. short or long). At each separable scale there are different phenomena. When things interact strongly, phenomena at all scales get coupled together. This inseparability of scales is often referred to as *chaos*. When interactions are weak, scales separate cleanly and what happens at a high level does not depend strongly on the details at a low level.
- Instead of control, we should talk about the limited certainty of outcome.
- To understand certainty, we need to understand scales sufficiently.
- Control-thinking or determinism has been ingrained in our culture since the time of the Enlightenment. Newton believed that there were laws that determined the outcome of a clockwork universe. The ability to formulate these laws depended on being able to separate concerns, which in turn assumed weak coupling.
- Only in the 20th century did we fully realize that weak coupling and determinism were the exception rather than the rule.
- Instead of determinism, we can shift to the safer idea of *predictability*.
- The foundation for predictability in any dynamical system is what physics refers to as stability, i.e. a persistence of state in spite of minor details. This is what we experience as control, but it is not just about us. It is about intrinsic stability in the total system.

2. Feedback Patterns and Thresholds

How the relative sizes of things govern their behaviours.

- How do we define stability? There are, in fact, many possible interpretations.

- It is useful to distinguish smooth dynamical behaviour from discrete or discontinuous processes. Today the words analog(ue) and digital have come to mean continuous and discrete.

- We need to understand how scales are measured, and what the units of measurement mean. The study of units of measurement is called dimensional analysis.

- The important characteristics of systems can be described entirely in terms of dimensionless ratios, i.e. ratios of similar quantities.

- Two systems are said to be dynamically similar if they have the same dimensionless ratios. It is this property that allows us to build scale models of aircraft to test in wind tunnels, etc.

- Not all systems are intrinsically stable. We have to keep any system inside a region of stability, by working constantly to maintain a persistent state, in a fluctuating environment.

- The language of operators is a key part of this chapter. An operator acts on a state to result in a new state. We write this

$$(\text{OPERATION}) \text{ state} \rightarrow \text{new state}$$

and we call this an operator mapping. This idea is used throughout the book to talk about change and stability.

- An operator mapping changes a current state into a new state.

- If the old state and the new state are the same, we say the state is a *fixed point* of the operator. Fixed points are like multiplication by zero.

- A fixed point is stable to perturbation by the operator.

- We may design systems with *desired end states* that are fixed points, so that they will be stable.

3. Digilogy: Cause, Effect and Information

How transmitted information shapes the world from the bottom up.

- System states may be described as discrete (in blocks or cells) or continuous (smooth).

- Everything in the world is really discrete if we look closely, but thanks to Newton and others, we have learnt to imagine that the world is smooth and continuous at a high enough level.

- Planck showed that we cannot understand the behaviour of the world we know without acknowledging the discreteness of states in nature, but he struggled to believe it himself. It was Einstein who showed that he was right and how this explained much about the physics we all rely on today for our technology.

- While physicists were discovering that energy and matter were discrete and digital, the development of the telegraph and cryptography was developing the notion that information was discrete and digital too.

- All information is about strings of symbols. Even DNA is just a symbolic code written in proteins.

- We can write the laws of physics in a form that shows the universe as a kind of computation, taking one state into another.

(Change) state → new state

Thus, what we learn about computers is what we learn about the world, and vice versa.

- When information is transmitted, it gets received by an independent party, who might not know the language in which the information was sent. Moreover, the symbols can be misread or distorted by environmental noise. Thus information has to be maintained. Shannon showed that information can be error-corrected.

- Physicists Feynman and Schwinger unwittingly made important links between information and physics that both physics and computing are learning from.

- Our challenge, in the modern world, is to understand the world in terms of states. This is the revised cultural norm, for the 21st century.

4. All the Roads to Nowhere

How keeping things in balance is the essence of control

- We can talk about the stability of an object or a crowd of objects. Statistical stability means that something looks stable on average, in a crowd. If the average is over time rather than population, it is known as an equilibrium, or detailed balance.

- To see stability emerge from detailed balance, we have to zoom out to a larger scale over longer times, and focus less on the individual transactions taking place.

- When we want to constrain the average state of something, we talk about setting a *policy* for it, rather than controlling it. We cannot control the details, but we might be able to constrain the average behaviour.

- Information itself is an average based on the transfer of symbols. The copying of symbols represents *dynamics*. The interpretation of the symbols at either end of a channel represents *semantics*.

- Equilibria can be unstable too. A queue is a good example. Either a queue is short, and what comes in goes out in a short amount of time, else it grows out of control above a critical threshold, and the time to pass through the queue grows to infinity.

- Most systems have some notion of balance. If they are not in balance, then they are spinning out of control. To understand stability, we therefore have to look for equilibria. This is called perturbation theory. It is the basis of much engineering.

- The concept of balance or equilibrium can be understood for both dynamics and semantics. Semantic equilibrium is about a constancy of interpretation. In game theory, it amounts to trying to balance the relative interpretations of merit in a competition or 'conflict of interest'.

5. Zero and the Building Blocks of Babel

How to forge the atoms of reliable infrastructure.

- Error correction in information transfer is a crucial process to understand. In semantic processes, with a desired outcome, we call this a *convergence* of the process to a desired end state.

- Convergence is the opposite of branching, hence it is the opposite of decision making or logical reasoning. In other words, reasoning leads to semantic divergence. A simple consequence is that decision logic (programming) is one of the main causes of instability in systems that perform some kind of reasoning.

- Semantic instabilities, including if-then-else logic, can happen in many different ways. Chinese whispers is an example where a noisy dynamical process coupled with a semantic instability leads to fundamental change in meaning of a message. This kind of error leads to big trouble in computer systems that are not designed with fault tolerant stability in mind.

- In mathematics, we can understand error correction simply by the number zero. Zero plays the special role of an operator for policy constraint, because no matter what state we start from, multiplying by zero gives zero: the desired state. It corrects a drifted state back to a calibrated origin, as long as we arrange for zero to be the policy state.

- This zero property was used by CFEngine to invent the concept of convergent (and idempotent) repair operations.

- The semantic freedom to interpret a digital message gives a great many possible structures and encodings. A pattern of symbols is called a language and its structure is called a grammar. Languages are the basis of how we represent meaningful information at the human level (say a document), but also how we create systems. By combining language with calibrated zeros, we can make a self-repairing language of states, and hence self-healing systems.

- Error correction is a fundamental part of digital electronics. However, as we rely on the integrity of digital patterns to make society's critical systems, the need for error correction or maintenance *at all scales* becomes more urgent.

Part 2: Certainty

Living with incomplete information

6. Keeping It Together by Pulling It Apart

How weak coupling strengthened human infrastructure

- The complexity of interrelationships in IT infrastructure is staggering. It mirrors the complexity of our real world. Without some emergent stability the complexity of our world could not hold together and persist.

- Thomas Hobbes, from the earliest times, underlined the importance of emergent behaviour as one of the important ideas in science. What we view as deterministic is often only emergent.

- Regulation of emergent behaviour brings us the certainty of outcome that allows us to trust systems. The key is to trust is to build a relationship in which we interact with something on a regular basis to learn its emergent characteristics. Learning is a substitute for naive belief in determinism.

- Programming is a problem. Statistical systems get more complicated when the parts that compose them are able to make decisions and determinations. This opens the door to unpredictability; unless the system is collectively stable at a larger scale, it invites the opposite of deterministic control. Reliance on programmability and software interfaces puts society in jeopardy from the amplification of small errors.

- Laws and rules don't bring stability in systems of many actors, as they don't account for emergent effects. The idea of autonomous behaviour ('voluntary cooperation') can be an effective way of understanding stability. The underlying stability that appears to obey rules comes from weak coupling ('less is more'): if a single agent can affect every other, there can be an avalanche instability, and cascade failure—a chain reaction. If agents only make their own mistakes, without propagation, the system can survive noisy individuals.

- The irony is that we need to relax and decentralize control, pull systems apart, to improve their stability and increase our level of certainty in systemic outcomes.

7. Seeing Is Disbelieving

How to explain what we see and make use of it

- Our contemporary culture is one of oversimplification. We value brevity over accuracy. This leads us to make mistakes.

- The notion that true and false are the two choices available to us has become a convenient fiction in Western culture, that does not accurately represent the world. That which is not known to be true, cannot be said to be false. Absence of knowledge is not knowledge of absence.

- To understand the world we need to measure it with greater nuance than true/false. Thus we have scales of measurement with multiple levels of intensity for phenomena we observe.

- When we observe, we sometimes measure incorrectly, so the result is not completely stable. If there are only two choices, the error we make is the maximum possible error (this is what causes many catastrophic failures in software). If we have more tolerance of error, with softer boundaries, there is less amplification of the error through the process of observation.

- If we are not able to observe at all, we have to deal with the uncertainty or perhaps incomplete information. But, even if we can observe, information is incomplete because we are not certain about errors (semantic and dynamic).

- The conclusion is that we have to make systems that are tolerant of errors in both process and interpretation. Logic is a poor framework for fault tolerance, because true/false divide amplifies errors.

- There are various approaches we can use to minimize uncertainty, like noise cancellation coding. We can also be inspired by the theories of physics, like statistical mechanics and quantum theory, that make the best of incomplete information with amazing success.

8. The Equilibrium of Knowing
Or how not to disagree with yourself

- Instability is not only about behaviour. Interpretations and meanings can also change and be unstable to errors of observation and reasoning.

- Knowledge is an effective antidote to instability, because it allows us to expect unpredictability and divergent behaviour, avoid it and measure out its consequences by averaging, rendering it less dangerous.

- The tools for bolstering stability include different forms of learning.

- Statistics is one form of learning that brings 'semantic stabilization'. Its conclusions are deliberately insensitive to small changes of detail. Statistics is all about semantics, but it is often misunderstood as a dynamical technique for computing certainty. There are plenty of ways to be fooled by naive use of tools like statistics, because the answer lie in interpretation.

- Bayesian methods allow us to interpret statistical learning as plausible belief. This is a very useful approach to estimating reliable knowledge about a changing system, often used in machine learning.

- Although he was too early to appreciate the significance, Bayes effectively redefined probability, taking it from an estimator of future predictions to a dimensionless scaling ratio in the renormalization of systemic uncertainty, thus avoiding the issues of causal inference.

- An oversimplified epithet for statistics is: *persistence* is truth. If we want certainty in IT infrastructure, we need to understand persistence rather than just change.

9. Clockwork Uncertainty
The arms race between reason and complexity

- Automation plays an increasingly dominant role in society. Robotic and mechanized systems creep into out lives in ways we do not expect.

- We tend to believe in logic (not persistence) as truth. Logical errors and observational uncertainties play into major system outages, both in the past and in the present. We trust our own complicated reasoning above simple mechanisms.

- Logic is unstable because it attempts to use precision to determine truth, but we know that imprecision is rife everywhere (Hume's contention).

- The alternative to logic is to use the stable property of fixed points, or 'zero' to redefine what we mean by truth in a mechanical world.

- The mathematics of symbols (algebra) allows us to approach predictable outcomes for dumb mechanisms with some sophistication, and more reliability than for complex logic. This is even true in the presence of indeterminism.

- If we can embrace indeterminism, rather than pretending it does not exist, it can be a powerful force for searching the world for answers. This kind of gambling on short-cuts can be proven to pay off in the solution of related problems in mathematics. Searching for information is one of the most important techniques in information technologies, because many other problems can be reduced to searches.

- Reliable infrastructure will thus come from not being too smart, and tolerating what we cannot control. The more we try to control by reasoning, the less stable systems are likely to be.

Part 3: Promises

The chemistry of autonomous cooperation

10. The Concept of Promises

Or why behaviour comes from within

- Logic fails us in understanding complex systems, so what else is there? Using the basic mathematics of certainty and uncertainty, we can come up with a formulation that strikes a balance between dynamical data and semantics: promise theory.

- Several attempts have been made to reduce the brittleness of logic, by introducing re-stricted or 'modal logics', have not succeeded at addressing the real problem, which is that logic is a branching process rather than a network process with convergence. It is fragile by design.

- Logics favour the notion of obligation over autonomous constraints. Obligations represent a non-local insistence of control. They impose states without regard for causation, and so they are too idealized to represent a realistic view of a causal system.

- Promises, on the other hand, are local, and are built around the concept of a network. They support the idea of distributed self-consistency. They fit neatly with ideas about learning, Bayesian belief and observer semantics. As a starting point, autonomous promises satisfy many of the properties we would like for a useful theory of distributed behaviour.

- Thinking in terms of promises represents a cultural shift. It is not hard, but it is unfamiliar.

11. The Human Condition

How humans make friends to solve problems

- Technology and machinery exist for the benefit of humans, and we should not forget that.

- We can work together with machinery, but to keep humans interested, we need to be involved in contributing to outcomes on a regular basis, building a relationship. One theory, of Dunbar, suggests that our brains evolved to process relationships, to be involved!

- Dunbar's work, together with studies of how we process language, indicate that humans can only relate to a handful of things over time: how many depends on the frequency of the relationship. Our relationships to technology and infrastructure need to be seen light of these limitations. So we should not try to feed humans too much information, nor too little.

- Knowledge management is relationship management, and it is one of our greatest challenges. It costs time and effort for a human.

- To deal with the issue of information overload on human partners, we use a variety of techniques. The classical approaches to categorizing information (putting things in boxes) adds cost and complexity. This is called taxonomy (or ontology). Everyone has to know the model of categorization for it to work. Thus it adds an overhead to each user which does not scale well with the amount of information.

- Using promise theory, and notions of autonomous agency, we can model knowledge in independent chunks that fit into individually meaningful contexts. This makes documentation of knowledge easy. Technology can then be used to help search for information based on context.

- With some redesign based on promises, semantic webs can be used to construct 'stories' or 'narratives' based on chaining together promises in a semantic space. This kind of reasoning can replace traditional logic, and it doubles as an expert system.

12. Molecular and Material Infrastructure

Elastic, plastic, and brittle design

- Everything in the world is discrete, but culturally we rely on the idea of continuity. This chapter is about recovering a meaningful understanding of continuity for infrastructure from discrete promises, as we scale things up to the size of tomorrows datacentres?

- To begin with, we need to place humans and machines in the right semantic roles. Using promises as the glue between these atomic parts, we can view a human-computer system as a single smart material.

- Then we can use a straightforward analogy to material science to understand the properties of this material: homogeneity, strength, brittleness, conductivity, etc. All of this can be understood from the chemistry of composition by promise bonds.

- This kind of predictive model allows us to see what structures will be weak or strong under different kinds of load, as well as predict how successful a human-computer fabric will be at any scale.

- Modern datacentres follow patterns that can be understood in this way already. A deeper understanding of the geometry of the structural relationships can still bring big improvements to smart material datacentres in the future, e.g. in network architectures.

- Not all infrastructure is in datacentres. Increasingly, it is both distributed and mobile. Our embedded and mobile devices behave like a gas of atoms that has a chemistry of its own. The attractive forces between devices is based on economics of cooperation.

- The concept of promises makes understanding infrastructure at a large scale plausible for the first time, as the physics of a smart material.

13. Orchestration and Creative Instability

Or why the conductor does not promise to blow every trumpet

- The holy grail of system design is the complete mastery of processes in time and space, as systems change both intentionally and unintentionally.

- The orchestral score is a sophisticated description of coordinated parallel behaviour, played by autonomous agents. However, current practice in information technology is still 'run book automation' or scripting, a serialized form of centralized coordination.

- Models of processes in computer science are largely based on serial execution and logic. At the other end of the spectrum, there are cellular automata, where the outcome of a computation can be considered emergent behaviour.

- We cannot disregard emergent behaviour in any collaborative system, so this needs to be part of any theory of intended outcome.

- The 'versioning' of plans of intent creates an evolving storyline for planned change. We should not confuse this story with the execution plan. The two are separable. Narratives are important to humans, but they represent a limited view of change. The implications of versioning, and local timelines, is very complicated and goes far beyond the scope of this book.

- Strongly ordered, sequential plans are fragile and non-maintainable, as the order forces us to unpick and then reconstruct something from the beginning if there is a problem.

- When delegating responsibility to multiple actors, a single storyline can still be created by merging the individual threads in a bow-tie process. This is facilitated by expressing every storyline in terms of promises with fixed-point (convergent promise) semantics, as we know that this makes conflicts of intent easy to discover and fix.

- Many worlds branching processes can be collapsed to a single set of convergent 'zero operations' to facilitate semantics continuity. This is the recommended approach for continuous delivery.

- Any plan of intent has to respect the physical constraints, like size, that prevent proper coordination (like CAP issues). Information travels at a finite speed, and thus there is always an event horizon beyond which we cannot see.

- Stability requires us to separate scales when planning intent. Rehearsing a promised plan enables learning feedback for humans. Rehearsal is human learning, and machine learning is rehearsal for machines.

- In summary, we should not confuse the best approach to executing change with the logical story that we want to tell about it afterwards. Confusing these two issues will quickly lead to a dynamical branching process and semantic divergence.

Chapter Notes

Notes

[1] I first proposed this similarity in the keynote at the International Conference on Autonomic Computing (ICAC 2008) held in Chicago, IL, from 2nd to 6th of June 2008.

[2] After the presentation of this paper, I was approached by an attendee from the University of New Mexico to ask whether I knew of Stephanie Forrest's research group. They had coincidentally just written some papers with a different focus also about the idea of Computer Immune Systems. Although our work did not overlap very much, we followed each others' work for a number of years, and kept in touch.

[3] This reminded me of cartoon I saw years ago of a slide-rule mounted in a glass case on the wall of a datacentre, with a sign saying: "Break glass in case of emergency."

[4] Physicist Kenneth G Wilson was awarded the Nobel prize for his work in scale and what is known in physics as the renormalization group. Renormalization is the an expression of the how the magnitude of an effect seems to be stronger or weaker depending on the scale at which you observe or interact with the phenomenon. His work points out that this goes far beyond mere perception. It has to do with *interaction* itself, and the finite range of information.

[5] Evolutionary biologists can no doubt speculate whether this quality of humans to separate local events from the bigger picture has evolved from a need to survive and adapt without going mad, or whether it is a side effect of being able to cope with the limitations of physics, i.e. do we choose not to try to swallow all information at once, or have we just adapted to not being able to? It is quite possible that our awareness and even our consciousness depend on this ability to shut out certain information, but let's get back to the idea of *control* and how we exploit that to build and advance our technologies to master our environments.

[6] Our brains seem to be limited in what they can perceive. This has been measured in many different kinds of studies. For example, Robin Dunbar has described how the human neo-cortex, i.e. that modern part of the brain responsible for thinking and analysis, has evolved to support a limited number of relationships. It can support a few relationships closely, or more relationships in a superficial manner, but there is a kind of conservation of the number multiplied by the intimacy. This seems to be a property of our brains.

[7] In particular, we talk about *deterministic systems*. Computing pioneer Admiral Grace Murray Hopper is quoted as saying: 'Life was simple before World War II. After that we had systems,'

Systems are often thought of as something complicated; but, irony aside, a system is merely an organized collection of methods that work together, like a computer system or an accounting system, an ecosystem, or a physical system.

[8]This is the principal of equivalence of inertial and gravitational masses, also referred to by Einstein in his special theory of relativity.

[9]Rumour has it, he also dropped a man and a woman from the top of the tower also, and seeing that they hit the ground at the same time, proved the equality of the sexes centuries before his time.

[10]Society itself has often been viewed this way. In the 1950s, science fiction author Isaac Asimov (1920-1992), even wrote his Foundation series of novels about the possibility to engineer the future of whole societies by what he called psychohistory, a kind of Hobbesian deterministic mathematical model of society, which was able to predict the future, but only on a large scale.

[11]The traditional theory of thermodynamics, from kinetic theory, to Boyle's law, and the differential relations of Helmholtz and Gibbs is a magnificent effective theory of fluids as bulk hydrodynamic fields.

[12]For a review of the history of subatomic particles, readers could do worse than to consult the readable accounts in Frank Close's excellent book Neutrino[Clo10], or Lawrence Krauss' Quantum Man[Kra12]. Although not comprehensive historical documents, these books convey a sense of the excitement and mystery of the time.

[13]Electrons and other things we assumed were 'particles' are now described by distributions (sometimes called probability clouds) whose best-case predictability is to be able to tell you what state some attribute of the electron is in at a given time and place. What is left of Newton and Leibniz? The concepts of space and time and the book-keeping economics of energy and momentum were more or less preserved, except for the additional surprise of being able to borrow energy from the 'bank' for periods of time. The concept of vacuum energy fluctuations arose in quantum mechanics when scientists tried to make the quantum theory compatible with Einstein's theory of relativity. The resulting predictions of spontaneous creation and annihilation of so-called virtual particles has been verified indirectly through experiments in high energy colliders.

[14]The fact that measurements are not determined by physical law in quantum theory, but rather by the act of measurement has a pleasing symmetry about it. We affect the system, and the system affects us at the same time. Interaction is mutual.

[15]The founders of quantum mechanics included Schrödinger, Heisenberg, Weyl, Bohr, Dirac and later many others including Bethe, Lamb, Feynman, Schwinger and Tomonaga, to name a few.

[16]I don't want to dwell too much on the details of the quantum theory here, but some interesting departures from intuition came out of it. In particular waves came to be important again: not waves in the classical sense, but rather waves of something only indirectly observable: probability of being found. As if the stuff of nature were playing a continuous game of hide and seek with itself, so-called particles were neither here nor there, unless you could actually catch them in the spotlight for a split second. The centuries long debate about whether light was a wave or a particle was thus compounded by a discussion about whether electrons and other particles were, in fact, not particles but waves.

[17]For instance, in the 1993 movie, *Jurassic Park*, Jeff Goldblum's character Dr. Malcolm explains chaos theory to Laura Dern's character using the butterfly effect as an example.

[18]A catastrophe has a special meaning in mathematics. The gradual rise of the oceans due to global warming might be devastating but it is not a catastrophe. A catastrophe would be if the

oceans suddenly rose or fell by 10 meters overnight. It is a sudden deviation from a predictable trend, a dent or a bend in an otherwise smooth behaviour.

[19]Non-linear systems are an example of what makes it hard to predict and control. We could try to affect the weather, perhaps by using giant solar mirrors in orbit to heat and cool the surface of the Earth in a controlled way. However, predicting the response would be just as hard as predicting the weather without the mirrors. Such a system is called *unstable*, because it tends to fly off into the unknown.

[20]Genetically modified foods are an example of a technology that has already been down this line of questioning already. In GM foods, engineers use information about the genes of plants and insects to engineer varieties of plant that repel insect parasites and pests. Environmentalists cite the fear that such genes would get out into the world and mutate into something harmful, or disturb the ecosystem somehow. No one knows if this will be the case, or if the mutation of a genetically modified plant would be anymore dangerous than the kind of natural genetic modification that is taking place all the time – but this is a concern that has captured people's imaginations. Information is a truly fundamental part of interaction and influence, but scale is also important: would a modification at the gene level be able to affect anything on a larger scale – it depends on the couplings. I do not know that answer to how strongly genetic change couples to other species, or the range of its transmission through spores and other agents. I suspect that it is strongly dependent on the nature of the genetic modifications themselves. It does, however, seem unlikely that artificially spliced genes would have radically different or more harmful properties than naturally mutated ones. I suppose only time will tell.

[21]According to my mother, her own mother discovered this rhyme in a letter while working at the British Censorship office during World War II. Since then, I have found references to variations on the rhyme in the Australian Town and Country Journal of Feb 26, 1887 [Unk87].

[22]I am inspired by one of the great books of popular science, *The New Science of Strong Materials* by J.E. Gordon (1913-1998), one of my favourite books growing up[Gor68].

[23]I will talk about 'systems' from now on in the general sense of the last chapter – meaning any identifiable arrangement of things that we wish to focus upon. There is some ambiguity to how we think of a system, because systems often have an environment around them with which they interact. Once they are interacting, the environment is arguably part of the system itself, and hence the boundaries are not necessarily clear. Processes of change are always measured in the context of the system and environment, relative to the boundaries and regions that defined the scales of the system.

[24]For a discussion of mitosis, see for example [Wol98]

[25]Interestingly, the time for half the amount of a substance to decay is constant for exponential decay. It does not depend on the size of the sample, or the amount left.

[26]My source for this fabulous bit of unverified information is [Cur11].

[27]Actually, Einstein changed the idea that space and time are completely orthogonal things. He showed that they are, to some extent interchangeable although time retains a special significance that is never entirely lost.

[28]Astute readers will note that bits are stored on disks or in transistor memory each of which takes up a certain physical size, so one could imagine making a relationship between the volume of silicon or other physical material L and information, which would then allow us to relate information to length. For instance, you could relate digits to the number of pages in a book required to print them, and hence the mass of paper. The difference between continuous measurements and binary digits is an important point, to which we'll return in later chapters. It has a profound

significance to our understanding of the world.

[29]For a comprehensive introduction and history, see [Gib11].

[30]Persons are discrete, or digital quantities like bits, so we could relate this measure to bits per second.

[31]For example, the so-called *Reynolds number* in fluid mechanics, is used to characterize solutions to the Navier-Stokes equations. This is relevant in aerodynamics and the flow of oil through pipes.

[32]Astute readers will realize that a small perturbation would start endless oscillations of the ball around the base of the valley if it were allowed to impart any momentum at all to the ball. To avoid that issue, perturbation theory assumes that the perturbation is vanishingly small – i.e. so close to zero that no measurable energy is transferred. If the system is unstable, as soon as the symmetry has been broken, it will do all the work by itself, without needing a sizable push from outside.

[33]See a discussion of the failure in [Var13c]

[34]I do not remember the details and hence the references to this story, which occurred early in the 2000s.

[35]Let's not kid ourselves; it's not that civil.

[36]Another case was the Apple Macbook battery shutdown caper. There, one had smart batteries that were controlled by chips with simple passwords to protect them. The passwords had been leaked publicly. Now all you need is some kind of virus that can access those passwords and enter them into a system. Since the passwords are not unknowable, it's just a matter of time before a virus or malicious piece of software arrives that pushes past that metastable barrier and the system destabilizes.

[37]A summary of the many sources of information around the causes of the flight are available, of course, on Wikepedia[Var13a].

[38]For a further discussion of systems drifting piece by piece towards catastrophic failure, see Sidney Dekker's book [Dek11].

[39]See Dawkins excellent written works on the mechanisms of genetic information and the analogy to cultural information[Daw90, Daw76].

[40]Precision and approximation play a major role in dynamical equivalence as all models work by selective approximation. We'll return to this issue under the part about certainty.

[41]The need for the laws of physics to be covariance under the effects of changes in viewpoint is basically the argument used by Einstein in formulating the Special Theory of Relativity.

[42]The diagram is actually called a Cayley tree—the result of a uniform branching process.

[43]Recall the pancake chain reaction collapse of the World Trade Center on the 11th of September 2001.

[44]For technical definitions of the terms of stability, see my book Analytical Network and System Administration[Bur04a].

[45]The immunity property was formalized by me in [Bur04b] for computer programmed immunity.

[46]Homeostasis (from the Greek for similar state) is the name used for the internal self-regulation of bodily functions.

[47]The CFEngine story is now a well known one in the computer automation world[Bur95, Bur03, Bur98].

[48]And be 'we' I mean those of you who are of this world, not counting robots, software agents, unicorns or other creations of the mind.

[49]The odd-ones-out amongst these things, and the things that have puzzled philosophers and scientists the most for centuries, are space and time. Whatever kinds of matter we put inside space and time, both space and time still give the illusion of being continuous. However, the assumption of continuous spacetime causes so many problems in fundamental physics that many believe that, if we could only observe it at a small enough scale somehow, we would find that spacetime itself were discrete.

[50]Later this same duality would appear for matter too.

[51]The details of infinite mathematics are fraught with subtlety, which is sure reason enough to avoid them, as science generally tries to do. However, I am oversimplifying for the sake of not getting trapped in a Zeno's paradox of story telling, with infinite regression.

[52]The translation of Planck's autobiographical notes was published in 1950, and many excepts have since appeared in other books and papers[Pla50, Lon84].

[53]This trend continues today. See for example Horgan's review[Hor96].

[54]See Longair's very nice summary [Lon84].

[55]Interestingly, Boltzmann also discussed the idea of a brain as an emergent property of statistical fluctuations. See references to the Boltzmann brain.

[56]The Imperial Wireless Chain was a strategic international telegraphy network, created to link the countries of the British Empire. Although the idea was conceived prior to World War I, it was not finished until the 1920s. See the discussion in [Var13b].

[57]Alan Turing is widely regarded as one of the key founders of information theory and computation. His influence from mathematical physics was profound. His first serious interest in mathematics apparently came through reading Einstein and Eddington and he had an understanding of the principles of general relativity and quantum mechanics while still at school. His first recorded serious scientific question was influenced by Eddington's 1928 book, The Nature of the Physical World: is there a quantum-mechanical basis to human will? [Hod92].

[58]An excellent introduction to encryption may be found in [Sin99]

[59]Hifi enthusiasts sometimes argue that the quality of vinyl records must be greater than that of digital, because vinyl is a continuous substance with infinite detail in its tracks. Digital has a sampling limit and therefore its resolution is limited. This argument is nonsense. Both media have limited resolution. The vinyl in which LPs are printed has a maximum grain size that limits the amount of detail that can be cut into it, and its imperfections lead to a level of noise that seriously reduces the ability to extract the signal from the records. Still, everyone loves the vinyl record player—it has an inexplicable soul about it that superior digital players will probably never have.

[60]Charles Babbage's difference engine, and successor the analytical engine were digital computers, based on mechanical rather than electronic machinery, so it would be wrong to refer to modern computers as the digital computers.

[61]This sounds suspiciously like the computer in *The Hitch Hiker's Guide to the Galaxy*, which came up with the answer '42' for life the universe and everything—but no one knew the question to which this was the answer! Douglas Adams was both a clever and a funny man.

[62]Linear response functions are also known as Green's functions, transfer functions, and a variety of other things in different branches of physics.

[63] In classical physics we usually start with the so-called *equation of motion* for a system, which models the rules for how it evolves over time. It might look something like this general

form, though the form is not important:

$$(\partial_t^2 + \ldots)q(t) = F(t),$$

where $F(t)$ is an edge state, or boundary condition that represents the input of known information to the system.

Written like this, we often say it represents a generalized force, but implicit in this statement are also so-called *boundary conditions*, which represent the information we have about the system at some given moment in time. External forces are, by definition, boundary conditions, in fact. No system can generate an answer about the current state of the world, without putting in some information about what is known from outside. The laws of physics allow us to infer future behaviour from current knowledge, but they don't work like a magical oracle containing knowledge of everything that happens.

This kind of equation of motion often arises from something like Newton's law of motion in the presence of a source or force $F(t)$, i.e. generic rules we have uncovered that seem to describe the way the world evolves in time and space. The term in parenthesis is related to a calculus recipe for working backwards to the 'act on' operator, in the form that physicists and mathematicians usually use to write the constraints of the system – but it is only when we've solved the constraints and found an 'evolution operator' that the mathematics start to resemble the operator formulation of the previous chapter, which is of most interest to us.

The differential operator in parenthesis determines how perturbations add up to change, and physics is about computing change. It can be solved using the rule that past causes lead to future effects. The idea that past causes lead to future behaviour is only one way of solving equations. It gives so-called retarded boundary conditions for the solution, starting in the now and working forwards. If, instead we happen to know the end-result but don't know the starting point of the evolution, the whole thing can be reversed to work backwards, by using so-called advanced boundary conditions[Bur02].

[64]Note that the same thing applies in quantum mechanics, for the Schrödinger equation and the state function (wave-function) with external source J. $\psi(t)$.

$$(\frac{\hat{p}^2}{2m} + V(\mathbf{x}) - E)\psi(t, \mathbf{x}) = J(t, \mathbf{x})$$

$$\psi(x) = \int (dx)G(x, x')J(x). \tag{14.1}$$

The source is just a model for linear perturbations to the system and can represent many different kinds of infinitesimal change.

[65]Yes, I made this word up, for fun.

[66]There is simply not the scope in this book to explain issues like perturbation theory, conformal models and scaling behaviour, to complete this picture in the wider case. That would make a fascinating book in its own right however.

[67]As far back as the 17th century, Fermat's principle of least time had been applied to explain how waves reflected and refracted. It suggested that nature somehow chooses to do what is least expensive. At the same time, Fresnel's principle concerned the paths taken by light during diffraction, interfering with one another and created patterns of light and dark. The same interference patterns had been observed in experiments with electrons, suggesting that electrons were both waves and particles at the same time—a confusing result to be sure.

[68]Although Feynman's vision has achieved much popularity, Schwinger has beaten him to a

fuller and more elegant formal theory[Gle92]. Later Schwinger remarked: "Like the silicon chip of more recent years, the Feynman diagram was bringing computation to the masses.".

[69]I would love to say more about this fascinating topic, but it goes far beyond this scope of this book. Some thoughts can be found in[Bur02].

[70]I occasioned to meet the Schwingers at the anniversary celebrations of the Nobel prize, where Schwinger and I sat next to one another at lunch. He asked me if I liked Mozart and I told him that I hated Mozart, to which he pursed his lips and asked me if I would like to die now or later. We settled on the soundtrack to Battleship Potemkin, and then moved on to a fondness for *Star Trek*. Schwinger's work had been central to my own studies as a PhD student. Although he won the Nobel prize with Richard Feynman and Sin Itiro Tomonaga for Quantum Electrodynamics, Schwinger was much less known than he flamboyant Feynman.

[71]See [Sch70]

[72]This is what is also called the mean field approximation. One often hears the expressions 'exact sciences' for the physical sciences. If this book has any purpose, it could be to show that the notion of an exact science is an oxymoron.

[73]We are, of course, a part of nature so this is not quite true, but such distinctions are artifacts of our mental models of the world, rather than an intrinsic part of it..

[74]As a teenager, I we used to watch the fuzzy dots at the end of a long evening of cheese sandwiches and brown ale, and wait for the rabbit on the bicycle to move along the bottom of the screen. The human mind has an extraordinary capacity to see patterns it wants to in data, which is surely a lesson for scientists and politicians.

[75]There are many ways of filtering out noise. One approach is to use frequency filters. This was common in sound studios before more advanced systems like Dolby encoding. We talk about the threshold of noise, an even the signal to noise ratio, which is a measure of the relative amounts of energy carried in the signal per unit time.

[76]I use the term grains, others use slices, buckets or cells for the units.

[77]The term static equilibrium is a misnomer, but it is a relic of a time before knowledge of atoms and their jigging motions on a tiny scale.

[78]The consensus problem is one of the classic issues in distributed systems. It relates to modern issues of wide area database consistency, for example. Banks too have to allow a finite equilibration time when processing financial transactions to allow the new balance to reach all their branches so that our account balances are the same everywhere. Many ideas and considerable confusion have resulted from trying to understand the semantics of consensus in information systems. Vector clocks,Paxos, Raft are examples that come to mind.

[79]Figure 4.5 shows the average length of the queue, whereas Figure 4.6 shows response time. By Little's law, we know that these things should be proportional for a Markov process. In addition, modern processor architectures have all kinds of complex internal details that invalidate the detailed picture of a Markov process. In spite of all this, the agreement is quite good.

[80]The idea of treating computers as a kind of empirical phenomenon, like any other subject of scientific study, was so unsettling to the establishment of computer science that it took as long as five years to publish much of this work in scientific journals. Science might be a self-correcting enterprise, but scientists are still human beings with their own agendas, and new ideas are rarely welcomed with open arms. As Niccolò Machiavelli wrote: "There is nothing more difficult to take in hand, more perilous to conduct or more uncertain of its success than to take the lead in the introduction of a new order of things, because the innovator has for enemies all those who have done well under the old condition and lukewarm defenders in those who may do well under

the new..". I later wrote in a textbook that we were still at the stage of zoologists observing the animals in the wild through binoculars to see how they behaved. See the closing words of [Bur00d].

[81] The published works on the similarities with the Planck spectrum can be seeing in refs[Bur00e, Bur00b, BHRS01].

[82] This observation later entered into my book on modelling human-computer systems[Bur04a].

[83] See the published edition of their work [NM44].

[84] For a more mathematical analysis, see [Bur04a].

[85] The original article on the subject by Hardin[Har68]. Much interesting work has been done in this area by Nobel laureate Elinor Ostrom[Ost90].

[86] Nash's story can be read in [Nas98] and his paper was reprinted in [Nas96].

[87] It shares some similarities with path integral methods of Feynman, insofar as one is exploiting a variational formulation of parameterized strategies. The construction of a mixture of strategies as a variational 'argmax' fixed point has some similarities with variational methods of least action, such as Feynman's diagrammatic variational formulation of particle pathways. For more details, see the simple discussion in [Bur04a].

[88] The prisoner's dilemma tournaments of Axelrod yielded simple but powerful insights into game theory as an iterative process[Axe97, Axe84, Axe86, Axe87]

[89] The University of Oslo, where I first started working on CFEngine was already quite sophisticated in writing 'scripts' that performed many regulatory maintenance tasks. CFEngine was certainly inspired by these smart engineers when I began writing it in 1993, in particular Knut Borge, Hans Petter Holen of USIT and Ola Borrabæk at the physics department were instrumental in my own initiation of Unix.

[90] For a discussion about network accretion and power laws, see for example, Barabási's book Linked[Wat99, Buc02, Bar02].

[91] Theorem 11 in Shannon and Weaver: Let a discrete channel have capacity C and a discrete source of entropy per second H. If $H < C$ there exists a coding system such that the output of the source can be transmitted over the channel with an arbitrarily small frequency of errors.[SW49]. His theory applies equally well to biological information[Sha40].

[92] I'm grateful to Andrew Hume for pointing out the studies on this topic. A study of Latent Sector Errors was performed in 2010[SDG10].

[93] I also referred to the periodic maintenance as the snow-clearing model[BR07].

[94] For an excellent introduction to material physics, there is the ever brilliant J.E. Gordon[Gor68].

[95] It is a frequently used phrase in computing to blame strange events on cosmic rays. This may mor may not be the case. In practice, there are plenty of other sources of stray radiation closer to computers, including earth faults, leaky microwave ovens and electrical sparks and surges that create electrical noise.

[96] A bifurcation is a forking of a pathway into two possible routes. It is one of the routes to chaos in the physics of complex non-linear systems.

[97] This begins to sound like a rendition of the song 'There was an old lady who swallowed a fly', which ends badly. The traditional song 'There was an old lady who swallowed a fly, don't ask me why she swallowed a fly – perhaps she'll die...'.

[98] Many worlds scenarios go back to Gottfried Leibniz who spoke of possible worlds in the mind of God. Then Saul Kripke worked on the concept of possible worlds in the 1950s and 1960s in the context of modal logic. Hugh Everett used the idea as an interpretation of quantum mechanics in 1957 in what is now the most famous many worlds interpretation.

[99]During the second millennium, standards of human governance were developed that are still used today. The bureaucratic approach to system oversight and resilience was the acme of information science during its time: discipline through process, form-filling documentation, review, consensus, redundancy, and so on. We make fun of bureaucracy and process thinking now, archaic as it seems, but during the Ottoman Empire, which imported the notion from Confucian China, being a bureaucrat was considered to be a high status function, like being an aristocrat. The German philosopher Max Weber formalized bureaucracy (rule by office) in the industrial revolution. Bureaucracy has a limited throughput however. It works at a slow human timescale, and just cannot respond fast enough to deal with the rate at which crises occur when working with large numbers of events.

[100]It has since been pointed out to me that E. Dijkstra, the now famous Dutch computer science pioneer, who seemed to think of pretty much everything, also considered the importance of idempotence and convergence, entertaining the idea of self-maintaining systems as a passing thought in 1974 [Dij74], though he did not develop the ideas as far as I can tell.

[101]Cauchy's residue theorem and analytic continuation are applications of this idea. As the math joke goes, after the accident the Polish test-pilot claimed: I was just a simple Pole in a complex plane.

[102]Like much of our mathematics and medicine, it was introduced to the West through the Islamic Empire and its bridge through the Ottoman Empire and Italy. The word zero comes from an Italian distortion of the Arabic word for zero 'sifr', from which we get cipher, and a host of other words in European languages.

[103]I developed this concept in a paper for my friend Jan Bergstra's 60th birthday, relating it to convergence and CFEngine[BC11].

[104]A good talk on this subject was given by Chas Emerick at QCon[cha14].

[105]The number of ideas about reducing software complexity and making it robust forms its own many worlds paradox. Ideas like Object Orientation and functional programming have claimed to provide the One True Answer, but none have yet taken on board the realities of general purpose programming. I have been particularly impressed by the talks given by software engineer Rich Hickey (author of the Clojure programming language and Datomic database), who applies physics-like thinking to software behaviour with great intuition. Probably Domain Specific Languages have the potential to solve part of the problem, by limiting capabilities rather than empowering ever more.

[106]The work on the maintenance theory was first presented in at LISA 2000 but spent several years in reviewer purgatory, as many unusual ideas do in academic circles. The final version was published here[Bur03].

[107]The concept of entropy goes back to the second law of thermodynamics, and it is frequently used and abused in popular ways, as if a gremlin, or agent of destruction. There are several very precise meanings of entropy that relate to information and conservation of energy. These things were related by Boltzmann, amongst others.

[108]This is not merely a wistful analogy: a recent BBC documentary reported that over 20 buildings per year collapse in Cairo due to illegal building by rogue developers, who fail to follow engineering standards and regulations.

[109]This is something of a sore point in technology design, especially software engineering, where many ideas about the perfect design language have been posited. The documentary film *Urbanized* by Gary Hustwit is an excellent description of how town planning has based itself on mistaken principles.

[110]The kind of pervasive computing that is finally taking off today in 2013, was was already discussed towards the end of the 1980s at the legendary Xerox PARC. Chief Technologist Mark Weiser and Chief Scientist John Seely Brown developed the notion of "ubiquitous computing" during the 1990s under their tenure at the Xerox Palo Alto Research Center (PARC). Ubiquitous computing was also known as pervasive computing and was later developed conceptually by research groups from many of the large computer corporations[WGB99]. Realistically, it took this long to develop the necessary level of communication and processing infrastructure required to support a useful information-rich experience, and then to see how it could be used to support an enhanced society.

[111]Statistics for human resource consumption are published by various organizations. These numbers are taken from[Cla62, Rep11] in February 2013.

[112]Windows are a perfect example. They are made by a highly sophisticated process of mixing common minerals like sand into an amorphous solid. The window has been around for centuries in different forms. The word window comes from the Norse root 'vindauga', meaning literally eye for the wind: a wind hole, but it has also gone through enormous technological changes: the invention of glass, the technology to make large, smooth, flat plates of it; the extraction of the raw materials, the generation of temperatures required to melt those materials, the containers to hold them while hot. The metal in the frames and the handles, sun reflective technology, heat insulating technology, sound insulating technology, the moulding of the parts. It is the very nature of infrastructure to disappear from view. We are intentionally unaware of it, and its mechanisms, most of the time. It is a question of trust. We trust in order to be relieved of the need to worry about certain aspects of life. Yet, it takes little more than a crack in the glass, or a brief power outage to shake that trust and feeling of invulnerability that nothing could go wrong.

[113]For a discussion of emergent behaviour in the mobile world, see [Rhe02, BDT99, Buc02].

[114]Psychologists might say that it replaces system 2 thinking with system 1. System 1 is our primitive, emotional and instinctive brain. System 2 is the cognitive neocortex and rational capability. Most of the time we prefer to rely on system 1, because system 2 is very costly. It uses up to 20 percent of our total energy consumption[Kah11].

[115]If there was ever any doubt that humans still played a major role in this new technology, one only had to look at the high profile exploitations now enabled by coupling infrastructure strongly to command and control systems. The attack by a disgruntled employee on water plant in Australia's Maroochy Shire water plant is now recorded in the hall of fame for security incidents. The more we strongly couple components together with network control systems, the easier they are to change, and the more vulnerable they become to abuse.

[116]See Douglas Hofstadter's excellent, classic book *Gödel, Escher, Bach: an eternal golden braid*[Hof81].

[117]See Alvin Toffler's excellent trilogy [Tof70, Tof80, Tof90]

[118]Mumford was a prolific if somewhat verbose writer and philosopher. See [Mum64], in its two volumes.

[119]See Anderson's paper from LISA 94 conference in [And94], and the related works of Evard, Couch and Finke[CD01a, Cou96, CG99a, Eva97, Fin97].

[120]The original paper by Sloman described the use of policy to describe access controls, based on deontic logic[SM93]. This was later used to design the Ponder access language.

[121]For a review of his ideas, see [Dem82].

[122]For example, the Management Information Base (MIB) made for SNMP, and later succeeded Common Information Model (CIM) both had tens of thousands of database tables, quite out of

control, because they modelled by manufacturer and product instead of by logical issue. A poor data model combined with static thinking in a dynamical environment quickly led to unwieldy solutions that were as expensive as they were inappropriate.

[123]For the OSI managed object model see [DZ83, Yem93]. Many pieces of these standards still survive in vestiges today, e.g. x500 networking, with x509 certificates used in the web. The ITU defined the TMN architecture (Telecommunication Management Network) in 1988, at the same time as SNMP. In the early 1980s the term FCAPS was introduced within the first Working Drafts (N1719) of ISO 10040, the Open Systems Interconnection (OSI) Systems Management Overview (SMO) standard and a common management information protocol (CMIP). The Distributed Management Task Force (DMTF) also contributed to management protocols.

[124]The name Unix was taken from the joke that the new operating system was EUNUCHS, a castrated version of MULTICS.

[125]Unix was made available under license by AT&T in the 1970s, and an open version of it was later released by the University of California, Berkeley. The legal wrangling over Unix ownership continued for years and would eventually kill off most of it in favour of open variants like FreeBSD, Linux, IllumOS and GNU.

[126]If an external user is supposed to supply a telephone number, for instance, then they should not be allowed to type in something else, like a command that could lead to dangerous side effects. Similarly, if a critical piece of software observes the state of information that might be altered by a third party. Global information is often considered to be information that can be altered by a third party, hence programmers view globally writable variables as problematic. Unfortunately, this includes all databases, that state should be validated for harmful side effects before trusting its integrity. Even a simple mismatch of alphabetic codes could lead to accidental trouble.

[127]For historical reasons, both are called observational 'errors', because it was thought that uncertainties were often the results of mistakes and inaccuracies made by the experimenter.

[128]Descartes writings are compiled in [Smi58].

[129]See the NASA article, *Unmasking the face on Mars*, or the movie *Mission to Mars* (2000).

[130]The name firewall itself comes from the world of civil engineering where it represents a barrier inside a building designed to limit the spread of fire. Whole countries block the free flow of information deliberately. The Chinese government is the most famous example of a government that censors information, but surveys show that every country in the world restricts access to some kind of information on a selective basis. For a less sinister example of intended and unintended partitioning, consider biology. Biology evolved skin and membranes around major organs to act as protective, semi-permeable barriers to different external influences, but faulty blood clots can also prevent the communication of blood to different parts of the body.

[131]In the computer science literature, CAP standard for consistency, availability and partition tolerance, but proximity is an easier way to understand the same thing. The CAP conjecture was a conjecture made by Eric Brewer, suggesting that one could have two but not three of the CAP properties at any one time[Bur12a, Bre00, Bre12]. The conjecture has since been shown to be inaccurate.

[132]I wrote about the relativity of knowledge in connection with databases, in more detail on my blog in 2012, see[Bur12a].

[133]Currently two examples of online social media channels come readily to mind: Twitter and Facebook.

[134]Recent experiments in quantum teleportation suggest that faster than light transmission of digital information might be possible, breaking Einstein's standing prediction that the speed of

light is a maximum limit. Keep your fingers crossed.

[135] With a solid ruler used to measure a book, the light which transmits the measurement messages has an absolutely negligible effect on the ruler or the book. But this is not always the case. Suppose we tried to measure a light-sensitive worm with a ruler. As soon as we switched on the light to read the graduations on the ruler, it would interact with the worm, causing it to shrink. The ruler would stay constant, but the total system would not be in equilibrium.

[136] Instead there can be a compatibility in the states that leads to certain observations not getting in the way of one another, but there are other measurements that share an underlying scale, such as distance and speed, which cannot be made without altering the system at a fundamental level. A 'particle-like excitation' cannot both be confined to a small region where we can say we know it's location *and* be moving in a uniform way at the same time. These states are logically incompatible in a transition system, although in a Newtonian continuum view they make perfect sense.

[137] Heisenberg went further and showed that there are certain things we seem fundamentally unable to measure at the same time, without a minimum of uncertainty. Recent experiments by researchers in China, around quantum teleportation, have suggested that there might be a way to circumvent Heisenberg's uncertainty limit, but this is currently speculative.

[138] For a fascinating and comprehensive overview of the history of statistics, see [Sti90].

[139] The culture of statistics sometimes gets in the way of its own goals, shrouding its agenda of clarity in a lot of technical jargon and standard tests whose semantics are given less attention than their application. Formal procedures can easily become bureaucratized to the point of obtuseness unless one keeps intentions clear.

[140] For an excellent telling of the story of cryptography see Singh's Code Book[Sin99].

[141] For an account of this, see also [Sin99].

[142] There, were met the Planck distribution which plotted the relative strength of each frequency of light emanating from a thermal system, which is the measured frequency with with quanta hit a detector, categorized by radiation-frequency (two different uses of frequency).

[143] In order for the noise to cancel out, it must be symmetrically distributed about the mean. This is true of several distributions, but it is particularly true of normally distributed noise, which is the kind of noise one would expect from experimental error.

[144] See Whittaker and G. Robinson, *Calculus of Observations*[WR29]

[145] The belief that there are universal constants in nature is not without controversy. In some theories of cosmology, these universal constants change over the age of the universe. I am not aware of any evidence one way or the other on this subject.

[146] For a review of Bayesian methods, see for example [Pea88, KN04].

[147] The distribution about the mean was unlikely to be normal, except in a few cases, and this could now be measured. As long as the distribution does not have long tail behaviour the expectation value and deviation are reasonable scales to characterize the data.

[148] Interestingly, the Boltzmann and normal distributions may both be derived from the Shannon information formula, by maximizing the information or uncertainty subject to certain constraints.

To get Boltzmann's distribution of energies, we just need to ensure that the probabilities predict an average total energy that is constant. To get the normal distribution, we just say that the average Pythagorean distance of data from the mean should be constant, like a kind of 'best fit'.

[149] For a more detailed derivation of the formula, see [Bur04a].

[150] John von Neumann is reputed to have told Shannon to call his measure the informational entropy, realizing the connection to Boltzmann's H-theorem, and telling him that he would have an advantage at conferences, where no one understood what entropy meant anyway.

[151] See his last book [Pri96], which I discovered to my amusement after choosing the title for this book. Physicists will find his message and viewpoint very similar to mine, for a completely different context.

[152] The formalization took some time to write in a language that computer scientists could accept, and appeared somewhat belatedly in [Bur04b].

[153] Parts of this chapter are based on a series of articles written in the USENIX ;login: magazine in December of 2000[Bur00c].

[154] See Asimov's story collection *I, Robot*.

[155] Ironically, though Asimov called his robot brain 'positronic', from the quantum theory, he was a chemist by training, so his view of causation was based on continuous potentials, like an analogue circuit.

[156] The Network File System had options for hard and soft mounting of file systems. Hard mounting was the default, and led to hanging computers when there were network problems.

[157] A phase transition in physics is a change-over to regime with different dynamics.

[158] A positive side effect of the episode was that one of my intrepid colleagues thought of all kinds of ways to improve the basic performance of the database interaction, so when we finally diagnosed the real problem, we had also made some important improvements to our own software too. Many software engineers would point to this as a reason why testing is important, but of course no test harness would ever have discovered such an unlikely combination of effects. To able to test something, you have to know what to look for. Testing is of limited value, because you mainly find what you expect. Its main purpose is to prevent an identical problem from happening again later due to a side effect of new changes.

[159] See for example his work [K.P59].

[160] See the text [Hod77].

[161] See George Dyson's excellent historical account in [Dys97]

[162] Per ratiocinationem autem intelligo computationem – by logic I mean computation. 1655

[163] see refs in [Dys97]

[164] See Boole's works in [Boo10b, Boo10a].

[165] See [vN95].

[166] The published work was [HA28], and the story behind it has been described in [Moo88].

[167] In fact the precise number changed in different versions of the challenge.

[168] Logic begins to get into trouble as it strays from simple discrete concepts, but this has not stopped it from trying to reason about continuum systems. Zeno's paradox is a good example. See also modal logic referred to in the next chapter. Semantic consistency can answer questions about continuum mathematics however if $x > 5$, this is consistent with $x > 0$.

[169] "It's Elementary, Dear Watson: Applying Logic Programming to Convergent System Management Processes"[CG99b]

[170] In Einstein's theory of relativity, this kind of parallelism is called a spacelike separation.

[171] See the review of system configuration[Cou07].

[172] See the short summary in the proceedings [BB07a].

[173] In the mathematics of causation, fixing the starting boundary condition is called a retarded solution; fixing the end-state is called an advanced solution. This is not a value judgement on the relative merits of the two!

[174] In CFEngine, guards were called classes before Object Oriented programming came into common use. This now leads to much confusion about the meaning of classes.

[175] See the paper om Maelstrom in [CD01a].

[176]Engineers usually want their solutions to be simple and elegant, but building for security sometimes means introducing ugly necessity into design to prevent harm from happening (no one thinks seat-belts and airbags improve the interior of a car, but we agree they represent necessary overhead to deal with statistical risk), even though they intrude onto the purity of *intended function.*

[177]Although convergent operator methods had been in use in CFEngine in 1993, I did not get around to describing their algebra until 1999, and this was not published until 2003. Couch and Daniels' work was presented at LISA in 2001, the same year that I chaired the conference as a pilgrimage back to the Town and Country hotel in San Diego. See [CD01b].

[178]See [Bur04a, Bur04b, Bur03].

[179]Related work is published in [CS03, CS04, SC07].

[180]See the excellent talk by Rich Hickey on this subject [Hic11]

[181]A few definitions of complexity relate directly to information. The Kolmogorov complexity, for instance, is defined as the length of the shortest program executable by a Turing machine that solves the problem. This is reminiscent of Shannon's intrinsic information.

[182]The reason why 'simple' is related to easy is due to the theorem proven by Chomsky, which relates structural complexity to the kind of computational automaton required to parse its structure. Descriptive complexity is a branch of computational complexity theory that characterizes complexity classes by the type of logic needed to express the languages in them.

[183]See [BK07].

[184]Could one characterize the complexity of reasoning itself? Asking such a general question leads to the vaguest answer, that it lies somewhere in **PSPACE**. The complexity of logic itself [HM92].

[185]In [Wes09], decision making based on continuous variables projected into discrete decisions is precisely the cause cited for software instabilities. The cited reference from Shapiro summarized it well:

> "From the 1960s onward, many of the ailments plaguing software could be traced to one principal cause-complexity engendered by softwares abstract nature and by the fact that it constitutes a digital (discrete state) system based on mathematical logic rather than an analog system based on continuous functions. This latter characteristic not only increases the complexity of software artifacts but also severely vitiates the usefulness of traditional engineering techniques oriented toward analog systems [emphasis added]. Although computer hardware, most notably integrated circuits, also involves great complexity (due to both scale and state factors), this tends to be highly patterned complexity that is much more amenable to the use of automated tools. Software, in contrast, is characterized by what Fred Brooks has labeled 'arbitrary complexity'" [Sha97].

[186]Programmable infrastructure goes by a variety of names: infrastructure as code, software defined networking, etc.

[187]A recent report by NASA draws similar conclusions in the flight systems of spacecraft. It is the logical decision-making that is culprit in triggering most instabilities [Wes09].

[188]According to the Philosopher John Searle, intentionality is that area of reason that includes beliefs, hopes, fears, desires, and so on. He writes that: 'Intentionality is that property of many

mental states and events by which they are directed at or about or of objects and states of affairs in the world'. He also writes: '...anyone who attempts to write too clearly runs the risk of being understood too quickly'! See [Sea83].

[189]When making policy for information infrastructure, we often need to be able to make decisions about cases of uncertain identity, for instance.

[190]See Daniel Kahneman's review of this effect in [Kah11].

[191]See references like [jCMWD98, CLM99]. In network management, the work of Moffet and Sloman was influential [SM93].

[192]See [Woo02, Cas93, Sin12].

[193]Interesting studies of deontics, i.e. rules in human institutions have been made by Nobel Laureate Elinor Ostrom [Ost05].

[194]The semi-empirical 'laws' of natural science are mere observations that capture the norms of reality.

[195]See the percolation approaches to security in [BCE03, BCS$^+$03]. Later we joined forces with Knut Engø Monsen to develop techniques for locating vulnerable and important points in networks.

[196]See an excellent review of security principles in Bruce Schneier's book [Sch00].

[197]John Sechrest was visiting the University College at the time, in connection withe establishment of an international masters degree in Network and System Administration. He and my Kyrre were interested in virtualization very early on, and together we came up with the term 'stem cell' machines for generic computers that would later be differentiated by CFEngine configuration. See [BBS94].

[198]We have been writing the definite technical monograph on the subject since 2005. The title and content of this book are in constant flux. It is currently known as *A Theory of Promises*.

[199]See [Bur05]. To my great surprise, this paper was informally voted 'best paper' in the plenum discussion after the conference.

[200]In moral philosophy it is conventional to use the spelling *promisor*. This seems too aggressive to me, and it is associated with the promissory obligation. In the promise theory of Jan and myself, a promise is a standalone primitive that does not require a notion of obligation at all. Thus, I distinguish the spelling of promiser.

[201]Why are promises not kept? Atiyah makes the point that it is often the promiser that benefits when a promise is kept. One is not necessarily looking for remuneration. See [Ati81].

[202]By using a simple typology for classifying promises, one can make detecting inconsistency very easy and precise.

[203]The same approach can be applied to any inanimate object. As long as a human can interpret something in the form of a promise, there is no particular problem to anthropomorphizing. Thus, it is okay to say, an electron promises to generate an electric field, or carbon atom promises to have 12 protons, or a gene promises to manufacture a certain protein, or a even that a book promises to explain a certain concept.

[204]See [BFb].

[205]We formulated a form of Newton's laws using promises in [BF07a].

[206]This is a little bit artificial. Strictly speaking, a use-promise $(-)$ does not have to be signalled back to the giver of something. The intention to receive or use could be kept private, or even signalled to a different party, but it is helpful to insist on it as part of model-building, to provide documentation of the intent to receive. A theory may differ from reality in details, if that is helpful

to understanding. A theory, after all, is meant to be a simpler idealization of reality that illustrates principles with clarity.

[207]This was quite annoying. I am supposed to be the physicist who knows about symmetry breaking. I should have been the one to phrase it in this way. Alas, Jan is quite brilliant.

[208]See [BFa, BFb].

[209]See [CD, Gil93, Fri81, She11, Sto52].

[210]In Schwinger's formulation of quantum field theory, the spacetime elements themselves were the promiser of the field. This was the power and the weakness of the formulation. It revealed symmetries and dynamics with great beauty, but also led to infinities arising from the assumption of continuous spacetime.

[211]When lecturing around the world, I often use this joke as a way of making engineers aware of how they think. How many system engineers does it take to screw in a light bulb? The answer would be quite a few, because you would naturally demolish the building in which the faulty light bulb existed and reconstruct it from the foundations with a working light bulb. Put like this, the idea of being without a mission-critical building for a year, just to get a working light bulb, makes the strategy seem irresponsible. Yet this is exactly what system engineers do if they find a small error in an otherwise perfectly good computer.

[212]See [Burb].

[213]For more details see Arthur C. Clarke's excellent account in [Cla92].

[214]In the popular science fictions series Star Trek, never a show goes by without hearing, "More power to the X, captain!", where X may be replaced by shields, engines, transmitters, or whatever. There is a common belief that brute force is the only way to solve problems.

[215]Gutta Percha is a natural substance from trees which is hard in air but malleable in water. It used to be used to mold electrical fittings for light bulbs and other before the invention of modern plastics.

[216]On the 10th June 1858, however, the re-fitted steam powered battleship Agamemnon left port from Plymouth carrying 1300 tons of cable in her hold and 250 tons on deck. As if to conspire against the attempt she hit a major storm about which the London Times wrote:

> "The massive beams under her upper deck coil cracked and snapped with a noise resembling that of small artillery... The Agamemnon rose heavily to the first (wave) and then went lower quickly into the deep trough of the sea, falling over as she did, so as almost to capsize completely."

This second attempt also had to be abandoned as the cable broke, but on a later voyage the cable was spliced and saved at least for a time.

[217]On the first day of operation the cable earned one thousand pounds. The American pioneer Cyrus W. Field funded the expedition.

[218]See [Kah11].

[219]See [Axe84, Axe97].

[220]See [Axe84, Axe97].

[221]Imagine trying to learn to play a piece of music on an instrument. First you study the music, analyzing how to play it, working out the fingerings laboriously with your analytical brain. Eventually, after sufficient repetition, it gets cached in 'muscle memory'. Today, we can dial up the music on any number of sound systems without having to use our brains at all, but this does not mean we 'know' the music very well. We never truly hear it in full unless we've played it and

analyzed it from every angle. We learn the words to songs only by listening over and over, but we only understand what the song is about if we take the time to analyze the text.

[222] See the work by Dunbar's group in [Dun96, HD03, ZSHD04].

[223] See the linguistic work of Fred Karlson in [Kar09].

[224] For excellent and readable reviews of research, see [Kah11, Ari12]

[225] As Lewis Mumford noted, we humans imitate machines, in the first instance, before freeing themselves to live with more dignity. Others associate their dignity with acting like a machine. The Myers-Briggs typology that came from Jung's psychology indicates that some humans prefer simple machine like work. Others are more intuitive.

[226] See counter examples in [McI91].

[227] See, for example, Daniel Pink's summary [Pin95].

[228] Network signals are digitized into packets (like TCP), computers are hardware is digitized into virtual machines (like VM elastic scaling), storage is digitized into sectors and pages (like RAID), tissue is digitized into cells, and the system becomes resistant to single cell death.

[229] In the interests of historical accuracy, this was not exactly the way things unfolded. Initially, the Business Driven IT Management (BDIM) workshops were brainstorming around ideas like security, governance, ITIL, eTOM, COBIT and a flurry of ideas about making web server performance better. It took me two years, and hearing Jacques Sauvé's presentation in Munich 2007 before I really paid attention to the role of promises in the discussion.

[230] See [Bura].

[231] I originally arranged a BDIM workshop at the LISA conference in 2008 and 2009, attended by Carolyn. We them wrote summaries of these workshops in [BR10a, BR10b].

[232] See for instance references in [Coa37, BF07a, Fox81, US, KT01, Hey07, Die06, ZMZ07, EKP98].

[233] Conversations with doctoral student Thomas Schaaf from Munich tipped me off to the connection with Deming.

[234] Jan Bergstra and I studied this in [BB06].

[235] See [BBJF05].

[236] Emergent behaviour is discussed in many references. See for example [BAJ00, Joh01, Hol98, BDT99, KE01] and our work is described in [BF07b, BB14].

[237] This what happens in market 'branding'. One tried to try to trick the human relationship-processor into thinking it is having a relationship with a popular product by compressing such a relationship into a single logo or symbol that we associate with popularity. But such short cuts are not sufficient: one does not become a doctor or a pilot simply by wearing the uniform.

[238] The project was part of the European Union's 6th Framework research programme which went my the name of EMANICS, and involved 13 partners from European countries.

[239] This was an idea first proposed by Joseph Mitola at the Stockholm Institute of Technology in 1998. It was to be a software-defined radio transceiver platform should evolve: a fully reconfigurable wireless transceiver which automatically adapted its capabilities to the availability of communications channels and user demands. To do that it needed certain smart features.

[240] See [Ada07].

[241] Demissie Aredo, Simen Hagen and I explained how to describe information relativity completely using promises in 2005-2006. See the different versions of this work in [AB07, ABH 6, Are04].

[242] See [Bus45].

[243] Nakarin Phooripoom and I explored the notion of promises in network routing in [Pho08].

[244] See [Bur09, Bur12b].

[245] I wrote about this in [Bur12b].

[246] See the excellent account of reading by Maryanne Wolf in [Wol07].

[247] Why we flirt with misunderstanding is an interesting question; perhaps as a test of our thinking, as a challenge to think along new lines, for metaphor.

[248] Dijkstra's shortest path algorithm is a method for finding the shortest journey between two points in a network. It refers to Dutch computer scientist Edsger Dijkstra who published the method in 1959.

[249] The patterns in associativity can be as significant as specifics of what is connected. Think of a chemical analogy: the chemical bond between oxygen and hydrogen (OH hydroxyl) is important in many situations of chemistry. As a single free radical, it plays a role in many processes. It is found in water H_2O, and in many organic molecules. Its significance is must greater than its size. Long chain polymers make much longer and more intricate chemical stories, but they are no more or less significant than they single-bond OH.

[250] See [Ost05].

[251] An illustration of what this could mean came to my attention in 2010, when I was asked to advise an international technology manufacturer about their use of CFEngine automation. They had already made extensive use of the software to automate their global infrastructure over a period of several years, but the engineering team, responsible for eight international datacentres, had hit a wall in terms of human cooperation: they were having trouble providing the services the company's business units wanted.

The business units of this manufacturing company wanted better assurances that their systems were compliant with security patches, in order to satisfy government regulations on export controls. The US government regulates technology companies with export controls, as well as financial Sarbanes-Oxley reporting against fraud. I had already had some ideas about using a new knowledge-based approach to address the matter. Graduate student Iman Dagnew and I had looked into modelling Sarbanes-Oxley (SOX) financial regulation in 2008, using promise theory, so the new promise model for CFEngine was well suited to reporting on that.

At the company, it was proving difficult for the engineers to keep their business unit meaningfully informed about the status of their systems, because the automation was driving the schedule of activity, leaving no room for compliance audits. Communication became an interruption to their daily work, instead of being an integrated aspect of the job. Managing any kind of knowledge is usually the last thing organizations think about, so status reporting was not an integrated process. The result was a series of disconnected episodes of computer system continuity, interrupted by human digressions for data collection, like cracks in the smooth operation. Human and computer processes were not integrated.

A colleague and I spent several days with the engineering team, in Texas, quizzing them about their set up, and their practices. After listening, it was clear that the engineers had a very good handle on the dynamics of their systems, but they had a highly insular view of its semantics. This was preventing them from building a collaborative relationship between business and engineering at the human level, and this was disrupting the machine level too.

As is often the case when human semantics are ignored, technology had become a collection of 'things' that lived for their own sake, at the behest of the engineers, without a sense of what they were for. This had happened to their information infrastructure. When the engineers looked at their system, they saw components, moving parts, and processes that kept the beast alive, but not a complete organism delivering a trusted service, and supporting the goals of the company.

One problem lay in communicating how engineering actually contributed to that business purpose, and how it could be improved. The engineers were proud of their relationship to the technology, but were not even aware of how remote their connection was to the business. Like most technology consumers, the business unit only cared about the purpose of the information system, not how cleverly it had been built. Everything was projected into two issues: how much does it cost, and does it meet our objectives? The engineers, on the other hand, found this viewpoint hard to digest. Thus there was a complete 'disconnect' between business and engineering. I noticed that the engineers discussed their work based on the knowledge they valued most: the details they had mastered, the names of the low level components that they had a regular relationship with (like the file of user registrations `/etc/passwd`) when making changes and repairs. When they described the system from this point of view, they name-dropped these particular files like cryptic symbols, and talked about running particular named programs with equally impenetrable names; they enthused over why one choice was much smarter than another, etc. It was like asking a carpenter what he was doing and hearing: 'I used a 30cm hacksaw from shelf 2 for three minutes, then switched to a shelf 3 jigsaw for 24 seconds, then hit one end of a plank with a hammer...'. The engineering department was promising things like the "SLA for the HPC was under 5 minutes" and "The passwords are encrypted with a seeded SHA256 cryptohash", and so on. What the business units heard was: "Blah blah blah password blah blah blah". None of these promises were of any value to them, because they could not understand what they meant. What they wanted to know was: are we obeying the law, are we meeting our commitments, are we cost effective?

There was not just a cultural divide, but a pedagogical gulf to be bridged. What they needed was not better engineers, but a way to communicate what all the technology meant for their business. There was a job here for some simple-minded knowledge engineering, as discussed in the last chapter. This could be the glue to bind the whole system.

I advised the engineers to take the lead in building a more human relationship to business, by promising to make the semantics if their activities transparent and comprehensible to their implicit partner. They should start with reformulating the way they thought about the technical promises of their infrastructure, and try to base them on a view of the problem that the business unit could relate to. Engineers often find this counter-intuitive because it is at odds with the engineering itself, where a top level view is a bad approach to designing systems. But for describing intent, it is good because it means one can start with an overview. If you have no intention to become an expert, you want to approach understanding from the top, from the semantic overview. You don't care about the dynamics much. In other words, they could begin to relate their promises to the stable core of slowly varying business concepts, rather than noisy trivia of fluctuating technology choices. It was their job to hide specialist detail and provide a usable and reassuring interface to their colleagues.

For example, at the business level, one might be interested in these kinds of topics:

customer service	Ensure excellence of experience in services
service availability	Keep online services running and available
productivity	Keep employees productive in their work
up-to-date infrastructure	Make sure we have the latest and greatest
support organizational agility	Keep infrastructure agile and adaptable

organizational growth	Handle planned and unexpected growth
IT efficiency	Keep performance to cost ratio high
regulatory compliance	Comply with audit in finance/security
information security	Policy for information security measures

The engineers reformulated not only their inter-personal promises but also their CFEngine machine promises to reflect these business objectives. That included, documenting the whys, the stakeholders in the outcomes, and which business objectives each detailed promise contributed to.

By offering such a bridge between their own promises and business objectives, we could actually help them to use their automation to improve human communication with larger *systemic thinking*. Promise theory turned out to be useful here, because it was already a model of information and intent. The result was fascinating to watch: the tension between humans and automation is often about machines replacing humans; here, there was no doubt in their minds that automation was good, indeed they mastered it, but now they could see a side of it they had not realized before. With just a little attention to the way they formulated their promises, the automation and compliance self-reporting capability that came out of CFEngine would also be accessible to everyone, without any additional work from the engineers. All they needed was a comprehensible summary. The result led to a prototype tool to track business goals, to enable this business level transparency. This goal tracker went through many revisions and improvements, but the idea of it was actually more important than the tool itself, because its function lay in stimulating the human aspect of cooperation in the fabric of promises. It had a campfire, water-cooler effect that created a reason for business and IT to talk.

Thinking of their own promises, as contributing to those of the company as a whole, forced engineers to confront the manufacturing business as well as the issues at a simple level, and form a continuous, seamless relationship to company objectives. Going the other way, the technology could easily report the state of compliance of all of its automated promises over time, and summarize that as a dollar business value which should get the business people interested in the results. Now they would be able to see a simple story about the existence of promises the engineers had programmed to address their high level concerns. If they didn't understand what they were seeing, then business and engineering would actually have to talk to each other face to face to ask the questions! The change was a win-win for cooperation, and promised to mend a crack between the two parts of the company that tended to open up when they were under pressure.

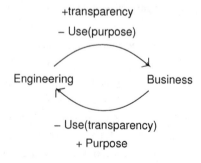

The engineers responded immediately to the simple suggestion of business goal alignment: not only was this straightforward to accomplish, it gave them a way to be better at doing their own jobs, and professional pride immediately kicked in. They could master this skill easily, and the result was that they felt that they were making a purposeful difference to the running of the whole organization.

[252]This discussion is based on the numerous talks and interviews with Adrian Cockcroft. I am grateful to Adrian for reading and verifying this description.

[253]Netflix refers to continuous improvement as anti-fragility, inspired by Taleb's book of the same name[Tal12].

[254]In the mid 2000s, the online retailer Amazon began to rent server infrastructure to online customers, and used the concept 'elastic scaling' to describe adding new virtual computers. This is not elastic scaling in the proper sense. The servers themselves are elastic up to the point the may be stretched to breaking point. Adding more servers is adaptive reinforced growth, but it is not elasticity.

[255]Non-metallic solids cannot normally generate dislocations that prevent cracks from spreading, and thus dissipate the energy of a failure process[Gor68].

[256]Few regard loosening system specification as a serious option, but a 'less is more' approach to certainty is a serious proposition. Not all materials can be magically molded to any shape and purpose. When there is no intrinsic bond within a material to satisfy a semantic transition, the only option is to combine the parts with some kind of joint. The expression 'when all else fails, use bloody great nails' goes perhaps a little too far, but the essence is correct.

[257]Recent trends in so-called Software Defined Networking might try to change that, but let us hope not for the sake of robustness.

[258]Paradoxically, the separation of concerns taught in software engineering courses is what leads to the plethora of interfaces between silos, which is the main source of complexity and brittleness. We have a long way to go to make information infrastructure into something as sophisticated as material science, nonetheless let's review just where we are today.

[259]I have been unable to find biographical dates for Charles Clos.

[260]It is related to the speed of waves in the solid, which in solids explains phenomena like refractive index, conductivity and other transport phenomena.

[261]See [Dis07, BD07].

[262]The first description of this concept in detail was given by Drexler in [Dre92].

[263]See my series of blog posts on this [Bur14a].

[264]We wrote about it in several versions before publishing the results in 2006[BF06].

[265]Today, the concept of information based money is coming to fruition, with phenomena like BitCoin.

[266]We eventually decided to present some of these methods in a short paper at the World Class Technology Summit in 2006. To my amazement, Siri came home with the prize for our work! We did not pursue the smart mall any further, but in 2008 I described the idea of molecular computing as a keynote to the International Conference on Autonomic Computing.

[267]Applying promises to spaces is a project that I began between the first and second editions of this book[Bur14b, Bur15a, Bur15b]. After laying out a necessary set of conditions to make a smart 'thinking space' I was intrigued to learn (via the 2014 Nobel prize) of the existence of place cells and grid cells in the brain, which seem to have the structure of a spatial coordinate system themselves[MKM08]. This work is nascent but fascinating.

[268] At the time of writing, much work is underway to build 'cloud computing' fabrics, composed of computational units called *process containers*. These fabrics are effectively shared semantic spaces, in which containers act as spacetime elements that keep certain promises. The Mesos project creates a management of spatial structure on top of a gas of these containers, while the Kubernetes project describes the self-healing promises to be kept by them, in a model which is an almost exact facsimile of CFEngine working at container timescales of seconds instead of minutes.

[269] See the work on Joint Cognitive Systems in [DH06].

[270] More recently, new media like film and video games could be added to the list, but the essential features are captured well by thinking about the ballet.

[271] There is still a prevalence of 'deployment' thinking in the industry. Information infrastructure is often planned out more like military maneuver. Each change is planned as a 'strike' scheduled as a campaign, a battle, or less destructively as house-moving operation. Once the battle is ended, the music is assumed to have ceased, the problem is conquered and one assumes that life continues. Organizations that operate in this manner even end up looking basically like military fire-fighting organizations. This practice is surely the legacy of an era in which change meant installing new equipment with a human workforce. The tools and challenges are different today, and the limitations of the old thinking are showing.

[272] Andrew Clay Shafer and Patrick Debois reputedly discussed the concept of agile infrastructure.

[273] In fact many of the concepts being revisited today were already present in IBM's mainframes in the 1960s, but in a closed proprietary form. The essential model was correct, and the following fifty years have rediscovered some of those basic truths by a circuitous route.

[274] However, the CFEngine vision has been bent somewhat under the inertia of thought in the information technology industry. It is still common for users to try to shoe horn CFEngine's promises into a linear timeline, one change at a time.

[275] The term recipe was used by Adam Jacob in his popular configuration management software Chef, but I am not making a particular association to Chef here. Adam chose this compelling name for a good reason, namely it is easy to understand.

[276] Measurements may be taken directly from CFEngine reports, as 'promises repaired'. The number depends on the detail with which companies orchestrate their infrastructure. From one customer, in a highly regulated industry, figures of between ten and a hundred minor corrections would be made per computer every few minutes. Some early work in this area was published in [Bur00a]

[277] See the work of Sydney Dekker in [Dek11] and related works.

[278] For a review of programming semantics in the context of infrastructure management, see Bergstra and Bethke[BB07b].

[279] Outages at Amazon and Netflix in 2012 number amongst the cases that I have privately confirmed were due to direct programming of infrastructure. I'm grateful to Adrian Cockcroft for insight into this.

[280] Today there is a focus on the notion of continuous delivery of new versions of software. Software itself is often cobbled together from many parts that do not interoperate smoothly, and a huge amount of complexity arises in trying to join the ouput of one piece to the input of another. File formats, information encodings, and all of the semantic and dynamic uncertainties of incompatible message formats come into play to make serial connection of parts a high risk sport. In the

future, we must develop more robust desired-end-state approaches to infrastructure components to get past the present fragility.

[281] Amdahl's law then says that the process will have a bottleneck which is the part that has to be serialized. It is sometimes said that a woman can make a baby in nine months, but 9 women cannot make a single baby in one.

[282] See the reviews and work by [BSF07, BSF, RB05, RB06].

[283] See a review in [Bae05, dA98]

[284] A review of cellular automata was given by Steven Wolfram, who has done a lot to study them over his career [Wol02].

[285] The game was published in Scientific American as a popular article [Gar70].

[286] See the article [BHS98].

[287] See Feynman's 1985 article reprinted in [HA96].

[288] See [RK12].

[289] For example, in music, a composer makes a solo voice loud by the vocal technique used by opera singers (before the age of microphones and amplification). Trying to use this individual technique in a choir would result in a mess of conflicting styles, rather than a homogenous texture. In information systems, a system engineer working with a single computer might make certain changes by hand, but trying to get two thousand people to make the changes to two thousand computers would not be a wise approach; and, mechanically copying one person's changes to two thousand computers would make it impossible to have a self-correcting feedback relationship between system and engineer. Progressing from agile improvisation to a programmed orchestration requires us to rethink methodology in a way that makes outcome as inevitable as possible.

[290] Staging environments usually go by less whimsical names like Development, Test, Production.

[291] Sanjai Narain presented a language called Alloy for attempting this in network management in 2005 [Nar05].

[292] See [Dem82].

[293] Ben Rockwood and John Willis have been instrumental in pointing this out to me.

[294] Martin Fowler reports that Kent Beck of the Three Rivers Institute in Switzerland, was deploying software every night on a project in the late '90s. See Beck's talk "Software G Forces" [Bec10].

[295] Timothy Fitz's blog based on what was going on at entertainment IMVU [Fit09]. John Allspaw and Paul Hammond's talk in 2009 [AH09] cemented many of the ideas and turned into a book by John Allspaw and Jessie Robbins' book [AR10] in 2010. Jez Humble and David Farley's also wrote a carefully written book [HF10] which grew out of the seed of a paper Humble co-presented at the conference Agile 2006: "The Deployment Production Line".

John Willis has written a good introduction to the history of DevOps in [Wil12]. It was Ben Rockwood who pointed out the connection between DevOps and Deming.

[296] The story about DevOps has grown particularly around its key orators, John Willis, Patrick Debois, Kris Buytaert, Damon Edwards, and others.

[297] See the review and reference in [Bur07].

[298] I don't want to use the specialist term closure here, because I that would be too strong. Closures are about trying to secure certainty. This approach is about dealing with uncertainty.

[299] Well known companies providing this service today are Akamai, Limelight and many others. These companies are likely to merge with 'cloud' providers over the years to come.

[300] In the future, cloud and content delivery networks are likely to converge into a single service, embedded into local devices in a highly pervasive way.

[301] Niles Eldredge and Stephen Jay Gould discussed the concept of punctuated equilibrium in evolutionary theory. The idea was that periods of little change persisted for some time, interspersed by bursts of sudden correlated change. There is no connection between their argument and my usage; it is simply a useful phrase.

[302] See [Gao09].

[303] Playing out an unfolding logic, in a convergent manner, is a problem that many engineers refuse to believe is possible without command and control logic. Melding on-the-fly interventions with a fully documented score is another. However, during the consulting with the technology company in chapter 12, I was asked to show how CFEngine could solve the following problem. In a computational pool it is important to keep a sufficient number of servers keeping their promises at all times, in order to keep the total business promise (the Service Level Agreement). However, this conflicts with another promise, which is to make sure that the machines are up to date. Certain fundamental updates require a computer to be restarted, but that means it has to be taken out of service. How then, can we make computers promise to update and restart only if doing so would not result in breaking the Service Level Agreement.

There are two aspects to this. It is possible to solve the problem entirely by orchestrating preconditions to satisfy sequencing (see chapter 9), and using machine learning to fill in the relationship role. It can also be constrained to happen between definite start and end times. This will not be deterministic: no one can predict the exact sequence of changes that will be played out, because the adaptation depends on jobs arriving from a completely unpredictable environment, fed by messages from multiple sources. The uncertainty, however is no greater than with a manual process.

The key challenge, however, was to make sure that no fewer than some number of machines was always running. If you believe in determinism, then you would say 'well, we poll the machines to see how many are running', but what about the case where machines are unable to respond to that signal? In this case, it doesn't matter. If some machines are running but do not respond to the coordination for some reason, then all is still well. However, not all problems can be solved in this way. What if the criterion had been 'make sure that no machines are running service X'? Then, the uncertainty about information becomes a liability. If the machines don't answer, it doesn't mean they are not there.

There is thus a class of problems that can be solved reliably, in spite of incomplete information, and another class that is fundamentally uncertain. This applies even to imperative methods, and it emphasizes why it is important to have some reliable knowledge about system state. Distributed convergent patterns, based on pre-conditions, as with CFEngine's periodic convergence and generalized by Alva Couch's maelstrom method, can be constructed to orchestrate this kind of problem. In 2012, I bit the bullet and published a few of the orchestration patterns, to prove a point. I wanted to illustrate how short performances could be interspersed throughout a continuous maintenance regimen, without introducing an ad hoc 'deployment' process. This is what I believe Rimsky-Korsakov meant when he wrote that orchestration was about planning out the totality of the performance, not just bits of it. Resistance to this kind of thinking is rife, however. We are still in the midst of a modern Newtonian to quantum shift in this area.

Inevitably, engineers find these cases hard to understand, compared to a more familiar linear flow chart approach, but this is an approach that will bring greater certainty, scalability and ultimately confidence and comprehension of infrastructure for the future.

Consider the benefits. Scale versus complexity is an interesting dilemma. Scale is a tangible problem, but complexity is somewhat abstract. As a result people tend to get more into trouble over complexity. With scale, one has plenty of issues: just managing the names and addresses of all the parts is a challenge by itself, for instance. With complexity, there are usually distinctions and hence decisions to be made.

Pools of machine resources bring scale without complexity. If machines play the same role in an infrastructure are usually known as *clusters*. Like the molecule in figure 12.9, a cluster consists of many 'identical' (or at least symmetrical) slave computers sharing the load of requests through a load balancing funnel. The approach is easily applied to web services, databases and other common functions. The so-called 'Map-Reduce' framework, reinvented at Google as a form of compute cluster, has been received a lot of attention in the industry as a data processing engine. It maps parallel tasks into threads and then collapses or reduces the results into a coherent unit. It can work across large numbers of computers. Its semantics are very low level and quite limited however. Its strength lies in reducing tasks to a dynamical scaling problem, by allowing only very simple semantics. The promises kept by each slave computer to a master controller are essentially so simple that dynamics can scale unimpeded.

Infrastructure itself is like a Shannon message. If there is a high level of redundancy or pooling, then the actual information involved may be compressed, so that, instead of thinking of a thousand single computers, one thinks of a single pool. However, if there is *semantic* diversity, a multitude of roles and purposes, the Shannon message cannot be compressed, and a system will be inherently complex. Scale with complexity is the killer.

For example, the world's largest search engines have massive scale, but their informational complexity is low, because the environments are highly compressible. A bank or manufacturing organization, on the other hand, might not have the same scale, but much higher complexity, due to the multiplicity of different lines of business and applications running.

This is just like an orchestra: the complexity comes not from the number of violins, but from how many different instrumental voices there are in the composition. Information infrastructure presents a harder problem, because the components of its orchestra may change roles quite often. The resulting collective behaviour starts to approach biological levels of complexity. Imagine then, when computers are literally everywhere, as they will be in just another decade, the casual observer simply won't know what is being used for what purpose, and yet infrastructure engineers will have to.

It is complexity that leads to the greatest difficulty in comprehending systems, because complexity implies strong coupling that prevents us from mere rescaling away patterns. The question we face going forward therefore becomes: what kind of tools and methods can one envisage to handle such complexity?

[304] An amusing episode in Jerry Seinfeld's comedy show has stuck in my mind over the years, in which the character George trying to maintain separate lives and personae (as many of us do) at work and in his private life. When someone from his workplace is inducted into the circle of friends, he screams: "Worlds are colliding, Jerry! Worlds are colliding!"

[305] When change is actually deployed, improper planning leads to mistakes. One of the things that astounds me the most in the field of computer science is the extent to which engineers want to believe in the existence of an 'undo' button for any possible change. Mistakes in orchestration can be undone, but mistakes in performance can't. Undo buttons are common in isolated software systems like editors, where a single timeline exists. Each change can be represented as a deterministic transaction, relative to the previous state. In such circumstances, each change

operation has an inverse because nothing else interferes with the data in between operations. This is a highly special case, however. As soon as there are multiple degrees of freedom, that allow data to change in parallel, undoing is provably impossible.

The larger the change, the greater the more irreversible a change becomes. In any parallel, open system reversibility is essentially impossible.

[306] My handwritten notebooks have contained sketches for a theory of 'network interferometry' since the idea occurred to me after a chance conversation with a geophysicist in 2005, about using constructive and destructive interference.

[307] There are many technologies and tools for building and maintaining information infrastructure, at the time of writing. I don't want to catalogue these here. Some of these were spawned from the CFEngine project over divergences of opinion about how to trade-off conflicting interests, some even use notions of self-repair. Even users of the CFEngine software do not hold exclusively to what I would consider the optimal approach. These are the realities of practice over ideology.

References

[AB07]   D. Aredo and M. Burgess. On the consistency of distributed knowledge. In *Proceedings of MACE 2007*, volume 6 of *Multicon Lecture Notes*. Multicon Verlag, 2007.

[ABH 6]   D. Aredo, M. Burgess, and S. Hagen. A promise theory view on the policies of object orientation and the service oriented architecture. *unpublished*, 2005-6.

[Ada07]   M.P. Adaa. Ontology for host-based anomaly detection. Master's thesis, Oslo University, 2007.

[AH09]   J. Allspaw and P. Hammond. 10 deploys per day: Dev & ops cooperation at flickr. Slideshare, 2009. http://www.slideshare.net/jallspaw/10-deploys-per-day-dev-and-ops-cooperation-at-flickr.

[And94]   P. Anderson. Towards a high level machine configuration system. Proceedings of the Eighth Systems Administration Conference (LISA VIII) (USENIX Association: Berkeley, CA):19, 1994.

[AR10]   J. Allspaw and J. Robbins. *Web Operations: Keeping the Data On Time*. O Reilly, New York, 2010.

[Are04]   Demissie B. Aredo. *Formal Development of Open Distributed Systems: Integration of UML and PVS*. PhD thesis, Department of Informatics, University of Oslo, Norway, 2004.

[Ari12]   D. Ariely. *The Honest Truth About Dishonest*. Harper Collins, New York, 2012.

[Ash52]   W.R. Ashby. *Design for a brain*. J. Wiley & Sons, 1952.

[Ash56]   W.R. Ashby. *An introduction to cybernetics*. J. Wiley & Sons, 1956.

[Ati81]   P.S. Atiyah. *Promises, Morals and Law.* Clarendon Press, Oxford, 1981.

[Axe84]   R. Axelrod. *The Evolution of Co-operation.* Penguin Books, 1990 (1984).

[Axe86]   R. Axelrod. An evolutionary approach to norms. *American Political Science Review,* 80(4):1095–1111, 1986.

[Axe87]   R. Axelrod. *Genetic Algorithms and Simulated Annealing (ed L. Davis),* chapter The Evolution of Strategies in the Iterated Prisoner's Dilemma, pages 32–41. Pittman, 1987.

[Axe97]   R. Axelrod. *The Complexity of Cooperation: Agent-based Models of Competition and Collaboration.* Princeton Studies in Complexity, Princeton, 1997.

[Bae05]   J.C.M. Baeten. A brief history of process algebra. *Theoretical Computer Science,* pages 131–146, 2005.

[BAJ00]   A.L. Barabasi, R. Albert, and H. Jeong. Scale-free characteristics of random networks: topology of the world-wide web. *Physica A,* 281:69, 2000.

[Bar02]   A.L. Barabási. *Linked.* (Perseus, Cambridge, Massachusetts), 2002.

[BB06]   J. Bergstra and M. Burgess. Local and global trust based on the concept of promises. *http://arxiv.org/abs/0912.4637,* 2006.

[BB07a]   K. Begnum and M. Burgess. Validating the promise theory syntax using rewriting logic. *Lecture Notes on Computer Science,* 4543 (Proceedings of the first International Conference on Autonomous Infrastructure and Security (AIMS)):203–206, 2007.

[BB07b]   J. Bergstra and I. Bethke. *Handbook of Network and System Administration,* chapter System Administration and the Scientific Method. Elsevier, 2007.

[BB14]   J.A. Bergstra and M. Burgess. *Promise Theory: Principles and Applications.* $\chi t \mathcal{A}xis$ Press, 2014.

[BBJF05]   K. Begnum, M. Burgess, T.M. Jonassen, and S. Fagernes. Summary of the stability of adaptive service level agreements. In *Proceedings of the 6th IEEE Workshop on Policies for Distributed Systems and Networks,* pages 111–114. IEEE Press, 2005.

[BBS94]   K. Begnum, M. Burgess, and J. Sechrest. Autonomic infrastructure in a virtual grid landscape from abstract roles. *unpublished,* 1994.

[BC11]   M. Burgess and A. Couch. On system rollback and totalised
            fields an algebraic approach to system change. *Journal of
            Logic and Algebraic Programming*, 80:427–443, 2011.

[BCE03]   M. Burgess, G. Canright, and K. Engø. A graph theoretical
            model of computer security: from file access to social engi-
            neering. *Submitted to International Journal of Information
            Security*, 2003.

[BCS⁺03]   M. Burgess, G. Canright, T. Hassel Stang, F. Pourbayat,
            K. Engo, and Å. Weltzien. Archipelago: A network security
            analysis tool. *Proceedings of the Seventeenth Systems Ad-
            ministration Conference (LISA XVII) (USENIX Association:
            Berkeley, CA)*, page 153, 2003.

[BD07]   M. Burgess and M. Disney. Understanding scalability in
            network aggregation with continuous monitoring. In *Lec-
            ture Notes on Computer Science, Proc. 18th IFIP/IEEE
            Distributed Systems: Operations and Management (DSOM
            2007)*, volume (submitted). Springer, 2007.

[BDT99]   E. Bonabeau, M. Dorigo, and G. Theraulaz. *Swarm Intelli-
            gence: From Natural to Artificial Systems*. Oxford University
            Press, Oxford, 1999.

[Bec10]   K. Beck. Software g forces: The ef-
            fects of acceleration. Slideshare, 2010.
            http://www.slideshare.net/KentBeck/software-g-forces.

[BFa]   M. Burgess and S. Fagernes. Pervasive computing manage-
            ment: A model of network policy with local autonomy. *IEEE
            Transactions on Software Engineering*, page (submitted).

[BFb]   M. Burgess and S. Fagernes. Voluntary economic cooper-
            ation in policy based management. *IEEE Transactions on
            Network and Service Management*, page (submitted).

[BF06]   M. Burgess and S. Fagernes. Autonomic pervasive comput-
            ing: A smart mall scenario using promise theory. *Proceed-
            ings of the 1st IEEE International Workshop on Modelling
            Autonomic Communications Environments (MACE); Multi-
            con verlag 2006. ISBN 3-930736-05-5*, pages 133–160, 2006.

[BF07a]   M. Burgess and S. Fagernes. Laws of systemic organiza-
            tion and collective behaviour in ensembles. In *Proceedings
            of MACE 2007*, volume 6 of *Multicon Lecture Notes*. Multi-
            con Verlag, 2007.

[BF07b]   M. Burgess and S. Fagernes. Norms and swarms. *Lecture
            Notes on Computer Science*, 4543 (Proceedings of the first

International Conference on Autonomous Infrastructure and Security (AIMS)):107–118, 2007.

[BHRS01] M. Burgess, H. Haugerud, T. Reitan, and S. Straumsnes. Measuring host normality. *ACM Transactions on Computing Systems*, 20:125–160, 2001.

[BHS98] M. Burgess, H. Haugerud, and A. Strandlie. Object orientation and visualization of physics in two dimensions. *Computers in Physics*, 12:274, 1998.

[BK07] M .Burgess and L. Kristiansen. *Handbook of Network and System Administration*, chapter On the Complexity of Change and Configuration Management. Elsevier, 2007.

[Boo10a] G. Boole. *An Investigation of the Laws of Thought*. Forgotten Books, New York, 2010.

[Boo10b] G. Boole. *The Mathematical Analysis of Logic: Being an Essay Towards a Calculus of Deductive Reasoning*. Forgotten Books, New York, 2010.

[BR07] M. Burgess and T. Reitan. A risk analysis of disk backup or repository maintenance. *Science of Computer Programming*, 64:312–331, 2007.

[BR10a] M. Burgess and C. Rowland. The business value of system administration. *USENIX ;login:*, 35(2):23–28, 2010.

[BR10b] M. Burgess and C. Rowland. *A Sysadmin's Guide to Navigating the Business World*. USENIX, 2010.

[Bre00] E. Brewer. Towards robust distributed systems. 2000.

[Bre12] E. Brewer. Cap twelve years later: How the "rules" have changed. 2012.

[BSF] R. Badonnel, R. State, and O. Festor. Probabilistic management of ad-hoc networks. In *Proceedings of 10th IFIP/IEEE Network Operations and Management Symposium NOMS 2006*.

[BSF07] R. Badonnel, R. State, and O. Festor. *Handbook of Network and System Administration*, chapter Management of Ad Hoc Networks. Elsevier, 2007.

[Buc02] M. Buchanan. *Nexus: Small Worlds and the Groundbreaking Science of Networks*. (W.W.Norton & Co., New York), 2002.

[Bura] M. Burgess. Business alignment through the eye-glass of promises. In *Keynote to BDIM workshop and NOMS2008, Brasil*.

[Burb] M. Burgess. Promise you a rose garden. http://research.iu.hio.no/papers/rosegarden.pdf.

[Bur95]   M. Burgess. A site configuration engine. *Computing systems (MIT Press: Cambridge MA)*, 8:309, 1995.

[Bur98]   M. Burgess. Computer immunology. *Proceedings of the Twelth Systems Administration Conference (LISA XII) (USENIX Association: Berkeley, CA)*, page 283, 1998.

[Bur00a]   M. Burgess. Evaluation of cfengine's immunity model of system maintenance. *Proceedings of the 2nd international system administration and networking conference (SANE2000)*, 2000.

[Bur00b]   M. Burgess. The kinematics of distributed computer transactions. *International Journal of Modern Physics*, **C**12:759–789, 2000.

[Bur00c]   M. Burgess. Needles in the craystack, when machines get sick. *USENIX ;login:*, 25(8), 2000.

[Bur00d]   M. Burgess. *Principles of Network and System Administration*. J. Wiley & Sons, Chichester, 2000.

[Bur00e]   M. Burgess. Thermal, non-equilibrium phase space for networked computers. *Physical Review E*, 62:1738, 2000.

[Bur02]   M. Burgess. *Classical Covariant Fields*. Cambridge University Press, Cambridge, 2002.

[Bur03]   M. Burgess. On the theory of system administration. *Science of Computer Programming*, 49:1, 2003.

[Bur04a]   M. Burgess. *Analytical Network and System Administration: Managing Human-Computer Systems*. J. Wiley & Sons, Chichester, 2004.

[Bur04b]   M. Burgess. Configurable immunity for evolving human-computer systems. *Science of Computer Programming*, 51:197, 2004.

[Bur05]   Mark Burgess. An approach to understanding policy based on autonomy and voluntary cooperation. In *IFIP/IEEE 16th international workshop on distributed systems operations and management (DSOM), in LNCS 3775*, pages 97–108, 2005.

[Bur07]   M. Burgess. *Handbook of Network and System Administration*, chapter System Administration and Business. Elsevier, 2007.

[Bur09]   Mark Burgess. Knowledge management and promises. *Lecture Notes on Computer Science*, 5637:95–107, 2009.

[Bur12a]   M. Burgess. Deconstructing the 'cap theorem' for cm and devops. part 1: The special theory of relativity for distributed systems. 2012.

[Bur12b]   M. Burgess. *New Research on Knowledge Management Models and Methods.*, chapter What's wrong with knowledge management? The emergence of ontology. Number ISBN 979-953-307-226-4. InTech, 2012.

[Bur14a]   M. Burgess. The making of a software wind-tunnel (1-3). http://markburgess.org/blog_windtunnel.html, April 2014.

[Bur14b]   M. Burgess. Spacetimes with semantics (i): Notes on theory and formalism. *http://arxiv.org/abs/1411.5563*, 2014.

[Bur15a]   M. Burgess. Spacetimes with semantics (ii): tenancy and the scaling of agency. *(in preparation)*, 2015.

[Bur15b]   M. Burgess. Spacetimes with semantics (iii): the structure of functional knowledge spaces. *(in preparation)*, 2015.

[Bus45]   V. Bush. As we may think. *The Atlantic*, 1945.

[Cas93]   C. Castelfranchi. Commitments: From individual intentions to groups and organizations. In *Proceedings of the AAAI Workshop on AI and Theories of Groups and Organizations: Conceptual and Empirical Research*, page 932, 1993.

[CD]   J.D. Carrillo and M. Dewatripont. Promises, promises. Technical Report 172782000000000058, UCLA Department of Economics, Levines's Bibliography.

[CD01a]   A. Couch and N. Daniels. The maelstrom: Network service debugging via "ineffective procedures". *Proceedings of the Fifteenth Systems Administration Conference (LISA XV) (USENIX Association: Berkeley, CA)*, page 63, 2001.

[CD01b]   A. Couch and N. Daniels. The maelstrom: Network service debugging via "ineffective procedures". *Proceedings of the Fifteenth Systems Administration Conference (LISA XV) (USENIX Association: Berkeley, CA)*, page 63, 2001.

[CG99a]   A. Couch and M. Gilfix. It's elementary, dear watson: Applying logic programming to convergent system management processes. *Proceedings of the Thirteenth Systems Administration Conference (LISA XIII) (USENIX Association: Berkeley, CA)*, page 123, 1999.

[CG99b]   A. Couch and M. Gilfix. It's elementary, dear watson: Applying logic programming to convergent system management processes. *Proceedings of the Thirteenth Systems Administration Conference (LISA XIII) (USENIX Association: Berkeley, CA)*, page 123, 1999.

[cha14]   Distributed systems and the end of the api. http://www.infoq.com/presentations/problems-distributed-systems, September 2014.

[Cla62]   A.C. Clarke. *Profiles of the Future*. Victor Gollancz, London, 1962.

[Cla92]   A.C. Clarke. *How the world was one*. Victor Gollancz, New York, 1992.

[CLM99]   E. M. Clarke, D. E. Long, and K. L. Mcmillan. Compositional model checking. MIT Press, 1999.

[Clo53]   C. Clos. A study of non-blocking switching networks. *Bell System Technical Journal*, 32(2):406424, 1953.

[Clo10]   F. Close. *Neutrino*. Oxford University Press, Oxford, 2010.

[Coa37]   R. Coase. The nature of the firm. *Economica*, 4(16):386–405, 1937.

[Cou96]   A. Couch. Slink: Simple, effective filesystem maintenance abstractions for community-based administration. *Proceedings of the Tenth Systems Administration Conference (LISA X) (USENIX Association: Berkeley, CA)*, page 205, 1996.

[Cou07]   Alva Couch. *Handbook of Network and System Administration*, chapter System Configuration Management. Elsevier, 2007.

[CS03]   A. Couch and Y. Sun. On the algebraic structure of convergence. *LNCS, Proc. 14th IFIP/IEEE International Workshop on Distributed Systems: Operations and Management, Heidelberg, Germany*, pages 28–40, 2003.

[CS04]   Alva Couch and Yizhan Sun. On observed reproducibility in network configuration management. In *Science of Computer Programming*, pages 215–253. Elsevier, Inc, 2004.

[Cur11]   J.P. Curry. Threshold monitoring, alarm fatigue, and the patterns of unexpected hospital death. *Newsletter of The Official Journal of Anesthesia Patient Safety Foundation*, Fall, 2011. http://www.apsf.org/newsletters/html/2011/fall/07_threshold.htm on 30/1/13.

[dA98]   W. Van der Aalst. The application of petri nets to workflow management. *Journal of Circuits, Systems and Computers*, 8(1):21–66, 1998.

[Daw76]   R. Dawkins. *The Selfish Gene*. Oxford University Press, Oxford, 1976.

[Daw90]   R. Dawkins. *The Extended Phenotype*. Oxford University Press, Oxford, 1990.

[Dek11]   S. Dekker. *Drift Into Failure*. Ashgate Publishing, Surrey, 2011.

[Dem82]   W.E. Deming. *Out of Crisis*. Massachusetts Institute of Technology, 1982.

[DH06]   D.D.Woods and E. Hollnagel. *Joint Cognitive Systems: Patterns in Cognitive Systems Engineering.* Taylor & Francis, New York, 2006.

[Die06]   J.L.G. Dietz. *Enterprise ontology.* Springer, 2006.

[Dij74]   Edsger W. Dijkstra. Self-stabilizing systems in spite of distributed control. *Commun. ACM*, 17(11):643–644, November 1974.

[Dis07]   M. Disney. Exploring patterns for scalability of system administration with topology constraints. Master's thesis, Oslo University, 2007.

[Dre92]   K.E. Drexler. *Nanosystems: Molecular Machinery, Manifacturing and Computation.* John Wiley & Sons, New York, 1992.

[Dun96]   R. Dunbar. *Grooming, Gossip and the Evolution of Language.* Faber and Faber, London, 1996.

[Dys97]   G. Dyson. *Darwin Among the Machines.* Penguin, London, 1997.

[DZ83]   John D Day and Hubert Zimmermann. The osi reference model. *Proceedings of the IEEE*, 71(12):1334–1340, 1983.

[EKP98]   R. Endl, G. Knolmayer, and M. Pfahrer. Modelling processes and workflows by business rules. In *Proceedings of the 1st European Workshop on Workflow and Process Management*, pages 47–56, 1998.

[Eva97]   R. Evard. An analysis of unix system configuration. *Proceedings of the Eleventh Systems Administration Conference (LISA XI) (USENIX Association: Berkeley, CA)*, page 179, 1997.

[Fin97]   J. Finke. Automation of site configuration management. *Proceedings of the Eleventh Systems Administration Conference (LISA XI) (USENIX Association: Berkeley, CA)*, page 155, 1997.

[Fit09]   T. Fitz. Continuous deployment. Blog, 2009. http://timothyfitz.com/2009/02/08/continuous-deployment/.

[Fox81]   M.S. Fox. An organizational view of distributed systems. *IEEE Transactions on Systems, Man and Cybernetics*, SMC-1:70–80, 1981.

[Fri81]   C. Fried. *Contract as promises.* Harvard University Press, 1981.

[Gao09]   W. Gao. Process management and orchestration. Master's thesis, Oslo University, 2009.

[Gar70]   M. Gardner. Mathematical games - the fantastic combina-
           tions of john conway's new solitaire game life. *Scientific
           American*, 223:120–123, 1970.

[Gib11]   J.C. Gibbings. *Dimensional Analysis*. Springer Verlag, Lon-
           don, 2011.

[Gil93]   M. Gilbert. Is an agreement and exchange of promises? *Jour-
           nal of Philosophy*, 90(12):627–649, 1993.

[Gle92]   J. Gleick. *Genius: The Life and Science of Richard Feynman*.
           Pantheon, New York, 1992.

[Gor68]   J.E. Gordon. *The New Science of Strong Materials, or Why
           You Don't Fall Through the Floor*. Penguin Books, London,
           1968.

[HA28]   D. Hilbert and W. Ackermann. *Grundzüge der theoretischen
           Logik*. Springer, Berlin, 1928.

[HA96]   A.J.G. Hey and R.W. Allen, editors. *Feynman Lectures on
           Computation*. Perseus, Reading, 1996.

[Har68]   G. Hardin. The tragedy of the commons. *Science*, 162:1243–
           1248, 1968.

[HD03]   R.A. Hill and R.I.M. Dunbar. Social network size in humans.
           Human Nature, 14:53–72, 2003.

[Hey07]   F. Heylighen. *Open Source Jahrbuch*, chapter Why is Open
           Access Development so Successful? Stigmergic organization
           and the economics of information. Lehrmanns Media, 2007.

[HF10]   J. Humble and D. Farley. *Continuous Delivery: Reliable Soft-
           ware Releases Through Build, Test, and Deployment Automa-
           tion*. Addison Wesley, New Jersey, 2010.

[Hic11]   R. Hickey. Simple made easy. Talk at QConn, 2011.
           http://www.infoq.com/presentations/Simple-Made-Easy.

[HM92]   J.Y. Halpern and Y. Moses. A guide to completeness and
           complexity of modal logics of knowledge and belief. *Artifi-
           cial Intelligence*, 54:311–379, 1992.

[Hod77]   W. Hodges. *Logic: An Introduction to Elementary Logic*.
           Penguin, London, 1977.

[Hod92]   A. Hodges. *Alan Turing, The Enigma*. Vintage, London,
           1992.

[Hof81]   D. Hofstadter. *Gödel, Escher, Bach: an eternal golden braid*.
           Penguin books., Middlesex, England, 1979/1981.

[Hol98]   J.H. Holland. *Emergence: from chaos to order*. Oxford Uni-
           versity Press, 1998.

[Hor96]   J. Horgan. *The End of Science*. Addison Wesley, New York, 1996.

[jCMWD98] J. j. Ch. Meyer, R. J. Wieringa, and F. P. M. Dignum. The role of deontic logic in the specification of information systems. In *Logics for Databases and Information Systems*. Kluwer, 1998.

[Joh01]   S. Johnson. *Emergence*. Penguin Press, 2001.

[Kah11]   D. Kahneman. *Thinking, Fast and Slow*. Penguin, London, 2011.

[Kar09]   F. Karlson. *Language Complexity As an Evolving Variable*, chapter Origin and maintenance of clausal embedding complexity, pages 192–202. Oxford University Press, 2009.

[KE01]   J. Kennedy and R.C. Eberhart. *Swarm Intelligence*. Morgan Kaufmann (Academic Press), 2001.

[KN04]   K.B. Korb and A.E. Nicholson. *Bayesian Artificial Intelligence*. Chapman and Hall, 2004.

[K.P59]   K.Popper. *The Logic of Scientific Discovery*. Basic books, New York, 1959.

[Kra12]   L.M. Krauss. *Quantum Man: Richard Feynman's Life in Science*. W. W. Norton & Company, New York, 2012.

[KT01]   I. Fosterand C. Kesselman and S. Tuecke. The anatomy of the grid: Enabling scalable virtual organizations. *International Journal of Supercomputer Application*, 15(3):200 222, 2001.

[Lon84]   M.S. Longair. *Theoretical concepts in physics*. Cambridge University Press, Cambridge, 1984.

[McI91]   R.J. McIntosh. Early urban clusters in china and africa. *J. Fld archeology*, 18:199–212, 1991.

[MKM08]   E.I. Moser, E. Kropff, and M.B. Moser. Place cells, grid cells, and the brain's spatial representation system. *Annual Review of Neuroscience*, 31:69–89, 2008.

[Moo88]   Gregory H Moore. The emergence of first-order logic. *History and Philosophy of Modern Mathematics*, page 95, 1988.

[Mum64]   L. Mumford. *The Myth of the Machine*. Ballentine, New York, 1964.

[Nar05]   S. Narain. Network configuration management via model finding. *Proceedings of the Nineteenth Systems Administration Conference (LISA XIX) (USENIX Association: Berkeley, CA)*, page 155, 2005.

[Nas96]   J.F. Nash. *Essays on Game Theory*. Edward Elgar, Cheltenham, 1996.

[Nas98]   S. Nasar. *A Beautiful Mind*. Simon and Schuster, London, 1998.

[NM44]   J.V. Neumann and O. Morgenstern. *Theory of games and economic behaviour*. Princeton University Press, Princeton, 1944.

[Ost90]   E. Ostrom. *Governing the Commons*. Cambridge, 1990.

[Ost05]   E. Ostrom. *Understanding Institutional Diversity*. Princeton University Press, 2005.

[Pea88]   J. Pearl. *Probabilistic Reasoning in Intelligent Systems: Networks of Plausible Inference*. Morgen Kaufmann, San Francisco, 1988.

[Pho08]   N. Phooripoom. A promising cfengine linux router. Master's thesis, Oslo University, 2008.

[Pin95]   D.H. Pink. *Drive*. Riverhead, New York, 1995.

[Pla50]   M. Planck. *Scientific autobiography and other papers*. Williams and Norgate, London, 1950.

[Pri96]   I. Prigogine. *The End of Certainty*. Simon & Schuster, New York, 1996.

[RB05]   O. Festor R. Badonnel, R. State. Management of mobile ad-hoc networks : Information model and probe-based architecture. *Journal of Network Management,*, 15:335–347, 2005.

[RB06]   O. Festor R. Badonnel, R. State. Fault montoring in ad-hoc networks based on information theory. *Networking*, pages 427–438, 2006.

[Rep11]   United Nations Report. Humanitys voracious consumption of natural resources unsustainable - un report. *United Nations Website*, 2011.

[Rhe02]   Howard Rheingold. *Smart Mobs: The Next Social Revolution*. Perseus Books, 2002.

[RK12]   N. Rimsky-Korsakov. *Principles of Orchestration*. Dover, New York, 1891,1912.

[SC07]   Yizhan Sun and Alva Couch. *Handbook of Network and System Administration*, chapter Complexity of System Configuration Management. Elsevier, 2007.

[Sch70]   J. Schwinger. *Particles, Sources and Fields (Volume 1)*. (Addison Wesley, California), 1970.

[Sch00]   B. Schneier. *Secrets and Lies*. J. Wiley & Sons, London, 2000.

[SDG10]   B. Schroeder, S. Damouras, and P. Gill. Understanding latent sector errors and how to protect against them. *Proceedings of USENIX FAST conference*, 2010.

[Sea83]   J.R. Searle. *Intentionality*. Cambridge University Press, Cambridge, 1983.

[Sha40]   C.E. Shannon. *An algebra for theoretical genetics*. Massachusetts Institute of Technology, Dept. of Mathematics, 1940.

[Sha97]   S. Shapiro. Splitting the difference: The historical necessity of synthesis in software engineering. *IEEE Annals of the History of Computing*, 19(1), 1997.

[She11]   H. Sheinman, editor. *Promises and Agreements*. Oxford, 2011.

[Sin99]   S. Singh. *The Code Book*. Fourth Estate, London, 1999.

[Sin12]   M.P. Singh. Commitments in multiagent systems: Some history, some confusions, some controversies, some prospects. In *The Goals of Cognition. Essays in Honor of Cristiano Castelfranchi*, pages 1–29, 2012.

[SM93]   M.S. Sloman and J. Moffet. Policy hierarchies for distributed systems management. *Journal of Network and System Management*, 11(9):1404, 1993.

[Smi58]   Norman Kemp Smith, editor. *Descartes: Philosophical Writings*, chapter Meditations on First Philosophy. Modern Library, 1958.

[Sti90]   S.M. Stigler. *The History of Statistics: The Measurement of Uncertainty before 1900*. Harvard University Press, Cambridge, 1990.

[Sto52]   S.J. Stoljar. The ambiguity of promise. *Northwestern University law Review*, 47(1):1–20, 1952.

[SW49]   C.E. Shannon and W. Weaver. *The mathematical theory of communication*. University of Illinois Press, Urbana, 1949.

[Tal12]   Nassim Nicholas Taleb. *Antifragile: Things that Gain from Disorder*. Allen Lane, London, UK, 2012.

[Tof70]   A. Toffler. *Future Shock*. Random House, 1970.

[Tof80]   A. Toffler. *The Third Wave*. Bantam, 1980.

[Tof90]   A. Toffler. *Power Shift*. Bantam, 1990.

[Unk87]   Unknown. Nonsense. Australian Town and Country Journal, 1887. http://trove.nla.gov.au/ndp/del/page/5100745.

[US]   Yathiraj B. Udupi and Munindar P. Singh. Multiagent policy architecture for virtual business organizations. In *Proceedings of the IEEE International Conference on Services Computing (SCC)*.

[Var13a] Various. Air france flight 447. *Wikepedia*, 2013. http://en.wikipedia.org/wiki/Air_France_Flight_447.

[Var13b] Various. Imperial wireless chain. *Wikepedia*, 2013. http://en.wikipedia.org/wiki/Imperial_Wireless_Chain.

[Var13c] Various. John hancock tower. *Wikepedia*, 2013. http://en.wikipedia.org/wiki/John_Hancock_Tower#Engineering_flaws.

[vN95] J. von Neumann. *The Neumann Compendium*. World Scientific, Singapore, 1995.

[Wat99] D.J. Watts. *Small Worlds*. (Princeton University Press, Princeton), 1999.

[Wes09] A. West. Nasa study on flight software complexity. Technical report, NASA Technical Excellence Program, 2009.

[WGB99] M. Weiser, R. Gold, and J.S. Brown. The origins of ubiquitous computing research at parc in the late 1980s. *IBM Systems Journal*, 38:693, 1999.

[Wil12] J. Willis. The convergence of devops. Blog, 2012. http://itrevolution.com/the-convergence-of-devops/.

[Wol98] L. Wolpert. *The Principles of Development*. Oxford Univeristy Press, Oxford, 1998.

[Wol02] S. Wolfram. *A New Kind of Science*. Wolfram Media, 2002.

[Wol07] M. Wolf. *Proust and the Squid: the story and science of the reading brain*. Harper Collins, New York, 2007.

[Woo02] M. Wooldridge. *An Introduction to MultiAgent Systems*. Wiley, Chichester, 2002.

[WR29] E.T. Whittaker and G. Robinson. *Calculus of observations*. Blackie and Son Ltd., London, 1929.

[Yem93] Yechiam Yemini. The osi network management model. *Communications Magazine, IEEE*, 31(5):20–29, 1993.

[ZMZ07] Y-E. Zheng, H. Ma, and L. Zhang. A temporal logic based grid workflow model and scheduling scheme. In *Proceedings of the 6th International Conference on Grid and Cooperative Computing*, 2007.

[ZSHD04] W.X. Zhou, S. Sornette, R.A. Hill, and R.I.M. Dunbar. Discrete hierarchical organization of social group sizes. *Proc. Royal Soc.*, 272:439–444, 2004.

Index

Acknowledgements

In this, my first attempt writing popular science, I have striven to tell a complex story of ideas—one that has lived implicitly inside my mind for many years, without particular form or narrative. The act of finally putting it down on the page precipitated many practical problems, such as how much foreknowledge to expect of readers, and how to keep the story both concise and interesting to a wide readership. It was a particular challenge to get everything into an order that would maximize the understanding of the reader, without becoming laborious. Inevitably my version of the story will have its shortcomings, and while potentially improved by the advice of friends and colleagues, I was not able to accommodate all suggestions, and I am entirely responsible for the final result. In some ways, this is the story of the thinking behind CFEngine, but I have avoided discussing details of CFEngine as it is now a commercial company, and I did not want to sully a good story with any taint of marketing or suggestion of competitive bias. Thus, I have not attempted to suggest that CFEngine is better or worse than its competition, I have limited to discussion to an estimation of its own success in solving certain issues.

My understanding of the issues in the book owes much to discussions with colleagues, students and friends over the years. I'd like to mention a few of those that have given me pause to think, in no particular order:

Siri Fagernes, Kyrre Begnum, John Sechrest, Steve Traugott, Kenth Skaar, Luke Kanies, Adam Jacobs, John Willis, Matt Disney, Æleen

Frisch Geoffrey Canright, Kenth Engø Monsen, Anil Somayaji, Juergen Schoenwalder, Olivier Festor, Rémi Badonnel, John Strassner, Rolf Stadler, Jacques Sauve, Claudio Bartolini, Carolyn Rowland, Nicole Forsgren Velasquez, Reynold Jabbour, and Steve Pepper.

A special mention must go to my friends and collaborators Alva Couch, and Jan Bergstra, without whom my work would surely have been far less than it became. I am also humbled by the response of many casual readers of my work who have come out in support of promise theory's aims and findings.

For the preparation of this book, I am grateful to Jez Humble for generous assistance with historical matters on continuous delivery, as well as excellent discussions and unprovoked encouragement. Thanks to John Allspaw for plying me with references in the field of Joint Cognitive Systems. The staff at Etsy generously answered many questions I had while testing the resilience of some of these ideas, and I've long profited from a sharing of ideas and goals with Mike Boyar and Mike Banker at 'the bank'. Also, I'm grateful to Andrew Hume for some statistics about error correction in storage. I was alerted to reference [Wes09] by Diomidis Spinellis, a highly significant find for which I am grateful. Glenn O'Donnel has been an outstanding gentleman, reading and enthusing with generous encouragement and helpful comments. Christopher Little read the manuscript with enthusiasm and proposed several improvements that I could not fully adapt to. Ted Zlatanov, Sven van der Meer, and Steve Traugott also generously read drafts of the manuscript with encouraging feedback. Finally, thanks to Jane-Ellen Long and Karen Mosman for careful readings, advice and encouragement and not least friendship.

For the second edition, I would like to thank Paul Borrill and Dinesh Dutt for precious and in-depth discussions on the challenges of large scale infrastructure. Thanks also to Adrian Cockcroft for reading and commenting, as well as Mike Loukides and Brian Anderson for their encouragement and flexibility, and all those who generously wrote reviews of (or wrote to me personally about) the first edition.

Finally, thanks to you, the reader, for taking the time to read these thoughts. I hope that some part of these ideas will stay with you and help to make sense of a journey that is only just beginning.

In closing, I would like to apologize to readers who might have felt rattled by my idiosyncratic form of English spelling. In such a personal book, I wanted to write in my own voice, representing my own culture and idiolect, and not be translated by the levelling machine of American publishing. I know that some readers will be stimulated by this decision, and others will be irritated by it. In my defense, all usage is accepted by the Oxford English Dictionary, and it ends up being oddly trans-Atlantic in its flavo(u)r.

About the author

Mark Burgess is a British theoretical physicist, turned computer scientist, living in Oslo, Norway. He is Emeritus Professor of Network and System Administration, and originator of the globally used CFEngine software and founder of CFEngine AS, Inc. He is the author of many books and scientific publications, and is a frequent speaker at international events.

Mark Burgess may be found at *www.markburgess.org*, and on Twitter under the name *@markburgess_osl*.

CPSIA information can be obtained at www.ICGtesting.com
Printed in the USA
LVOW04s1855150615

442535LV00034B/252/P